RURAL TRENDS
IN DEPRESSION YEARS

This volume contains a third survey of 140 village-centered agricultural communities. The first was published in 1927, the second in 1933. The Bureau of Agricultural Economics of the United States Department of Agriculture and the Columbia University Council for Research in the Social Sciences co-operated in this study.

RURAL TRENDS IN DEPRESSION YEARS

A Survey of
Village-centered Agricultural Communities
1930–1936

By EDMUND deS. BRUNNER
and IRVING LORGE

New York : Morningside Heights
COLUMBIA UNIVERSITY PRESS
1937

Published 1937

Foreign Agents

OXFORD UNIVERSITY PRESS
Humphrey Milford, Amen House
London, E.C.4, England

KWANG HSUEH PUBLISHING HOUSE
140 Peking Road
Shanghai, China

MARUZEN COMPANY, LTD.
6 Nihonbashi, Tori-Nichome
Tokyo, Japan

OXFORD UNIVERSITY PRESS
B. I. Building, Nicol Road
Bombay, India

Printed in the United States of America

Introduction

THIS report has two purposes. The first is to present the results of a study of changes in rural social life in the United States between the years 1930 and 1936, which included the Great Depression that began in 1930.

The second purpose is to trace the life story of 140 village-centered agricultural communities through another, or third, phase of their development and history, so that it may be studied in relation to the phases revealed by two earlier surveys of the same villages. The second purpose lends added value to the first.

This is the third time these same centers have been studied under the same director. The initial investigation, made in 1923–24 under the auspices of the Institute of Social and Religious Research, was the first national study of farmers' towns of less than 2,500 population. It was a beginning of a sociology of village life in the United States. It showed that rural America was becoming increasingly centered in villages and towns, rather than in the crossroads hamlets. It revealed the villages as interpreting the country to the city, and the city to the country.[1]

The second study of these places was begun in the late summer of 1929 by the Institute of Social and Religious Research. Shortly afterward, it became the rural section of the study carried on by President Hoover's Research Committee on Social Trends. Field work was begun in December, 1929, and completed in the early summer of the following year. This study showed important

[1] This investigation was reported in five volumes, of which three are important: *American Villagers* (1926), by C. Luther Fry, an analysis of the census data of the villages; *American Agricultural Villages* (1927), by Edmund deS. Brunner, Gwendolyn S. Hughes, and Marjorie Patten, a report of the field survey; and *Village Communities* (1927), by Edmund deS. Brunner, a summary of the entire investigation. These are publications of the Institute of Social and Religious Research, distributed by Harper & Brothers, New York.

changes, and also revealed that some phenomena noted in the first study seemed to be clear trends.[2]

The third and present investigation was begun in January, 1936, and completed in the summer of the same year. The same 140 villages were surveyed, about one-fourth of them by the same fieldworkers who had surveyed them in one or both of the earlier studies.

The report opens with a summary of the basic changes in and adjustments of agriculture from 1930 to 1935 as shown by the census and illustrated in the communities studied. There follows an analysis of changes in population and in communities as such and in the relations of village to country. The discussion then turns to changes in institutions such as those of trade, industry, banking, education, religion, and social life. In connection with education, special attention is given to the rise of adult education during the depression years. Finally, consideration is given to the question of relief, a phenomenon previously almost nonexistent in these communities.

So far as the writers know, this is the first time in rural social research that a nation-wide sample of communities has been thrice visited and studied. They trust that the resulting body of data may make a real contribution to an understanding of rural social trends, of the development of agricultural villages and communities, and of their importance in the national life.

In this series of studies, an agricultural village is considered as an incorporated center of more than 250 and less than 2,500 population situated in the midst of a farming area for whose inhabitants it supplies the usual commercial and social services.

As has already been implied, the chief source of data for the study here reported was field work by competent investigators. In the first two investigations, use was also made of the popula-

[2] The results appeared in *Rural Social Trends,* by Edmund deS. Brunner and J. H. Kolb (New York, McGraw-Hill Book Company, 1933). This study covered more ground and made more use of non-field-work sources of data covering all of rural life than had the earlier investigation.

tion census data for the villages for 1920 and 1930 respectively. This was specially tabulated. The 1930 censuses of agriculture and distribution were also largely used. The third investigation had no such source of data on population, but use was made of the 1935 census of agriculture and the 1933 and 1935 censuses of distribution or of retail trade. A discussion of methodology appears in Appendix A.

It is important to draw attention to two matters at this point. In the first place, all tables and factual statements not credited to other sources are taken from the field-work data. In the second place, it should be noted that the field work of this study was practically completed before the drought of 1936 became serious.

No investigation of this kind can be carried to completion without the aid of many agencies and individuals. Detailed acknowledgments are made in Appendix A, but special indebtedness must be noted at this point to:

(1) The Carnegie Corporation and the American Association for Adult Education, whose generous grants for this study to the Council for Research in the Social Sciences of Columbia University made the project possible.

(2) The Bureau of Agricultural Economics of the United States Department of Agriculture, under whose auspices the study was undertaken jointly with Columbia University. Through its Division of Rural Life and Population Studies (Dr. Carl C. Taylor, chief), the Bureau extended its facilities and assigned staff members for field work, which covered 11 communities.

(3) The Division of Social Research Unit of the Works Progress Administration, Dr. T. J. Woofter, Jr., co-ordinator of Rural Research. The state men of this unit conducted or supervised the field surveys in 69 communities.

(4) The Secretary of Agriculture, Henry A. Wallace, and the Undersecretary, M. L. Wilson, without whose interest and cooperation the study could not have been undertaken.

(5) Edmund deS. Brunner, Jr., released to this study by the

Resettlement Administration. He had charge of indexing by topics the field-work reports, and prepared 671 classified cards of illustrative material, almost three-fifths of which were used in this report. He also prepared factual first-draft write-ups of Chapters V and X, and is responsible for most of the final drafts of these chapters as they appear in this report.

EDMUND DES. BRUNNER
IRVING LORGE

Teachers College
Columbia University
March 1, 1937

Contents

Tables

RURAL TRENDS IN DEPRESSION YEARS

I

Changing Agricultural Backgrounds

THE YEARS covered by this study, 1930 to 1936, were among the most eventful in the history of modern agriculture. In his 1929 report, the Secretary of Agriculture, Arthur Hyde, stated that the long agricultural depression of the 1920's appeared to be drawing to a close, and that a new stabilization between agriculture and industry was in prospect. Before his report was in print, the tragic era of the Great Depression had begun. Farm and rural non-farm purchasing power dwindled seriously, affecting industrial employment and profits. Bank failures in villages, foreclosures and tax sales of farm property, multiplied. Organized resistance to the legal processes of foreclosures and tax sales developed here and there. The dispossessed tended to proposals and action deemed radical by the more conservative. Schools, churches, social agencies, and organizations suffered severely.

With the coming of the new administration in March, 1933, a series of laws was enacted intended to remedy the situation both on the farm and, indirectly, in the nation. In effect, these attempted a degree of social control over agriculture unprecedented in American history.

It is the purpose in this chapter, first of all, to describe briefly a few of the economic trends that illustrate the developments of these years, because a knowledge of them is necessary if one is to understand the social trends. Then attention will be called to the effect upon the communities studied of the legislation of 1933, and their reaction to that legislation. Finally, the changes among economic agencies that were in existence before 1930, notably the co-operatives, will be recorded. The reader will not find in this chapter, however, detailed discussions of such legislation as the

Agricultural Adjustment Act, or of other legislative or administrative devices concerned with improving the position of agriculture; nor will he find any attempt to strike a final balance sheet of their alleged benefits and losses.

It is well to understand, however, that these years since 1930 have brought agriculture to a position of importance in the national economy not hitherto attained. Since the days of Jefferson and Hamilton, the interests of agriculture and industry have clashed again and again. In the 1930's, a growing volume of literature, and of space devoted to agricultural affairs in the metropolitan press, has emphasized the idea that the prosperity of the nation is bound up with the prosperity of agriculture. The neatly columned regiments of figures released by the 1930 Census of Distribution [1] drove home that idea. The Agricultural Adjustment Act of 1933 and the subsequent amendments to the Soil Conservation Act in 1936 have made the nation conscious through taxation of the illness and the necessities of American agriculture. The lesson has not been palatable to all; but it has been learned, as the competing promises to farmers of the major parties in the presidential campaign of 1936 give abundant evidence.

It is against this general background that the prosaic story of changes in the number, size, and value of farms in the first half of the 1930's, the shifts in farm population, and the results of crop control and credit legislation must be viewed.

CHANGES IN NUMBER OF FARMS AND FARM POPULATION, 1930–35

Number of farms increases.—Perhaps the most dramatic result of the Great Depression is the increase in the number of farms and in the total farm population. Throughout the 1920's, the number of farms had been slowly declining, though a bit more rapidly in the latter half of the decade than in the earlier. The total decline was about 160,000 farms, or 2.5 per cent. In the 5 years from April, 1930, to January, 1935, there was the largest 5-year in-

[1] Brunner and Kolb, *Rural Social Trends*, Chapter VI, especially pp. 161-65.

crease in over half a century: 523,702 farms, 8.3 per cent more than in 1930. In fact, it was a larger gain than in a number of 10-year periods. It carried the total number of farms in the United States to the all-time high of 6,812,350.

Every census region shared in this increase; but it was most marked in the heavily industrialized eastern areas and in the Far West. The New England states led with a gain of 26.7 per cent. The Middle Atlantic, East North Central, Mountain, and Pacific all added more than 11 per cent; but none exceeded 14.5. Table 1 gives the regional story.

As is always the case, these regional figures obscure very sharp

TABLE 1

THE INCREASE IN FARMS, 1910–35 [a]

Number of Farms by Divisions

Division	*In Thousands*					*Per Cent Increase*	
	1910	*1920*	*1925*	*1930*	*1935*	*1920–30*	*1930–35*
United States	6,361.5	6,448.3	6,371.6	6,288.6	6,812.3	*– 2.5*	*8.3*
New England	188.8	156.5	159.4	124.9	158.2	*–20.2*	26.7
Middle Atlantic	468.4	425.2	418.8	357.6	397.7	*–15.9*	11.2
East North Central	1,123.5	1,084.7	1,051.6	966.5	1,083.7	*–10.9*	12.1
West North Central	1,109.9	1,097.0	1,111.3	1,112.7	1,179.8	1.4	6.0
South Atlantic	1,111.9	1,159.0	1,108.1	1,058.4	1,147.1	*– 8.7*	8.4
East South Central	1,042.5	1,051.6	1,006.1	1,062.2	1,137.2	1.0	7.1
West South Central	943.2	996.1	1,017.3	1,103.1	1,137.5	10.7	3.1
Mountain	183.4	244.1	233.4	241.3	271.4	*– 1.1*	12.5
Pacific	189.9	234.2	265.6	261.7	299.5	11.8	14.5

[a] Source: United States Censuses of Agriculture.

differences among the states. On the one hand Connecticut gained 87 per cent,[2] while Georgia lost 2 per cent in the number of farms. Twenty-five of the 48 states showed gains larger than the national average. The state picture is broadly sketched in Table 2.

Farm population gains.—This sharp gain in the number of farms was owing in large measure to a flight from the cities and their economic insecurity. It was apparently a great, uncontrolled mass movement to the succoring breast of Mother Earth. The urban emigrees hoped at least for subsistence. The gain began in

[2] Part of this may have been due to an under-enumeration in 1930.

1930 and reached its peak in 1932–33. Since 1933 there have been indications that the situation has either stabilized, or that pre-depression trends have begun to reassert themselves. Nonetheless, the agricultural census of 1935 records an all-time high for the farm population of 31,800,907 persons, a gain of 1,355,557 over 1930, or 6.3 per cent.

TABLE 2

THE INCREASE IN FARMS, 1930–35 [a]

States Grouped by Percentage Gain in Number of Farms

States Gaining [b]

MORE THAN *30%*	*20–30%*	*10–20%*	UNDER *10%*
Massachusetts	West Virginia	New York	Maine
Rhode Island	Florida	New Jersey	Vermont [c]
Connecticut		Pennsylvania	Illinois
New Mexico		Ohio	Minnesota [c]
Arizona		Indiana	Iowa
		Michigan	Missouri [c]
		Wisconsin	North Dakota [c]
		Virginia	South Dakota
		Kentucky	Nebraska
		Tennessee	Kansas
		Utah	Delaware
		Washington	Maryland
		Oregon	North Carolina
		California	South Carolina
		New Hampshire	Alabama
			Arkansas
			Louisiana
			Oklahoma
			Texas
			Montana
			Idaho [c]
			Wyoming [c]
			Colorado
			Nevada

[a] Source: United States Census of Agriculture, 1935.

[b] In 2 states the number of farms declined: Georgia, 2.0 per cent; Mississippi, 0.3 per cent.

[c] These states gained from 8.3 per cent, the national average, to 9.7 per cent.

This gain was not evenly distributed over the nation. Despite the fact that 46 of the 48 states showed increases in the number of farms in 1935 as compared with 1930, only 35 recorded gains in the total farm population. Of the 13 states that registered declines, the loss in 6 was one per cent or less. The sections most involved in these population losses included the tobacco-cotton area in northeastern North Carolina, the Yazoo-Mississippi delta, the Black Belt of Texas, southwestern Oklahoma, the old plantation section of Georgia, and the drought-stricken area extending from Montana eastward to western Iowa and southwestern Minnesota. Thus, South Dakota lost over 8 per cent and Montana nearly 5 per cent.

Deducting the total losses of about 162,000 in these 13 states, it is clear that the gain in the other 35 exceeded one and a half million persons.

Character of migration.—The distress character of this migration is evident from the 1935 census data on "Movement to Farms," which show that 44.6 per cent of the increase occurred in the New England, Middle Atlantic, and East North Central regions, comprising only three-tenths of the states, and which had in 1930 only 22 per cent of the farm population, but which are our most highly industrialized areas.

It was further found when this census was taken that over 671,000 farms, on which lived nearly 2 million persons, were occupied by families who, 5 years earlier, had had a non-farm residence. This group alone would more than account for the increase in the number of farms. Thirty-five per cent of the farms occupied by former non-farm residents were in the 3 regions already noted. But the movement was particularly marked within certain areas. The largest of these includes the Appalachian subsistence-farming area extending along the hills and mountains from Pennsylvania to Alabama. Unemployed miners, lumber workers, factory employees, and others who were unable to find work in industrial pursuits, totaling in all between a third of a million and a half-million persons, returned to the small hill and valley farms which were once abandoned, or to farms being operated by their relatives or friends. Areas around the industrial centers of New England, New York, Michigan, and Ohio furnish typical examples of other regions where there has been a large influx of people to farms. Between a third of a million and a half-million persons from these industrial centers have resettled on idle farms, or have engaged in part-time farming in the surrounding farm areas. The 3 other regions in which the movement to farms was extensive included the cutover lands of northeastern Minnesota and northwestern Wisconsin, the Ozark Mountain and eastern Oklahoma area, and the Pacific Coast valleys. Into each of these 3 areas, more than 100,000 persons have moved from cities, towns, villages, or other non-farm residences.

This shift of population was also influenced to some extent by the proximity of cities. The previous study, *Rural Social Trends*, demonstrated that the influence of proximity of cities was not simply a matter of regions but was applicable and measurable throughout the nation,[3] that there was a gradient pattern of relationships of tiers of counties to urban centers. When concentric tiers of counties grouped around the county containing a major city are analyzed, significant relationships are revealed. In using this device, all counties bordering that in which a city is located are called tier one counties. All counties bordering on tier one are called tier two and so on.[4] This procedure was followed for 18

[3] Brunner and Kolb, *Rural Social Trends*, pp. 115, 116, 136-39, 342.

[4] The population of these cities in 1930 ranged from 20,760 to 634,394. Three were less than 50,000 population. Six had between 50,000 and 80,000; five, between 110,000 and 183,000; and four, over 300,000. The cities were Binghamton, New York; Columbia, South Carolina; Des Moines, Iowa; Fargo, North Dakota; Fort Worth, Texas; Harrisburg, Pennsylvania; Lincoln, Nebraska; Milwaukee, Wisconsin; Montgomery, Alabama; Nashville, Tennessee; Pine Bluff, Arkansas; Portland, Oregon; Richmond, Virginia; San Francisco, California; Springfield, Illinois; Toledo, Ohio; Wichita, Kansas; Williamsport, Pennsylvania. With the exception of San Francisco, all metropolitan groups such as New York, Chicago, or Boston were omitted to avoid, as far as possible, complicating the story of rural-urban relationships by the factor of suburbanism.

Whenever there was any doubt as to the tier number to be assigned to a particular county, the entire trade area was tiered by several people and the mean of their determinations selected. In the metropolitan area of San Francisco, in which San Francisco takes up all of the city county and in which are included a number of large cities in what would have been tier one counties, all counties that would have been tier one are designated as the city county tier, and further tiering is based on that assumption. In the Richmond area, the independent city of Richmond, together clusters of counties grouped about as many cities and involving, all told, 347 counties.

This device was applied to an analysis of the relation of the proximity to cities to the proportion of the 1935 farm population that was living in non-farm areas in 1930. In these 18 groups of counties studied, almost 10 per cent of the 1935 farm population in the city county had been in the non-farm population in 1930. In tiers one to three inclusive, this ratio was between 6 and 7 per cent; in tier four, 8 per cent. The differences among the tiers were not significant within regions, as Table 3 shows.

The average of 3 persons per family on the farms occupied by those who were not on farms in 1930, and the increase of

TABLE 3

FARM POPULATION: RATIO OF PERSONS AGED 5 YEARS OR OVER WHO WERE NON-FARM IN 1930 TO THE TOTAL FARM POPULATION IN 1935

By Region and by Tiers of Counties, 18 Areas

Region	*City County*	*Tiers of Counties*			
		1	*2*	*3*	*4*
All regions	9.3	6.7	6.1	6.9	8.0
Middle Atlantic	10.4	8.8	7.4	8.6	...
South	7.7	3.5	4.0	3.6	4.0
Middle West	9.6	6.3	5.5	6.5	6.8
Far West	11.6	14.3	12.5	14.5	16.6

over a half-million farms since 1930, suggest that this has been largely a movement of recently established families rather than the migration of single individuals. These families have returned to farms once abandoned, to new farms, and to unoccupied houses on farms operated by their relatives and friends.

Most of this migration of families has been to small farms, on which these families have sought to produce at least part of the

---

with the counties of Henrico and Chesterfield, was considered to be the city county.

The wholesale-grocery areas of the United States, published as a map supplement to the *Market Data Handbook* (United States Department of Commerce, 1929), were used as a guide in determining how far out from the city county to go.

food, particularly vegetables, eggs, and milk, needed for their own use. These families have probably augmented very little the total production of farm products for sale.

This whole movement of population raises some very interesting considerations. It occurred at a time when there was much talk, and some effort, in the direction of planned population distribution. It is too much to expect that efforts so new to the American habit could control so strong a ground swell as this movement represents; but the type of migration and its location on the land all indicate problems as to the support of these people. Many of them will fall back to a mere subsistence level or below it. With improved economic conditions, they will doubtless seek to return to the city, so that permanent expansion of social utilities to care for their needs would be questionable. Possibly an extension of the type of land-zoning legislation now in force in Wisconsin would help solve these difficulties; but this involves the slow process of action by state legislatures.

This migration was true, of course, to the American tradition. Migration founded the nation, peopled the West, crowded the cities. The American has freely moved elsewhere when opportunity seemed to beckon. He has never been forced, to the extent that the European has, to work out his salvation in some one spot. And, in the main, his moves were profitable. But with the end of free land, with erosion damage to millions of acres, the question arises as to whether migration can any longer be an effective mass answer to the problems of economic distress.

Farmers in the 1934 drought area also moved in large numbers to more favorable land elsewhere, as the chapter on population shows. This, like the exodus from cities, was a distress migration.

Sixty-nine, or practically one-half, of the 140 village-centered rural communities on which the field work of this study was based, experienced significant influxes of new farm population. The sources and destination of this new population are discussed in

Chapter III. Suffice it to say here that 3 in 10 of the places reporting received this new population from nearly urban centers, one in 4 from nearly farming country, and the rest, largely those in the Far West, from other geographic areas, usually from drought-stricken sections. In almost half the cases, they settled on land variously described as cheap, poor, vacated, or submarginal. In more than one-third of the communities, they acquired good land; and in the other cases, average.

One surprising feature of the 1935 enumeration was the continued decline in the number of Negroes on farms. It will be recalled that between 1920 and 1930, the number of native white farmers increased somewhat, while the number of Negroes and other non-whites declined. The number of colored persons on farms reported a further decline of approximately 190,000 persons between 1930 and 1935. With respect to the Negroes, who make up the great bulk of the non-white population, this is probably a reflection of the displacement of cotton-croppers as a result of the A.A.A. program.

In many instances, villages as well as farms shared in the increase in population. These movements are worthy of further analysis. They had very real effects on social organizations. They complicated problems of relief. But these considerations are discussed in Chapter III. The important fact at this point is the sharp reversal in the trend toward fewer farms and a smaller farm population, and the significant increase in both during the first half of the present decade.

Size of farms declines slightly, total acreage increases.—With an 8.3 per cent increase in the number of farms, and a 4.5 per cent gain in farm population, it would appear reasonable to expect a decline in the average size of farms. The average size did in fact decline in 6 of the 9 census regions, and in 34 of the 48 states, in 10 of which the declines were more than 10 per cent. The average size increased in only 14.

Two-thirds of the increase in the number of farms in the United

States between 1930 and 1936 took place in those ranging from 3 to 19 acres. An additional one-eighth of the increase ranged from 50 to 99 acres. This seems to indicate that the increase in much of the farm population came from those who could not afford large holdings and who will become part-time or mere subsistence farmers. The total drop for the nation in the average size of farm was, however, barely 2 acres: from 156.9 in 1930 to 154.8 in 1935. This small decline has various explanations. In the first place, the total number of acres in farms increased nearly 68 millions to 1,054,515,111. This is the equivalent of 130 acres for each of the new farms reported. Therefore the new farms were not only carved out of the acreage existing in 1930; there was a considerable expansion of the total agricultural plant. Also, in one area and in several states within other areas, there was a considerable consolidation of farms and a considerable acreage brought under cultivation with a negligible increase in the number of farms. This applies especially to the West South Central states, where, with an increase of barely one per cent in the total number of farms, or 34,437, there was a gain of almost 17.2 million acres.

Another factor of interest in considering size is the fact that manager-operated farms gained on the average from 1,109 to 1,261 acres. Tenants increased their average acreage from 115 to 117.6 acres; but the owner-operated farms declined in size, those of full owners from 128 to 122 acres. Consolidation of foreclosed holdings under managers and the smaller acreages of farms purchased by those newly turning to the soil are partial explanations of these facts.

Not only does the size of farms vary by census divisions, but also by distance from the city. The nearer to the city, generally speaking, the smaller is the size of the farms, as is shown in some detail in the previous study.[5] This is in part a function of crops raised. Food such as fruit, vegetables, and dairy products tends to be raised near the urban market and on smaller farms than

[5] Brunner and Kolb, *Rural Social Trends*, Chapter V.

those devoted to grain, livestock and fiber. Farms in the city county are also smaller; because, as is shown later in this chapter, a larger percentage of the farm operators in these counties engaged in off-farm work, and for more days than was the case in the outlying tiers of counties. The increase in total land in farms indicates, of course, a change in the ratio of land in farms to the total area of the nation.

As has already been noted, the national figures are the highest ever reached; the increase between 1930 and 1935 being 3.6 points, or almost 7 per cent, with the result that 55.4 per cent of the nation's land is now in farms. As would be expected, the proportion of land in farms was less in the city counties than elsewhere. But even these counties with urban centers reversed the

TABLE 4

FARM SIZE: AVERAGE ACREAGE PER FARM

By Region and by Tiers of Counties, 18 Areas, 1935

Region	*City County*	*Tiers of Counties*			
		1	*2*	*3*	*4*
All regions	108.4	126.4	149.9	199.1	315.8
Middle Atlantic	92.1	103.4	95.4	114.9	...
South	74.2	94.5	107.1	132.5	167.8
Middle West	150.0	175.6	177.4	209.2	454.3
Far West	90.0	84.3	263.9	419.2	260.7

steady downward trend in the proportion of their land in farms, by showing an increase; in the Middle Atlantic and Southern regions, a greater increase than in a number of the more rural tiers.

It seems quite certain that the trend toward an increase in the number of both larger and smaller farms noted in the 1930 census has continued. The newer areas are still developing, holders of foreclosed properties are consolidating them into large farms; but thousands of other persons, many of them part-time farmers, are taking to small holdings. This includes, of course, many of the families in the Resettlement Administration communities.

Thus, the average acreage at Crossville, Tennessee, is about 15 acres; at Dyess, Arkansas, 30 acres; at Arthurdale, West Virginia, under 5 acres.

Some understanding of the effects of these processes is gained from the field survey. In 3 of the Southwestern communities studied, tractor farming had greatly increased. One landowner

TABLE 5

FARM LAND: PROPORTION IN FARMS OF ALL LAND AREAS

By Region and by Tiers of Counties, 18 Areas

Region and Year	*City County*	*Tiers of Counties*			
	PER CENT	PER CENT *1*	PER CENT *2*	PER CENT *3*	PER CENT *4*
All regions					
1910	74.5	78.6	76.9	73.9	65.4
1920	70.7	76.0	75.8	73.4	65.7
1930	65.2	72.5	73.5	71.6	66.6
1935	67.9	75.8	75.9	75.0	71.1
Middle Atlantic					
1910	67.1	69.4	77.3	63.4	...
1920	64.2	67.2	75.1	58.8	...
1930	56.2	60.2	67.1	54.6	...
1935	57.3	60.6	67.5	56.7	...
South					
1910	70.2	75.4	72.6	74.0	70.4
1920	61.9	71.1	68.9	71.8	64.6
1930	56.5	64.4	64.2	65.4	66.8
1935	63.9	71.0	68.9	72.2	73.8
Middle West					
1910	87.9	93.1	89.9	91.0	86.8
1920	85.6	92.4	90.3	91.6	90.5
1930	80.8	91.9	90.9	91.8	89.5
1935	81.9	94.0	93.0	93.3	94.3
Far West					
1910	51.1	50.8	43.9	32.9	15.0
1920	54.3	46.1	46.7	37.8	17.9
1930	50.1	46.5	49.8	43.1	20.4
1935	47.2	49.1	50.1	45.6	20.8

with 33 farms averaging 60 acres each purchased 5 tractors, consolidated his holdings, retained a few selected laborers to operate the machines, and forced 30 families, 150 people in all, to vacate the land. His example was followed by a number of others. In another place, 5 tractor agencies are competing for business; and all are doing well. In the third center, 1,000 head of work cattle and 35 families have been displaced. In at least 2 of these places, farming with tractors was believed to be still in the "experimental" phase, and their purchase was said to have become a "craze," especially in the spring of 1936. Certain it is that one of these 2 communities, though it is on the edge of the Dust Bowl, is rapidly going from grass to farm, perhaps under the pressure of low livestock prices.

In another community in the Old South, the acreage in farms doubled between 1930 and 1935, and there was a 40 per cent gain in the number of farms. Part of this area had long since been abandoned as cotton land, and part of it was cutover. The new settlers were former lumber and sawmill hands trying to re-establish themselves through agriculture. These for the most part had small holdings.

Value of farms declines.—The size of a farm is, of course, one of the factors in its value, though only one. The 1935 census of agriculture showed a further large drop in the total capital value of America's largest single industry. Land and buildings declined from $47,879,838,358 in 1930 to $32,858,844,012, or practically 30 per cent. The total decline from 66.3 billions in 1920 to the 1935 valuation was 50.5 per cent. This terrific deflation is a major explanation of the epidemic of foreclosure sales, bankruptcies, and bank failures that has afflicted rural America since 1921.

Before considering some of these phenomena, it is important to analyze further the matter of the value of farm land and buildings. It is encouraging that the 1935 valuation figures represent at least some upturn from the low point in farm real estate. This low point is estimated by the Bureau of Agricultural Economics to have been reached on March 1, 1933. Each March since then has recorded a slight rise. Between 1932 and 1933, values dropped 18 per cent. Since then there has been a rise of 12.3 per cent. In other words, the total valuation at the low point was down to approximately 30 billions, or nearly 55 per cent below that of 1920.

Expressed in the index numbers used by the Bureau of Agricultural Economics, the trend in farm real estate, using 1912–14 as 100, is shown in Table 6.

This table also shows the sharp regional variations. The declines have been most pronounced in the areas devoted to one crop or to only a few crops. Thus, two of the three Southern regions dropped about 60 per cent between 1920 and 1932. The areas within the industrial regions that are devoted to specialized crops

TABLE 6

FARM LAND VALUES: ESTIMATED VALUE PER ACRE OF FARM REAL ESTATE BY DIVISIONS [a]

(1912–14 = 100)

Division	*1920*	*1925*	*1930*	*1931*	*1932*	*1933*	*1934*	*1935*	*1936* [b]
United States	170	127	115	106	89	73	76	79	82
New England	140	127	127	126	116	105	104	104	105
Middle Atlantic	136	114	106	101	96	82	83	85	88
East North Central	161	116	96	87	73	62	65	68	72
West North Central	184	126	109	97	81	64	67	68	71
South Atlantic	198	148	128	116	96	80	87	93	97
East South Central	199	141	128	117	97	79	85	93	96
West South Central	177	144	136	121	97	82	88	91	94
Mountain	151	105	102	100	82	69	69	70	73
Pacific	156	146	142	140	118	96	97	101	105

[a] Source: United States Department of Agriculture, Bureau of Agricultural Economics, Release of May 21, 1936.

[b] Preliminary.

neither rose as rapidly nor fell as far as elsewhere. This is particularly true of the New England and the Pacific states. These estimates of the Bureau of Agricultural Economics are confirmed by the experience of the insurance companies with farm mortgages and foreclosed farms on their hands, and by the Farm Credit Administration. Both report sales at strengthening prices. Foreclosed farms are bringing slightly more than the value of the mortgage, though they never on the average dropped much below 85 per cent. Real estate dealers in the communities surveyed in every region also declared that the demand for farms was strong, that it often exceeded the supply, and that the market was rising. Among other causes accounting for this, such as rising farm income, the loan program of the Farm Credit Administration and its practice of basing loans on the "normal" value of farms may have helped.

Values per farm showed, naturally, similar trends and regional fluctuations, as appears in Table 7. From a per farm valuation of $10,284 in 1920 and $7,614 in 1930, the 1935 per farm valuation went to $4,823, lower even than in 1910. It is easy to see how, with his equity declining about 3.5 per cent per year on the average, the farmer with a mortgage had a difficult problem to keep afloat.

TABLE 7

FARM VALUES: AVERAGE VALUE PER FARM BY DIVISIONS [a]

1920–35

Division	*1920* [b]	*1930* [b]	*1935* [b]
United States	$ 10,284	$ 7,614	$ 4,823
New England	5,860	7,530	5,696
Middle Atlantic	7,061	7,880	5,385
East North Central	13,771	9,660	6,087
West North Central	22,307	13,623	7,954
South Atlantic	4,488	3,639	2,434
East South Central	3,484	2,528	1,684
West South Central	6,316	5,263	3,542
Mountain	12,958	10,188	6,531
Pacific	19,941	18,431	11,099

[a] Source for 1920 and 1930: Fifteenth Census, Agriculture, General Report, p. 72; source for 1935: United States Census of Agriculture, 1935, Vol. I, p. xx.

[b] Covers land and buildings only.

The previous study, *Rural Social Trends,* showed that land values on a per acre basis were higher in the city county than in the tiers, that they decreased as the distance from the city increased, and that the deflation in land values proceeded less drastically in the city county than elsewhere. The first two of these generalizations is still true; the third did not hold between 1930 and 1935. Per acre valuations declined in all tiers at about the same rate, varying nationally from 40 to 47 per cent. Regional rates varied, of course, as Table 8 shows; but the trend was similar throughout. It should be noted also that in every instance, except tier four in the South and tier one in the Far West, 1935 per acre valuations were lower than the pre-war 1910 values.

Farm income lower.—Drastically as farm values fell, the in-

TABLE 8

FARM LAND VALUES: VALUE PER ACRE OF ALL FARM PROPERTY

By Region and by Tiers of Counties, 18 Areas

Region and Year	*City County*	*Tiers of Counties* 1	2	3	4
All regions					
1910	$ 99.90	$ 66.82	$ 56.50	$ 49.64	$ 37.31
1920	154.73	122.75	102.95	94.86	77.28
1930	143.60	94.25	71.82	65.93	61.56
1935	83.20	52.60	38.11	35.98	33.45
Middle Atlantic					
1910	54.20	51.20	43.00	46.80	...
1920	81.00	78.70	66.60	72.40	...
1930	86.20	77.60	63.60	69.30	...
1935	45.70	38.96	30.74	32.00	...
South					
1910	50.40	27.50	24.10	20.90	18.40
1920	97.10	60.40	51.50	44.80	41.10
1930	80.90	42.90	35.40	37.80	35.70
1935	48.99	23.33	18.99	18.94	21.16
Middle West					
1910	138.90	99.50	93.30	80.80	49.80
1920	220.70	182.90	170.80	159.80	112.70
1930	199.00	121.90	107.50	97.30	73.50
1935	108.36	68.09	57.96	54.68	40.29
Far West					
1910	180.30	93.90	45.30	30.90	40.80
1920	207.50	165.50	74.20	47.60	60.70
1930	223.60	176.50	68.50	38.80	76.60
1935	154.02	106.65	37.04	26.43	38.22

come of farmers declined even more precipitously. Gross farm income dropped almost 70 per cent by 1932 from the 1919 level of almost 17 billion dollars, or to 5.3 billions. From 1923 to 1929, inclusive, it fluctuated between 11 and 12 billions. The net income figures show a somewhat smaller, but none the less severe, fall, even when 1929 is compared with 1933. In this period there was a drop from 6.74 to 2.89 billions, or 57 per cent. As will be noted from Table 9, the drop in the amount available for capital return and management declined even more drastically; but it has also recovered impressively since the lowest point, even if the A.A.A. benefit payments be deducted.

The decline varied, of course, according to crop. The export

TABLE 9

GROSS FARM INCOME, EXPENDITURES, VALUE OF OPERATORS' AND FAMILY LABOR, AND INCOME AVAILABLE FOR CAPITAL AND MANAGEMENT,[a] 1924–34[b]

(In Millions)

Year	*Total Gross Income*	*Total Expenditures*[c]	*Balance Available for Capital, Unpaid Labor and Management*	*Value of Operators' and Family Labor at Rates Paid Hired Labor*	*Income Available for Capital and Management*
1924	$11,337	$4,276	$7,061	$4,405	$2,656
1925	11,968	4,632	7,336	4,447	2,889
1926	11,480	4,734	6,746	4,534	2,212
1927	11,616	4,706	6,910	4,501	2,409
1928	11,741	4,998	6,743	4,491	2,252
1929	11,941	5,203	6,738	4,519	2,219
1930	9,454	4,446	5,008	4,096	912
1931	6,968	3,304	3,664	3,218	446
1932	5,337	2,450	2,887	2,460	427
1933	6,406	2,439	3,967	2,297	1,670
1934	7,300	2,679	4,621	2,586	2,035

[a] Source: United States Department of Agriculture, Bureau of Agricultural Economics, Circular No. 382, December, 1935, Table 6.
[b] Gross income and government payments for 1935 amounted to 8,508 million and for 1936 to 9,530 million.
[c] Includes operating expenditures, wages to hired labor, and taxes payable.

commodities, as is well known, suffered most. Table 10 makes this clear and indicates that even at the worst in 1932, when corrected by 1929 prices, certain types of farming were not seriously inconvenienced. These include, of course, dairying, poultry, fruit, and vegetables, though the first two of these ran into more serious difficulties later on.

Totals like these mean little unless they are reduced to a per farm basis; and this the United States Department of Agriculture has estimated annually for more than a decade, using from 6,100 to 16,000 representative farms. For the United States, the average net result of the owner-operators for their own farms has ranged from $66 in 1932 to $1,334 in 1928. From the 1932 low there was

TABLE 10

AGRICULTURAL INCOME: PERCENTAGE OF 1929 GROSS AGRICULTURAL INCOME BY SELECTED GROUPS [a]

	At 1932 Prices				*At 1929 Prices*			
Item	*1929*	*1930*	*1931*	*1932*	*1921*	*1930*	*1931*	*1932*
Grains	100.0	66.0	52.9	18.4	100.0	79.9	101.5	50.5
Fruits and vegetables	100.0	94.0	74.5	56.4	100.0	80.9	103.3	108.0
Cotton and cotton seed	100.0	56.2	31.6	27.0	100.0	79.9	72.8	85.2
Meat animals	100.0	87.1	60.3	39.4	100.0	101.4	101.2	97.5
Poultry products	100.0	85.4	65.8	49.0	100.0	107.8	108.9	97.4
Dairy products	100.0	87.4	69.5	54.2	100.0	99.4	103.6	108.4

[a] Source: *National Income, 1929–32*, 73d Congress, 2d Session, Senate Document 124, p. 49, Tables 32 and 33.

a recovery to $624 in 1934. In addition, each farm used about $200 worth of food and fuel produced on the home farm. The regional variations are quite wide, as will be noted in Table 11.

Data are not available for all states; but some idea of the

TABLE 11

AGRICULTURAL INCOME: FARM RETURNS: AVERAGE NET RESULT OF OWNER-OPERATORS FOR THEIR OWN FARMS FOR THE CALENDAR YEARS 1922–34 [a]

Geographic Division	*1922*	*1925*	*1928*	*1929*	*1930*	*1931*	*1932*	*1933*	*1934*
North Atlantic	858	1,352	1,105	1,254	882	445	180	619	733
East North Central	928	1,370	1,170	1,178	604	202	119	542	873
West North Central	1,235	1,680	1,798	1,684	595	−178	− 98	502	339
South Atlantic	623	616	639	764	214	215	41	435	554
South Central	735	824	1,121	987	217	216	88	432	539
Western	986	2,047	2,171	1,994	868	242	178	738	1,023
United States	917	1,297	1,334	1,298	538	154	66	516	624
Number of Reports									
United States	6,094	15,330	11,851	11,805	6,228	7,437	6,383	6,855	7,626

[a] Source: United States Department of Agriculture, Bureau of Agricultural Economics, Circular No. 382, December, 1935, p. 19.

trends of the last years is given in the 1935 report of the College of Agriculture of Indiana, reproduced in part in Table 12. This shows the varying fortunes of farm-family incomes during the last few years. These figures indicate that there were serious losses in 2 of the 6 years included; and that, except for dairying, the returns in 1934 were better than in 1929. Another indication of the extent of agricultural recovery is in an Iowa study showing an average cash income of $1,990 in 1933 and $2,764 in 1934.

TABLE 12

LABOR INCOMES BY SELECTED TYPES OF FARMING IN INDIANA 1929–34

		Types of Farming			
Year	STATE TOTAL	DAIRY	GRAIN AND LIVESTOCK	CORN AND WHEAT	SOUTHERN GENERAL FARMING
1929	$1,091	$1,177	$1,039	$1,541	$742
1930	9	67	67	45	*−569*
1931	*−875*	*−663*	*−1,060*	*−568*	*− 88*
1932	*−511*	*−622*	*− 550*	*−496*	*−213*
1933	584	570	640	693	85
1934	1,285	506	1,684	1,832	911

The "parity" index.—Even income figures do not tell the whole story. The real factor is the purchasing power of that income. For more than 25 years, the United States Department of Agriculture has estimated the ratio of the prices received by the farmer to prices paid by him, using the period from August, 1909, to July, 1914, inclusive as 100. These are the parity years made famous by the A.A.A. act. The stability of the relationship in these years is easily apparent from the data below. They chart the brief war and post-war prosperity, and the stages of the long agricultural depression that began in 1921.

1910 — 104	1919 — 105	1928 — 96
1911 — 94	1920 — 105	1929 — 95
1912 — 100	1921 — 82	1930 — 87
1913 — 100	1922 — 89	1931 — 70
1914 — 101	1923 — 93	1932 — 61
1915 — 93	1924 — 94	1933 — 64
1916 — 95	1925 — 99	1934 — 73
1917 — 117	1926 — 94	1935 — 86
1918 — 115	1927 — 91	1936 — 92

The difficulties that many farms have had in making both ends meet during recent years is quite apparent from the various sets of data thus far given. One adjustment that farmers have attempted to make, especially those who have small holdings and those near cities and large towns, is to secure an additional source of income in some occupation off their own farm.

Part-time farming.—During the 1920's, increasing numbers of farmers began to seek sources of income to supplement that from their soil. The importance of this additional source of family income was first noted and studied in southern New England and Ohio. There appeared to be a direct relationship between proximity to cities and the proportion of farmers gainfully employed on a part-time basis away from their own land.[6] It was assumed that with the large urban-rural migration of the 1930's, this movement had increased; and the 1935 census of agriculture gathered data on the subject.

These data disclose that slightly more than 2 million farmers worked off their farms in 1934 for pay or income, 9.1 per cent more than in 1929. The increase in this practice, therefore, was only slightly greater than the increase in the number of farms, so that the gain in the proportion of all farmers so engaged in 1934 as against 1929 was only from 30.3 to 30.5 per cent. These data include all farmers on work-relief projects.

The data also show that 22.7 per cent worked 150 or more days; an almost equal proportion, from 50 to 149 days; and 28.6 per cent, less than 25 days. The hypothesis that rurality and nonfarm employment were negatively associated seems to be borne out by the 1935 census in two ways.

In the first place, the more urban and industrial the region, the larger the proportion of farmers so employed for 150 days or more, and the smaller the proportion employed off the farm less than 25 days. This is indicated also in the average number of days worked, as is shown in tabulations by regions. In the second place, the more urban and industrial the region, the higher was the pro-

[6] Brunner and Kolb, *Rural Social Trends*, pp. 49-50.

portion of part-time farmers engaged in non-agricultural occupations. Thus, in the more rural regions the proportion engaged in agricultural as against non-agricultural occupations and the proportion of farmers working for hire less than 25 days were alike higher than elsewhere. Probably in these regions a somewhat neighborly exchange of services at times of peak load is the characteristic pattern. These statements are shown statistically in Table 13.

TABLE 13

PER CENT OF ALL FARM OPERATORS REPORTING DAYS WORKED OFF FARMS FOR PAY, 1929 AND 1934[a]

Division	*1929*	*1934*
New England	44.7	41.4
Middle Atlantic	34.9	32.0
East North Central	28.6	28.7
West North Central	23.6	31.6
South Atlantic	31.8	30.1
East South Central	32.7	25.7
West South Central	29.2	29.7
Mountain	33.2	43.1
Pacific	37.2	36.4

[a] Source: United States Census of Agriculture, 1935.

The urban influence on off-farm work is also shown very clearly by the tier analysis technique already employed in this chapter. In every region, the farm operators of the city county averaged more days of labor off their farms than operators in the other tiers, by from 33 to 42 days. There was clearly less such off-farm work in the Middle West, regardless of the tier, than in the other regions, and sharply more in the Far West. But, as would be expected, the ratio of agricultural off-farm workers to all off-farm workers was higher in the outlying tiers than in the city county. Tables 14 and 15 detail these facts.

All told, each part-time farmer averaged 97 days in outside employment in 1934, three less than in 1929. Thus a total of more than 202 million days was put in. The census makes no estimate of total wages received; but it seems reasonable to assume that the earnings from outside employment increased the total net income of the farmers of the United States by from 8 to 10 per cent in 1934. In the communities studied there was a noticeable increase

TABLE 14

AVERAGE NUMBER OF DAYS WORKED OFF FARMS BY FARM OPERATORS SO REPORTING

By Tiers of Counties, 18 Areas, 1935

Region	*City County*	*Tiers of Counties*			
		1	*2*	*3*	*4*
All regions	131.4	98.3	93.4	96.8	89.3
Middle Atlantic	118.4	108.0	96.1	104.1	...
South	144.9	94.3	94.3	98.1	95.2
Middle West	112.7	83.9	77.5	78.4	63.9
Far West	176.1	145.8	137.7	141.9	131.4

in the number of roadside markets and in the number of old large houses opened for tourist trade. This latter was a depression adjustment in the villages.

TABLE 15

RATIO OF AGRICULTURAL OFF-FARM WORKERS TO ALL OFF-FARM WORKERS

By Region and by Tiers of Counties, 18 Areas

Region	*City County*	*Tiers of Counties*			
		1	*2*	*3*	*4*
All regions	13.0	17.3	16.5	16.3	15.6
Middle Atlantic	3.6	5.3	4.7	3.9	...
South	16.1	20.4	13.9	19.1	15.3
Middle West	15.8	18.7	21.7	18.5	17.9
Far West	8.3	21.1	23.8	14.9	11.6

For many farmers, part-time farming was impossible; and it is necessary to examine some of the results of the untoward conditions that have been sketched. One of these relates to changes in the tenure of farm operators.

Farm tenure fluctuates.—As the depression deepened, many farmers who had been foreclosed were permitted to remain as tenants on the land they once had owned. Certain creditors, especially some insurance companies and some banks, consolidated their holdings and employed managers. At the same time, as already has been noted, there was a considerable demand for farms during the years of returning optimism. The data on farm tenure of the 1935 census of agriculture were therefore awaited with keen interest and some anxiety.

The net result of these varying trends was that the 1930 all-time record for the proportion of tenant-operated farms, 42.4 per cent of the total, declined slightly to 42.1 per cent in 1935. The number of owner-operated farms gained over 9 per cent, as compared with an increase of 8.3 per cent in the total number of all farms. Tenant-operated farms rose 7.5 per cent in number. As already pointed out, the additional owner-operated farms were relatively small in size. In general, the increase in farms operated by owners was greatest in states where the gain in the number of farms was largest. Apparently those who moved from the city were able to purchase their farms.

But, as often happens, the national statistics conceal some regional trends, not all of which are encouraging from the point of view of those who believe that a stable and prosperous rural life in America can best be built on the basis of the family-owned and family-operated farmstead.

The decrease in the national figures on tenancy was the result of the decline in the number and per cent of tenant-operated farms in the three census divisions that comprise the South. This region of 16 states has about one-half of all farms, and about two-thirds of all tenant-operated farms in the United States. The drop in the proportion of tenant-operated farms in this region from 55.5 to 53.5 per cent accounts, therefore, for the slight national decline.

Outside the South, the proportion of farms operated by tenants rose from 28.5 to 30.6 per cent of all farms. In these 32 states not in the South, the greatest gain in tenancy was in the Middle West where the proportion was already high. In Iowa, South

Dakota, and Nebraska, the number of farm owners actually declined, while the number of tenant-operators gained from 6 to nearly 10 per cent. Half of Iowa's farms, and more than half the acreage, are now operated by full tenants; another 12 per cent by part-tenants and part-owners; and it is estimated that more than 10 per cent of the land is owned by absentee corporations, largely insurance companies. But even in the New England and Middle Atlantic states, where the proportion of tenant-operated farms had been declining for decades, there were increases between 1930 and 1935.

Even in the South, the decline in tenancy is an indication more of a new problem than of the solution of an old one. The number of cropper-tenants declined 60,000. Three-fourths of this decrease was in the West South Central states, where the number of other tenants also dropped by over 10,000. Most of this was in Texas and Arkansas, where the number of croppers decreased 27 per cent and 12.5 per cent, respectively. This is a reflection of the growing mechanization of the farms in this area noted earlier in the chapter, and also of the displacement of croppers and some other tenants as a result of the A.A.A. reduction programs. With the added reduction of the 1935 crop year, which followed the census, the situation may have grown worse.

This issue as to the plight of the cotton-cropper as a result of the developments since 1930 is highly controversial. It will be considered in relation to the 140 communities of this investigation in the section on the A.A.A. (pages 44-55). Here it may be of interest to draw attention to an article on "Agricultural Adjustment and Farm Tenure" by D. W. Watkins of Clemson, South Carolina, Agricultural College,[7] in which he presents a summary of his own and certain other studies.

He shows that less than one-third of the farm-tenants on relief rolls came from farms signing A.A.A. contracts, which of course were a huge majority of all farms; that in shifts up and down the

[7] *Journal of Farm Economics,* Vol. XVIII, No. 3, pp. 469-76.

agricultural ladder, the cropper and share-tenants fared much better in 1934–35 than in 1931–32; that the net cash income of the croppers, which was 54 per cent below that of the farm owner-operator in 1932, was 50 per cent below in 1934. The studies summarized in this article are concerned only with the south-eastern cotton belt, where conditions were not as serious as in the West South Central states. That they were not good, however, is shown by Dr. Calvin Hoover's report to Secretary Wallace on "Human Factors in the Cotton Acreage Reduction Program." [8]

It is interesting to observe the changing relationship of land tenure and distance from the city. In 1910, and to a less extent in 1920, the farther a county was from a major city, the larger the proportion of farms operated by owners. This is no longer true. Nationally speaking, the proportion of owner-operated farms in the city county has steadily risen; but in the other counties it has as steadily declined. The drop was most rapid in the fourth tier of counties out from the city county. While this trend is not shown in every county tier in each region, there is considerable conformity to the national trend, except in the Middle Atlantic states, as Table 16 shows.

These data must be interpreted in the light of the ratio of owners to tenants discussed above. They indicate that the check in the increase of tenant-operated farms in the United States between 1930 and 1935 was due to the increase in owner-operation in city counties, where farms are small and are often operated on a part-time basis. Among the larger farms, of the more traditional American pattern, farther out from the city, tenancy increased. This is clearly a depression influence which most commentators would consider unfortunate, especially in view of the fact that while only 42 per cent of our farm operators are tenants, owner-operators possessed only 42 per cent of the total value of all farm real estate in 1930.

One interesting development relating to tenancy was discovered

[8] United States Department of Agriculture, 1934 (mimeographed).

in the field work, which should be checked when census data are fully available. In a number of places, especially in the Far West, there was a marked tendency to lower or abolish cash rent and substitute share-rental as fairer to all concerned.

Another interesting revelation of 1935 is the decline in the number of manager-operated farms; a category which includes, of course, corporation farms. The 1935 total of 48,104 such farms is almost 8,000 below the 1930 total, and about 20,000 below that of 1920. Moreover, the decrease was reported from every census division. However, the number of acres in such farms dropped by only 2 per cent to 60.6 million. The average acreage of such farms rose, as has already been noted, from 1,109 to 1,261 acres.

In only 4 census regions—the New England, Middle Atlantic, Mountain, and Pacific—does the proportion of manager-operated farms exceed one per cent. In the first 2 of these, the proportion of the area is around 3 or 4 per cent; but in the West South Central, Mountain, and Pacific, this proportion runs from approximately 10 to 12 per cent. Elsewhere, despite the consolidation of holdings, the manager-operated acreages run only around 2 per cent of the total farm acreage.

It is evident, from this brief summary of the 1935 census data, that the depression has operated in different ways in different areas. Even the increase in the number of farms and of the farm population was unequally distributed, not shared by every state. The only common experiences were the decline in the value of farms and in farm income.

The difficulties of the depression were aggravated by two factors which interacted with its development. These two factors were debt and taxation. They will now be discussed, after which various adjustments to the total situation will be described.

FARM INDEBTEDNESS

The volume of debt on owner-operated farms in the United States rose rapidly with the increase in land values that began in

TABLE 16

FARM TENURE: PROPORTION OF FARMS OPERATED BY OWNERS AND BY TENANTS [a]

By Region and by Tiers of Counties, 18 Areas

Region and Year	Per Cent Operated by									
	Owner					Tenant				
	CITY COUNTY	TIERS OF COUNTIES				CITY COUNTY	TIERS OF COUNTIES			
		1	*2*	*3*	*4*		*1*	*2*	*3*	*4*
All regions										
1910	57.7	62.1	63.5	64.2	66.5	40.7	36.8	35.5	34.9	32.2
1920	57.6	60.8	61.2	61.6	60.4	40.8	38.0	37.7	37.3	37.6
1930	60.9	60.4	60.3	58.9	56.0	37.6	38.5	38.7	40.2	42.9
1935	61.3	59.7	58.7	57.7	55.7	37.6	39.3	40.5	41.5	43.6
Middle Atlantic										
1910	74.8	70.2	73.6	70.3	...	23.0	28.5	25.1	27.9	...
1920	76.5	71.5	72.6	70.1	...	20.6	26.6	26.3	28.3	...
1930	82.7	77.9	80.3	77.2	...	15.1	20.2	18.8	21.6	...
1935	83.1	79.1	79.6	76.3	...	15.3	19.3	19.5	22.8	...
South										
1910	43.2	51.2	52.7	55.3	54.8	55.9	40.2	46.9	44.3	45.0
1920	45.6	50.2	51.8	53.1	51.0	53.4	49.3	47.7	46.5	48.5
1930	45.9	46.4	47.3	46.8	42.1	52.8	53.1	52.2	52.7	57.5
1935	48.6	46.8	46.6	47.9	43.7	50.3	52.7	53.0	51.7	55.9
Middle West										
1910	60.4	62.7	63.9	65.9	69.8	38.2	36.4	35.2	33.1	29.0
1920	58.0	58.3	59.6	62.1	61.9	40.5	39.2	39.1	36.7	36.8
1930	60.8	58.5	57.9	57.7	56.8	38.1	40.6	41.3	41.5	42.2
1935	59.4	57.0	55.5	54.5	54.1	39.7	42.3	43.7	44.8	45.0
Far West										
1910	66.3	80.4	79.2	74.9	77.4	30.5	16.6	18.3	23.4	19.6
1920	63.6	80.4	77.7	72.5	71.7	34.0	17.0	20.0	25.0	22.8
1930	73.6	82.5	78.2	74.6	75.2	24.1	15.0	19.1	23.3	22.3
1935	73.1	79.1	74.4	73.3	76.7	25.3	18.8	23.4	25.0	22.3

[a] The per cent of managers, making up the total, does not appear in this table.

the 1890's and continued until 1920. In that year, it amounted to 4 billion dollars, having risen to that total from 1.7 billions in 1900. By 1925, an additional half billion had been added to the burden, and an average loan, per mortgaged farm, was $4,004. As the agricultural depression deepened in the latter half of the 1920's, credit sources began to dry up; by 1930, total indebtedness dropped to 4.08 billions, and the average mortgage to slightly less than $3,600. The proportion of owner-operated farms that were mortgaged reached 42 per cent in this year. Meanwhile, the value of farms was declining, as has been shown, so that the farmer's equity was decreasing. In 1932, the B.A.E. estimated that the ratio of farm debt to farm value reached an all-time high, and that 7 per cent of all farms were mortgaged at more than their depression values. The data given above concern only owner-operated farms and only mortgages. They take no account of crop liens and other short-time obligations, or of loans on tenant-operated farms placed by the landlords.

Unfortunately, the data on farm mortgage indebtedness in 1935 have not yet been released. It is probable that there has been an increase in the mortgage debt of perhaps 10 per cent since 1930. This estimate is based on estimates of farm mortgage loans to farmers made periodically by the B.A.E. In 1929, 39 life insurance companies, member banks in the Federal Reserve system, and the joint-stock land banks now being liquidated had outstanding 2.6 billion dollars in loans; and the Federal Land Banks, 1.2 billions. In January, 1936, the Federal loans, including those of the land bank commissioner, had risen to 2.869 billions, and those of the other agencies had declined to 1.25 billions. The total outstanding loans of these agencies, therefore, had risen from 3.8 billions to 4.12.

Forced sales.—One evidence of the prosperity or the distress of agriculture is to be found in the number of foreclosures or tax sales. A clear indication of the post-war agricultural depression is to be found in the unprecedented totals to which such sales went during the 1920's. From 1926 to 1930, inclusive, foreclosures ranged from 14.8 per 1,000 farms to 18.2, while tax sales fluctuated from 4.2 to 5.2 per 1,000, a total forced sale of from 19.5 to 23.3 farms per 1,000. The high year was 1927, the low 1929. In 1930, the total of forced sales was 20.8; in 1931, 26.1; in 1932, 41.7; and in 1933, 54.1. The emergency legislation began to take effect in 1934, when the proportion dropped to 39.1. In 1935, the drop was more pronounced, to 28.3. There were, of course, sharp regional variations within these national figures, as Table 17 shows.

The most fortunate regions were the New England and Middle

TABLE 17

FARM INDEBTEDNESS: NUMBER OF FORECLOSURE SALES PER 1,000 FARMS, 1926–35 [a]

Division	*1926–31*	*1932*	*1933*	*1934*	*1935*	*Total 1932–35*	*Grand Total*
U.S.	102.4	28.4	38.8	28.0	21.0	116.2	218.6
N.E.	40.5	10.3	13.2	12.8	12.1	48.4	88.9
M.A.	53.2	12.4	19.6	18.0	16.2	66.2	119.4
E.N.C.	100.8	27.8	38.3	27.8	20.8	114.7	215.5
W.N.C.	151.9	43.8	61.5	44.4	34.6	184.3	336.2
S.A.	92.7	26.1	32.2	22.5	13.7	94.5	187.2
E.S.C.	81.2	24.6	36.4	24.7	18.6	104.3	185.5
W.S.C.	71.5	27.0	35.2	22.1	17.0	101.3	172.8
Mt.	162.7	27.0	33.6	28.7	23.7	113.0	275.7
Pac.	74.4	26.8	36.0	30.6	19.8	113.2	187.6

[a] Source: United States Department of Agriculture, Bureau of Agricultural Economics, Circular No. 354, April, 1935, and Circular No. 382, December, 1935.

Atlantic. Those hit hardest were the Middle West and Mountain. In areas where in a decade the equivalent of one-third of the farms have changed hands by foreclosure sale, there is obviously a serious economic maladjustment. This situation explains some of the phenomena described later in this chapter; and, along with the data on income, indicate the urgency behind the emergency agricultural program of 1933.

Even within regions, some states were harder hit than others. The equivalent of almost one-half of South Dakota's farms, and well over one-third of Montana's, changed hands by foreclosure in the decade 1926–35, as did almost two-fifths of Iowa's and one-third of Minnesota's. These ratios are based on the total number of farms. If the base were the total number of owner-operated farms that were mortgaged, it is clear that in some states the equivalent of almost the entire area, owner-operated but mortgaged, suffered foreclosure. In other words, it is probable that many who purchased at distress prices early in the decade 1926–35 were themselves unable to continue operations as the depression deepened, despite their lower capitalization.

As is noted elsewhere, tax sales in this same decade involved an additional 78.7 farms per 1,000, so that the total forced sales were equal to almost 30 per cent of all farms for the decade. From 1930 on, forced sales have exceeded voluntary transfers in the worst years by over three times. In 1934 and 1935, however, the general improvement was registered in a sharp decline in forced transfer and a small but steady increase in voluntary sales and trades. The total of forced sales does not include, of course, the number of tenant-operators who defaulted on crop liens, chattel mortgages, and other such obligations.

The basic reason, of course, for this deflation, the effect of which on the capital value of American agriculture has already been noted, was the unprecedented decline in the price of farm products and the static nature of interest and debt payments. The purchasing power of money has fluctuated tremendously from 1914 on; but the obligations of the debtor have had to be paid in dollars, not in the equivalent of the purchasing power he borrowed. Therefore, when farm purchasing power collapsed, foreclosure and tax sales were an inevitable sequence.

The Farm Credit Administration.—It was to ease this situation somewhat that the various Federal agencies lending to farmers were consolidated in the Farm Credit Administration; and the Administration was authorized to sell bonds to the public and lend to the farmers on advantageous terms, and at low rates of interest.

On September 1, 1936, as noted, the Administration had almost 2.9 billions of dollars outstanding in loans to farmers. During the peak of the emergency, loans sometimes reached 10 million dollars a day; and the average for 1934 was 5 million dollars. Almost 90 per cent of these loans went to refinance existing obligations due others. In almost one-fifth of the cases, the farmer's debt was adjusted downward to avoid foreclosure. At times, the F.C.A. was writing 70 per cent of the farm loan business; and even though the peak has passed, farm loans by outstanding life insurance companies decreased from May 1, 1935, to May 1, 1936, by 115 million dollars, while those of the F.C.A., through the land banks and commissioner, increased 176 million dollars. Outstanding bank loans also declined. In May, 1936, however, Federal agencies supplied only 22 per cent of the funds loaned on farm mortgages. The question arises, nonetheless, as to whether or not the Federal government is monopolizing the rural credit field; and, if so, how this may be changing local banking practice.

These general facts about the Federal Farm Credit Administration and its place in the rural credit situation are interestingly enough illustrated in the reactions of farmers, merchants, and bankers to the local activities of the organization.

Farm credit in the 140 communities.—The outstanding conclusion from this phase of the field survey is that no Federal activity touching these communities between 1930 and 1936 was more wholeheartedly approved. In only 2 of the 140 communities was there real opposition to the Farm Credit Administration. In both of these, a strongly partisan local paper has compaigned against it; and in both there was a strong local bank that stood in well with the farmers because of years of efficient and intelligent service. In 10 other places, the bankers were somewhat opposed, holding that now that the emergency was past the F.C.A. should retire from the mortgage, and especially from the production loan, business as rapidly as possible. In each of these places, however, the farmers, and in most of them the merchants, took an opposite view and pointed to the lowered interest rates, the "fair" method of appraisal on the basis of "normal value," as decided and lasting benefits.

In one such place, the banks had refused to lend money on what the community considered good security. With the advent of the Farm Credit Administration, the banks began to solicit business, including some they had refused, and offered to accept security formerly rejected. In a few cases the banks offered inducements, or used pressure, to prevent the transfer of loans from them to the F.C.A. One of the banks most opposed to the F.C.A. still will lend nothing under 8 per cent. Any farmer meeting its conditions could secure a Federal loan, according to local real estate men.

In 2 villages, the Farm Credit Administration program was opposed because no help had been extended in 1931 and 1932 by the old Federal Farm Loan Bank, and half the farms were foreclosed; but in one of these, the new agency took over enough farm mortgages to enable the local bank, which had closed, to pay a 30 per cent dividend. The opposition forthwith melted away. In about one-eighth of the communities studied, the Farm Credit Administration is credited with having saved the local bank. In the 128 communities where no opposition was discovered, there was general, and often enthusiastic, approval of the policies and procedures of the Farm Credit Administration; but this approval was tempered in 13 cases, most of them in the Middle West and the South, by the statements of the bankers that the Federal agency had taken the poorer class of business.[9] But in 4 cases out of 5, no significant critical opinion was expressed; and in these communities the interest and amortization payments were up to, or above, the average for the district as reported by the Farm Credit Administration. In 46 communities, all agreed that the F.C.A. had "helped greatly" or "saved the situation"; and in 68, that it had

[9] It is quite possible that this is true in some of the communities. In one, for instance, there was a page of the local newspaper given over to the advertising of foreclosure sales in the county, proceedings having been initiated by the Farm Credit Administration. In only a few other places, however, were such advertisements noted, and these in each case concerned only a few farms.

been of real assistance. In each case, one-half of these reports came from the Middle West, in which region lay three-sevenths of the communities studied. A regional summary of these comments is given in Table 18.[10]

Some idea of what the F.C.A. meant can be shown by summaries of the fieldworkers' reports. In one village, damaged by a hurricane as well as by the depression, 84 per cent of the growers utilized its facilities. In another, 500 seed loans were made in 1935; but with the better conditions of 1936, only 130. In a third, in which a desperate situation existed, the county agent, by working day and night with farmers and F.C.A. representatives, finally saved 156 farmers from impending foreclosures. In 24 places in which there was no opposition to the F.C.A. few or no loans were made. Curiously, there were no borderline cases. In places where more than 20 loans were made, the number was considerably larger, in some cases running up to two-thirds or four-fifths of all farmers. The banking situation in these villages, as described in Chapter VI, also throws considerable light on the contribution of, and the necessity for, the Farm Credit Administration.

TABLE 18

ATTITUDES OF COMMUNITIES TOWARD FARM CREDIT ADMINISTRATION

Region	*No. of Villages*	*Helped Greatly* [a]	*Helped* [a]	*Helped a Little* [a]	*No Help or Loan Application*	*Opposed*
All	140	46	68	8	16	2
M.A.	28	2	11	2	11	2
South	30	12	17	0	1	0
M.W.	60	22	33	4	1	0
F.W.	22	10	7	2	3	0

[a] For explanation of these terms, see Footnote 10.

This summary, of course, gives no indication of the many comments dealing with the value of the credit extended to the community and its farmers. The refunding and consolidation of

[10] "Helped Greatly" in the table means that the F.C.A. prevented bank failures or a large number of foreclosures. "Helped" indicates that without its assistance there would have been seriously inadequate credit facilities to handle the situation. "Helped a Little" means that fewer than 20 loans were made.

indebtedness enabled farmers to pay off merchants, doctors, tax collectors, and others. In some cases, debts were scaled down; but confidence in the credit structure was restored because creditors exchanged government obligations for doubtful, slow-paying, or frozen assets. Lowered interest rates and expansion of credit adequate for the need were mentioned again and again as outcomes of the Federal farm loan policy. The production and seed loans were greatly appreciated; but where local banks were strong, the F.C.A. apparently did not enter into the short-term credit business to any great extent. In the main, in these communities, the banks have reduced, or even retired from, long-term mortgage loans, but have kept the best of this business and all, or a generous share, of the short-term loans. In the main, also, the air has been cleared by the cessation, or the sharp slackening, of foreclosures, and by the strengthening of the whole credit structure. This process has given many communities a greater sense of stability and security than in the years when even leading farmers feared the loss of home and land.

TAXATION PROBLEMS

Throughout the discussion of farm credit, mention has been made of tax sales of farms. This situation was only less serious than the foreclosure problem. Land values and taxes alike skyrocketed during the prosperous years of 1917 to 1920, inclusive. Indeed, real estate taxes increased slowly through the 1920's, while land values were declining and prices were low in comparison with costs. Counting 1910–14 as 100 for taxes, the fluctuations were as follows, so far as real estate taxes are concerned:

1915	110	1922	224	1929	241
1916	116	1923	228	1930	238
1917	129	1924	228	1931	217
1918	137	1925	232	1932	188
1919	172	1926	232	1933	161
1920	209	1927	238	1934	153
1921	223	1928	239	1935	154

Stated another way, taxes in 1932 were $1.50 for each $100 of valuation; in 1934, $1.11, or 37 per cent below the 1929 peak of $1.76.

In other words, during the period from 1929 to 1932 taxes fell less than half as rapidly as farm producing power. In the latter year, according to a study of *The Farmer's Tax Problem* by the Bureau of Agricultural Economics, the average tax per acre in 1932 was about 10 per cent higher than in 1919; but real estate values had declined one-half. The tax per $100 of full value consequently increased more than 100 per cent.

Like debts, these taxes had to be paid in dollars of greater purchasing power than formerly. Thus they took an ever larger share of the declining farm income. Eventually farmers became delinquent in their payments, and then defaulted. In the whole country, in the 10 years from 1926 to 1935, inclusive, almost 8 per cent of the farms were sold to satisfy these claims. In the Old South, the proportion was about 12 per cent, as Table 19 shows; in the Middle Atlantic states, 13 per cent. As with foreclosures, the greatest trouble occurred in the areas devoted largely to a single crop.

What this meant in the 140 communities was shown in the

TABLE 19

FARM INDEBTEDNESS: TAX SALES PER 1,000 FARMS, 1926–35[a]

By Census Divisions

Division	*1926–31*	*1932*	*1933*	*1934*	*1935*	*Total*
U.S.	31.7	13.3	15.3	11.1	7.3	78.7
N.E.	22.2	5.2	6.6	7.3	6.8	48.1
M.A.	21.1	5.6	8.7	8.2	7.7	51.3
E.N.C.	24.0	6.5	5.6	4.2	2.7	43.0
W.N.C.	28.0	8.7	10.5	6.5	6.0	59.7
S.A.	49.5	21.0	27.3	18.2	10.8	126.8
E.S.C.	34.1	26.0	27.1	20.2	12.0	119.4
W.S.C.	24.0	13.2	16.0	12.2	5.9	72.0
Mt.	67.1	16.5	19.2	15.4	12.0	130.2
Pac.	24.9	10.8	8.1	6.5	4.8	55.1

[a] Source: United States Department of Agriculture, Bureau of Agricultural Economics, Circular No. 354, April, 1935, and Circular No. 382, December, 1935.

previous report, *Rural Social Trends.*[11] Therefore only two illustrations will be given. In one Middle Atlantic county, in November, 1932, 665 pieces of property, mostly farms, were sold for taxes. In a one-crop western community, the growing seriousness of the situation is shown by the percentage of land sold for taxes and the percentage delinquent.

	Per Cent of Land	
	SOLD FOR TAXES	DELINQUENT
1930	0.6	17.0
1931	0.7	34.4
1932	16.9	72.2
1933	24.4	60.0

This text table shows the cumulative effects of the difficulties and also a quite typical hesitancy on the part of the taxing authority before exacting the final penalty.

It has already been shown that taxes have begun to turn downward. Unlike the credit situation, there could be no Federal aid in effecting an improvement. Three causes account for this: decreased government services, substitute taxes such as sales and income taxes, and increased efficiency in government. The reduction in services was frequently forced by taxpayers' leagues; and evidence of the effect of this on schools, health services, and the like will appear in other chapters. In the Middle Atlantic county cited above, the taxpayers, acting through the Grange, secured a 70 per cent reduction in the highway appropriation and a 50 per cent cut in the tax for testing cattle for tuberculosis and that for public health. There were taxpayers' leagues in about one-eighth of the 140 communities. Invariably they struck blindly at existing services. No case was found in which they tried to make government more efficient by consolidating outmoded taxing units, such as counties, townships, or school districts, or by combining county offices.

The discussion of the last two problems, mortgage debt and

[11] Pages 46-47.

taxation, have indicated also certain adjustments and solutions arrived at. There remain three types of effort, each designed to combat the depression and its effects. One of these was overt action on the part of farm groups by use of the strike technique. The second was the Federal program of agricultural adjustment. Finally, there came the changes these years brought to the agricultural co-operatives. These three phases of the agricultural background will be discussed in the next chapter.

II

Agricultural Adjustments in Rural Communities

ONE OF the first indications of the need for adjustments to assist farmers to continue in business was a series of strikes that began in 1932. About one-eighth of the 140 communities included in this survey experienced such disturbances, which reached their peak in late 1932 and in 1933. The strikes were of two kinds: those that offered resistance to foreclosure sales, and those by which an effort was made to raise prices by keeping products from reaching market.[1] In addition, there was one strike of farm laborers in a fruit-growing area.

The strikes to prevent foreclosure sales occurred almost exclusively in the Middle West, which had three-fourths of all strikes of both kinds in these villages; but there were a few in the Middle Atlantic states. The usual procedure was for a group of farmers to assemble at the place of sale in advance of the announced time. When the officers who were to dispose of the property arrived, they were told that the sale would be opposed. If the proceedings were carried through, the farmers sometimes made bids of a few cents, and returned the property to the debtor. In one state the slogan was started, "They can't take our homes away." In the communities studied, the participants in these farm strikes were largely farmers. Often they were aided by sympathetic villagers. In one community, the initial stimulus came from the proprietor of a pool hall in a city of some 30,000 population about 30 miles away. He brought with him 2 trucks loaded with unemployed. Apparently

[1] No community studied was affected by the strike centering in Arkansas of the cotton tenants and croppers in the spring of 1936. This represents a third and highly significant type. Perhaps the fairest brief discussion of this movement is to be found in a special number of the *Information Service* of the Federal Council of the Churches of Christ in America issued June 27, 1936.

his leadership was accepted; but after 3 sales had been successfully prevented, the farmers took over the movement. In this section, farmers were organized and traveled hundreds of miles over the state on call to assist in organized resistance elsewhere. With one exception, this was the only case in the 140 villages where any evidence could be found of outside leadership in disturbances of this kind. In the other instance, it is alleged that the two leaders came from a very large city about 150 miles distant. Those opposed to the strike effectively discouraged it by attempting to lynch the men, who escaped, not by the aid of officers of the law, but through the kindly offices of a few friendly farmers. The local leaders in most of the places studied seem to have been farmers who were heavily in debt. The greater number of them were men in their forties. In a dozen cases, farmer leaders of these movements had themselves suffered foreclosure. In several other communities, committees of farmers investigated the facts in regard to every foreclosure and tax sale; and in a number of instances secured adjustments and a scaling down of the debt by suggesting that foreclosure proceedings would be resisted.[2]

The "holiday" movement.—The efforts to withhold products from market centered in the Middle West, where most of them were under the auspices of the Farmers' Holiday Association, and in the dairy communities in the New York City milk shed. In 2 communities, the local tax league shifted over into the holiday movement. In one, a "motorcade" was organized which kept milk from the creamery for a week and secured a slight increase in price. The employees in the creamery refused to handle such milk as trickled through; but village unemployed eagerly took their places. Eventually the original employees were taken back, partly because of farmer pressure.

The milk strike in the Chicago shed illustrated anew for the

[2] In one community, farmers successfully resisted the forced sale of the equipment of a village dentist to whom many of them owed money. His difficulty, they contended, was due to theirs. When the A.A.A. checks arrived the following fall, they paid their bills and the dentist satisfied his chattel mortgage.

farmers the problems arising when state lines bisect economic areas. Wisconsin tested its milk cattle for tuberculosis before Illinois, and quickly gained a larger share than formerly of the Chicago fluid milk trade. After Illinois required this test, it had naturally sought to recover its losses. With more fluid milk available than could be consumed in the Chicago shed, the price dropped. The 1936 opinion in such Wisconsin dairying communities as were studied was that only an interstate milk authority could effect a permanent solution for the problems of dairymen in this area. Much milk was dumped during the strike, and more was converted into cheese, but there was no extreme violence.

Several of the communities in the Middle Atlantic states were involved in the milk strike in the New York City milk shed in the summer of 1933. In this strike there was some violence. In one of the communities surveyed, a group of unarmed farmers were congregated at a strategic crossroad intent on persuading farmers on their way to the creamery to return home. There had been no violence. Several trucks had complied with the request not to deliver the milk. Drivers of these trucks reported that all conversation between them and the pickets was "good natured." The local leaders, as well as the local newspaper, had urged that there be nothing beyond a campaign of persuasion. Thirty-five state troopers were in the village guarding the creamery. For some reason they left the creamery in cars, driving toward the crossroad. Stopping near the farmers, the troopers, without provocation, suddenly attacked them and bystanders indiscriminately with clubs and tear gas. There was no resistance, but troopers struck old men, children, and farmers again and again, even those already wounded. One woman with a baby in her arms was struck down in her own garden as she was watching the proceedings. No milk truck was even in sight at the time of the attack.[3]

The effect on the community was interesting. Its rural news-

[3] The above paragraph is a summary of the testimony given at a hearing subsequently held in the high-school auditorium under the commanding officer of the troopers.

paper, one of the best in the United States, had been sympathetic to the dairymen's problems, but had been influential in promoting peaceful picketing in the event that a strike should come. After the attack, it published a very fair analysis of the conflicting issues and stories, and came out unequivocally against the state police. The village was immediately swung wholeheartedly to the side of the farmers. The physicians who treated the wounded, some of the attorneys practicing in the village, and various social organizations all wired protests to the governor and asked for an investigation of the incident and a removal of the troops. The few Jewish citizens made a similar appeal on religious grounds. The local businessmen's association wired:

> The ——— Club of ——— protests the extreme cruelty and absolutely unwarranted brutality of your Cossack State Troopers who have severely beaten, clubbed, and wounded old men, children, and innocent by-standers in conjunction with milk holiday here. We demand immediate withdrawal of these irresponsible half-crazed thugs and the substitution, if necessary, of responsible officers who have a knowledge of and respect for human rights.

The troopers were shortly withdrawn. The newspaper and several other agencies also wired the United Press asking that a staff member be sent to investigate and report. The request was granted.

For several reasons, this particular incident has been elaborated rather than others which occurred in these villages. Excellent newspaper accounts were available, as was also the testimony taken at a hearing. The community is an old, historic, conservative eastern one. It has always been overwhelmingly Republican in politics. Village-country relations have been highly co-operative since before the first study in 1923. Over 85 per cent of the population was native born. The leaders of the "holiday" were well-known, highly respected local citizens, holding offices in Grange, co-operative, church, and social organizations. They were loyal to the American system and satisfied that their peaceful picketing was well within the law.

In a number of other communities, fieldworkers were told that incidents similar to this were averted only by the conciliation committees of the Farm Credit Administration and the payments of the Agricultural Adjustment Act. It is to a consideration of the adjustment of the latter of these agencies that the discussion now turns.

THE AGRICULTURAL ADJUSTMENT ACT

With the coming in of the Roosevelt administration, energetic steps were taken to assist agriculture through the passage of the Agricultural Adjustment Act. As was stated in the introduction to this chapter, only the effect of the act in the 140 communities included in this survey will be here discussed. The reader must look elsewhere for detailed explanations of the law, and for appraisals of its effectiveness in assisting both rural and national recovery.[4]

The act was the first attempt at national social control of agriculture; and, as such, is of prime importance even though it was invalidated by the Supreme Court 32 months after its passage. A vast majority of the commercial farmers who were raising the crops included under the law co-operated with the Administration; and nationally as well as in the communities studied, with two or three exceptions, the proportion increased each year.

It is not easy to summarize the thousands of comments made to fieldworkers about the law and its administration. In more than one-fifth of the communities the benefits derived were deemed "invaluable." The payments made to farmers "saved the situation," "prevented complete ruin." In such statements local bankers, farmers, merchants, newspaper editors, tax collectors, and others all agreed. In about half the communities, the consensus of these individuals was that it had "helped considerably," "prevented serious losses," "saved a number from relief," "kept some farmers from bankruptcy." In these places a few were found who disagreed with the great majority. A few bankers believed that the existing

[4] Perhaps the best single source of information on the pro's and con's of the Agricultural Adjustment Act is to be found in the *Journal of Farm Economics*, especially Vol. XVII, Nos. 1, 2, and 3, and Vol. XVIII, Nos. 1 and 2.

measure of recovery would have come without Federal aid to agriculture. A few others believed the act to be "basically unsound," "useful only as an emergency measure." In another fifth of the communities, the act had been of little help or none, because crops locally raised were not included in the provisions; yet the consensus of opinion was either favorable to the act or neutral. In the remaining centers, there was active opposition on the part of the majority, even though in 4 such places it was admitted that the act had been of considerable local assistance. "But who would refuse Santa Claus?" In 10 places it was felt that the law as administered was unfair to tenants or owner-operators with small acreages. These attitudes are summarized in Table 20, which reveals that about two-thirds of the places were considerably helped

TABLE 20

REACTIONS TO THE AGRICULTURAL ADJUSTMENT ACT

Region	*Number of Communities*	*Invaluable*	*Helped Considerably*	*Little Help but Approved*	*No Help No Opposition*	*Helped but Opposed*	*No Help Opposed*
All regions	140	29	67	10	15	4	15
Middle Atlantic	28	...	4	4	10	...	10
South	30	12	14	...	2	1	1
Middle West	60	12	40	3	0	2	3
Far West	22	5	9	3	3	1	1

by, and also approved, the act; and that, all told, more than three-fourths approved it.

Naturally enough, for the most part the attitudes correlated with the benefits received. There was more opposition in the dairy sections and in fruit and truck areas than elsewhere. This represents the situation in summary form. The facts and opinions lying behind it will now be presented.

Trade increases.—Almost everywhere the act operated, merchants reported not only increased sales but also large payments on indebtedness. In one village which had suffered from both low prices and drought, one merchant had carried farmers for 2 years, especially for purchases of food and gas. The Agricultural

Adjustment Act saved him from bankruptcy. Within a few weeks after the receipt of the checks, farmers paid off $40,000 on their charge accounts, an equivalent of almost a year's average business. Similar stories came from every region except the Middle Atlantic, in which few communities benefited. Banks had notes paid off or restored to good standing. Tax collectors also reported large payments on back taxes as the checks rolled in. In one community, the banker traced the results of the first check to come in, a fairly large one. The farmer paid the hardware merchant, grocer, doctor, dentist, and tax collector. Both doctor and dentist turned over the farmer's checks to others in the community whom they owed, including again the tax collector, who was able thereby to make an overdue payment to the School Board, which forthwith made a 2 weeks' payment on back salaries due teachers, who in turn immediately put the money into circulation. As other checks arrived, there was a general circulation of the funds, wiping out old obligations and securing much-needed consumer goods, which cleared up the whole credit situation and stabilized the entire community.

With back debts cleared away, subsequent payments went quite generally for repairs, clothes, painting of houses and barns, and for capital expenditures such as farm equipment and automobiles. Many merchants reported trade increases of 50 to 100 per cent after the Agricultural Adjustment Act; and, like the farmers, credited this to the payments and increased prices of farm commodities which they felt were the result of the act.

In drought areas.—In the communities hard hit by the drought of 1934, enthusiasm for the Agricultural Adjustment Act was unbounded. "It saved most of our farmers and business concerns from complete ruin," said a banker in one community which had made only 20 per cent of its normal crop. "The Agricultural Adjustment Act was insurance against drought; and, with our crop 50 per cent below normal, it prevented foreclosures and staved off farmers going on relief," said another. These were quite typical comments from such places.

There was also testimony that in some communities the arrival of the Agricultural Adjustment Act checks cut the ground out from under those who were urging overt resistance to foreclosure and tax sales and promoting an extension of the Farmers' Holiday movement.

Striking the balance in the community.—In several places thoughtful leaders attempted to strike a balance between the credits and debits of the Agricultural Adjustment Act. "It both helped and hindered; but helped much more than it hindered," remarked two leaders in widely separated communities, both of whom favored the act. On the credit side, these and many others put down the increase in farm income and village trade, the stimulation of more scientific methods in cultivating the acres allowed under the contracts, the increased planting, especially in the South, of food crops and increased diversification in general, and the great increase in interest in, and thinking about, economic and social issues.

In many of the 96 communities that benefited considerably from the Agricultural Adjustment Act, intangible values were emphasized by farm and village leaders alike. It was said that the morale of the farmers, and of villagers who depended on their business, was lifted to the best levels since 1920, not only by the receipt of the benefit payments but also by the realization that agriculture had become a matter of national concern. Great values were seen too in farmers' working together instead of individually to meet their problems, in their being brought to see their problems in relation to the nation and world status of agriculture, in their dealing on terms of equality with government officials in planning the details of local administration of the act. It was stated many times that a new sense of responsibility had grown up among farmers as well as an increased comradery and spirit of co-operation; and that frequently the effects of this had carried over into other community affairs.

Debit items.—On the debit side, it was pointed out that the alert farmer who had, before the Agricultural Adjustment Act, reduced his acreage of cotton or grain and diversified his crops, was in effect penalized by the act either because of a lowered base acreage or because his rotation scheme would not permit further reduction. This, it was feared, would also prevent such farmers from sharing in the new Soil Conservation Act.

It was also stated in some places in every region, but especially in the South, that tenants were not given their full share of the benefit payments; and, in the South, that they were displaced. However, in several places in this region, owners were prosecuted under the Agricultural Adjustment Act for failure to live up to the sections of the contract relating to tenants.

One of the fieldworkers, a professor in a Middle Western university, attempted to explore the problem of displaced tenants in the Southern villages which he studied and one of the authors' students made a similar attempt in another state. These two covered, all told, one-fourth of the Southern villages. They both found that there had been displacement of tenants, especially croppers, in all communities. They agreed that this had swollen the relief rolls. As one tenant put it, "The government wouldn't let us plant, so we had to go on relief." They also agreed that this displacement was but a new phase of the already serious problem of cotton tenancy. The displaced tenants were clearly the less efficient, the more shiftless, and to some extent those in poorer health. Many of them found relief a relatively pleasant avenue of escape from the grueling toil of the cotton fields, and were not sorry to take it. County welfare workers essentially corroborated this analysis. This statement of the situation is no excuse for it, nor does it give consideration to the displacement of tenants through mechanization. Some leaders are already concerned as to eventualities when, as, and if Federal aid is withdrawn, especially with the growing mechanization of the cotton plantations. It must be remembered that the immediate problem has developed out of a situation thus described by Johnson, Embree, and Alexander in their *The Collapse of Cotton Tenancy.*[5]

> The cultural landscape of the cotton belt has been described as a "miserable panorama of unpainted shacks, rain-gullied fields, straggling fences, rattle-trap Fords, dirt, poverty, disease, drudgery, and monotony that stretches for a thousand miles across the cotton belt. . . ."
>
> The present system is so constructed that the landless remain landless and the propertyless remain propertyless. To accumulate property, to increase independence, is to oppose the system itself. . . . Not only is it impossible to develop a hardy stock of ambitious farm owners—the persistent American ideal—but it is impossible to avoid physical and moral decadence.

There were also some criticisms of alleged "red tape," and a few of inefficient administration on the part of the local committee. It is significant, however, that in only 3 communities of the 96 that benefited was there any criticism of the basic procedures, such as allotment of individual base acreages. Everywhere else this essentially democratic device seems to have operated to the satisfaction of the great majority so far as the field surveyors could discover.

The above criticisms were made in communities where the consensus of opinion was strongly in favor of the Agricultural Adjustment Act. Elsewhere the basis of the criticism was broader. In many communities, the better-educated expressed grave doubts as to the restoration of prosperity by the application of the principle of inducing scarcity. These, for the most part, favored the idea of adjustment and control because of the necessities of a suddenly changed situation; and many of them were hopeful of the soil conservation features of the new act. A few ministers added their voices to this criticism on moral and religious grounds; though far fewer than was expected in view of the newspaper pub-

[5] Charles S. Johnson, E. R. Embree, and W. W. Alexander, *The Collapse of Cotton Tenancy* (Chapel Hill, University of North Carolina Press, 1935).

licity given to clerical opinion on this point. Only two were found who averred that the drought was sent by God as punishment for plowing up cotton and for slaughtering hogs before they had attained normal weight.

Buyers of farm produce in 2 or 3 places and one large canner complained that the act had made the farmers "unreasonable" in their bargaining and "apt to question the set price." This was interpreted by these critics as indicating a dangerous increase in "radicalism."

There were also the familiar expressions of doubt as to the wisdom of the government's setting quotas of the number of acres to be planted. These comments were heard chiefly in the places that could not share in the benefits. In 3 communities, there seemed to be a well-defined idea that the benefits received would somehow be taken away again through taxation. In one place this idea was fostered by the banker, who, it is alleged, also stated that he would withdraw credit facilities from those who signed contracts. Politics was also charged in some places. It is perhaps significant that, despite some bitter attacks on the Agricultural Adjustment Act to which fieldworkers listened, especially in the East, no one alleged that benefits were being paid for not raising crops that never had been raised.

The Supreme Court decision.—It is quite natural that with so large a proportion of these communities benefiting from the Agricultural Adjustment Act, the values and benefits should be emphasized more than the mistakes and criticisms. The only purpose of this discussion has been to report local opinions and evidence. It is equally understandable that the decision of the Supreme Court invalidating what, to the benefiting farmers, were the essential features of the act, produced great disappointment. In only one of the 96 communities profiting considerably from the act was the decision received "calmly." In the others it left them "infuriated," "very critical," "hostile to the Court," "confused and angry."

Editorials found in local newspapers by those engaged in this study were unanimously condemnatory.

One newspaper announced the decision in the following headline:

SUPREME COURT VOIDED TRIPLE A
Rights of State Invaded Says Court
Holy Smokes!

A few editorials charged that the decision had been "dictated by the money bags."

The grounds of the decision were particularly resented. It was pointed out that neither markets nor the winds and floods that produced erosion problems were respecters of state boundaries or state rights. As one local editorial put it, "The grounds rather than the decision destroys our confidence in the Sanctity of law as so interpreted." The subsequent decision returning the processing taxes paid by the consuming public to the processors aroused even more criticism. In no one of the 140 villages could any approval of this action be discovered except on the part of a few processors.

Villagers in general agreed with the farmers on the decision. Quite representative of this feeling was the action in one large county-seat village. After a mass meeting of the contract signers, the following telegram was sent to all Senators and Congressmen of the state: "Eleven hundred contract signers of ——— county urge immediate substitution which will permit continuation present production control program." This telegram was paid for by the village merchants. This raises the question of the Soil Conservation Act substituted for the old Agricultural Adjustment Act.

The revised program.—It was too soon in most communities, at the time when field work was being conducted, to learn much about attitudes toward and the support of this new Soil Conservation program of the Agricultural Adjustment Administration. In the crop areas covered by the old law, support, as measured by contracts signed, was off from 8 to 12 per cent. In 24 communities, there was general approval of the new plan; in 3, opposition; and in 4, a good bit of questioning. In the other 109, no consensus of opinion existed; local leaders said they did not as yet know enough about the plans to express themselves.

It was perhaps significant that the new program was being received with interest and even enthusiasm in some places where the original plans had aroused opposition. This applied especially to dairying and truck- and fruit-farming areas, though these attitudes were not unanimous in all such communities.

County agents reported that attendance at meetings to explain the new program was as good as, or often better than, when the old Agricultural Adjustment Administration was being initiated. It is interesting to note that in one community where the planning and discussion program under the Agricultural Extension Service (described in Chapter VIII) had been very successful, the whole new program was carefully considered, and committees were appointed to go into every phase of the matter. Leading farmers in a number of the Southern and Mid-Western communities were quite enthusiastic about the new program, believed that it was basic to much-needed soil conservation, and that it would be helpful in many ways. They approved, too, of the payment being given for what involved work rather than "as a gift for not working."

But it is evident that elsewhere the new program will have a harder row to hoe. "This program is only good farming and I don't propose to be paid extra by tax money for what I'm doing for my own profit," said one master-farmer. On the other hand, it was pointed out in several places that one value of the new program is that it fosters practices which the best farmers have used and advocated for some years. In another community, one-sixth of the audience left a Farm Bureau meeting when the new program was to be explained and returned afterwards. In 2 communities farmers were saying, "We don't believe it's right, but if Uncle Sam insists on giving away money we might as well get ours." All these comments came from areas of specialized farming.

In grain and cotton areas, there was some objection that the basic acreage allotted was too small to make co-operation profitable, especially for the small farm; and quite naturally in a presidential year some of those interviewed suspected that the whole program was a political device. The relation of the new program to the small farm was arousing concern in some of the 140 communities, because small farms often need soil conservation most and are harmful to the region when the care of their soil is neglected; yet can hardly support proper procedures, even under the scale of payments adopted for the new Agricultural Adjustment Administration program.

Quite obviously and naturally, the gigantic effort to exert social control over agriculture to benefit both agriculture and the nation is, in its new form, not fully understood. The necessity for haste in drafting the present law to take the place of that invalidated by the Supreme Court left weak spots. The educational program faced and faces a huge task in re-educating the nearly 7 million farmers of the nation in both the basic principles and the necessary procedures, if these 140 communities are at all representative in this particular.

Soil erosion and conservation.—Perhaps one of the greatest assets of the new Agricultural Adjustment program is its tie-up with soil conservation; for one of the most significant changes in agricultural practices and attitudes in these communities was indicated by the growing interest in a permanent soil-conservation program, chiefly for individual farms or communities, but also for the state and the nation. It is not yet generally recognized as a problem in all these centers; but in previous studies it was never discussed even by leaders. In 1936, it was no unusual thing for leading farmers and bankers to raise with fieldworkers the problems of soil erosion and conservation. In 10 communities in 7 states, everyone seemed alert at least to the local aspects of the problem. In one, a flood had hastened action. The Farm Bureau informed the government it needed flood and erosion control, reforestation, and soil conservation to keep its lands from becoming submarginal; and both offered and asked for co-operation to these ends. In another, a tractor was purchased for terracing, which was done at cost under the supervision of the county agent. In at least 2 Southern communities, the owners are making rigid demands of their tenants in regard to cover crops and similar soil-conserving procedures. Undoubtedly a few more years will see more progress in this direction.

One community that in the words of the county judge, "has seen the light at last," became active in terracing and crop rotation in 1933. Three years later, it reaped an unexpected reward when the floods of 1936 arrived. Formerly, in floods, a small creek went on the rampage, inundating many acres. This year, with three-fourths of the land in that sector terraced, the creek was tamed completely, crops were saved, and erosion held to a minimum. This experience, according to the agricultural teacher in the high school, was "worth 100 lectures."

Such progress is, of course, overdue. The Soil Conservation Service and the National Resources Board both reported in 1936 on the serious ravages of erosion by wind and water. Nearly 160 million acres have lost all or most of their topsoil and are already entirely or nearly useless for cultivation. Over a half-billion more have lost from one-fourth to three-fourths of their topsoil; and the cultivated portion will be useless in time unless drastic steps are taken. All told, an area equal to about three-fourths of our present farm acreage has been affected. Only the Northeast among the regions has escaped the results of our prodigal soil mining.

It is encouraging, therefore, that the discussion of the problems of, and remedies for, erosion by wind and water has begun to be a topic of current interest in at least some of the communities studied. It shows that the experts who for years seem to have been voices crying in the wilderness are at last being heard.

What can happen when erosion runs its course unopposed is

shown by one of the field surveys. In 1924, there was a place of some 700 persons on the fringe of the trade area of one of the 140 villages. It had a bank, 14 stores, a good school, and churches. In 1930, the bank and 6 stores had closed, the population had dropped below 500, farms had been abandoned. In 1936, farming had all but disappeared. There were but 3 struggling stores, the population was about 300. The children were transported to the village for school. The bulk of the adult males were commuting to work, or were living on relief. Topsoil was gone, huge gullies scarred the earth. The neighborhood was a rural slum still on the downgrade.

CHANGES IN FARM PRACTICES

Thus far the discussion has dealt with a legal adjustment to the depression conditions, participation in which was, however, voluntary but very general. Other adjustments were made on an individual or community basis. In exactly one community out of 7, there was marked progress to a rather wide diversification over and above changes effected by the Agricultural Adjustment Act. In most of these, the growing of garden truck for home consumption played a prominent part. This was especially true in the South, where in some communities the owners had decided that it was cheaper to have their tenants "grow their groceries than to furnish them." The 1935 agricultural census reports an increase of 34 per cent for the nation in acreage devoted to vegetables, other than potatoes. But even this brings the total to only about one per cent of the improved land in crops.

In one community in 20, the farmers had turned to some new crop that was proving unexpectedly important and profitable. In one, it was Ladino clover; in another, flower seeds, the demand for which was said to have increased all through the depression. In a third, soy beans were raised for an automobile manufacturer, and peppermint and certain other specialties flourished profitably on what had once been considered wasteland. Back of each of these decided shifts was a story of ingenuity and leadership on the part of one man, or of a few men at the most.

Two communities, previously devoted to a few special crops, increased the number of these. In the first, which enjoyed a 10 months' growing season, the processes of cultivation, harvesting, packing, and marketing were thus spread over the entire year. This solved a stubborn transient-labor problem, which was giving the community much concern at the time of each previous study. In the other, the increased sources of income, together with the decreased living costs, left this community relatively as well off as in 1929. It was one of 3 that appeared to have suffered little if at all during the depression.

In one-tenth of the communities, but especially in those studied in Texas, Nebraska, and Kansas, there was a sharp increase in mechanization. The influence of this on the size of farms was discussed in Chapter I. In some of the villages in the latter 2 states, tractor sales in the last 2 crop years had averaged round 200, two-thirds of them in 1935–36. Half of these were new; half, second-hand. In some places this was a drought development. Drought and dust had killed off the horses. Power was needed; and it was proving cheaper to buy a tractor than to restock with work horses. Bankers and county agents were against this trend. Few of the machines were being purchased for cash; and the bankers and county agents feared overproduction. They pointed out that the farm "grows nothing that serves as oil, gasoline, or grease." The farmer retorted, "Yes, but when I'm not using the tractor I don't have to feed it, nor do I have to curry it." In 2 places, the battle seems to be joined between the recommended mixed and livestock farming and mechanized cash-grain farming.

That these communities represent at least one type is borne out by the Census Bureau report on *The Manufacture and Sale of Farm Equipment and Related Products: 1935.* This shows practically a 50 per cent drop in the value of farm equipment sold by manufacturers in 1931 as compared with 1930. But in 1935, unit sales were only 21.1 per cent below 1930.

On tractors alone, 1930 saw a sale of 202,458. In 1931, only 71,104 were disposed of; but in 1935, the total sold exceeded 161,000.

DROUGHT

The drought of 1936, which came on just after the field work for this study was completed, may be doubly serious in some of these villages. What it means can be seen by comparing yields per acre, in bushels, for one Nebraska community by years:

Commodity	*1930*	*1932*	*1934*
Corn	34	37	5.9
Wheat	20	17.2	3.0
Barley	32	25	6.4
Rye	32	17	3.8
Oats	34	34	7.0
Alfalfa (tons)	2.9	2.0	0.0

Why, under such conditions, the Agricultural Adjustment Act payments were declared lifesavers is explicable. The efforts to do anything that might stave off the effects of some similar calamity is also understandable.

In the main then, agriculture in the communities studied is in flux. Where cotton-bolls whitened the landscape, there are green-topped turnips, red-cheeked tomatoes, lacy asparagus plants. Aging orchards yielded their last fruit, and have given their last service as firewood; and in their stead chickens eternally scratch for worms, or grain waves once more. Shifts like these have been discussed more often than they were found. Where found, they have been preceded by conferences in Farm Bureau and Grange meetings, in hardware stores and over the home supper table. They have brought new problems for county agents, but they demonstrate that the farmer is ready to move in new directions.

THE CO-OPERATIVES

One adjustment to the problems of agriculture long antedated the depression. For years, American farmers have practiced co-operation, especially in the marketing field, as the best means of increasing their net return on goods marketed, and to reduce their costs on supplies purchased. The trend in this movement as summarized by R. H. Elsworth of the Farm Credit Administration is as follows:

Year	*Number of Associations*	*Volume of Business in Thousands*	*Members*
1915	5,424	$ 635,839	651,186
1925	10,803	2,400,000	2,700,000
1930	12,000	2,500,000	3,100,000
1934	10,900	1,365,000	3,200,000
1935	10,900	1,530,000	3,280,000

Of these associations, about one-fifth are purchasing organizations only; the rest are marketing or both. The decline in the number of associations is not significant. There have been some liquidations; but there have also been consolidations of local co-operatives into federations, national or regional terminal market sales-agencies, and large-scale centralized associations. It will be noted that the total gross membership has increased fivefold in the first 15 years covered by the table, and slowly throughout the 1930's. The trend has been toward fewer but larger associations, and this was clearly noted in the 140 villages in the 1930 study. The decline of 40 per cent in the dollar volume of business is largely, if not wholly, explicable on the basis of the sharp decline in the price level.

There is a possibility that these figures are underestimates, especially those giving the number of associations. Mr. Elsworth kindly opened his records on the 140 communities to the authors. These disclosed that the fieldworkers reported about 50 per cent more co-operatives than were listed in the Farm Credit Administration files. Part of the discrepancy may be accounted for by differences in definition. Some of it is probably due to the fact that the data for this study were gathered by field work, whereas the Farm Credit Administration's come by correspondence. Assuming that this ratio of difference would hold nationally, there are probably nearly 15,000 co-operatives. Even if this is a reasonably correct estimate, there would not be proportionate increases in volume of business and membership, since the Farm Credit Administration would obviously not miss the larger co-operative organizations.

The co-operative movement is far stronger in some regions than in others. Sixty-three and six-tenths per cent of the membership is in the Middle West, which also transacts more than 55 per cent of the business. California, with 2.5 per cent of the membership, has nearly 12 per cent of the business. The rest is shared by all the other states.

W. I. Myers, governor of the Farm Credit Administration,[6] estimates that, all told, there are more than 20,000 farmers' business co-operatives in the United States. This includes those already noted, credit unions, and nearly 2,000 mutual insurance companies. Co-operatives purchasing oil, gasoline, insurance, and electricity are among the fastest growing in number and volume of business at present. The 1934 volume of business for these consumer or purchasing co-operatives was 365 million dollars, and 1936 may run to half a billion, or 5 or 6 per cent of the total rural retail trade and one-tenth of the farm retail trade. These are probably conservative estimates. Gas and oil sales of the Ohio Farm Bureau co-operatives in the first half of 1936 were almost 3 million dollars, a gain of almost 50 per cent over the same period in 1935. The Central Co-operative of Wisconsin, the Eastern States Farmers Exchange, the Grange Co-operative Wholesale, and others reported 1936 business running from 27 to 63 per cent over 1935, which in turn was sharply higher than in 1934. For the crop year 1935–36, the Farm Credit Administration reports that the co-

[6] Press release of July 22, 1936.

operative purchase of farm supplies was 25 per cent over the previous year, bringing this item alone to 315 million dollars.

With this national background, it is of interest to get a close-up on local situations as given in the 140 villages. But the tendency toward consolidation, even on a county basis, makes it difficult to present as clear-cut a picture as in 1930. Time and again, field-workers reported that local marketing organizations had consolidated, or had been absorbed in county or district agencies, so that local memberships were difficult or impossible to secure. The data on marketing co-operatives that follow contain, therefore, a considerable but unestimatable understatement. On the other hand, some co-operatives that existed in 1930 were liquidated during the depression years. This was especially true in the Southern and Middle Atlantic villages.

The net result of these two forces was to reduce the number of local co-operative organizations in the 140 village-centered communities from 233 to 201, and their membership from 40,340 to 37,200.[7] It is conservatively estimated that without the consolidation noted above, the number of co-operatives would be at least 10 per cent higher, and the membership from 10 to 15 per cent larger. The average membership for each co-operative in these centers increased from 173 in 1930 to 186 in 1936. It seems from these data as if the co-operative movement in these villages had followed national trends or possibly bettered them a little.

The decline, already noted, in the number of local co-operatives with local organizations, which began in these communities between 1924 and 1930 despite increased memberships, continued in all regions except the Far West. It was particularly severe in the South, where the depression took a heavy toll. The total volume of business for the 127 co-operatives reporting, both marketing

[7] This 1936 membership figure is estimated on the basis of the 88 per cent of the co-operatives reporting on membership. For the first time in this series of studies, some of the larger co-operatives, 12 per cent in all, declined to give membership figures. A number of these were located in communities where there was strong opposition to their activities on the part of non-co-operative producers or middlemen.

and consumers' and excluding three insurance organizations, was $14,427,257, or $113,600 for each organization; a volume far exceeding that of the average mercantile establishment in these communities.

It should be emphasized that the above text on the number of co-operatives has dealt only with totals. As Table 21 shows, the number of purchasing co-operatives increased from 47 to 63; and between 1930 and 1935 there was a gain in the number that both marketed and purchased. The loss in the number of associations that were exclusively marketing groups produced the entire net loss, and has three explanations: first, the considerable number of marketing co-operatives which in the inter-survey period began also to purchase supplies co-operatively for their members and therefore changed their classification; second, the movement already noted for local organizations to be absorbed completely in district or regional agencies; third, and least important, the small number of co-operatives that liquidated their affairs as a result of the depression.

Exactly 60 per cent of these co-operatives distributed profits on a patronage basis only; 6 per cent more used both patronage and profit dividends. The others required all members to hold stock, and dividends were declared on the stock held regardless of patronage. In practice, there appeared to be a high correlation between the number of shares held and the patronage; some at least of this type nevertheless controlled their affairs on the basic co-operative principle of one man—one vote. The plan of declaring dividends on stock only was especially frequent in the Middle West. In the other regions, the patronage or dual base was used in three-fourths to nine-tenths of the co-operatives. Some of these data are summarized in Table 21.

Back of these statistics lie some interesting and probably quite typical stories, especially in connection with purchasing organizations. Local merchants have become quite worried by the co-operatives in about one village of every 12, but have been unable to withstand them except in a single village where the farmers liquidated a very successful purchasing co-operative for the sake of good village-country relations, but only after securing certain concessions. In one village under banker leadership, the businessmen organized *sub rosa* to wreck the purchasing co-operative. Propaganda was skillfully spread that it was being run by "reds" financed from Russia, and that it was illegal. An attempt was made to arrest the manager. When this failed, his life was threatened. The co-operative, under wise and courageous leadership, carried the war into the enemies' country, and the opposition has ungraciously accepted defeat. The bank will not lend to co-operative members, but they have turned successfully to the Farm Credit Administration. The 1935 business of this farmers' consumer co-operative in a very hard-hit Southern community, reached the astounding total of $244,000. There are 400 members. In most of the consumer co-operatives that have been formed in the inter-survey period, both farmers and villagers are members except in such conflict situations as have just been described. In one community the $10 membership certificates, which drew 6 per cent interest all through the depression, are much sought after by farmers and villagers alike, and circulate almost as legal tender.

In several communities where farmers had trouble with the local creamery, co-operatives were organized. All, thus far, have been successful, not only in raising prices but in their management. In one of these places, by agreement, dividends are not to be paid until the private concern is "liquidated." One of these co-operative creameries, instead of paying dividends, is setting aside a cent for every incoming pound of milk to create a fund with which to buy out the opposition, which has lost a great amount of business.

An interesting sidelight on co-operation was found in connection with the farmer-owned telephone companies. In virtually every case it was reported that disconnections during the depression were far fewer in the co-operative companies than where the Bell system had a monopoly. The co-operative rates were, of course, lower.

TABLE 21

TYPES OF CO-OPERATIVES

Region	*Number of Villages*	*Number with Co-operatives*			*Total Co-operatives*			*Buy Only* [a]			*Sell Only* [b]			*Both*		
		1924	*1930*	*1936*	*1924*	*1930*	*1936*	*1924*	*1930*	*1936*	*1924*	*1930*	*1936*	*1924*	*1930*	*1936*
All regions	140	120	114	93	263	233	201	47	40	62	140	141	65	76	52	73
Middle Atlantic	28	22	23	16	41	39	30	15	18	13	19	19	13	7	2	4
South	30	23	19	16	44	33	23	7	0	2	22	21	11	15	12	10
Middle West	60	54	53	42	114	110	92	22	20	33	50	59	22	42	31	37
Far West	22	21	19	19	64	51	56	3	2	15	49	42	19	12	7	22

[a] That is, consumer co-operatives.
[b] That is, marketing co-operatives.

The co-operatives obviously did not come through the depression without trouble and losses. In 2 Middle Western communities hard hit by the depression and drought, the 4 co-operatives existing in 1930 all found themselves losing money and liquidated, though without loss. In one Far Western town, 3 big growers bought orchards at foreclosure on tax sales, constructed their own drying yards, and refused to work with the co-operatives; thereby wrecking the local unit of a regional agency in this community.

The Farm Credit Administration data for these 140 communities includes information as to the defunct co-operatives. Since the compilation began some 20 years ago, a total of 115 have liquidated for one reason or another. The least stable group seems to have been the marketing association of specialized crops like raisins, olives, and vegetables; and in proportion to the existing number of co-operatives, liquidations were more frequent in the Middle Atlantic and Southern regions than elsewhere.

This summary of the co-operative movement emphasizes the fact that it is a well-established device whereby farmers attempt to adjust their economic problems. It was not born of the depression. Rather, as an established agency, it is shown as making its own institutional adjustments to the changing conditions of 1924–36; adjustments not dissimilar to those of non-co-operative commercial agencies. Some co-operatives have succumbed. But, in the main, the trend is to a smaller number of local organizations and a larger and stronger membership, as well as to consolidations into regional, district, or county agencies. These consolidations have been made possible by the improved facilities of communication and transportation, and by a growing interest in consumer co-operation, which is broadening out to include the handling of many more kinds of supplies and household necessities.

III

Population Changes

THE SURVEY of the 140 American agricultural villages in 1936 undertook to discover what population changes had occurred during the depression years, 1930 to 1936. The field work was limited to a rapid survey of the status of each village with respect to a large number of variables. But in 1936, independent enumerations of the village populations were not available, as they had been in 1930 when the official enumeration which the Bureau of the Census made available in 1930 was a significant advantage.

To lessen the resulting disadvantage in 1936, the field surveyors were required to report estimates of population. Each fieldworker was instructed to return an estimate of village, of open-country, and of total community population. Each estimate was to be an average of the judgments of postmaster, school superintendents, assessors, telephone supervisors, and other officials or authorities in a position to know of population and migration. It is recognized that such estimates might be subject to errors of bias or of ignorance. Yet the data are perhaps better than results obtained by extrapolating trends, since local migrations are evaluated. The inferences based on these recorded estimates are limited by the validity of the judgments, and this cannot be too much emphasized. Nevertheless, since the estimates are the best approximations to the total population, the statistics are presented as a background for the relative growth of American agricultural villages and the processes of migrations in the last half decade. In previous studies, field-work estimates agreed closely with final census figures. This time, however, the larger amount of population movement may have introduced an element of error.

In Table 22 are given the average population per village in

1930, and the average estimated population per village in 1936, for the 140 villages.

In 1930 the total village population in the 140 villages was 188,893; in 1936 the estimated population was 201,425, an increase of 6.67 per cent, which may be compared with the gain of 2.7 per cent from 1924 to 1930.[1] In each region, except the Far West, increase in population in the villages surveyed averaged about 5 per cent. In those of the Far West it was about two and a half times as great, almost 13 per cent. The increase averaged about 6 per cent for the small, for the medium, and for the large

TABLE 22

VILLAGE POPULATION: THE AVERAGE POPULATION PER VILLAGE IN 1930 AND THE AVERAGE ESTIMATED POPULATION PER VILLAGE IN 1936

140 American Agricultural Villages: by Region and by Size of Village in 1930

Region and Size	*Number of Villages*	*Average Population per Village 1930*	*Average Estimated Population per Village 1936*	*Relative Change since 1930 (1936–1930)/1930*
All regions	140	1,349	1,439	+ 6.67%
Middle Atlantic	28	1,192	1,250	+ 4.86
South	30	1,385	1,466	+ 5.84
Middle West	60	1,318	1,385	+ 5.08
Far West	22	1,586	1,790	+12.86
Small villages	48	707	749	+ 5.94
Medium villages	57	1,283	1,353	+ 5.54
Large villages	23	2,041	2,164	+ 6.02
Towns	12	2,906	3,211	+10.49

villages. Those villages, however, which between 1924 and 1930 had passed out of the census classification for villages grew at a faster rate. The villages which by 1930 had become towns grew from an average population of 2,906 to an estimated 3,211, an increase of 10.5 per cent.

VILLAGE GROWTH RAPID IN DEPRESSION

These estimates of 1936 population indicate, not only that American agricultural villages did not decline in size during the

[1] The 1924 population was estimated in the same manner as the 1936 population.

depression, but even that their population probably increased at more than twice their rate for the period from 1924 to 1930.

It is not surprising that the village populations increased. Migration from farms to villages, coupled with the fact that fewer villagers emigrated from the villages, makes the estimated increase very probable. The surveyors reported migration to the villages as well as curtailment, though not the cessation, of emigration from them. Table 23 gives the sources of the villages' new population between 1930 and 1936. The new population is classified as coming from near-by urban centers, surrounding open country, or

TABLE 23

THE ORIGIN OF NEW VILLAGE POPULATION IN 1936

140 American Agricultural Villages: by Region and by Size of Village in 1936

	Villages Reporting New Population from:				
Region and Size	NEAR-BY URBAN CENTERS	SURROUNDING OPEN COUNTRY	OTHER REGIONS	*No Change in Village Population*	*No Answer*
All regions	21	47	22	43	7
Middle Atlantic	6	6	2	13	1
South	4	10	5	8	3
Middle West	9	28	4	16	3
Far West	2	3	11	6	...
Small villages	7	9	6	17	3
Medium villages	9	24	8	17	3
Large villages	3	9	1	7	...
Towns	2	5	7	2	1

other geographic areas. When the field reports indicated population "mostly from city communities," "from large centers," or "from large cities of surrounding territories," the origin is given as *near-by urban centers;* the new population reported as "moved in from the country," as "farm laborers who moved to the village on WPA," as coming "from inside the county," or "from the trade areas," is classified as of *surrounding open-country* origin; the new population reported as "part came from nearby open country and part from other places," as coming "from outside district," or "from the dust bowl," is classified as from *other geographic centers;* and when the reports were "only slight movement from nearby" or "some left, and a few others replaced them," the classification is *no change of village population.*

Ninety of the 140 villages reported some new population by migration, whereas 43 villages showed no migrational influx, and 7 did not answer the question. Half of the Middle Atlantic, more than 60 per cent of the Southern, almost 70 per cent of the Middle West, and more than 70 per cent of the Far West villages reported increase in population due to migration to the villages. A little more than half of the small-sized, more than two-thirds of the medium-sized, and almost two-thirds of the large-sized villages, as well as over four-fifths of the towns, reported migrational influx.

WHERE THE NEW VILLAGE POPULATION CAME FROM

The new population varied in origin, however, from region to region. In the Middle Atlantic areas, it was primarily from near-by urban centers and from surrounding territory; in the South and the Middle West, it was chiefly from the open country; while in the Far West, the other geographic areas were the dominating sources.

The Middle Atlantic migration to the villages was undoubtedly a depression phenomenon. The curtailment of economic opportunity in the Middle Atlantic manufacturing centers sent people to the villages in search of new opportunities, or at least to find lower living costs. One New York village reported, "the depression forced migration from cities to cheaper homes and low taxes of villages. When mills shut down, some 40 families came to the village and took up farming." A Pennsylvania village reported "influx of new population from Elmira, Binghamton, Endicott, and Johnson City into village and open country. They moved into anything they could get, so that some village homes were converted into apartments."

In the South, the migration to the village was due in part to the attractiveness of relief, in part to the opportunity for work on P.W.A. projects, and in part to the mechanization of the farms.

The A.A.A. also had some influence; some displaced croppers moved to the trade centers. A typical Southern report is, "People moved in to get relief benefits and work on government projects." A Southern village reported, "the new inhabitants are employed in the area E.R.A. and W.P.A. offices and in the new stores, filling stations, and the remodeled hotel . . . the county relief worker believes that 45 to 50 new families moved into the village in the last five years." The other type of migration is shown in the report of a Southern village, which increased its population from 1,131 in 1930 to 1,500 in 1936, that "dual factors are responsible: an embryonic oil boom in the vicinity and the tractor-forced tenant displacement on adjacent farms which has driven scores of farming families to the village and the safety of relief and W.P.A."

Contrasting with the urban depression of the Middle Atlantic area and with the reduction of farm work plus the lure of relief in the South, the drought was probably the cause of the Middle West villageward movement. The reports were, "population came from Middle West drought areas," and "influx from drought-stricken sections in Missouri." A Kansas village, however, listed four sources for the new population of 120 persons: "(1) the movement of people from open country to the village; (2) generally stimulated business conditions; (3) stranded oil-field workers from other parts of the county; and (4) officers from a C.C.C. camp who established residence." Another Mid-West village, which increased its population by 725, points to farm consolidation as the cause in a report referring to the new residents as "tenants from neighboring farms, as they 'were required to vacate small farms in the trend toward larger ones.' "

Just as in the Middle West, the drought regions and the Dust Bowl contributed new population to the Far West villages. A California village reported an added population of 121 persons "from the Middle West, Texas, and the South"; another village reported "a steady influx of people from Missouri"; and another reported its new population as coming "from all sections of the U.S. by word of friends, and promises of employment." A proud Oregon village reported "a considerable population increase, mostly from drought areas and busted California communities."

BETTER TIMES WILL LURE MANY FROM VILLAGES

In general, the migration of the people to villages has been unusually heavy in the last 5 years. The urban depression, the lure of relief and work relief, mechanization of farms, and the unfortunate severity and length of the drought have forced unusual migration. The source of the migration in the Middle Atlantic may mean that the Middle Atlantic village population increase is temporary. Readjustments will probably follow on the improvement of urban employment opportunities. It may be expected that an exodus from the village to the cities will occur shortly in the Middle Atlantic region. Such an exodus, however, is less likely to occur in the South. The farm tenants, farm laborers, and Negro croppers will probably remain in the villages to which they emigrated, unless the North should again offer opportunity. With the abatement of relief and government projects, the Southern population increase may cause a serious problem unless economic opportunities can be provided the people whose farm and relief sources of livelihood have been eliminated. Increase in farm prices and a good farm year or two may bring a realignment of population in the next 5 years in the Middle West and the Far West.

The estimated increase in village population may be temporary; but it is probable that 1940 will find in agricultural village communities more people, by about 3 per cent, than there were in 1930.

OPEN-COUNTRY POPULATION ALSO GAINED

It should be repeated that these are estimates, although the changes in school enrollments checked closely with reported changes in population in most villages. It should also be noted that there was doubtless some migration from villages, though this was not studied. Moreover, not all villages grew. Many, as in previous studies, showed slight change. Some lost, a few, such as one or two that suffered severely from drought or floods and a few whose above average-sized industries closed down, quite sharply. The figures given are an estimate on a regional basis for entire groups of villages.

The village in an agricultural community acts as a service center for the surrounding open country. In the last 5 years, as is reported in Chapter IV, the trade areas of village centers increased. With the increase of the area within the community boundaries, it was to be expected that farm population would show an increase. But the growth from 1930 to 1936 shows an acceleration not much less than that which obtained in the village center, except in the Middle West, in the same period. Table 24 gives the average open-country population in the trade area per village.

TABLE 24

THE ESTIMATED AVERAGE OPEN-COUNTRY POPULATION COMMUNITY AREA PER VILLAGE IN 1930 AND IN 1936

140 American Agricultural Villages: by Region and by Size of Village in 1930

Region and Size	*Number of Villages*	*Average Estimated Open-Country Population per Village* 1930	1936	*Relative Change since 1930* (1936–1930)/1930
All regions	140	2,099	2,433	15.91%
Middle Atlantic	28	1,544	1,584	2.59
South	30	3,414	3,569	4.54
Middle West	60	1,638	2,244	37.00
Far West	22	2,271	2,477	9.07
Small villages	48	1,352	1,580	16.86
Medium villages	57	2,173	2,507	15.37
Large villages	23	3,169	3,716	17.26
Towns	12	2,683	3,031	12.97

Each region showed an increase in the number of persons in the surrounding trade area. Against an increase of 2.1 per cent in the period 1924–30, the open-country population in Middle Atlantic service areas increased 2.6 per cent in the last 5 years; in the South, however, the increase in the last quinquennium was 4.5 per cent, as against 12.9 per cent in the period 1924–30; in the

Middle West, the greatest relative increase of open-country population, 37 per cent, was reported, in contrast with a loss of 3.1 per cent in the period 1924–30; in the Far West, the open-country increase in the last 5 years was 9.1, as compared with 22.6 per cent in the period 1924–30. It should be pointed out that this gain came in part because about one-third of the centers increased the area which they served, while few lost area. Moreover, it is obviously more difficult to estimate the population of the area tributary to a center than to estimate that of the center itself, for such areas do not conform to definite political boundaries. (The problem of determining the community area is dealt with in the next chapter.) Part of the increase in the open-country population here reported was also due to the growing trend in some places of people to settle outside of, but near, the legal boundaries of the center. In only one such case had the village boundaries been changed to include these people and the area they occupied.

The open-country population increase was almost uniform for areas around small-sized, medium-sized, and large villages. The population surrounding towns did not increase as rapidly as the average. This was largely because of the exodus of open-country population from the territory around the towns in the New York flood areas.

WHERE THE NEW FARMERS CAME FROM

Just as the sources of new village population were classified, so were the origins of the new farm population in the community. The source was classified as *urban* when the report was that the population "came from large industrial centers," or that it consisted "mainly of city people"; as *from surrounding open country* when reported as due to "increase in trade area," or as from "nearby areas," or "nearly rural areas"; as *from other regions,* if the new farm population came from "Middle-West drought areas," or was made up of the "sons of farmers and farm boys returning from cities," or was brought by "resettlement"; as *unchanged* if the report was that the "increase was by birth," or "about constant from one farm to another." Table 25 shows the sources of new farm population by the defined categories.

Thirty-six per cent of the Middle Atlantic communities, 53 per cent of Southern communities, 43 per cent of Middle West communities, and 73 per cent of Far West villages reported immigration of new farm population. Moreover, as the village population came from sources related to various economic and agricultural points of stress, so did the movement of farm population represent the same primary origins. The main source was from near-by

TABLE 25

THE ORIGIN OF THE NEW FARM POPULATION IN VILLAGE-CENTERED COMMUNITIES IN 1936

140 American Agricultural Communities: by Region and by Size of Village in 1936

	Communities Reporting New Farm Population from:				
Region and Size	NEAR-BY URBAN CENTERS	SURROUNDING OPEN COUNTRY	OTHER REGIONS	*No Change of Farm Population*	*No Answer*
All regions	21	17	31	64	7
Middle Atlantic	6	3	1	15	3
South	6	5	5	12	2
Middle West	9	8	9	31	3
Far West	...	...	16	6	...
Small villages	7	2	9	20	4
Medium villages	9	12	8	29	3
Large villages	4	1	5	10	...
Towns	1	2	9	5	...

urban centers in all regions except the Far West, to which the new farm population came from other regions.

In the Middle Atlantic region, there were some reports of village population moving "to small farms to gain lower costs and advantage of some subsistence income." A Pennsylvania village reported, "all farms occupied. The school census showed five children of school age in 1934 and 21 in 1935. Movement to farms came late. In another township, three schools about to close in 1934 now have 18, 23, and 28 pupils," respectively. A New York village reported, "when mills closed down, forty families took up subsistence farming." Another Pennsylvania village reported, "due to the depression, there is less drifting to the cities on the part of youth who stay at home on the farms."

In the South, industrial centers and the mines contributed new population to the open country. An Alabama village found that "ex-miners from abandoned coal mines went to farms, the majority to old farms which they reclaimed. Others, especially the young men, cleared woodland in real pioneering. Young people also stayed at home." The field story of another Southern village shows the community "gained sixty farms during the five-year period. Part of this influx is accounted for through the migration of ten families from the vicinity of Morgantown, West Virginia. Most of the remainder appears to consist of families who have come into this area from Wilmington, Chester, and Philadelphia. These families have almost invariably settled on the smallest and poorest farms." The report from a Kentucky village emphasizes the subsistence aspect of farming in the report that "the open-country service area was thought to have grown from 2,550 to 3,000 because many have returned from industrial centers, some have come from near-by counties, while others moved from neighboring small towns to the country. Many in the latter group would have been on relief if they had not gone to farms." Another Alabama village reports local depression as a source of farm population by referring the increase in open-country population to "*out-of-works* from the city, and bankrupt merchants from the village center."

In the Middle West, villages reported movement to the farm due "largely to drought and poor feed conditions existing in neighboring states," or to "influx of drought-stricken farmers from Missouri and Nebraska." The other source is "some folks returning from industrial centers," and "many younger families moved back to area to farm when they lost jobs in the city." In the Far West, too, the drought forced people to seek new farm opportunities. One report shows the "increase is from Dust Bowl drawn by good markets, pasture, and cheap water." Another reported, "farmers from the Mid-West drought areas, tenants from the South, and ranchers from Colorado, Nevada, and Utah." Against this influx in some communities, the stricken drought areas report losses, especially from the Dust Bowl.

THE KIND OF LAND THE NEW FARMERS SETTLED

Another view of the farm immigration can be obtained by looking on the kind of land the new farm population settled. The land was classified as *cheap, poor, vacated, or submarginal* when the report indicated that such land was "old farm," " new reclaimed land," "cut over," "unimproved," "erosion," or "subsistence" farm land; it was classified as *average* when the reports were "tobacco land," "tillable soil," "average" or "general" farms; and as *good* when reported "good for truck farming" or as "better lands," "dairy farms," "first grade."

In Table 26 is given an analysis of the number of communities reporting new farm population and the land settled.

TABLE 26

TYPE OF LAND ON WHICH NEW FARM POPULATION SETTLED, 1930–36

140 American Agricultural Villages: by Region

Region	*New Farm Population Settled on:* CHEAP, POOR, VACATED OR SUBMARGINAL LAND	AVERAGE LAND	GOOD OR BETTER LAND	*No New Farm Population*	*No Answer*
All regions	27	11	23	64	15
Middle Atlantic	5	...	5	15	3
South	7	4	5	12	2
Middle West	9	6	6	31	8
Far West	6	1	7	6	2

The balance shows that in 44 per cent of the cases in which new farm population was reported, the land settled is poor, in 18 per cent average, and in 38 per cent good land. The cheap land was settled primarily by the people from urban centers; the average and good land, by farmers forced out of their original land by floods in New York and the drought in the Middle West. The problem of subsistence farming has been intensified, in part by the coming of city emigrees with little or no farm experience, and in part by incoming farmers' lacking in knowledge of local soils.

INCREASED POPULATION RAISED VILLAGE PROBLEMS

The great mobility of the village and farm population obviously raised many problems for these communities. From one village came the complaint, "it is hard for community organizations to function and remain intact because the mobility rates are so high." But the problems raised by the mobility of population were not the only ones. The new population, arising as it did in part out of urban depression, drought, and mechanization of farms, brought problems of schooling, relief, housing, and social and economic conflict. In Table 27 the kinds of problems that were created are tabulated, as well as the number of villages experiencing any problem because of the migrational influx.

More than half of the villages do not feel that the increased population caused any problem. But in nearly 40 per cent of them, such problems were felt to exist. Relief needs and school costs were the problems most frequently mentioned. "Relief loads were somewhat increased because new population was mostly unskilled laborers." "Some of the new population are 'floating population' from Kentucky, Virginia, and Tennessee. They work on one farm a season, but are so shiftless that they have to move on. During the past five years, the 'floating population' has become more stable in order to get relief." A Middle West village reported, "new population increased relief load, swamped schools, had to employ more teachers." In general, the new population "increased pressure and competition for both jobs and relief"; it caused a greater unemployment problem. The new population seriously affected living standards in at least one community where "the unemployed took to farming on a subsistence scale. Gardens

TABLE 27

THE TYPE OF PROBLEM RAISED BY THE NEW POPULATION IN THE COMMUNITY

140 American Agricultural Villages, 1935: by Region

Region	*No Problem Created*	*Problem Created*	*Type of Problem Created*						*No Answer*
			SCHOOL	RELIEF	SCHOOL AND RELIEF	SCHOOL AND OTHERS NOT SPECIFIED	RELIEF AND OTHERS NOT SPECIFIED	OTHERS NOT SPECIFIED	
All regions	76	53	11	16	13	2	4	7	11
Middle Atlantic	17	6	3	1	1	...	...	1	5
South	13	14	3	3	6	...	1	1	3
Middle West	37	20	3	7	4	1	2	3	3
Far West	9	13	2	5	2	1	1	2	...

sprang up on every vacant lot in town and small patches on the edge. Families quit buying at the stores and attempted to become self-sufficient. The standard of living dropped to an unprecedented low."

The new population also created a somewhat new problem for agricultural communities. Rather widespread were the complaints of a housing shortage, especially in villages. Every region has 2 or more communities with complaints of "wretched, crowded conditions, as many as four families in a house. No one cares to invest money in new houses for rent. This is one of the bad results of the depression"; or "houses scarce, people doubling up. No building because rents are low."

It is unusual for villages to protest against an increase in population. Yet the general character of the migration increased school enrollments, relief loads and competition for jobs, according to the testimony of many local leaders in the places reporting problems, at the same time that standards of living were lowered and housing standards were abated.

One evidence, however, of the difficulty of estimating population is made clear by a study undertaken by the Youth Commission of the American Council on Education, with the support and cooperation of the present survey. The total population of a representative sample of 45 of the 140 American villages was enumerated. This enumeration shows a population of 50,077 in 15,696 families in 1936, as compared with a population of 56,457 in 15,404 families in 1930.

In the enumerated sample of 45 villages the census shows for 1936 a decline of more than 11 per cent from the Federal enumeration of 1930. Relative decreases ranged from one-half of one per cent to more than 42 per cent. Only 7 of the 45 enumerated villages show an increase over 1930 in total population in 1936. Using the ratio of the difference between the population enumerated in 1936 and in 1930 to the enumerated population in 1930,

4 villages increased more than 6 per cent (one per cent a year), 3 increased from 0 to 6 per cent, 8 declined from 0 to 6 per cent, 10 declined from 6 to 12 per cent, 7 declined from 12 to 18 per cent, 8 declined from 18 to 24 per cent, 3 declined from 24 to 30 per cent, and one declined 39 per cent, and another 42 per cent. The estimates of the population of these same 45 villages, on the contrary, indicate that 3 increased 32 per cent, 27 per cent, and 47 per cent, respectively, that another 3 increased from 12 to 18 per cent, 9 increased from 6 to 12 per cent, 24 increased from 0 to 6 per cent, 4 declined from 0 to 6 per cent, and one declined 8 per cent, and another 16 per cent.

There is little substantial agreement between the special 1936 enumeration and the 1936 estimates of population.[2] In the villages where there were sharp differences between the enumeration and the estimates, the enumeration was generally considerably lower. In the case of the villages that had suffered from natural calamities, this is explicable. Local people may have assumed that those who left would return. Enumerators would count only those who were then actually resident.

In other cases the result was so much at variance with the estimates of the fieldworkers, with the school enrollments, and with the general character of field reports that the present writers believe the population to be under-enumerated in them. It should be noted that, as shown in Chapter VII, the school enrollment was secured according to the residence of the pupils in the village municipality and from the outside separately. In many of these communities in which the enumeration showed a decline in population, to such an extent that the average size of family declined by one or even one and a fraction persons, the village school enrollment showed increases. In large part as a result of this, the enumeration of all 45 villages showed a reduction of average fam-

[2] As a matter of fact, the ratios of change between estimate and enumeration have a negative correlation.

ily size from 3.67 in 1930 to a family average of 3.19 in 1936. In several of these centers fieldworkers produced evidence of housing shortages and doubling up of families.

It should be added that a complete enumeration of the entire 140 villages would probably have shown a small decline in the size of family. Many of the families moving to these villages consisted of young married people, former residents, with no children or children below school age. This is in line with the very small change in elementary-school enrollment reported in Chapter VII. On the other hand, part of the large increase in the high-school enrollment was to have been expected on the basis of the age distribution shown in the 1930 census enumeration. In addition, however, unexpected increases were due to a larger proportion of junior-high-school students continuing with the work of the senior high school and to the great number of graduates of senior high schools remaining for additional instruction as postgraduates. Many of the latter group formerly left the village, and their remaining at home tended to increase the village population.

The population estimates, as indicated, unquestionably cannot be completely accurate, but when they are so sharply at variance with the enumeration in some communities, it suggests at least that the population trends in American villages during the depression cannot be determined from the enumeration of these 45 villages. It also may be that the trend can never be completely determined because by the time the 1940 population census is taken, new migration trends may have obscured the 1930–36 picture.[3]

The estimated increase of open-country population in the trade areas of the 140 villages was 15.91 per cent over 1930. The data and reports presented thus far, while concerned only with the 140 village communities under survey, indicate a greater farm population than in 1930. The May, 1935, estimate of the Bureau of Agricultural Economics as of January 1, 1935, shows a presump-

[3] It is hoped that it may be possible to present a more complete analysis of the Youth Commission's study and the estimates at some future time in an article discussing population estimates in village communities.

tive increase in the farm population of 2,610,000 persons in the period from January 1, 1930, to January 1, 1935, or almost 8.7 per cent, which checks fairly well with the material returned from the communities surveyed, when consideration is given to the relatively greater population density near a village center as compared with areas more remote. The total farm population was thus estimated in the Bureau's press release of May 2, 1935, as 32,779,000 as of January 1, 1935. The census results, as reported in the first chapter, give 31,800,907 persons. This is another illustration of the difficulty of estimating population. In any event the farm population showed increases in all regions and a majority of the states. The old and revised estimates are shown in Table 28.

There are many reasons for believing that the 1935 Census of Agriculture was better done than that of 1930. But the relatively slight change in the number of farms of less than 3 acres raises

TABLE 28

MOVEMENT TO AND FROM FARMS [a]

Year	*To Farms from Cities*	*To Cities from Farms*	*Net Movement* [b]	
			TO FARMS FROM CITIES	TO CITIES FROM FARMS
1920	560,000	896,000	...	336,000
1921	759,000	1,323,000	...	564,000
1922	1,115,000	2,252,000	...	1,137,000
1923	1,355,000	2,162,000	...	807,000
1924	1,581,000	2,068,000	...	487,000
1925	1,336,000	2,038,000	...	702,000
1926	1,427,000	2,334,000	...	907,000
1927	1,705,000	2,162,000	...	457,000
1928	1,698,000	2,120,000	...	422,000
1929	1,604,000	2,081,000	...	477,000
1930	1,611,000	1,823,000	...	212,000
1931	1,546,000	1,566,000	...	20,000
1932	1,777,000	1,511,000	266,000	...
1933	944,000	1,225,000	...	281,000
1934	700,000	1,051,000	...	351,000
1935	825,000	1,211,000	...	386,000

[a] Source: United States Department of Agriculture, Bureau of Agricultural Economics, Release of October 27, 1936, p. 9. Births and deaths not taken into account.
[b] In the release of May 2, 1936, the Bureau estimated the net movement from cities to farms as follows: 1930, 17,000; 1931, 214,000; 1932, 533,000; and a net movement from farms to cities in 1933 of 277,000 and in 1934 of 211,000.

a theoretical possibility of under-enumeration in this single category.[4] Regardless of this, there is every indication in these 140 communities that the rural non-farm population which was also non-village increased markedly between 1930 and 1936, and there are reasons in many of these communities to suspect that if urban prosperity is fully re-established, this population will decrease more rapidly than the farm or village population.

SUMMARY

On the basis of the data as presented, much of it admittedly estimated, it is believed that in 1935 the open-country and the rural population were probably at their highest point in our national history. It is further estimated that from that high of 1935 there will be an important recession due to cityward migrations in the next 5 years, but that the 1940 census will probably show a gain for the decade and that for the rural non-farm group this gain will be slightly larger than between 1920–30.

This impending migration will bring about many readjustments, and will sharpen some of the differences, between rural and urban communities. Agricultural communities that bonded themselves or secured government grants in aid to give educational, social, and economic advantages to their new inhabitants, may find that expected income will be seriously cut. Another consequence will be the necessity for the equalization of opportunity for the rural inhabitant as compared with the urban resident.

[4] Despite an increase of nearly 70 per cent in the number of farms under 10 acres, there is at least the possibility of under-enumeration in the 1935 agricultural census in regard to the small farms. Many of these small-scale ventures would have been classified as farms in 1930, when the index number of farm prices for produce grown in 1929 was at 146, but they could not be so classified when the index number of farm prices for produce grown in 1934 for report in 1935 was at 90. A small-scale farm that produced $250 worth of produce in the census of 1930 would for comparable farm yields have produced $155 worth in 1934. Moreover, farm production was reduced from an index number of 101 for 1929 to 91 for 1934. These two facts would indicate that for a small-scale farm to be included as a census farm it would have been necessary to produce almost 80 per cent more farm products in 1934 than in 1929.

IV

Village–Country Relations

THE OPENING chapters of this report described those changes in the basic industry of rural America, agriculture, that occurred between 1930 and 1935 and were fraught with social implications because they affected the security, the attitudes, the behavior, or the social organization of rural people. So far as was possible, data from census and field-survey reports concerning the rural population and the changes in its structure during the same period were summarized; and attention was recalled to the well-known fact that the people of rural America fall into two major categories, farm and non-farm, the latter group made up largely of people in villages. This chapter turns to a discussion of the interaction of these two groups within the area of closest association, the local community. Later chapters will report the fortunes of certain institutions which among them account for the large majority of village-country interactions.

Those who have worked on this series of studies believe that the facts revealed demonstrate that the village or town center has become the capital of rural America. The crossroads neighborhood is no longer the chief integrating social factor in rural life. Despite fluctuations, farmers are steadily increasing their use of the village or town center for education, especially on the high-school level; for the ministries of religion; for social life; for professional service of various sorts; and for the purchasing of daily necessities. The evidence for this is given in the various chapters dealing with these topics.

The degree to which these village services are utilized varies within each community, as it certainly varies among the regions;

but the trend is clear, even though it has been slowed during the depression. Rural social trends can therefore best be studied in the village- or town-centered agricultural community. This is the dominant type of social organization in rural America today; and it was never more dominant, even though there is also a closer relationship with the city in some particulars.

This being so, it is important to discover the areas within which the interactions operate, and to appraise the relations of village and country people, their attitudes toward each other. Are the increasing associations forced by the compulsion of changed conditions, or are they entered into cordially and happily? Friction is always possible and always unfortunate in such relationships, just as it is within the far more closely knit social organization—the family.

Service areas.—Implicit in the concept of the rural community as village or town centered is the fact that the center serves its hinterland in a variety of ways such as were sketched earlier in this chapter. When the center fails in this function, the people of the hinterland seek a new focal point or orientation; and the former center becomes disorganized, declines, and in the end sometimes becomes a small satellite or neighborhood within the area of influence of some other center. This has happened to many of the incorporated places of less than 500 population, and especially of less than 250 population. There are nearly 3,000 of the latter group in the United States, a disproportionately large number of them, more than one-half, in the Middle West.

It is important, therefore, to analyze the fluctuations in the extent of these communities. This is done in Chapter III in reference to the changes in population tributary to a given center. The present discussion deals only with the total community. The boundary of this so-called community area was drawn to include that area from which a majority of the country people came for a majority of their required services, such as education, trade, recreation, and so on. The line so drawn might or might not represent the area or pull of any one particular service or institution. Rather it represented the modal situation against which any particular service could be compared.[1]

In summary, it may be said that the community areas increased significantly in just under one-third of the places studied, 32.8 per cent, or 46 of the places, to be exact. All regions but the Middle West fell slightly under this. The Middle West region showed increases in 26 of the 60 villages, or 43 per cent. Among small villages of under 1,000 population, only 9 of the 42 reported gains. Curiously enough, the next poorest record was made by the 17 towns of 2,500 to 5,000 population, only 4 of which showed significant gains. Probably they had reached the greatest possible limits previously, as they grew out of the village category in the years from 1923 to 1936. Twelve of the 20 large villages of from 1,750 to 2,500 population, and 21 of the 59 villages of from 1,000 to 1,750 population, increased their service areas.

All but about half a dozen of the remaining 92 villages showed no appreciable change since 1930. In the main, the conclusions of the 1930 study were confirmed in 1936. Trade areas were more difficult to determine than in 1924, except for the services of such specific lines as banking, hardware, and co-operatives. The areas of social service were much more clearly defined, but seldom as large as the trade areas of the more successful or better-established commercial institutions. However, where a village by excellent service had won a very high degree of allegiance to its economic services, the social and cultural agencies tended to approximate the areas of trade service; and where such areas had enlarged, the areas of other services tended to enlarge. The converse of this

[1] For a detailed discussion of the method employed, see Brunner, Hughes, and Patten, *American Agricultural Villages,* Chapter II; this chapter also contains a series of maps for selected villages giving community and specific service areas as found in 1924. See also Brunner and Kolb, *Rural Social Trends,* pp. 92-99, for a full discussion of the situation as it existed in 1930.

was not true. Except in a very few stranded and rapidly declining centers, when a trade area shrank it tended to approach a more stable area of social and cultural service.[2]

The previous studies showed that the high school was increasingly influential as a determinant of the community. More than that of any other service, its area coincided with or approximated the community boundary. This is but natural. The high-school country youth form associations with village youth. As they grow into adulthood there is some intermarriage between the two groups. As they graduate from high school and drop the connections with its extracurricular activities, many of the open-country youth eventually join the social organizations of the village. In some communities this process has been accelerated by the depression. Young folk of farm and village alike have been unable to find opportunities elsewhere, and to a greater extent than previously have remained in their home communities and sought outlets for their social life together. In other places, however, the depression has had an opposite effect. There simply has not been money enough to share in any organized social life. In some such situations, the little neighborhoods in the open country to be discussed later in this chapter have become more important than formerly. The question now arises as to relationships between villagers and farmers within these community areas, for changes concern both external factors like area and internal factors making for co-operation.

One of the most marked changes in the 140 villages between 1924 and 1930 was the great improvement in the relationships of farmers and villagers. These were judged to be co-operative in 100 cases in 1930, as against only 27 in 1924. Whether the strain and tensions of the depression and drought, the foreclosures and breakup of homes that had afflicted some of the communities, the

[2] The data on p. 85 showing increases and decreases in trade areas are therefore quite, though not wholly, representative of the increases in areas of the cultural and social services and of the degree of stability in such service areas, but are not representative of decrease.

TABLE 29

VILLAGE AND COUNTRY RELATIONS

140 Villages: by Region

Region	Number of Villages	*Co-operative*			*Neutral*			*Conflicting (Poor)*		
		1924	*1930*	*1936*	*1924*	*1930*	*1936*	*1924*	*1930*	*1936*
All regions	140	27	100	85	89	34	42	24	6	13
Middle Atlantic	28	5	19	17	20	8	7	3	1	4
South	30	4	26	14	22	4	9	4	0	7
Middle West	60	9	41	38	37	16	20	14	3	2
Far West	22	9	14	16	10	6	6	3	2	0

sharp shifts in population that had occurred in a large minority of the places, had had a detrimental effect on the active co-operation found 6 years before was one of the important questions of this inquiry.

The reader can interpret the results summarized in Table 29 for himself. To the authors, they seem, all things considered, encouraging. Active co-operation in many ways, which will be illustrated shortly, was found in 85 communities, 15 fewer than in 1930. The larger part of the loss was absorbed by that category which, for want of a better term, is called "neutral." In "neutral" situations, the active co-operation in numerous activities that characterized the co-operative group was not present in the same degree. But neither was there any active conflict or antagonism. There was antagonism, however, in 13 cases, as against 6 in 1930. But this increase is accounted for entirely by the South. In the Middle West and Far West, there were fewer conflict situations. Moreover, conflict situations, despite the depression difficulties, were only half as numerous as in 1924.

Cause of conflict.—These ratings are obviously somewhat subjective despite the instructions given fieldworkers and the number of interviews held in each community.[3] A close reading of the reports suggests that the conflict category should be changed to "conflict or poor," for some of these 13 places were put in this group rather because former co-operative activities had lapsed on account of the pressure of the depression than because actual conflict had broken out over some issue. In fact, actual conflict was found in only 7 places. In 2, it was due to what hard-pressed village merchants felt were "unreasonable" demands by hard-pressed farmers for credit at the stores. In 2 others, the villagers deeply

[3] Fieldworkers were told to list communities as co-operative where there was active co-operation between village and country groups on significant social projects and where the farm population was well represented in the social organizations of the community. The conflict category was to be used when the two parts of the community were divided on some issue. "Neutral" included all other situations, obviously many where there might be a considerable degree of cordiality between village and country though little or no active co-operation.

resented the formation of consumer co-operatives by farmers. In another case, the village acquired a "pay roll" when oil was struck and the merchants were accused of having ceased to cater to the farmers' trade. Again the farmers tried to secure their necessities by barter, and were irritated by the objections of villagers. Quarrels over relief also entered into this situation. The worst conflict was over the issue of rural electrification. In one community the village wished to co-operate with the Rural Electrification Administration in securing service. The farmers wished to share in this. The villagers opposed extending lines to the farms because it would increase the cost.

This is quite a different list of causes of antagonism than that found in 1924. Then sheer inability by one group to realize the legitimate necessities of the other ranked high. Ten communities were split asunder by conflicts over school policy or consolidation. Politics, and prices in village stores, were sore points. None of these frequent causes of misunderstanding of a dozen years ago played any part in 1936. This in itself is indicative of significant social change. The later conflicts clearly grew out of the depression, and it is worth repeating that the entire net increase in the poor or conflict category is accounted for in the South in 7 communities among the one-third hardest hit by the depression in this region.

It is probable that if 4 other communities of the 13 were visited a year later, a better rating would be given; for in all of these 4, steps were being taken to improve relations, or to restore the former co-operation. In 2 of these communities, villagers were making overtures to farmers looking toward better understanding. In another, the county judge and county agent were jointly calling a series of meetings to stress mutual interests, especially in regard to county finances, credit, health and mosquito control. A somewhat similar effort was being made in the fourth place.

It should be added, however, that without the partial recovery in the prices of farm commodities and the A.A.A. checks, the situation might have been worse than it was. In 6 places, co-operative activities and relationships were being strained by the inability of farmers to pay their bills; but when they received cash, they cleared off these obligations as soon as possible, and these clouds soon disappeared.

Co-operative activities and attitudes.—The variety of activities and events that illustrate the co-operative relationships existing in 3 communities out of 5 is noteworthy. In 6 more, doubling the 1930 figure, fire protection was extended throughout the trade area on a tax basis rather than a rental charge per fire. Sometimes this lowered the insurance rates. In several places, the Chamber of Commerce or comparable organization was changed into a community association with half the members from the farm. In one such place, when a severe blizzard proved too much for the county snow-fighting apparatus, 148 men about equally divided between villagers and farmers worked together opening roads and lanes. In all places where relations were good and which experienced farm strikes, the village newspaper backed the farmers. One such instance was described in another connection.[4] In another case, the village weekly newspaper carried the headline, "Our Farmers Right or Wrong!"

The 1930 survey drew attention to the growing importance of the village high school in determining the area of social service, as well as to the practical disfranchisement of open-country patrons in non-consolidated districts. In several such cases, at village initiative, the village and township school boards have begun to meet jointly for a discussion of high-school policy; and in one case, where a consolidation took place, the boards were similarly consolidated. In a number of villages with non-consolidated schools that drew largely from the open country, tuition was reduced in the depression, sometimes in even larger proportion than teachers' salaries. As was noted in the previous studies, the schools through their community and extracurricular programs

[4] *Supra*, p. 42.

were often highly important factors in building community cohesiveness.

Farm Bureaus and such luncheon clubs as the Kiwanis and Rotary were also important in this connection. In a number of places, these were carrying on many joint activities. In several, the joint activities culminated in an annual dinner on the closing day of the annual meeting of the County Farm Bureau or Grange. Speakers on such occasions were always persons of importance, including the presidents or deans of the state colleges of agriculture, heads of state departments, and in one case a United States Senator. In other communities there were annual fairs or harvest festivals with free barbecues, pageants, plays, or other recreations. Stores closed on such days. Merchants have co-operated in lowering prices, and the farmer has responded. In one case, the farmers even liquidated a successful consumer co-operative to preserve community good will; apparently they have never regretted their decision.

In the main, in the communities enjoying these cordial and co-operative relationships between village and open country, the people realize that the welfare of each group is bound up with that of the other. The years 1933 and 1934 did a great deal to teach the merchants that they were dependent on the good will of the farmers, and that in community affairs their role was one of leadership. The absence of any speech reactions indicating conflict or even lack of sympathy is evidence of this, as is also the growing number of farmers in village social organizations. The proportion of open-country members in village-located social groups in the 85 places in the co-operative category, considerably exceeds the average for all communities as given in Chapter X.

Neutrality.—And the places classed as "neutral" are also mindful of the common interests and reciprocal relationships that exist. In one such place, the sense of social distance between farmers and villagers dated back to the very founding of the village in 1791. Within the village itself, there was little interchange between the retired-farmer group and the others. There was no antagonism, or setting of class against class, in this or comparable situations. Villagers and farmers respected each other and their respective functions. Little or no feeling of superiority was detected by field-workers. There was co-operation on specific projects when the need arose in some places. In some, greater and more continuous co-operation seemed to be developing out of these specific projects. The Rotary club in one village, for instance, was putting on a series of "rural relations" nights.[5]

Communities classed as "neutral" were not therefore all at a single point on the scale between "co-operative" and "conflict." Most of the "neutral" group were closer to co-operative relationships than to conflict. Indeed, of the 71 changes in the relations that were reported from these 140 communities, it was stated that in 52 there had been improvement since 1930. In each region, improved relations were found in about three-fourths of the places in which there were changes. The size of the center seemed to have little influence, the slightly poorer record of the small villages probably being too small to be significant.

Neighborhoods decline in number.—Rural Social Trends, the report of the 1930 study, gave a number of illustrations of neighborhood life and organization.[6]

These activities have been little changed. Typical of some of the neighborhoods that, because of economic difficulties, had had to satisfy their own social needs is the program of a Missouri neighborhood of 21 families. Its Community Club and Home Bureau were responsible for quite a program of home-talent plays and musicals, classes in current events and homecrafts and gardening. In another neighborhood, the activities centered in a church, and included educational, social, and athletic events. In fact, the athletic field was lighted for night games, despite the

[5] For previous descriptions and more detailed discussion of village and country relations in these communities, the reader is referred to the reports of the two earlier surveys: Brunner, Hughes, and Patten, *American Agricultural Villages,* Chapter III; and Brunner and Kolb, *Rural Social Trends,* Chapter IV.

[6] Pages 70-72, 326-32.

depression. The neighborhoods described in detail in the reference above were continuing their activities, as were others. There was no change in the factors integrating these neighborhoods. Any one of the following factors, or any combination of them, bound these population groups together into neighborhoods: school, church, social or economic organization such as Grange or Farm Bureau local, store, racial group, topographic isolation, family (i.e., clan) group.

It is most important to note, however, that while neighborhood life had taken on new vitality in some communities and had sustained activity in others, the depression years of the inter-survey period saw a heavy mortality among these minor centers. The number had declined from 513 to 429 between 1924 and 1930, and in 1936 fieldworkers classed as active only 286 of these 429, a decline of 34 per cent. However, 31 new neighborhoods were found; and 17 which had been judged not sufficiently active in 1930 to be listed as such were clearly functioning in 1936, and their leaders refused in most cases to admit that the 1930 decision had been correct. Clearly, however, neighborhoods can experience resurrection if conditions change. The net total of neighborhoods in these communities in 1936 was 328,[7] a net decline of 36 per cent since 1924, and of 23.5 per cent since 1930. The regional details are shown in Tables 30 and 31.

The first table shows that over the 12-year period, the ratio of neighborhood decline has been more rapid in the South, where hard-surfaced roads came later than elsewhere. The migration of Negroes also helped along the decline.

The significant thing about Table 31 is not so much the average number of neighborhoods for each community as the fact that by 1936, 33 of these communities had no active neighborhood, as against only 3 in 1924. This in itself is an evidence of closer village-country integration.

In view of the vitality of some of these minor centers, it is

[7] This deducts 6 active neighborhoods no longer within their communities because of changes in boundaries.

important to determine as far as possible the reasons for this decrease in the number of neighborhoods.

In the first place, those which in 1930 had had only a single integrating factor, like a school, church, or Grange, suffered a

TABLE 30

NEIGHBORHOODS IN COMMUNITY AREAS

Number of Neighborhoods by Regions, 1924, 1930, 1936

Region	*1924*	*1930*	*1936*	*Per Cent Decline* *1924–36*	*1924–30*	*1930–36*
All regions	513	429	328	36.0	16.4	23.5
Middle Atlantic	110	96	78	29.1	12.7	18.6
South	151	105	77	49.0	30.4	36.3
Middle West	175	154	122	33.5	12.0	26.2
Far West	77	74	51	20.8	4.0	31.1

heavy mortality. Thus places depending only on a school disintegrated rapidly as neighborhoods when this institution was consolidated with a new district centering in a village.

Again the great development of farm-to-market roads during the depression proved a disturbing factor in neighborhoods which had

TABLE 31

NEIGHBORHOODS IN COMMUNITY AREAS

Number of Neighborhoods by Size of Village Center, 1936

Size	*Number of Villages*	*Number with Neighborhoods*	*Total Number Neighborhoods*	*Average No. per Center 1936*	*Average No. per Center 1924*	*No. Villages by Size 1924*
All villages	140	107	328	3.0	3.7	140
Towns	17	12	45	3.75	. . . [a]	4
Large villages	20	15	37	2.5	3.9	31
Medium villages	61	50	170	3.4	3.2	58
Small villages	42	30	76	2.5	3.2	47

[a] There were only 4 towns in 1924, all less than 2,800 population; they are not separately tabulated.

previously experienced some degree of geographic isolation. There seemed to be a direct relation between the scope of this program and the mortality of neighborhoods. Thus the decline was especially heavy in Pennsylvania, where Governor Pinchot's administration measurably kept its promise to "get the farmer out of the mud." The phenomenon was quite akin to that of earlier years when the main hard-surfaced roads disturbed the life of neighborhoods lying in their path and accounted for the demise of many.

The depression was a third factor in the death or quiescence of neighborhoods. While it brought new life to some, its rigors caused others to suspend activities. It should be recorded here for future researches that some at least of these neighborhood centers may be dormant rather than dead. But this will not apply to all; for, as the earlier portion of this chapter shows, the social life of these communities is increasingly centering in the village; whereas a generation ago, in the horse-and-buggy era, it was very much a neighborhood affair.

Population migration was another cause for the lapse of neighborhood activities both in drought-stricken neighborhoods that lost population and in a few which received an influx they could not assimilate. The former consideration was particularly operative in the Middle West, and both these factors played a part in the Far West.

Of the newly-born neighborhoods, some were a result of a desire for social life nearer home than the village because there was no money to spend on extra evening trips to town. Others were small places, once communities, that had lost out in the effort to readjust to the automobile age and that lapsed into the status of a satellite to a larger village center. A considerable number of the "new" neighborhoods were simply resurrections. It is this tendency of neighborhoods to reappear in new relationships and with new integrating factors that makes it exceedingly difficult to generalize as to their eventual place in the American rural scene. Obviously, successful ones have a very important place in the open-country social organization in their communities. It is equally obvious that as a group, neighborhoods are less important and influential in the places studied than at any time since this series of investigations began.

The story of neighborhoods is, and will continue to be, one of adjustment and readjustment to the series of changes in the physical and social environment. Some will die; some will be dormant for a period to be called into new activity later; some will be newly formed. Probably there will be fewer neighborhoods in 1940 than there are today; but certainly there will still be several hundred actively functioning when that time comes.

These data indicate that village and country relations have reached a considerable degree of harmonious interaction. The pattern of a village- or town-centered community has been accepted, with some variation of course, among the regions. The area over which this pattern operates has stabilized in many cases, is still enlarging in some, declining in only a few. The closer integration of village and country is shown also in the decline of neighborhoods. The village center is often taking over the functions of the old neighborhood; but the process will not, for some time if ever, entirely eliminate such primary groups from the rural scene.

V

Business and Industry[1]

HERE begins the consideration of social trends that came into evidence in the period between 1930 and 1936, inclusive, in those broad phases of collective behavior that have long been recognized and institutionalized, such as trade, industry, religion, recreation, social welfare, and education.

When the 140 villages of this study were surveyed in 1930, the depression had not yet affected them to any great extent. By the close of 1935, the year of the present survey, these villages, like the nation, had experienced the unhappy times prevalent during 1931–33 and also the partial recovery of the 2 succeeding years. Naturally, the half decade just passed, with its profound disturbances to agriculture and business, caused many changes in the economic life of the American village. These changes have been reflected in such things as the varying number of its stores, banks, and industries, the amount of its retail sales, and the amount and type of its industrial employment, all of which are related to the size of a village and the geographic region in which it is located. Here the attempt will be made to trace, and in some measure to explain, certain of these economic changes that have occurred since 1930. Particular attention will be paid to retail trade and to the industrial life of the communities studied.

The outstanding development in the trade of these centers was the amazing increase in the number of stores, despite the sharp drop in retail sales. The increase in the average number per community was from 38.6 to 52.5, or 36 per cent.

These figures are based on field-work reports which in 1930 checked closely with the Dun & Bradstreet reports and with the

[1] Edmund deS. Brunner, Jr., is co-author of this chapter.

1930 *Census of Retail Distribution.* It was not possible to arrange for a comparison of the field-work data with the former source in this study. Through the co-operation of the *Census of American Business,* limited data on their 1932 and 1934 studies were made available. These were work-relief projects; and not only was information refused in some cases, but some stores were overlooked in the enumeration. The census authorities, in making the data available, drew attention to decided under-enumeration in a number of communities. Therefore, this chapter uses the field-work data of this study in reporting the number of stores, though it is probable that the definitions employed differed in a few particulars from those of the census and that the total number of establishments reported is therefore slightly in excess of the number that the *Census of American Business* would have listed even if their count had been complete. The trends, however, are clear.

This general increase was shared by every region and by every size group of centers, as Table 32 shows, though rates of gain varied.

The increase in number of stores was especially marked in the Middle West and the Far West, where the villages had about 40 per cent more stores in 1936 than in 1930. There was a corresponding increase in the average number of stores per village for every size of village. In the South, the total number of stores rose by one-third; and in the Middle Atlantic region, by more than one-fifth. The town-sized center in the Middle Atlantic region alone experienced a decline in its number of stores. It was the only exception to the upward national trend.

Obviously despite the depression, the birth rate of rural stores was considerably higher than the death rate; though with both social organizations and churches the reverse was true. The whole situation was a complex of conflicting forces, some of which, however, are reasonably apparent. It is remarkable that in spite of the low condition of purchasing power so many rural storekeepers were able to carry on and even to establish new enterprises.

Perhaps this is an indication of their adaptability to depression environment. Many village merchants the country over, realizing the nature of the struggle they encountered, took active measures to combat it. They sought to establish or improve good relationships with the open-country population, particularly with the farmers. Not only did some of the proprietors of village stores give as liberal credit and as square a deal as possible to the farmers, but they also attempted to make their countryside neighbors feel more important in the total community life.[2]

TABLE 32

THE INCREASE IN RETAIL OUTLETS: AVERAGE NUMBER OF RETAIL STORES PER VILLAGE

By Region and by Size of Village

Region and Size	*1930*	*1936*
All regions		
Town	71.1	88.1
Large	57.7	70.2
Medium	37.7	50.8
Small	22.3	32.2
Total	38.6	52.5
Midde Atlantic		
Town	68.0	61.0
Large	54.0	67.3
Medium	38.6	43.3
Small	24.9	30.8
Total	34.9	42.8
South		
Town	82.5	90.7
Large	54.5	65.8
Medium	35.5	49.9
Small	16.9	24.6
Total	38.7	51.8
Middle West		
Town	81.0	81.7
Large	59.8	69.7
Medium	37.7	54.1
Small	21.1	34.6
Total	37.7	52.6
Far West		
Town	62.8	93.2
Large	65.3	103.0
Medium	40.8	55.8
Small	26.9	36.4
Total	45.7	65.4

[2] *Supra*, pp. 90-91, in chapter on Village-Country Relations, giving illustrations.

In some villages the merchants rallied the populace to their aid by conducting "buy at home" campaigns, and, not content with this, they attempted, often with success, to enlarge the size of their trade areas. In this connection, the improved roads and new highways in many of the village areas played an important part. In one way, they served to help the merchant by providing easier and more comfortable access to the village from the open country; but, on the other hand, they also facilitated the farmers' realizing their desires for the varied attractions and big stores of larger centers. In the majority of the cases in which there were better road conditions, the net result was favorable to the village stores, particularly where their proprietors had aggressively taken steps to build up their open-country trade.

TABLE 33

INCREASE IN RETAIL OUTLETS: PERCENTAGE CHANGE IN TOTAL NUMBER OF RETAIL STORES

By Region and by Size, 1930–36

Region		*Size*	
All regions	36.0	All villages	36.0
Middle Atlantic	22.6	Town	23.9
South	33.8	Large	21.7
Middle West	39.5	Medium	34.7
Far West	43.1	Small	44.4

These and other factors affected the birth rates and the death rates of village stores in recent years. Primarily, of course, they affected retail sales; but these in turn determine whether stores shall live or die. In some villages, bank failures disrupted the economic life of the entire community and proved disastrous to its stores, as trade went to other centers where it could be carried on more conveniently. Conversely, however, bank failures in near-by neighborhoods were the means of increasing the business of other villages, thus aiding their merchants. The inability of some stores to keep an adequate stock of goods lost them considerable trade. Customers gradually went to other towns where their wants could be immediately filled.

After 1933, the pocketbook of the farmer, swelled by higher crop prices and A.A.A. benefit checks, provided the purchasing power which revived the business life of village stores. The various work projects and the relief trade available by Federal agencies furthermore sustained trade. County-seat towns in which offices of Federal emergency agencies were located, especially benefited because of the large number of persons who came to transact business there and while in town traded at the local stores.

In the returning agricultural prosperity, of course, the village people shared and benefited by buying more from one another. A further explanation of the larger number of stores in 1935 rests with the increase in the population of some of the 140 villages since 1930.[3] This larger population undoubtedly was able to sustain more stores to service its needs. A similar effect resulted from the enlarged trade areas of about one-third of the villages, as the larger areas naturally included more customers. Moreover, as will be noted, there were several entirely new types of stores which did not exist in 1930. But beyond these factors was another, quite important, which can be stated in a fieldworker's description of the situation in an eastern village of 1,800 population, with a trade area with twice as many. It is quite representative of what went on in a considerable number of places:

> Twenty-four new places of business were established between 1930 and 1936. One-half of these were started by persons who were natives of the community. More than half of the new proprietors were young persons just beginning their careers. Only two had previously left the village and returned as a result of the depression. Nearly all of the new businesses were ones which required little capital investment and were devoted to specialties, some of which had not been previously available.

Other comparable reports often stressed the value of these services new to the community, and told of inroads made in the trade of urban stores. Whether such stores continue to be able to compete with cities remains to be seen. But during the depression, when less money for travel was available, they did. Beauty shops

[3] *Supra*, pp. 66-68, in chapter on Population Changes.

or parlors offer conspicuous examples of this situation. These were almost nonexistent in 1924 in these villages. There were some in 1930, especially in the Middle Atlantic villages. In 1936, there was an average of one and one-fourth beauty parlors per village.

Types of retail stores.—Not all types of stores increased in number, however. The changes in the types of stores in the 140 villages are shown in Table 34.

TABLE 34

RETAIL OUTLETS: NUMBER OF STORES PER VILLAGE BY TYPE OF STORE

	Number Local Stores per Village			*No. Local Stores per Village*	*No. Chain Stores per Village*	*Total Stores per Village*
	1910	*1920*	*1930*	*1936*	*1936*	*1936*
All retail stores	27.7	32.1	39.6	49.7	2.8	52.5
Grocery [a]	2.4	3.1	4.3	3.9	1.0	4.9
All other food	2.5	2.1	3.3	2.5	.1	2.6
General	5.5	5.2	4.4	2.2	.2	2.4
Apparel [a]	3.7	3.6	3.7	1.7	.1	1.8
Automobile accessories	0.2	4.4	8.8	10.3	.8	11.1
Furniture	1.0	1.0	1.0	.9	.0 [c]	.9
Lumber	1.2	1.2	1.3	.5	.1	.6
Hardware	1.6	1.7	1.8	2.2	.1	2.3
Feed and farm supplies	1.4	1.4	1.4	.6	.0 [c]	.6
Restaurants and soft drinks	1.2	1.6	2.4	5.2	.0 [c]	5.2
All other retail [b]	7.0	6.8	7.2	19.8	.3	20.1

[a] Does not include chain stores in 1910, 1920, or 1930.
[b] In 1936 this category included for the first time liquor stores, tourist camps, and boardinghouses.
[c] Less than .1.

It will be noted that the number of grocery stores per village has increased steadily from 1910 to the present. By 1936, however, some local grocery stores had been displaced by chain stores. The number of all other food stores declined somewhat, probably because of the complete stocks of food which grocery stores, particularly those belonging to a chain, have kept in recent years. The village general store continued on the general decline which it began between 1910 and 1920. It may be that, as a result of the ever increasing specialization of rural mercantile enterprises, the general store will gradually die out.

Apparel stores suffered heavily during the depression. The previous survey pointed out the special force of urban competition in this line of goods. Lumber stores also fell upon evil times, as there was little building done between 1930 and 1936. Stores selling feed and farm supplies decreased in number, partly because there were fewer livestock to feed, and partly because the farmer was unable to buy equipment. The automobile accessories group continued the steady increase that it has shown ever since 1910, as did the hardware stores, although in this latter group the increase has been less spectacular. The fact that many people were getting along with the old cars doubtless affected the former group. The number of restaurant and soft-drink establishments rose substantially. The greatest increase, however, occurred in the "all other retail" group. This group includes beauty parlors, barber shops, drugstores, novelty stores, tourist camps, boardinghouses, etc., and in 1936, liquor stores. Many such enterprises were established during the depression by unemployed persons who still had some capital remaining to them.

The first and last types in this category of "all other retail" are especially interesting. There was an average of nearly one liquor store per village. This was an entirely new group since, for obvious reasons, bootleg outlets of liquor were not listed in the previous studies which were made during the prohibition regime. The beauty-parlor gain has already been noted. This is an indication of the spread of an urban service despite the depression, or perhaps because of it. Each of these places had, of course, a small trade in various cosmetic preparations.

Chain stores fail to increase.—There are those who have predicted that the chain store would increasingly displace that of the small local merchant. In the case of the 140 villages, however, this prophecy has not yet reached fulfillment. The number of chain stores per village in 1936 was 2.8, the same figure as in 1930.[4] In some places younger businessmen credited the chains with "waking things up." And in some villages chain stores have pressed the local merchants very hard and have even aroused considerable resentment among the citizens. The notes of a fieldworker who surveyed a village in the Far West throw some light on the people's attitudes:

> The establishment of several new chain stores has hurt the business of local merchants considerably and the cry of the local business man is "out with the chain store," in spite of a few recognized benefits.
>
> Local merchants and citizens are very much opposed to the chain stores, being apparently of the opinion that these chain stores take more out of the community than they put in. The prevailing attitude towards these stores seems to be that the managers are usually "small frys" who have no personal capital, do not own property or pay taxes, or support community enterprises, and are not interested in building up the community. They have not co-operated with local merchants, are ruthless in their price cutting, and fail to observe regulations as to hours and wages. Another general complaint is that the chain grocery stores offer an inferior grade of merchandise. Although furnishing employment for a few local people, these stores often require employees to work long hours for a small salary. One of the local bankers stated that he regards the accounts of these chain stores entirely as an expense, since they make large deposits and almost immediately draw out the entire amount to send to head offices outside the community.

In villages where situations like this exist, the people often rally around their local merchants. There have been many instances in recent years in which chain stores, because of their policies, have been unable to become firmly established in communities and have had to close up shop and move away. Chain stores that have taken an interest in their communities and that have employed local men known in the village and themselves interested in the store, have been much more successful than their less social fellows.

On the whole, the presence of chain stores in small villages does not appear to have been harmful to the local stores. In some in-

[4] Brunner and Kolb, *Rural Social Trends,* p. 149.

stances, the chain stores, even when located in centers several miles off, have undoubtedly brought grief to village merchants; on the other hand, the competition caused by chain stores has more often than not served to awaken local merchants to such an extent that they have not only held their own but have improved their businesses with consequent benefits to themselves and to the community. These statements explain attitudes and happenings in specific communities. The outstanding fact for the whole group is, however, that, despite an increase in the number of stores, the number of chain units remained constant between 1930 and 1936.

Trade areas.—As noted in the chapter on village-country relations, the size of the trade areas has remained the same between 1930 and 1936 in 86 of the 140 villages, decreased in 6, and increased in 46. Improved transportation, which is one of the most important factors affecting trade areas, was mentioned earlier in the chapter. Better roads, trucks, and pleasure cars have provided better access to villages over larger territories, and in this way have served to enlarge trade areas. But the increased ease of motor transportation has also served to allow rural people to satisfy their desires to trade in larger towns and cities. The effect of new or improved highways on a village's trade area has depended largely upon its distance from more populous centers, and upon the type of merchant in the village. In those instances in which better facilities for motor-car transportation have come to isolated villages, the result has been materially to enlarge the size of the trade areas, and also to encourage their residents to come to the village more frequently. With respect to villages near larger centers, improved transportation has caused some gain in size of trade areas, but has also caused the residents to shift some of their trade to the attractive stores of towns and cities.

As a result, some villages are adjusting to services for which they are best fitted, and are leaving more specialized services to competing towns. This is a function of density of villages as much as of roads, as these places draw from wide areas for services in which they excel. Thus the trade area in some places is larger but thinner. It should also be noted that occasionally a new trunk highway through a village has brought it trade not only from tourists but also from city people who have come for the ride, or to benefit from lower prices for certain goods, or to obtain fresh farm produce.

The effect of improved transportation facilities upon village trade areas has been determined in some measure, also, by the activities of local merchants. In some cases they have been shrewd enough to foresee the probable consequences of better roads and cars, and have taken active measures to protect their interest in the countryside trade. It has already been noted that many village merchants have put on fairs or bargain days for the benefit of the open-country people and have co-operated with them in various ways, as already noted in Chapter III. In one Middle West village of slightly less than 1,000 population, the program of the merchants included co-operation with farm organizations in securing better farm-to-market roads, free band concerts, home-coming days, old settler picnics, open-air loud speaker for reception of market reports, the Farm and Home Hour, as well as other features of special interest to farmers or of high cultural value, and finally active co-operation with the local drama group, including villagers and farmers, in a series of home-talent plays and entertainments financed on a 10-cent admission charge. These policies here and elsewhere have often been amply repaid by their recipients in the loyalty which they have shown to their village merchants in spite of opportunity of trading elsewhere. The story is very different where the merchants have continued their own way, sometimes to gradual failure, disregarding changed conditions and the necessity to understand, and co-operate with, farmers or other rural folk.

The presence of one important economic or social organization, or more, in a village is a strong determinant of its trade area. One village is the location of a large patron-carrying creamery. Farmers from miles around periodically come to the village to transact business with this creamery, and consequently patronize the local stores. The same situation obtains in varying degrees when a village possesses a strong farmers' co-operative, or offices of Federal agencies, county offices, large schools, or a motion-picture theater, an apparently sound bank, or combinations of these and other organizations. The condition of village banks affects their trade areas considerably; where banks sink and fail, portions of trade areas are often lost to villages that do have good banking facilities. Similarly, live village newspapers were credited with helping the situation in several places. Whenever there is weakness of any sort in the stores, in the community spirit, or the institutions of a village, its trade area contracts and it may even be absorbed by those of other and relatively stronger villages. This was the fate of some formerly functioning villages, now reduced to neighborhood status.

This summary, of course, merely says that some communities are succeeding in meeting new conditions and some are not. For that reason, several illustrations are selected from representative but contrasting situations. The first concerns a medium-sized village nearly a hundred miles from Philadelphia and about 50 miles from a city of over 100,000 population.

> Some of the ——— and Philadelphia department stores maintain regular delivery service for furniture and some other items; but if any trade has been lost to ——— merchants as a result, it has been more than offset by the advantages gained through the moving-picture theatre, the consolidated school, and the growing importance of the county seat in the everyday affairs of the county's residents. The paved highways which link ——— with the larger cities have been in existence for at least ten years, and whatever effect they may have had in the past apparently was altered little between 1930 and 1935. At least one of the recently established women's clothing stores appears to have secured some of the trade which formerly went to the city, and there is one new men's clothing store which apparently has succeeded in securing some of the local business.

The second case is from a proud, historic, and formerly self-satisfied village in the deep South.

——— shows signs of decline in the last five years. There are vacant business buildings; several of the stores are just barely hanging on; discouragement over the outlook is not at all infrequent; interest in community affairs is not strong, the young people from the "best" families are leaving or are planning to leave as soon as the opportunity offers. There are physical indications of a lack of civic pride; the sidewalks are in a bad state of repair, and in a number of places cave-ins have not been repaired. Except in the business blocks, one needs to be constantly on the lookout to avoid mud puddles in the sidewalk after a rain; and the paved portion of the main street is so covered with mud and dust that a person glancing at it casually might fail to notice that it had been surfaced.

In spite of decreased incomes and enforced reductions in expenditures, the insistence upon styling in clothes and other merchandise is gaining in importance as a factor and customers continue to demand a large variety of goods from which to make their selection.

———'s merchants are finding it impossible to carry the stocks necessary to meet the demand for women's ready-to-wear, men's clothing, furniture, etc., and this trade goes largely to other places. With it there has gone some of the incidental shopping which might have been done in ———.

The third case, from the Middle West, stresses the economic value of a strong cultural and social life. This community had more than held its own, though less than 25 miles from a city of over 100,000 population.

The favorable position of L———, it would appear, is largely traceable to two things: first, the progressive attitude, a willingness to make adjustment to changes in the situation; and, second, a successful organization of the cultural interests.

The community enterprises referred to in the report are the channels into which the latent cultural life of the people has been directed.

The community pride and initiative, in evidence today, is capable of further development and is largely dependent upon leadership. The improvement shown in the community morale evidently has had economic effects, though this does not readily lend itself to tabulation.

In addition, a housing shortage in the city mentioned and the high reputation of this community resulted in a desirable influx of population. The village leaders are emphasizing this advantage.

RETAIL SALES DURING DEPRESSION

During the period 1930–33, total retail sales in the 140 villages drastically declined, 52.1 per cent. Total retail sales for the nation declined approximately 49 per cent in the same period. The extent of the decrease in the amount of sales in the rural villages undoubtedly resulted largely from the greatly reduced income of the farmer in those years. The farmer curtailed drastically his purchases of all sorts, thus causing the business of the village stores to sink, and their proprietors consequently bought much less from one another. The smaller purchases by rural people were reflected in a lowered standard of living. Observations of fieldworkers record that people demanded cheaper grades of merchandise, including clothing, farm and household supplies, hardware, and groceries, and bought these goods in smaller amounts. Much of this curtailment was made possible by delaying the replacement of equipment for both farm and home. Families, furthermore, did without electricity, water, and telephone service. Many of them, unable to keep their own houses, shared living quarters with other families, often with unemployed children returned from the city, or else relinquished their houses for small shacks or barns.

While the unfortunate agricultural situation was largely responsible for the reductions in retail sales in all the villages the country over, there were other causes which operated with similar effect in the various geographic regions. In some portions of the Middle West and the Far West, the drought struck farmers a hard blow, so that they were deprived of the greater part of even the income that might have remained to them in the depression. In some villages, particularly in the South, bank failure so damaged the economic life that business suffered greatly. Bank failure caused trade to be transacted on a strictly cash, instead of on a credit, basis. Stores deprived of bank credit were unable to acquire sufficient stock and had their ordinary means of financing otherwise disturbed. Customers not only lost funds in the deceased banks, but found it inconvenient to trade in a village without banking facilities. Thus trade moved from those villages in which banks failed, much to the detriment of retail sales. Another reason for the reduction in the dollar amounts of retail sales is that much trade was accomplished by barter. The owners of village stores accepted various kinds of food from the farmers in payment for goods. Village people also bartered with one another for what they needed. This was especially true in the South, though it occurred elsewhere. It went to surprising lengths. In one store, a share-cropper traded half a dozen eggs for 2 oranges; and in another a Negro girl received some candy for one egg. The wholesale price of eggs went as low as 8 and 10 cents a dozen in a number of the communities. One village resorted to the use of scrip. A further adjustment to the depression, perhaps partially an outgrowth of barter trade, was made by rural people, particularly farmers, who attempted to raise or to make at home goods which they formerly purchased.

Still another factor somewhat reducing local retail sales was the sales tax. In states where it operated, the postmasters of the communities studied almost without exception reported sharply increased purchases of money orders in favor of mail-order houses. In one center near a state line, the proprietor of a hardware store had his main store in a state with a sales tax, the other in a neighborhood just over the state line where there was no sales tax. His combined business in 1936 was ahead of any year since 1929; but the April gross in the store where the sales tax was in effect was way off. The figures by years for this month are:

1930	$4,482
1932	2,561
1936	1,733

Most of his customers were carrying their accounts and receiving their goods over the state line to avoid the tax.

A number of communities showed that trade lost because of the opening of hard-surfaced roads may be regained when the novelty wears off. In one wheat-belt village, a new trunk highway was opened in 1929 and drained away some trade. In 1933, the novelty began to wear off; and this, coupled with a more aggressive policy on the part of the merchants, brought back both the trade and the territory that had been lost.

Village retail sales suffered not only from agricultural depression, but also from industrial depression. Several of the 140 villages had in them small industrial plants which failed between 1930 and 1933. The workers, who were thus deprived of employment, made poor customers for village stores, and a number of the jobless subsequently went on relief. Technological unemployment appeared in a few villages. New machinery in mills and quarries was responsible for displacing some gainfully employed workers.

A statistical picture of the decline in retail sales in the 140 villages is presented in Table 35, which shows the amount and percentage of change, the average retail sales per village, per store, and per capita by region and by size of village for the period 1930–35.

In the main, this table shows that the decline in per capita sales was most severe in the South and in the small villages, whether the comparison is on the basis of 1933 or 1935. The table does show a sharp increase in per capita purchasing power in 1934–35 over 1932–33. Judging by field-work reports, this increase for the South may be underestimated.

In scanning the data in this table, three things should, however, be borne in mind. In the first place, the census does not report sales taking place outside a given municipality but within its trade area. This was estimated as equal to about $10 to $12 per capita in 1930; and if the ratio of decline was the same in the open country as in the village, the per capita figures given for 1933 are understated by about $5 or $6, and those for 1935 by about $7 or $8. Again, if these censuses, as would seem to be quite possible, are under-enumerated, the per capita sales would be understated likewise. Finally, the decline in the dollar volume of sales does not represent a proportionate drop in the volume of goods sold, since 1932–33 prices were sharply lower than in 1929–30.

It is interesting to compare the figures in Table 35 with the replies of village merchants in the 140 villages to fieldworkers'

TABLE 35

RETAIL SALES: AMOUNT OF AND PER CENT CHANGE IN AVERAGE RETAIL SALES FOR COMMUNITY POPULATION

Per Capita, by Region and by Size of Village

Region and Size	*1930*	*1933*	*1935*	*1930–33*	*1930–35*	*1933–35*
	DOLLARS			PER CENT CHANGE		
All regions						
Town	$401	$163	$222	*−59.3*	*−44.6*	36.2
Large	332	152	218	*−54.2*	*−34.3*	43.4
Medium	277	166	162	*−58.1*	*−41.5*	39.7
Small	244	90	134	*−63.1*	*−45.1*	48.9
Total	301	128	180	*−57.4*	*−40.2*	40.6
Middle Atlantic						
Town	412	281	302	*−31.7*	*−26.7*	7.5
Large	409	204	262	*−50.1*	*−35.9*	28.4
Medium	310	135	199	*−56.4*	*−35.8*	47.4
Small	260	129	160	*−50.4*	*−38.5*	24.0
Total	314	150	204	*−52.2*	*−35.0*	36.0
South						
Town	265	95	115	*−64.1*	*−56.6*	21.1
Large	252	121	179	*−51.9*	*−29.0*	47.9
Medium	178	83	108	*−53.3*	*−39.3*	30.1
Small	142	41	57	*−71.1*	*−59.9*	39.0
Total	208	87	117	*−58.1*	*−43.8*	34.5
Middle West						
Town	460	201	268	*−56.3*	*−41.7*	33.3
Large	412	156	220	*−62.1*	*−46.6*	41.0
Medium	319	124	166	*−61.1*	*−48.0*	33.9
Small	278	101	161	*−63.7*	*−42.1*	59.4
Total	345	137	191	*−60.3*	*−44.3*	39.4
Far West						
Town	430	183	269	*−57.4*	*−37.4*	47.0
Large	333	187	343	*−43.8*	3.0	83.4
Medium	327	127	207	*−61.1*	*−36.7*	63.0
Small	273	98	159	*−64.1*	*−41.8*	62.2
Total	356	155	238	*−56.5*	*−33.1*	53.5

inquiries concerning the extent of recovery. Rural storekeepers and bankers the country over were almost unanimous in their opinion that trade in the first half of 1936 was much better than in 1932, and in many cases better than in 1930. Bank deposits and clear-ings have risen as the next chapter shows. Retail sales have made notable gains, as has employment, use of utilities, and new construction. The reasons for improvement have already been discussed under the earlier section on the number of stores. Larger farm income and the activities of Federal agencies have been of prime importance in quickening the tempo of economic life, and in some villages the credit rests with the success of small industrial plants. Table 36 summarizes the estimates of improvement in business given to fieldworkers by village businessmen and bankers.

TABLE 36

ESTIMATES OF IMPROVEMENT IN BUSINESS 1935-36 OVER 1930 AND OVER 1932

140 Selected American Agricultural Villages, by Region and by Size of Village

Region and Size	*Is Business Better or Worse than in 1930?*				*Is Business Better or Worse than in 1932?*			
	BETTER	WORSE	SAME	N.A.	BETTER	WORSE	SAME	N.A.
All regions								
Town	10	4	3	...	15	1	1	...
Large	13	4	2	1	20	...	...	...
Medium	34	18	5	4	54	2	2	3
Small	15	22	5	...	37	4	1	...
Total	72	48	15	5	126	7	4	3
Middle Atlantic								
Town	...	1	...	...	...	...	1	...
Large	2	1	...	...	3	...	...	...
Medium	5	9	...	1	12	1	1	1
Small	3	6	...	...	8	1	...	...
Total	10	17	...	1	23	2	2	1
South								
Town	3	1	...	...	3	1	...	...
Large	5	1	...	...	6	...	...	...
Medium	11	1	...	...	11	1	...	...
Small	5	2	1	...	6	2	...	...
Total	24	5	1	...	26	4	...	...
Middle West								
Town	2	2	...	...	4	...	...	...
Large	6	2	1	1	10	...	...	...
Medium	15	6	4	3	25	...	1	2
Small	5	11	2	...	17	1	...	...
Total	28	21	7	4	56	1	1	2
Far West								
Town	5	...	3	...	8	...	...	...
Large	...	...	1	...	1	...	...	...
Medium	3	2	1	...	6	...	...	...
Small	2	3	2	...	6	...	1	...
Total	10	5	7	...	21	...	1	...

In more than three-fourths of the villages, this improvement was estimated on a percentage basis by a sufficiently large proportion of the business houses to afford an estimate for the community. The medians of these estimates are presented in Table 37.

TABLE 37

ECONOMIC IMPROVEMENT: THE MEDIAN OF REPORTED PER CENTS OF IMPROVEMENT IN BUSINESS: 1935–36 OVER 1932

140 Selected American Agricultural Villages: by Region and by Size of Village

Region and Size	*No. of Villages Reporting*	*Median Per Cent*
All regions		
Town	14	22.5
Large	13	25
Medium	49	20
Small	31	25
Total	107	22
Middle Atlantic		
Town	...	...
Large	2	20
Medium	11	10
Small	3	20
Total	16	10
South		
Town	4	12.5
Large	6	25
Medium	11	20
Small	8	22.5
Total	29	20
Middle West		
Town	4	57.5
Large	4	35
Medium	21	20
Small	17	25
Total	46	20
Far West		
Town	6	30
Large	1	30
Medium	6	23.3
Small	3	24
Total	16	27.3

For the whole group, improvement in 1935–36 over 1932 is 22 per cent. There is some evidence that this estimate may be an understatement. The Department of Commerce on November 12, 1936, estimated that sales in rural areas for October of that year were 21 per cent above 1935 and 42 per cent higher than in 1934. During the latter half of 1936 the "parity index," i.e., the ratio between prices paid to farmers and prices paid by farmers, has been close to 100, and this unquestionably has brought some improvement in rural retail trade. Recovery has proceeded at a rapid pace; and it is entirely possible that 1936 rural trade, in volume at least, will approximate 1929–30 totals. The data already given for 1932–33 on per capita sales represent probably the absolute low of the depression.

The Department of Commerce estimates for the period under review, expressed in index numbers as given in Table 38 and Table 39, show in the main a steady improvement and clearly indicate the significance of gains in 1936 over 1935 in every region.

The way in which the recovery actually worked out in many

TABLE 38

INDEX OF DOLLAR VALUES OF RETAIL SALES OF GENERAL MERCHANDISE IN RURAL AREAS

(1929–31 = 100)

	Without Seasonal Adjustment				*With Seasonal Adjustment*			
Month	*1933*	*1934*	*1935*	*1936*	*1933*	*1934*	*1935*	*1936*
January	47.2	66.0	72.6	79.9	57.0	79.5	87.5	96.5
February	50.8	73.1	82.0	84.2	56.0	80.5	90.5	93.0
March	44.2	74.0	90.6	99.2	47.5	79.5	97.5	106.5
April	59.1	70.8	97.0	105.5	61.5	74.0	101.0	110.0
May	60.9	74.9	87.6	106.5	65.0	79.5	93.0	113.5
June	62.1	68.3	94.2	106.2	65.5	72.5	99.5	112.5
July	54.9	58.2	74.7	88.3	71.5	75.5	97.0	114.5
August	64.7	68.1	79.8	96.2	75.0	79.0	93.0	112.0
September	73.2	97.9	103.7	122.3	74.0	99.0	105.0	123.5
October	97.5	108.7	127.6	...	80.0	89.0	104.5	...
November	105.1	110.4	127.6	...	85.5	90.0	103.5	...
December	110.3	134.2	155.9	...	77.5	94.5	110.0	...
Annual Index	69.2	83.7	99.4					

places is shown in the following report from a hard-hit Southern community, quite typical of many.

At the close of 1930, the fertilizer people held $25,000 worth of notes given by farmers of ——— community to pay for fertilizer used. These notes could not be collected. Because it was necessary for the farmers to have fertilizer if they were to raise a crop, this concern continued to supply a minimum amount to the farmers of the region during the years 1931 and 1932. Until 1933, its customers went deeper and deeper into debt. Some owed twice the annual value of the crops produced. Many had not paid loans on homes and farms and taxes. The banks could not finance them. These people could not pay the interest on their obligations; but the sheriff did not foreclose on property. People economized upon fertilizer, food, clothes, automobiles. Homes were dilapidated, stock and equipment run down, and terraces, land, and fences were not kept up.

At the end of 1933, the fertilizer concern collected 99 per cent of bills made by farmers for fertilizer during the year and 10 to 15 per cent on back notes. In 1934, the farmers were converted to the A.A.A. They began to buy new mules and better fertilizer. The fertilizer concern collected 20 per cent on old notes and practically all of its bills for the year 1934. In 1935, the same concern had collected 60 per cent of all back debts on fertilizer notes and 98 per cent of accounts for that year. Most of the farmers had paid back taxes, and in some cases they had paid off loans on farms.

Several new stores opened in 1935 and are making a go of it. By 1935, one of the leading merchants had entirely recovered from the depression, and business had increased 50 per cent. During the past twelve months the first wire fencing since 1929 was hauled out of ——— and merchants have had trouble supplying the demand for it.

TABLE 39

INDEXES OF DOLLAR SALES OF GENERAL MERCHANDISE IN SMALL TOWNS AND RURAL AREAS BY REGIONS, 1930 AND 1935[a]

(1929–31 = 100)

Seasonally Adjusted

	1930				*1935*			
Month	EAST	SOUTH	MIDDLE WEST	FAR WEST	EAST	SOUTH	MIDDLE WEST	FAR WEST
January	93.9	120.2	86.9	111.3	84.5	101.9	85.6	95.4
February	94.7	111.4	87.0	105.8	88.8	108.5	88.1	95.3
March	107.2	127.4	103.1	114.4	95.9	119.7	95.5	97.9
April	109.7	127.2	100.7	119.6	98.2	118.2	95.6	100.4
May	110.7	127.6	105.4	125.4	86.5	106.8	88.2	101.2
June	107.8	132.5	102.6	129.8	95.2	115.5	94.0	106.8
July	108.9	140.9	103.9	129.8	91.4	112.7	91.5	104.0
August	110.6	136.0	101.3	123.1	87.5	109.8	86.0	102.7
September	119.7	156.7	107.5	126.3	103.9	122.0	94.7	103.7

[a] Source: United States Department of Commerce, Press release of October 28, 1936.

Other evidences of recovery were reports from many communities that the sale of better grades of groceries and cuts of meat picked up in 1936. Car trades and sales also increased, beginning in the fall of 1935. Thus one fieldworker reported from a Middle West village: "The probabilities are that the standard of living of the area is as high as in 1930, or higher, since a large number of luxury items, such as radios, and electric refrigerators, fuel heaters and gas heaters, have been introduced within the last 5 years, especially within the last 18 months."

INDUSTRY

Despite the fact that these communities are agricultural, they do have some industry, most of it related to the food and fiber crops in the immediate vicinity of the communities. About one-eighth of the gainfully employed in these villages in 1930 were engaged in these plants, which represent, therefore, an important element in the economic life of these villages.

Number of industries declines.—The turnover among these industries was quite high between 1924 and 1930, but between 1930 and 1936 both the death rates and the birth rates increased. Of the 593 industries in existence in the former year, two-fifths succumbed to the depression. In the previous period only about half as many liquidated. On the other hand, 161 new enterprises were initiated. In 1936, 513 were operating, an average of 3.7 per village as against 4.2 in 1930 and 4.6 in 1924. The number of industries declined in every region. This is shown in Table 40.

A smaller number of industries reported full-time workers in every region except the Middle West; though the average number of full-time employees per industry declined only from 25 to 21. There was, however, a fourfold increase in the number reporting part-time workers, an increase shown in each region. Counting both full-time and part-time employees, there were more people receiving wages in 1935 than in 1930. On the basis of these figures, it seems probable that many workers who were employed full time in 1930 were receiving only part-time employment in 1935, and that new employees were often hired on a part-time status. There was a notable increase in the number of concerns employing full-time workers from the open country, a result brought about in some measure, possibly, by the decrease in farm production under the A.A.A. program, and possibly also by the removal of village workers to small farms to compensate for reduced wages. It is evident that farmers displaced some village people in industrial work, as the proportion of full-time employees from the open country rose from 7 per cent of all full-time employees in 1930 to 20 per cent in 1935. This change is especially startling in the South, where undoubtedly displaced share-croppers and renters turned to village industries for their livelihood and profited by the recovery in the textile industry. Table 40 gives the regional details. Another explanation of this phenomenon is to be found in the number of women who sought and received places in industry. Illustrative of this aspect of the situation, not everywhere observed, is the record of a Middle Atlantic village. In it a comparison of the number of people in industry in 1930 and in 1936 reveals that the number employed rose from 345 to 583. This tremendous jump is explained by the fact that formerly only the men worked; with the depression and the consequent drop in wages and number of hours, more women sought employment. In other words, this village had in 1930 a large labor reserve which was called into service by the demand for more workers (who, however, worked only intermittently and at rush periods) and offered its services because of the need for more income for the family.

Table 41 shows that, for all industries, the average number of both full-time and part-time employees fell between 1930 and 1935.

The decrease in the average number of part-time employees, in spite of a considerable rise in their total number, resulted from the great increase in the number of concerns employing workers on this basis. The average number of part-time employees per

TABLE 40

VILLAGE COMMUNITY INDUSTRY: THE NUMBER OF FULL-TIME AND PART-TIME WORKERS EMPLOYED IN INDUSTRIES REPORTING, THEIR AVERAGE WAGES AND THE NUMBER OF FULL-TIME WORKERS FROM THE OPEN COUNTRY

140 Selected American Agricultural Villages, 1930 and 1936: by Region

Region	*Number of Industries Reported*		*Number of Villages Reporting Industries*		*Full-Time Workers*				*Part-Time Workers*				*Full-Time Workers from Open Country*			
	1930 [a]	*1936*	*1930*	*1936*	NO. REPORTING	*1930*	NO. REPORTING	*1936*	NO. REPORTING	*1930*	NO. REPORTING	*1936*	NO. REPORTING	*1930*	NO. REPORTING	*1936*
All regions	593	513	128	130	520	13,002	464	9,954	50	4,280	206	9,014	90	915	155	2,019
Middle Atlantic	155	119	27	27	151	3,894	108	3,038	14	726	47	1,224	34	349	44	591
South	156	119	29	27	119	3,010	108	2,123	11	255	57	1,122	18	86	40	545
Middle West	195	191	51	54	168	2,503	179	2,371	14	1,109	67	2,482	29	194	41	304
Far West	87	84	21	22	82	3,595	69	2,422	11	2,190	35	4,186	9	286	30	579

[a] The totals for 1930 in this and subsequent tables differ slightly from the 1930 data as published in *Rural Social Trends*, for the following reasons: (1) industries were reclassified and a slightly different definition of industry was used; (2) it was possible to secure 1930 information during the 1936 study on a few plants incompletely enumerated in the former year. Data for 1924 were not retabulated on the present basis and hence are not given in these tables.

industry decreased in every region. The Far West particularly specializes in part-time employees, largely because of the seasonal type of industry in that region. The average number of full-time employees decreased in every region except the Middle Atlantic.

It is evident that a striking increase in the number of concerns employing 10 or fewer part-time employees occurred between 1930 and 1936, and also a decrease in the number of plants with 100 or more full-time employees. This is undoubtedly a result of the depression. Smaller increases in the number of concerns employing larger numbers of part-time employees are also apparent. The number of concerns employing fewer than 10 full-time employees dropped slightly for all 140 villages, but increased in the Middle West and the Far West. The computation of the figures on industrial employment on a percentage basis, in Table 42, serves to make clearer the trends in employment.

A case helps to make clear what happened in many places. A certain farm implement plant was closed from early in 1932 to the spring of 1934. This threw slightly more than 100 persons out of employment. In 1934, the plant reopened with 13 workers. In 1935, the number was stepped up to 35. When the plant was visited in April, 1936, 81 were being employed.

Industrial wages.—It has always been very difficult to obtain wage data from the industries in these communities. In some cases there was natural unwillingness to make the data public. In others the books were kept so that it was impossible, without a name-by-name study, to separate full-time from part-time workers. Again, in many of these small industries, the owner worked with his employees and often failed to differentiate between the wages he paid himself and the profits he withdrew from the business.

In this survey, because of depression conditions, a special effort was made to determine the average wages of full-time employees. Reasonably accurate data were secured from almost two-thirds of the industries. In the Middle Atlantic and the 2 Western regions, the average varied from $19.87 to $20.18, a remarkably close

TABLE 41

VILLAGE COMMUNITY INDUSTRY: THE AVERAGE NUMBER OF EMPLOYEES, FULL-TIME AND PART-TIME, FOR INDUSTRIES REPORTING PERSONNEL, AND THE NUMBER OF INDUSTRIES REPORTING BY THE NUMBER OF EMPLOYEES, FULL-TIME AND PART-TIME

140 Selected American Agricultural Villages, 1930 and 1936: by Region

Region	*Average Number of Employees*				*The Number of Industries Employing*															
					LESS THAN 10 EMPLOYEES				10 TO 50 EMPLOYEES				50 TO 100 EMPLOYEES				100 AND UP			
	1930		*1936*		*1930*		*1936*		*1930*		*1936*		*1930*		*1936*		*1930*		*1936*	
	Full Time	*Part Time*	*Full Time*	*Part Time*	*Full Time*	*Part Time*	*Full Time*	*Part Time*	*Full Time*	*Part Time*	*Full Time*	*Part Time*	*Full Time*	*Part Time*	*Full Time*	*Part Time*	*Full Time*	*Part Time*	*Full Time*	*Part Time*
All regions	25	86	21	44	302	10	300	131	154	19	105	46	29	8	33	10	35	13	26	19
Middle Atlantic	26	52	28	26	84	2	63	29	45	6	27	13	11	2	7	2	11	4	11	3
South	25	23	20	20	71	4	74	44	34	5	20	8	4	2	9	1	10	...	5	4
Middle West	15	79	13	37	114	4	121	47	42	5	45	12	7	1	9	3	5	4	4	5
Far West	44	199	35	120	33	...	42	11	33	3	13	13	7	3	8	4	9	5	6	7
					The Percentage of Industries Reporting Employment of Personnel															
All regions					58.1	20.0	64.7	63.6	29.6	38.0	22.6	22.3	5.6	16.0	7.1	4.9	6.7	26.0	5.6	9.2

correspondence. In the South, the average was $12.50. In 1930, the nearest estimate possible was about $25.00 a week. In 1929, the director of the present investigation made a study of 70 industrial villages, each devoted to a single industry. The median average wage in these communities, except in the South, ranged from $24.00 to $28.00 for males, and was $15.50 in the South. Females averaged $21.00 in all except the South, and $12.00 in the South. Judged by these data, and in the light of the depression, the weekly rates for full-time workers in agricultural villages does not seem to be out of line.

Type of industry.—Other characteristics of the industrial organization of the 140 villages appear in Table 43, which shows the percentage distribution of manufacturing industries by region and by type of industry classified on a more detailed basis than was used in 1930 and 1924. Outstanding is the fact that much rural industry is devoted to processing and packing food and allied products. This is particularly true in the Far West. There has been little change, a slight increase, in the percentage of industries dealing with food, though a noticeable gain in this category occurred in the Middle West. Industries concerned with lumber and furniture are next in importance, especially in the South. In the Far West the proportion in this category has dropped considerably. In this region a larger percentage of industries is now manufacturing iron, steel, and other metal products.

During the depression years, village industries experienced some changes, notable among which was the appearance for the first time of labor unions. The employees of a small industrial plant in one Pennsylvania village were organized during 1934 by men sent out from the union's headquarters. A strike resulted in a slight increase in wages. One of the plant's executives said that insistence on the higher wages simply meant increased costs and prices, less business, and consequent unemployment. Nevertheless this concern seems to be prospering for all that, and everyone in the community is now satisfied. A similar occurrence took place

TABLE 42

VILLAGE COMMUNITY INDUSTRY: PERCENTAGE DISTRIBUTION OF INDUSTRIES

By Number of Employees and by Region

Number of Employees	*All Regions*				*Middle Atlantic*				*South*				*Middle West*				*Far West*			
	1930		*1936*		*1930*		*1936*		*1930*		*1936*		*1930*		*1936*		*1930*		*1936*	
	F	P	F	P	F	P	F	P	F	P	F	P	F	P	F	P	F	P	F	P
Less than 10	58.1	20.0	64.7	63.6	55.6	14.3	58.3	61.8	59.6	36.4	68.6	77.2	67.9	28.5	67.6	70.2	40.2	0.0	60.9	31.4
10-50	29.6	38.0	22.6	22.3	29.8	42.8	25.0	27.6	28.6	45.5	18.5	14.0	25.0	35.8	25.1	17.9	40.3	27.2	18.9	37.2
50-100	5.6	16.0	7.1	4.9	7.3	14.3	6.5	4.2	3.3	18.1	8.3	1.7	4.2	7.1	5.0	5.5	8.5	27.3	11.5	11.4
100 up.	6.7	26.0	5.6	9.2	7.3	28.6	10.2	6.4	8.4	0.0	4.6	7.0	2.9	28.5	2.3	7.5	11.0	45.5	8.7	20.0

TABLE 43

DISTRIBUTION OF MANUFACTURING INDUSTRIES BY TYPE OF INDUSTRY AND BY REGION

140 Selected American Agricultural Villages, 1936

Type of Industry	Percentage Distribution									
	ALL REGIONS		MIDDLE ATLANTIC		SOUTH		MIDDLE WEST		FAR WEST	
	1930	*1936*	*1930*	*1936*	*1930*	*1936*	*1930*	*1936*	*1930*	*1936*
Total	100.0	100.0	100.0	100.0	100.0	100.0	100.0	100.0	100.0	100.0
Food and allied	41.2	43.6	32.1	34.3	37.3	37.1	46.1	50.4	51.8	51.1
Textile and clothing	4.2	4.1	7.7	10.1	5.1	5.9	2.6	1.0	...	...
Iron and steel, machinery and vehicle and other metal	6.9	8.2	12.3	11.8	4.5	5.0	5.6	5.2	4.6	14.3
Lumber and furniture	20.8	18.9	18.1	19.3	27.6	31.1	15.4	13.6	24.1	13.1
Leather	.8	1.2	2.0	3.4	...	...	1.0	1.0	...	...
Paper, printing, and allied	3.2	1.9	7.1	3.4	...	.8	4.1	2.6	...	...
Chemical and allied	2.9	3.3	2.6	4.2	3.8	2.5	3.6	4.2	...	1.2
Clay, glass, and stone	5.2	4.1	5.2	2.5	.6	.8	8.2	6.8	6.9	4.8
Cigar and tobacco	5.5	1.4	2.6	3.4	...	...	2.1	1.6	...	...
Transportation	4.1	.8	...	...	1.9	.8	1.0	1.0	1.1	1.2
Miscellaneous	5.2	12.5	10.3	7.6	19.2	16.0	10.3	12.6	11.5	14.3

in a silk mill in a North Carolina village where, with the aid of sympathetic citizens including the high-school principal, the employees were finally successful in forming a union. The formation of unions in village industries, however, has made small headway. One reason for the lack of union organization among the employees of small concerns in the villages is that these concerns appear to have a genuine interest in the welfare of their employees. The relationship between employer and employees in such small companies is, of course, much more personal and informal than is the case in large industrial plants. In this connection, the notes of a fieldworker on a small plant in a Far Western village are of interest.

> Mr. G. pays his men well, as they are expected to work for him during their whole lifetime, and he is directly interested in their welfare. All of them own their own homes in town, have some farm land in the district and are well insured, and are holders of fairly large bank accounts.

The owner of a plant in another village stated that although some of his men were too old to be properly efficient, they had spent their lives in his employ and he would never let them go.

In general, it appears that between 1930 and 1936, there was a decided shift among rural industries toward smaller plants and more part-time employment, there was slightly greater dependence upon the locality as the source of raw materials, and problems of employer-employee relationship began to emerge.

VI

Rural Banking

AT THE time *Rural Social Trends* was published, the statement was made "Perhaps more than any other institution, banks showed the effects of the depression. The decade of 1921–1931 will go down in modern history as a period of unprecedented mortality among banks. Failures averaged about 600 a year during that period, and in 1931 exceeded 2,000. A great majority of these failures were in places of under 10,000 population." [1]

Number of banks continues decline.—"The 140 villages give a clear indication of these difficulties. One-fifth of the 254 banks found in 1924 had failed or merged by 1930." The banks continued to show the influences of the continuing depression in the quinquennium from 1930 to 1935. Using data, compiled from the Rand McNally Banker's Directory, of the reports as of June, 1930, January, 1931, 1932, 1933, 1934, 1935, and June, 1935, for the 140 villages in this study, Table 44 was computed. The table gives the history throughout the depression of the banks of the 140 villages in terms of number of banks surviving the depression. Of the 214 banks found in these villages in the spring of 1930, 5 banks had either failed or merged by June, 1930. By the following January there were 201 banks in the 140 villages. January, 1932, found 16 fewer banks; now there were 185. By January, 1933, these had been reduced to 175. Then came the banking holiday of March, 1933. Only 4 more banks were lost by January, 1934.

By January, 1935, the tide had turned. There were 174 banks in the 140 villages, which was the number found in June, 1935. From the time of the first survey in 1924 to the end of June, 1935, the 140 villages lost 80 banks, almost six-tenths of a bank

[1] Page 165.

TABLE 44

AGRICULTURAL VILLAGE BANKS: THE NUMBER OF LOCALLY OWNED AND BRANCH BANKS EXISTING, THE NUMBER MERGED AND THE NUMBER CLOSED, AS OF SPECIFIED DATES

140 Villages, by Region and Size

Region and Size	No. of Villages	June, 1930				January, 1931				January, 1932				January, 1933			
		No. Locally Owned	No. Branch	No. Merged	No. Closed	No. Locally Owned	No. Branch	No. Merged	No. Closed	No. Locally Owned	No. Branch	No. Merged	No. Closed	No. Locally Owned	No. Branch	No. Merged	No. Closed
All regions	140	194	15	...	3	186	15	1	9	173	12	3	18	161	14	2	11
Mid.Atlantic	28	39	...	...	...	38	...	...	1	38	...	...	...	35	...	2	1
South	30	33	6	...	...	30	6	1	2	29	3	...	7	29	4	...	1
Middle West	60	96	...	...	3	92	...	...	6	83	...	1	9	75	1	...	8
Far West	22	26	9	...	...	26	9	...	...	23	9	2	2	22	9	...	1
Small	42	55	...	...	...	51	...	...	4	48	...	2	2	43	...	...	5
Medium	61	82	5	...	3	83	5	...	...	75	3	1	11	71	5	2	3
Large	20	37	3	...	...	34	3	1	2	33	3	...	3	31	3	...	2
Town	17	20	7	...	...	18	7	...	3	17	6	...	2	16	6	...	1

TABLE 44—*Continued*

AGRICULTURAL VILLAGE BANKS: THE NUMBER OF LOCALLY OWNED AND BRANCH BANKS EXISTING, THE NUMBER MERGED AND THE NUMBER CLOSED, AS OF SPECIFIED DATES

140 Villages, by Region and Size

Region and Size	*No. of Villages*	*January, 1934*				*January, 1935*				*June, 1935*			
		NO. LOCALLY OWNED	NO. BRANCH	NO. MERGED	NO. CLOSED	NO. LOCALLY OWNED	NO. BRANCH	NO. MERGED	NO. CLOSED	NO. LOCALLY OWNED	NO. BRANCH	NO. MERGED	NO. CLOSED
All regions	140	155	16	1	6	152	22	...	1	152	22	...	...
Mid.Atlantic	28	32	...	...	3	32	2	...	...	32	2	...	...
South	30	30	4	...	...	30	5	...	...	30	5	...	...
Middle West	60	74	1	1	1	74	2	...	1	74	2	...	...
Far West	22	19	11	...	1	16	13	...	...	16	13	...	...
Small	42	41	...	...	3	39	1	...	...	39	1	...	...
Medium	61	68	5	1	3	68	9	...	...	68	9	...	...
Large	20	31	3	...	...	31	3	...	1	31	3	...	...
Town	17	15	8	...	...	14	9	...	...	14	9	...	...

per village. The total number of banks, moreover, does not fully indicate what happened in the 5 years. The number of locally owned or managed banks decreased from 194 in June, 1930, to 152 in June, 1935, and the number of branch banks increased from 15 in June, 1930, to 22 in June, 1935. The Middle Atlantic and the Middle West villages which had no branch banks in 1930 had 2 each by 1935. In the Far West, branch banking has been forging ahead. The 22 Far West villages had 26 locally owned banks and 9 branch banks in June, 1930; by June, 1935, there were but 16 locally owned banks and 13 branch banks.

The depression reduced sharply the average number of banks per village, curtailing banking facilities in many communities and even eliminating them in some. From 1924 with an average of 1.8 banks per village, there was a steady decline to 1935, with an average of 1.2 banks. In Table 45 is given the number of villages

TABLE 45

AGRICULTURAL VILLAGE BANKS: THE NUMBER OF VILLAGES WITHOUT BANKS AS OF SPECIFIED DATES

140 Villages, by Region

Region	*June 1930*	*January 1931*	*January 1932*	*January 1933*	*January 1934*	*January 1935*	*June 1935*
All regions	2	7	9	11	11	8	8
Middle Atlantic	0	0	0	0	2	1	1
South	1	3	5	5	3	2	2
Middle West	1	4	4	6	5	4	4
Far West	0	0	0	0	1	1	1

without banks on specified dates. These increased from 2 in June, 1930, to 11 in January, 1933 and 1934; and in 1935 there were still 8 villages without a bank. Table 46 gives the average number of banks per village and the number of villages having a specified number of banks. In 1924, 44 villages had only one bank, 78 had 2, 15 had 3, and 2 had 4. By 1935, 97 villages had only one bank, 32 had 2, and 3 had 3. There is a grave possibility that this sharp reduction in the number of banks per village and the tendency to one locally owned bank and to branch banking will seriously affect the credit relations in a village. The banker may, and sometimes does, make some very arbitrary credit distinctions. The farmer or village merchant becomes dependent upon a single village banker for credit funds, or he must go to a larger community.

Banks in places under 2,500 were particularly affected by the depression trend. Of the 8,916 bank suspensions in the decade 1921 to 1931, almost three-quarters were located in places having a population of less than 2,500. The actual percentages show that 62.5 per cent of national banks, and 76.6 per cent of state banks suspending operation in the decade 1921–31, were in villages or hamlets.

Balance sheets show trend toward greater liquidity.—Another view of the banking situation in the 140 villages is given by the table showing the average resources and liabilities of the solvent banks at each period. Table 47 gives the averages per bank according to the shortened form of bank report.

For all regions, there was a steady decline in the average resources per bank from $670,400 in June, 1930, to $536,900 in January, 1934. January and June, 1935, brought about a reversal in trend with increases to $579,200 and $586,300, respectively. The average capitalization changed but little in the 5 years. The Banking Acts of 1933 and of 1935 caused certain bookkeeping adjustments, but if "capital," "surplus," and "profit" be used as an indication of the capital structure of the bank, the averages vary slightly, being $90,300 in June, 1930, $93,100 in January, 1931, $89,400 in 1932, $83,100 in 1933, $86,600 in 1934, $89,400 in January, 1935, and $89,900 in June, 1935.

The primary change in the structure of solvent village banks has been in the ratio of loans and discounts to deposits and in the ratio of cash due from other banks to deposits. The ratio of loans and discounts to total deposits hovered around 66 per cent in the period June, 1930, to January, 1933. After the banking moratorium of March, 1933, the ratio changed to 59 per cent in January, 1934, and then to 45 per cent in January and June, 1935. The

TABLE 46

AGRICULTURAL VILLAGE BANKS: THE AVERAGE NUMBER OF BANKS PER VILLAGE, AND FREQUENCY

140 Villages, by Region

Region	*Average Banks per Village*				*Villages with Specified Number of Banks*														
					NONE			ONE			TWO			THREE			FOUR		
	1924	*1930*	*1932*	*1935*	*1924*	*1930*	*1935*	*1924*	*1930*	*1935*	*1924*	*1930*	*1935*	*1924*	*1930*	*1935*	*1924*	*1930*	*1935*
All regions	1.8	1.5	1.3	1.2	1	1	8	44	70	97	78	63	32	15	6	3	2	...	...
Middle Atlantic	1.4	1.5	1.4	1.2	...	...	1	19	16	21	9	11	5	...	1	1	...	...	...
South	1.7	1.4	1.1	1.1	1	1	2	12	16	21	13	13	7	4	...	...	...	...	...
Middle West	2.1	1.6	1.3	1.3	...	...	4	6	28	39	44	28	15	9	4	1	1	...	...
Far West	1.8	1.6	1.5	1.3	...	...	1	7	10	16	12	11	5	2	1	1	1	...	...

TABLE 47

AGRICULTURAL VILLAGE BANKING

A. THE AVERAGE LIABILITIES OF LOCALLY OWNED OR MANAGED BANKS AS OF SPECIFIED DATES 1930–35

By Region

Region	*No. of Banks*	*Capital*	*Surplus*	*Profit*	*Deposits*	*Other Liabilities*	*Total*
		IN THOUSANDS OF DOLLARS					
All regions							
June, 1930	193	43.0	47.3	...	553.1	27.0	670.4
January, 1931	186	43.8	49.3	...	544.9	24.8	662.8
January, 1932	172	43.2	46.2	...	503.4	27.3	620.1
January, 1933	159	43.5	39.6	...	422.3	39.9	545.3
January, 1934	149	45.3	30.4	10.9	424.4	26.9	536.9
January, 1935	151	52.6	24.7	12.1	473.8	16.0	579.2
June, 1935	152	52.5	24.2	13.5	485.5	10.6	586.3
Middle Atlantic							
June, 1930	38	47.1	106.0	...	826.8	55.3	1,035.2
January, 1931	38	48.4	105.9	...	838.9	44.7	1,037.9
January, 1932	38	48.4	90.7	...	784.9	50.3	974.3
January, 1933	35	51.1	75.7	...	705.0	78.5	910.3
January, 1934	31	48.8	65.5	18.4	679.8	52.7	865.2
January, 1935	32	69.5	60.3	27.4	742.3	28.8	928.3
June, 1935	32	71.2	57.2	30.8	738.5	16.9	914.6
South							
June, 1930	33	47.1	43.9	...	428.9	27.5	547.4
January, 1931	30	47.2	45.5	...	394.3	29.6	516.6
January, 1932	29	45.7	42.6	...	248.2	22.6	443.1
January, 1933	27	44.0	41.3	...	311.3	27.0	423.6
January, 1934	29	55.1	29.1	14.2	358.4	28.0	484.8
January, 1935	29	48.7	17.8	8.1	330.6	11.6	416.8
June, 1935	30	48.6	17.0	10.9	320.5	10.8	407.8
Middle West							
June, 1930	96	39.6	28.4	...	507.4	16.4	591.8
January, 1931	92	40.5	30.3	...	492.9	16.1	579.8
January, 1932	82	38.9	28.8	...	451.4	18.1	537.2
January, 1933	75	38.3	24.4	...	348.6	28.5	439.8
January, 1934	71	38.7	16.3	7.0	346.0	14.3	422.3
January, 1935	74	46.1	11.1	7.5	405.4	10.8	480.9
June, 1935	74	45.2	11.7	7.3	432.4	7.4	504.0
Far West							
June, 1930	26	44.6	35.9	...	479.4	24.2	584.1
January, 1931	26	44.6	37.9	...	473.0	21.1	576.6
January, 1932	23	46.9	39.3	...	448.4	19.5	554.1
January, 1933	22	48.0	32.1	...	359.8	33.1	473.0
January, 1934	18	49.4	27.6	8.3	400.1	22.6	508.0
January, 1935	16	55.9	29.4	9.7	512.8	22.7	630.5
June, 1935	16	55.9	29.4	12.5	534.2	12.9	644.9

TABLE 47—*Continued*

AGRICULTURAL VILLAGE BANKING

B. THE AVERAGE RESOURCES OF LOCALLY OWNED OR MANAGED BANKS AS OF SPECIFIED DATES 1930–35

By Region

Region	*No. of Banks*	*Cash Due Banks*	*U.S. Gov't Securities*	*Other Securities*	*Loans and Discounts*	*Other Resources*
		IN THOUSANDS OF DOLLARS				
All regions						
June, 1930	193	88.8	...	189.3	364.5	27.8
January, 1931	186	90.0	...	191.2	354.3	27.3
January, 1932	172	81.7	...	180.8	332.0	25.6
January, 1933	159	65.1	...	171.5	280.7	28.0
January, 1934	149	93.2	54.8	110.8	250.7	27.4
January, 1935	151	127.0	90.3	124.3	212.1	25.5
June, 1935	152	132.7	89.8	118.5	220.0	25.3
Middle Atlantic						
June, 1930	38	84.8	...	482.5	433.9	34.0
January, 1931	38	94.5	...	461.4	447.2	34.8
January, 1932	38	88.9	...	402.9	452.0	30.5
January, 1933	35	73.9	...	391.4	412.0	33.0
January, 1934	31	81.5	71.7	286.1	389.1	36.8
January, 1935	32	114.7	148.8	270.6	355.1	39.1
June, 1935	32	130.1	129.6	279.2	337.3	38.4
South						
June, 1930	33	81.8	...	63.0	373.9	28.7
January, 1931	30	74.8	...	65.1	348.0	28.7
January, 1932	29	59.5	...	64.6	292.3	26.7
January, 1933	27	61.2	...	68.7	263.1	30.6
January, 1934	29	116.7	50.6	48.4	233.7	35.4
January, 1935	29	98.8	49.2	69.3	170.1	29.4
June, 1935	30	80.8	44.3	59.0	195.6	28.1
Middle West						
June, 1930	96	91.8	...	127.2	345.9	26.8
January, 1931	92	91.4	...	132.6	330.4	25.4
January, 1932	82	82.6	...	126.9	302.9	24.8
January, 1933	75	61.6	...	116.5	234.7	27.0
January, 1934	71	85.6	50.4	67.7	197.6	21.0
January, 1935	74	134.6	80.7	85.0	162.6	18.0
June, 1935	74	142.8	92.3	75.0	175.5	18.4
Far West						
June, 1930	26	92.8	...	150.7	319.5	21.1
January, 1931	26	95.9	...	149.4	310.8	20.5
January, 1932	23	94.9	...	152.6	287.7	18.9
January, 1933	22	67.9	...	135.8	249.6	19.7
January, 1934	18	105.1	49.9	79.6	249.5	23.9
January, 1935	16	167.5	91.8	113.0	231.6	26.6
June, 1935	16	188.9	83.3	110.3	236.7	25.7

TABLE 47—*Continued*

AGRICULTURAL VILLAGE BANKING

C. THE AVERAGE LIABILITIES OF LOCALLY OWNED OR MANAGED BANKS AS OF SPECIFIED DATES 1930–1935

By Size

Size	*No. of Banks*	*Capital*	*Surplus*	*Profit*	*Deposits*	*Other Liabilities*	*Total*
				IN THOUSANDS OF DOLLARS			
Towns							
June, 1930	20	56.2	34.3	...	661.2	29.8	781.5
January, 1931	18	55.0	36.4	...	619.9	22.2	733.5
January, 1932	17	52.4	32.6	...	572.7	22.2	679.9
January, 1933	16	53.8	26.4	...	445.7	46.0	571.9
January, 1934	14	51.8	13.7	10.6	461.4	26.9	564.4
January, 1935	14	64.2	13.1	10.7	531.1	22.5	641.6
June, 1935	14	65.5	13.5	9.4	533.7	3.9	626.0
Small villages							
June, 1930	54	32.7	32.6	...	352.3	21.0	438.6
January, 1931	51	33.4	32.8	...	346.7	20.4	433.3
January, 1932	48	32.9	31.4	...	311.9	15.4	391.6
January, 1933	43	31.2	30.4	...	258.5	26.8	346.9
January, 1934	40	29.1	21.6	7.7	256.1	10.6	325.1
January, 1935	39	33.0	19.4	8.3	322.8	11.4	394.9
June, 1935	39	33.0	19.1	9.2	345.1	8.8	415.2
Medium villages							
June, 1930	82	43.0	54.1	...	567.6	25.2	689.9
January, 1931	83	43.8	54.5	...	552.8	21.8	672.9
January, 1932	74	44.6	52.1	...	522.6	30.2	649.5
January, 1933	69	45.5	40.8	...	433.3	43.0	562.6
January, 1934	65	44.2	30.2	9.4	382.6	26.6	493.0
January, 1935	67	51.3	24.2	15.6	429.3	15.0	535.4
June, 1935	68	50.8	23.0	17.4	446.2	11.8	549.2
Large villages							
June, 1930	37	50.9	60.7	...	755.7	38.3	905.6
January, 1931	34	53.4	68.0	...	783.0	40.2	944.6
January, 1932	33	50.5	61.4	...	703.2	40.9	856.0
January, 1933	31	50.5	56.8	...	612.6	48.2	768.1
January, 1934	30	66.3	50.3	18.6	722.2	44.5	901.9
January, 1935	31	74.9	37.9	9.7	734.3	21.1	877.9
June, 1935	31	74.9	38.0	12.2	726.4	13.5	865.0

TABLE 47—*Continued*

AGRICULTURAL VILLAGE BANKING

D. THE AVERAGE RESOURCES OF LOCALLY OWNED OR MANAGED BANKS AS OF SPECIFIED DATES 1930–35

By Size

Size	*No. of Banks*	*Cash Due Banks*	*U.S. Gov't Securities*	*Other Securities*	*Loans and Discounts*	*Other Resources*
		IN THOUSANDS OF DOLLARS				
Towns						
June, 1930	20	124.0	...	158.2	456.3	43.0
January, 1931	18	131.1	...	171.7	395.4	35.3
January, 1932	17	131.5	...	169.6	344.6	34.1
January, 1933	16	82.7	...	163.6	286.2	39.4
January, 1934	14	129.2	66.5	107.3	219.2	42.2
January, 1935	14	161.7	97.3	150.3	190.1	42.2
June, 1935	14	181.7	94.1	108.0	203.9	38.3
Small villages						
June, 1930	54	58.2	...	112.7	242.6	25.1
January, 1931	51	57.2	...	117.2	233.4	25.5
January, 1932	48	53.5	...	119.2	197.5	21.4
January, 1933	43	43.7	...	118.4	162.6	22.2
January, 1934	40	70.0	34.9	71.7	129.9	18.6
January, 1935	39	107.4	54.1	85.3	131.5	16.6
June, 1935	39	106.3	61.0	87.0	144.6	16.3
Medium villages						
June, 1930	82	86.9	...	198.9	381.5	22.6
January, 1931	83	90.7	...	188.1	372.6	21.5
January, 1932	74	81.3	...	195.0	351.2	22.0
January, 1933	69	63.2	...	180.5	293.9	25.0
January, 1934	65	73.3	42.4	107.6	248.8	20.9
January, 1935	67	114.8	86.2	116.5	198.1	19.8
June, 1935	68	120.4	86.3	112.2	208.8	21.5
Large villages						
June, 1930	37	118.8	...	296.9	454.8	35.1
January, 1931	34	115.6	...	320.1	469.4	39.5
January, 1932	33	98.2	...	244.3	478.0	35.5
January, 1933	31	90.1	...	229.6	412.0	36.4
January, 1934	30	150.3	102.8	171.8	430.9	46.1
January, 1935	31	162.4	141.6	178.5	353.9	41.5
June, 1935	31	170.9	131.6	176.8	346.5	39.2

ratio may be interpreted as a measure of relative liquidity (though it be a poor one). It is obvious that the banks are becoming more liquid either through greater caution, easier liquidation, or the operation of the Federal credit agencies. Certainly cash due from other banks is a definite indicator of liquidity. The ratio of cash to deposits was approximately 16 per cent before the banking holiday, and then increased to 22 per cent and 27 per cent in 1934 and 1935, respectively. The relatively greater amounts of free cash are probably due to the restrictions in the Banking Acts of 1933 and of 1935, particularly the latter with its limitation of investment for banks by its correspondents. The Middle Atlantic villages are more fortunate in being able to invest in the New York market, as the cash ratio of 18 per cent shows, whereas the Middle West has a much larger surplus of free cash, as is indicated by their ratio of 33 per cent. The Southern banks, which always had the highest ratio of loans and discounts to deposits, still maintain that questionable lead, although the reduction from a ratio of about 87 per cent before the moratorium to 61 per cent in June, 1935 (the date of the Middle Atlantic and the Middle West ratios above), is a step towards liquidity of resources. These ratios may also reflect changes in the economic functions performed by these banks. They may indicate, too, the varying degrees of shock experienced by the banking structure in the different regions.

It is very difficult to analyze the shortened form of bank statement, since neither portfolio nor rediscounts are adequately presented. Nevertheless, the course of the depression to the upturn is adequately shown in the decrease of deposits and the total amount invested in loans and discounts.

Failed banks clearly weaker than others.—The bank statements of the 50 banks that suspended activity through insolvency or voluntary liquidation were also analyzed. These banks suspended operation during the period 1930–35. Of the total, 27 were banks operating under state charters and 23 were national banks. The

TABLE 48

POSTAL SAVINGS DEPARTMENTS IN 140 AMERICAN AGRICULTURAL VILLAGES, 1930–36

By Region and by Size

Region and Size	*1930*			*1931*			*1932*		
	NO. OF DEPOSITORS	NO. OF VILLAGES HAVING POSTAL-SAVINGS DEPTS.	TOTAL AMOUNT OF MONEY ON DEPOSIT	NO. OF DEPOSITORS	NO. OF VILLAGES HAVING POSTAL-SAVINGS DEPTS.	TOTAL AMOUNT OF MONEY ON DEPOSIT	NO. OF DEPOSITORS	NO. OF VILLAGES HAVING POSTAL-SAVINGS DEPTS.	TOTAL AMOUNT OF MONEY ON DEPOSIT
All regions	946	63	$499,931	1,614	70	$840,136	4,008	69	$1,947,533
Middle Atlantic	11	11	459	9	11	326	42	6	13,595
South	22	6	10,622	176	10	72,068	602	9	296,063
Middle West	558	29	338,753	887	31	540,240	2,312	36	1,195,738
Far West	355	17	150,097	542	18	227,502	1,052	18	442,137
Small	246	13	161,712	283	14	169,608	703	14	299,754
Medium	237	23	103,331	414	27	204,329	1,137	26	537,438
Large	91	13	30,395	184	15	76,341	672	15	326,941
Town	372	14	204,493	733	14	389,858	1,496	14	783,400

TABLE 48—*Continued*

POSTAL SAVINGS DEPARTMENTS IN 140 AMERICAN AGRICULTURAL VILLAGES, 1930–36

By Region and by Size

Region and Size	*1933*			*1934*		
	NO. OF DEPOSITORS	NO. OF VILLAGES HAVING POSTAL-SAVINGS DEPTS.	TOTAL AMOUNT OF MONEY ON DEPOSIT	NO. OF DEPOSITORS	NO. OF VILLAGES HAVING POSTAL-SAVINGS DEPTS.	TOTAL AMOUNT OF MONEY ON DEPOSIT
All regions	7,113	74	$3,296,485	7,823	81	$3,584,821
Middle Atlantic	62	6	20,870	66	11	19,002
South	860	11	411,309	1,082	13	479,415
Middle West	4,511	39	2,154,030	4,901	39	2,403,618
Far West	1,680	18	710,276	1,774	18	682,786
Small	1,055	17	416,762	1,206	19	433,548
Medium	2,181	29	1,001,246	2,566	33	1,148,895
Large	1,428	14	636,311	1,462	14	707,886
Town	2,449	14	1,242,166	2,589	15	1,294,492

Region and Size	*1935*			*1936*		
	NO. OF DEPOSITORS	NO. OF VILLAGES HAVING POSTAL-SAVINGS DEPTS.	TOTAL AMOUNT OF MONEY ON DEPOSIT	NO. OF DEPOSITORS	NO. OF VILLAGES HAVING POSTAL-SAVINGS DEPTS.	TOTAL AMOUNT OF MONEY ON DEPOSIT
All regions	8,193	85	$4,130,225	8,258	83	$4,208,059
Middle Atlantic	69	13	20,958	73	11	21,762
South	1,147	14	488,997	1,217	14	519,998
Middle West	5,306	40	2,976,282	5,300	40	3,019,411
Far West	1,671	18	643,988	1,668	18	646,888
Small	1,163	21	454,817	1,163	19	440,345
Medium	2,779	35	1,417,236	2,936	35	1,455,477
Large	1,657	14	904,693	1,634	14	964,787
Town	2,594	15	1,353,479	2,525	15	1,347,450

average resources and liabilities for each type of bank are given below:

Resources			*Liabilities*		
	STATE	NATIONAL		STATE	NATIONAL
Loans and discounts	$253,952	$224,951	Capital	$ 41,667	$48,261
U.S. Govt. securities	3,050	44,560	Surplus	16,163	8,326
Other securities	77,600	105,708	Undivided profits	8,872	36,681 [a]
Cash and reserves	17,932	42,745	Total deposits	311,524	311,075
Other assets	63,097	38,137	Bills payable	24,764	51,672
Total resources	415,271	456,101	Other liabilities	14,210	86
			Total liabilities	417,199	456,101

[a] Includes circulation.

The average size of the closed banks is significantly smaller than of those that remained solvent in the 5 years. The ratio of loans and discounts to total deposits was 82 per cent for state banks and 72 per cent for national, which was higher than the average for all solvent banks. All in all, the 50 banks that were closed represented total resources of $21,703,000. The ratio of repayments in liquidation dividends was available only for state banks, for which group they varied from 0 per cent to 80 per cent, with a median of 45 per cent. In the 140 villages, the loss sustained approximates to date about 8.5 million dollars in the quinquennium.

GREAT INCREASE IN POSTAL SAVINGS

At the same time that the number of banking units in the 140 villages was decreasing, the number of postal savings departments was increasing. In 1930, there were 63 such designated departments in the 140 villages; in 1935 there were 85. Two basic factors are responsible for this increase: the loss of banking facilities and the fear of bank failures. Since bank failures predominated in the Middle West, it is not surprising that half of the new depositories were in that region.

An analysis has been made of the number of village postal savings departments, the number of depositors, and the gross deposits for the year 1930–36, inclusive. Table 48 gives the data.

In the quinquennium, postal savings depositors in these villages

TABLE 49

POSTAL SAVINGS: AVERAGE NUMBER OF DEPOSITORS AND AVERAGE AMOUNT OF MONEY ON DEPOSIT PER POSTAL SAVINGS DEPARTMENT IN THE 140 AMERICAN AGRICULTURAL VILLAGES, 1930–36

By Region and by Size

Region and Size	*1930*		*1931*		*1932*		*1933*		*1934*		*1935*		*1936*	
	AVERAGE NO. OF DEPOSITS	AMOUNT OF MONEY ON DEPOSIT	AVERAGE NO. OF DEPOSITS	AMOUNT OF MONEY ON DEPOSIT	AVERAGE NO. OF DEPOSITS	AMOUNT OF MONEY ON DEPOSIT	AVERAGE NO. OF DEPOSITS	AMOUNT OF MONEY ON DEPOSIT	AVERAGE NO. OF DEPOSITS	AMOUNT OF MONEY ON DEPOSIT	AVERAGE NO. OF DEPOSITS	AMOUNT OF MONEY ON DEPOSIT	AVERAGE NO. OF DEPOSITS	AMOUNT OF MONEY ON DEPOSIT
All regions	15	$7,935	23	$12,002	58	$28,225	96	$44,547	97	$44,257	96	$48,590	99	$50,700
Middle Atlantic	1	42	1	30	7	2,266	10	3,478	6	1,727	5	1,612	7	1,978
South	4	1,770	18	7,207	67	32,896	78	37,392	83	36,878	82	34,928	87	37,143
Middle West	19	11,681	29	17,427	64	33,215	116	55,232	126	61,631	133	74,407	133	75,485
Far West	21	8,829	30	12,639	58	24,563	93	39,460	99	37,933	93	35,777	93	35,938
Small	19	12,439	20	12,115	50	21,411	62	24,515	63	22,818	55	21,658	61	23,176
Medium	10	4,493	15	7,568	44	20,671	75	34,712	78	34,815	79	40,492	84	41,585
Large	7	2,338	12	5,089	45	21,796	102	45,451	104	50,563	118	64,621	117	68,913
Town	27	14,607	52	27,847	107	55,957	1,749	88,726	173	86,299	173	90,232	168	89,830

increased over eightfold, from 946 to 8,258; deposits increased from less than a half-million to more than 4 million dollars. Each region and each size participated in this increase. In Table 49 is shown the average number of depositors and the average amount of money on deposit for each village postal savings department. For all regions the average number of depositors increased six and three-fifths times; in the Middle Atlantic the increase was 7 times; in the South over 21 times; in the Middle West 7 times; and in the Far West over 4 times. And deposits corresponded to this rapid increase in depositors. This increase in deposits and depositors, moreover, was due not only to the greater number of postal savings departments but rather to the search for guarantee of deposits with the Federal government.

Summary.—The incidence of bank failure was greatest in places with populations under 2,500. The 140 villages lost more than 30 per cent of their banks in the period 1924 to 1936. It is obvious that something was lacking in the kind of managership, or in the kind of supervision and regulation these small village banks had in the period. Social and economic planning must safeguard thrift in the population by preventing cataclysmic elimination of the savings of foresighted villagers and farmers.

The entire history of the depression and its results on the banking situation in these villages indicate three things: first, a great financial loss in terms of money lost by depositors; second, the curtailment and elimination of banking facilities; and third, an increased tendency towards branch banking. It is apparent that readjustments in banking are necessary to prevent similar recurrences of bank failures and to prevent monopolistic banking practice in villages and their surrounding communities.

VII

Rural Schools in the Depression

WITHIN the field of education, the school is but a single agency. Many others are educative, either directly or otherwise. The last years have seen a considerable development of agencies other than schools in the realm of adult education, and into this sphere the school itself has entered. Because of these developments and their significance, it seemed wise to undertake a far more extensive study of rural adult education than has been attempted hitherto in this series of reports, and to include therein the activities of the school. This chapter, however, will be concerned only with the public school as a social institution dealing with children and youth.[1]

The public schools of the communities surveyed are a major social and educational interest. In the first inter-survey period, 1924–30, their progress was marked, as measured by the usual indices. The Great Depression threw American education into reverse. Salaries were slashed, services dispensed with, terms shortened, and schools closed. Rural schools were more severely wounded than urban; those in the open country more than those in the village. The beginnings of this process were noted in the previous report, *Rural Social Trends,* as a result of correspondence with school authorities in the 140 communities in the spring of 1932. The present study finds the schools once more on the upgrade in most communities. The low point was reached in rural

[1] Private schools are omitted because they were few in number and because they varied from an old and nationally known academy to rather small and weak parochial schools of Roman Catholic and Lutheran denominations. The number of these parochial schools declined from 35 in 1924 to fewer than 20 in 1936. Furthermore, it should be stressed that this survey considered the school as a *social* institution. No attempt was made to study the educational output of the school in terms of pupil achievement or to rate school plants according to the score-card devices employed in technical administrative investigations, nor were curriculum studies made.

public education in the school year 1933–34. The data to be presented, therefore, are not a measure of the full effect of the depression upon these schools, though its influence is still clearly to be seen.

The depression and education.—Between 1920 and 1934 the total of public educational expenditure dropped from 2.54 billion dollars to 1.97, or 22.4 per cent, despite a sharp increase in enrollment. The rural schools suffered more than the urban. Typical, in the areas hardest hit, were such situations as follow, culled from fieldworkers' reports. There were frequent reports of buildings that had deteriorated, a condition recently checked by W.P.A. projects for painting, repairs, and other renovations. Salary cuts of from 10 to 60 per cent from 1930 levels, half of them from 30 per cent up, were made, and new teachers were being employed at even lower rates. Since 1934, some of these cuts have been restored in part. Four areas lost school funds through the failure of banks, and 23 village districts reported decreased assessments or tax rates and difficulty in collecting taxes. In some of the Southern villages, even in county seats, terms had been cut to five and a half or 6 months, as against the previous 8 to 9. Even these terms, in 2 or 3 villages, were to be reduced by from a month to 6 weeks in the school year 1936–37. In one village, the taxpayers' league discovered that almost one-half the parents, who had two-thirds of the children, were not taxpayers, and the league had started an agitation to exclude these children from the schools unless they paid tuition. Instances like these, as stated, show the worst side of the educational situation in these 140 village-centered rural communities. The general state of affairs will become clear as the discussion proceeds.

Number of open-country schools declines.—As in the previous inter-survey period, the number of open-country schools declined. There were 1,333 in 1936, as against 1,505 in 1930. This was a net decline of 11.4 per cent. The gross decline was slightly larger, since some open-country schools were added because of enlarged community boundaries. Most of the decline was caused by consolidation, or because pupils were transported to village schools under contracts. A few schools were closed because there were no longer children in a one-room, one-teacher district. These consolidations quite generally simply enlarged the areas of previously consolidated districts. In one county, for example, 18 schools were closed, and the pupils were sent to 2 village schools. In another village school, which had long had contractual relationships with outlying open-country districts, consolidation was put through which affected 17 schools, 10 of which were closed and 7 of which retained only the first four to six grades.

As pointed out before in these studies, there is unfortunately no one satisfactory definition of a consolidated school. Fifty schools are so called, and there are about a score of union, independent or otherwise-named schools which are in effect consolidations; so that about one-half these village schools operate on that basis.

Farm children use village schools.—The considerable open-country enrollment in the village schools of the 140 communities was alluded to in the last chapter. The proportion continued to increase, so far as the elementary schools are concerned, between 1930 and 1936. In the high schools the proportion of country pupils to the total declined very slightly for the total group of communities but increased for those 123 that remained villages. As in 1930, it still stands at approximately one-half. The regional details are given in Table 50.

The steady increase in the use of village elementary schools for country children is almost certainly a result either of the consolidation of country schools with those in the village, or of the transporting of children from such school districts by contract. It is most marked in the small villages of the Far West and South, where one-half and almost two-thirds, respectively, of the enrollment originates outside the village center. The decline in proportion of open-country youth in the total enrollment of the high school has a number of possible explanations, not more than one or two of which operated in any given situation.

In the first place, the depression kept open-country youth from attending high school in some communities. They could not afford it, especially in non-consolidated districts where no transportation was provided.

In the second place, there were a number of communities in which the proportion of youth of high-school age altered as between village and open country because of changes in population. Thus in the drought areas, there was migration from the farms

TABLE 50

OPEN-COUNTRY CHILDREN IN VILLAGE SCHOOLS

Proportion of Country Pupils in Village High and Elementary Schools, by Region and by Size

	High School			*Elementary School*		
Region	*1924*	*1930*	*1936*	*1924*	*1930*	*1936*
All regions	45.6	49.5	48.2	24.0	25.7	29.2
Middle Atlantic	41.2	54.8	52.1	12.1	14.0	17.0
South	41.6	51.3	48.2	34.6	44.4	45.4
Middle West	45.2	47.6	48.2	17.3	18.3	16.2
Far West	49.1	46.7	44.8	27.1	22.7	35.0

	High School		*Elementary School*	
Size	*1930*	*1936*	*1930*	*1936*
Small	55.5	54.1	36.4	43.3
Medium	49.3	49.1	25.9	27.7
Large	45.8	51.7	19.9	20.8
Town	... [a]	38.1 [a]	... [a]	28.0

[a] Not computed for 1930. Included with large villages.

but not as much from the villages. In some other communities, the people who moved to the farms were younger than those who left and had no children of high-school age.

Again, as noted in the previous report, competition of city schools on the one hand and those in hamlets or small villages nearer the farm on the other, reduced open-country attendance, not in the aggregate, but in these village and town centers.

Finally, it should be noted that more than one-tenth of the 140 centers are now towns. Nine of these have populations ranging from 3,000 to 4,500. As the last chapter showed, they have not increased their open-country service areas proportionately; nor has the open-country population grown as rapidly as that in the center. Moreover the ratio of villagers to countrymen always increases with the size of the center. This biases the result; yet these centers must be retained to carry through the comparisons with former years. It is significant, however, that only 38.1 per cent of the high-school enrollment in the towns came from the open country, while in the village centers the proportion exceeded 50 per cent.

The use of these village schools by rural people raises, of course, problems of village-country relations. It was pointed out in Chapter IV that the area of high-school service was increasingly becoming the most important measure of the general area of community influence. Consolidation seems to be the fairest and most democratic way of safeguarding the interests and dividing the burden of support for both village and country. Otherwise, the open-country people are at the mercy of the village board of education as, for instance, in one Middle Atlantic community where 80 per cent of the pupils in the village high school are from farm homes while the control of the school is solely in the hands of directors elected by the village voters.

The villagers are recognizing the problem. The few consolidations that took place between 1930 and 1936 were motivated in part by the desire of the villagers to share the control. Moreover, in a few centers, the schools were actively recruiting for open-country pupils, offering to try to secure National Youth Administration aid if needed, organizing "courtesy" classes to assist the open-country pupils to overcome the handicaps resulting from school hours shortened by the necessity of depression economy.

New buildings.—The use of the village school by the open-country population in the large proportions shown in the preceding tables means of course that the physical plant must be large enough to take care of the load. Villages have met this need quite adequately. In 1924, nine-tenths of the school plants were rated as fair or better. Despite this, increasing population, consolidation, rising standards, and civic pride accounted for the erection of 65 new school buildings and additions to existing buildings in 21 additional villages by 1930.

In 1931, 10 more villages built new schools or additions to old ones. Construction then ceased until the various emergency provisions embodied in Federal legislation in 1934 and 1935 made funds available, and times generally improved. Thirty-three villages then expanded their school plants, 19 of them with Federal assistance so that a total of 43 new buildings were erected between 1930 and 1936, two-thirds as many as in the previous 6 years. This means that within the 12 years from 1924 to 1936, the school plants in the centers of these communities have been practically reconstructed, 128 of the 140 villages having either secured new buildings or sizable additions to those already possessed.

The total cost of the buildings erected from 1930 to 1936 was about $2,500,000, the average per building $62,600, or less than one-half of the average between 1924 and 1930. In this earlier period, only one in 6 of the new buildings cost less than $75,000. Between 1930 and 1936, only 3 in 10 cost more than this amount.

Interestingly enough, the average cost of the schools built without Federal aid exceeded that of the aided buildings by over $10,000, the two figures being $67,650 and $57,310, respectively. There is some evidence that Federal participation and review of the plans held down the costs. The Federal government, under P.W.A., in the average case advanced 38 per cent of the cost of the aided buildings, or $21,842. In the South and Far West, more than two-thirds of the schools erected were Federally assisted, in the Middle Atlantic villages, 2 out of the 5 were helped, in the Middle West, 2 out of 13.

School expenses tend downward: state aid upward.—Building costs were not the only aspect of education costs that turned downward. Between 1930 and 1936, the median school budget declined 16.1 per cent, despite a 12.3 per cent gain in total enrollment, per village school system, as against an advance of 9.5 per cent between 1924 and 1930. This total average obscures important regional differences. The Middle Atlantic villages actually managed to increase their operating expenses by 12.9 per cent. The most serious decline was in the Middle West, where median budgets dropped 26.6 per cent. The South, proportionately, lost only one-half as much, 13.2 per cent. The decline in the Far West was 7.6 per cent.

One explanation of these sharp differences lies in the policies of the states toward aiding local school systems. In the Middle Atlantic states this policy is now well established, more than one-half the expenses coming from the state. In California, which supplies almost two-thirds of the operating expenses, the total expenses actually increased by 5 per cent; so that the decline noted above was caused by the villages in the other states in this region, where it amounted to about 16 per cent. The South has also initiated state aid in a number of states. North Carolina's school system is now entirely on a state basis. Texas is quite liberal. In the villages of these 2 states, the total operating expenses increased 2.9 and 1.5 per cent, respectively, by 1936 over 1930. On the other hand, only 2 of the states of the Middle West extend aid in ratios comparable with the states already mentioned. In these 2, the decline in school costs was less than 10 per cent, or only about two-fifths as much as for the region as a whole. At the other extreme in this area is Kansas, still as always lowest in state aid; and here school budgets declined most drastically. Tables 51 and 52 give the details on average school expenses and on state aid.

The first of these tables reveals, among other things, that the decline in the costs of schools in small villages has been less than the average; that of the large villages, about average; but that of the medium-sized group, considerably above average. These places probably over-extended themselves in the 1920's, and were less able to meet the depression strains. The large village-town group registered a small gain. For the first time it was possible in this study to secure dependable cost figures for some Negro schools in the South. The median expenditures were $4,500, less than one-fifth that of the white schools.

State aid almost doubled, and increased in almost all states and in every major region. This is clearly a depression-borne trend. The pressure of low prices and debt, described in Chapter I, coupled with high taxes archaically levied, made it necessary for the states to step in if the school program was to be maintained at anything like 1920 levels. Moreover, there was a demand for some measure of tax relief. The two needs coalesced in persuading legislatures in increasing numbers to assume a larger share of the educational burden.

Teaching costs decline.—In proportion to the total operating expense of the village school systems, teaching cost, which is the largest single item in the budget, continued the decline noted in 1930. This charge absorbed 61.3 per cent of the expenses in 1935–36, as against 66.2 per cent in 1929–30, and 70.1 per cent in 1923–24.

Variations from this total figure by size of village were slight, though greater than in 1930, when the largest deviation was two-tenths of one per cent. Small village systems used only 56 per cent of their budgets for paying teachers, large villages 65.8 per cent. This was the range. Among the regions, the South, as previously, had the largest ratio, 65.4 per cent, a decrease of 7 points over 1930; and the Far West had the lowest, 59.0 per cent. Probably these figures mean that the bulk of the economy induced by the depression resulted from reducing teachers' salaries disproportionately as compared with other costs, especially since there are two more teachers per village than in 1930.

Teaching costs per pupil, counting both the elementary and high-school students, which had slightly exceeded $49 in both

TABLE 51

SCHOOL EXPENDITURES: AVERAGE EXPENDITURES OF VILLAGE SCHOOLS

140 Villages: by Region and by Size of Village

(Dollars in Thousands)

Region and Size	*1924*			*1930*			*1936*		
	NO. REPORTING	MEAN	MEDIAN	NO. REPORTING	MEAN	MEDIAN	NO. REPORTING	MEAN	MEDIAN
All regions	87	$32.3	$28.3	122	$37.0	$30.9	133	$34.8	$26.0
Middle Atlantic	6	20.6	19.9	26	30.0	25.5	27	38.3	28.8
South	15	16.9	15.3	20	24.2	21.9	25	23.0	19.0
Middle West	45	30.5	29.6	54	33.6	32.7	59	28.0	24.0
Far West	21	50.4	42.3	22	65.5	54.2	22	62.3	50.0
Small	25	19.0	19.5	40	22.8	22.2	40	22.5	18.8
Medium	37	31.7	30.1	54	36.3	32.9	58	29.8	25.1
Large	25	46.5	43.2	28	53.9	49.0	18	45.8	40.8
Town	...[a]	...[a]	...[a]	...[a]	...[a]	...[a]	17	69.0	63.5

[a] Included with large villages.

1924 and 1930, decreased to $39.46 in 1936, a drop of over 20 per cent, as against a decline of 16 per cent in total operating expense. The variation by size of village was in no case significant. Regional differences, however, were striking. They ranged from $57.83 in the Middle Atlantic villages to $23.89 for Southern white schools and $7.63 for Negro schools. The Far West and Middle West teaching costs per pupil exceeded $50 and $40, respectively, by a few cents. In the main, per pupil high school

TABLE 52

STATE AID TO SCHOOLS IN STATES HAVING 5 OR MORE VILLAGES IN THE STUDY, 1930–36

140 Villages

	No. Villages Reporting		*State Aid Per Cent of Total Expense*	
	1930	*1936*	*1930*	*1936*
Grand total	87	92	22.8	43.1
Middle Atlantic	27	27	48.4	56.3
New York	13	13	55.5	61.8
Pennsylvania	14	14	36.0	42.5
South	9	8	24.2	68.2
North Carolina	6	5	9.7	100.0
Texas	3	3	50.5	41.4
Middle West	42	48	9.6	16.3
Illinois	6	5	4.5	6.7
Indiana	5	4	2.7	17.5
Iowa	11	10	2.8	3.7
Kansas	4	7	0.8	1.5
Minnesota	3	5	37.9	48.7
Missouri	5	5	27.7	43.0
Nebraska	2	5	5.3	3.8
Wisconsin	6	7	12.0	6.7
Far West				
California	9	9	19.9	64.4

costs averaged two and one-half times those in the elementary school.

In the open country, per pupil teaching costs dropped from $39.23 to $27.71, with all regions except the South exceeding the average by a considerable margin. The range was from $42.01 in the Far West to $18.67 for Southern white and $8.67 for Negro schools. The decline for the open-country schools was therefore almost 30 per cent, half again as great as in the village schools. This is a clear indication of the effect of the depression on these small institutions.

In an effort to determine more exactly the effect of the depression, reports of state boards of education were consulted and the county data were tabulated by tiers according to the plan described in Chapter I. The data for this procedure, in this case, were secured by special tabulation from the annual reports of state departments of education, all of which include a considerable amount of data on a county by county basis.[2] The data so used disclosed several interesting facts. In the school year 1929–30, the greatest variation in current expenses per enrolled pupil was $11, between the city-county schools and those in tier two. Tiers one, two, and three were approximately equal at this level. Tier four stood above the city-county schools by $7.10. By 1933–34, the low point of the depression for education and the latest one for which data from these reports were fully available, tier four had dropped below the city county, and was approximately equal to the other tiers at a level about $12 below the city, or tier zero county. It is quite clear from the data, also, that the decline gained momentum with the years in most tiers, except for the fourth, where there was a sharp drop between 1930 and 1931, then a slight pick-up for 2 years and another serious decline in 1933–34. With some variations, this was the pattern in all regions. The Middle Atlantic states, as in the villages, resisted the deflation, as did the South, surprisingly enough. Probably in that case the level was so low even in 1929–30 that any decline was of intensified seriousness. Moreover, the South had a larger proportion of schools that closed entirely; and these weakest districts were consequently eliminated from the statistics. Tables 53 and 54 tell the story, and show clearly the disadvantageous position of the fourth and most rural tier. This is but another indication

[2] This material was compiled by Charles J. Bornman. It is expected that the data not here used will be published elsewhere.

that the more rural the area the harder was public education hit.

In the main, the same story appears when the data are assembled on the basis of current expenses per pupil in average daily attendance. The differences are to be accounted for by varying habits of attendance in the various regions.

TABLE 53

CURRENT EXPENSES PER ENROLLED PUPIL

By Tiers of Counties, 1929 through 1934 Inclusive, 18 Areas

Year	*Tier 0*	*Tier 1*	*Tier 2*	*Tier 3*	*Tier 4*
1929–30	$69.57	$59.10	$58.31	$59.21	$76.67
1930–31	68.18	57.57	56.59	56.38	58.30
1931–32	64.60	55.19	51.83	55.64	60.70
1932–33	61.06	50.04	48.09	47.69	59.25
1933–34	55.36	45.65	43.08	42.51	43.84

When all expenses per pupil enrolled are considered, the critical situation of rural education appears at its worst. All expenses, of course, include those for buildings, interest, and the like. Here the declines by tiers from 1929–30 to 1933–34 from the city-county through tier four, expressed in percentages, are 30, 38.2, 27.7, 32.2, 50.9.

TABLE 54

SCHOOL EXPENSES: PER CENT DECLINE IN CURRENT EXPENSES PER ENROLLED PUPIL, FROM 1929–30 TO 1933–34

By Regions and Tiers of Counties, 18 Areas

Region	*Tier 0*	*Tier 1*	*Tier 2*	*Tier 3*	*Tier 4*
All regions	20.4	22.8	26.1	28.1	42.9
Middle Atlantic	11.2	2.5	12.1	11.0	. . .
South	9.4	23.1	22.8	21.2	26.9
Middle West	24.5	28.2	29.3	27.7	33.6
Far West	24.1	35.2	28.3	40.7	59.6

Teachers' salaries decline.—It has been suggested that the proportion of instructional to total school costs indicates a severe decline in teachers' salaries. This indeed occurred. In 1933–34, one-half of all the rural teachers in the United States received less than $750 annual salary, less than the "blanket-code" minimum of the N.R.A. for unskilled labor. At least 40,000 of this low-salaried group had an annual salary of less than $500. These trends operated also in the communities studied.

The average annual compensation of the village schoolteachers declined from $1,373 in 1930 to $1,148 in 1936, or 17.2 per cent. In the open country, for the white teachers, the decrease was from $872 to $666, or 23.6 per cent. Even these salaries represented some increase from the lowest point. As Table 55 shows, the declines have not been uniform among the regions. Despite increased budgets in the Middle Atlantic villages, salaries are 4.3 per cent below 1929–30 levels, though above 1924. In the South they have fallen steadily since the first study, by about 30

TABLE 55

AVERAGE SALARY OF WHITE[a] TEACHERS IN VILLAGE AND COUNTRY SCHOOLS

By Regions

Region	*Village Salaries*			*Country Salaries*		
	1924	*1930*	*1936*	*1924*	*1930*	*1936*
All regions	...	$1,373	$1,147	...	$ 872	$ 666
Middle Atlantic	$1,244	1,454	1,391	$ 870	925	851
South	1,153	1,071	820	689	694	573
Middle West	1,365	1,342	1,026	700	632	574
Far West	1,670	1,633	1,486	1,157	1,090	887

[a] The average salary of Negro village teachers in 1936 in the South was $460; in the open country, $333.

per cent. The decline in the Middle West was not quite as drastic as this; and that in the Far West amounted to only 9 per cent. By size of village, the chief variation was in the towns, which exceeded the average of all villages by almost $200; and the small villages, which fell below it by $140. One of the surprising items in the table relates to the essential equality of salaries in the Middle West and South, in the open-country schools, despite a considerable disparity in favor of the Middle West in the compensation of village teachers. This again may be in part a difference in regional policy on state aid. In fact in Kansas, which, as shown, had the least state aid, the salary of the open-country teachers in the communities studied was only slightly above the level of the salary of the teachers in Negro open-country schools in the South. Since the terms in the South are considerably shorter than in Kansas, the per diem wage for these Negro teachers was actually higher.

Here again an attempt was made to use the tier measurement. Once more it becomes apparent that the more rural the district, the worse the deflation, in this case the worse the cut in salary. This is shown in Table 56.

Teachers' training improved.—Despite the lower salaries of the teachers, the improvement in their professional preparation noted in 1930 continued. In 1936, 63.5 per cent of the village teachers were holders of college degrees, as against 54.6 per cent in 1930,

TABLE 56

INSTRUCTIONAL COST PER TEACHER

By Tiers of Counties, 1929 through 1934 Inclusive, 18 Areas

Year	*Tier 0*	*Tier 1*	*Tier 2*	*Tier 3*	*Tier 4*
1929–30	$1,701.76	$1,129.57	$1,069.67	$1,094.00	$1,091.93
1930–31	1,602.91	1,124.81	1,021.78	1,039.84	893.85
1931–32	1,627.51	1,087.14	1,008.52	1,055.48	967.48
1932–33	1,514.83	936.41	874.50	879.72	874.59
1933–34	1,334.96	857.37	798.75	800.33	659.52
Per cent decline 1929–30—1933–34	21.5	24.1	25.3	27.0	39.6

and 41.3 per cent in 1924. This represents an increase of over 53 per cent in 12 years in the proportion of village teachers who were college graduates. Indeed, one-seventh of these persons, or one-eleventh of the total teaching force, were holders of postgraduate degrees. On the other hand, the proportion of those who were teaching without more than a high-school diploma, one out of 13, remained constant because a sharp increase in this group in the South balanced declines in the Middle Atlantic and Far West villages. Only the proportion of teachers with normal-school diplomas decreased. This reflects in part the tendency to change 2-year and 3-year normal schools into 4-year teachers colleges. Among the regions, there was but little variation in respect to the

professional preparation of teachers. In the Middle Atlantic states, 57.4 per cent had completed college; in the other regions, 64 or 65 per cent. By size of village, the deviation from the average was even less. Table 57 carries the detailed facts on this point. It is possible that there may be a connection between the sharp increase in the professional preparation of these village teachers and the notable improvement in the school curricula described later in the chapter.

Quite obviously, one of the elements in this trend toward better-prepared teachers has been the competitive situation produced by the depression. With many services being curtailed or discontinued, and classes being increased in size, better-trained teachers became interested in, and available to, the school boards in these smaller communities. The long-time campaign of state boards of education for high standards played directly into this other tendency and complemented it.

County and village superintendents and village boards were found to be much interested in better-trained teachers. In the Middle West, a number of county superintendents had come to require at least 2 years of college even for open-country schools; and in some communities this was credited with having spurred the interest in school consolidation. In 1924, 4.5 per cent of the open-country white teachers held college degrees. In 1936, the proportion was 21.7 per cent. Even among the Negro open-country teachers, 6.4 per cent held college degrees in 1936 as against almost none in 1924.

Pupils.—The enrollment in the schools of these communities, village and open country, increased 9 per cent in the inter-survey period to 109,452, and was divided as follows:

Village elementary	42,849
Village high school	28,729
Country schools	37,874

In terms of the village schools alone, therefore, the high-school enrollment in 1936 was 40 per cent of the total, as against 34.2

per cent in 1930, and 31.7 per cent in 1924. The enrollment in these village high schools was more than 10,000 over the 1924 figures, an increase of 57.7 per cent. The elementary-school increase over 1924, on the other hand, was only 3,736, or 8.7 per cent above 1924; and more than nine-tenths of this increase took place before 1930. The open-country school enrollment was 60 less than in 1924.[3]

It is clear that the increase in school enrollment has been, for all the communities, primarily a matter of the high school, as Table 58 shows. However, in the elementary schools there were increases in the 2 Eastern regions that balanced declines in the 2 Western divisions. The Middle West decline in elementary-school enrollment has been especially sharp. In the open country, there were increases in all regions except the Middle West, that in the South being quite sharp. These enrollment data should be considered in the light of the data presented in the chapter on population, which shows an increase of 2.7 per cent in the village population between 1924 and 1930, and of 6.7 per cent between 1930 and 1936. The comparable per cents for the open country are 6.8 and 15.9.

The high-school gain is in harmony with national trends, especially trends since 1930 when there has been a tremendous influx into the high schools of the nation. The regional and size comparisons are given in Table 58.

National Youth Administration.—One factor in sustaining, or even in increasing, the high-school enrollment was the extended aid to needy students under the National Youth Administration. This help was being given in 114, or more than four-fifths of the communities, in the school year 1935–36. All regions exceeded this average except the Middle Atlantic. In 4 of the 6 Negro high schools, National Youth Administration grants were also made. Quotas varied; but averaged about 12, or 6 per cent of the enroll-

[3] It should be noted that there are 20 open-country high schools in these communities. The proportion of high-school students to total school enrollment is 30 per cent, an increase of 5 points over both previous studies.

TABLE 57

TRAINING OF VILLAGE SCHOOLTEACHERS

Percentage Distribution by Region: 140 American Agricultural Villages, 1924–36 [a]

Region	1924			1930			1936		
	LESS THAN NORMAL	NORMAL SCHOOL	COLLEGE AND POSTGRAD.	LESS THAN NORMAL	NORMAL SCHOOL	COLLEGE AND POSTGRAD.	LESS THAN NORMAL	NORMAL SCHOOL	COLLEGE AND POSTGRAD. [b]
All regions	19.3	39.4	41.3	7.3	38.1	54.6	7.2	29.3	63.5
Middle Atlantic	24.1	46.6	29.3	10.6	38.8	50.6	4.3	38.3	57.4
South	22.1	33.3	44.6	6.9	36.3	56.8	14.7	20.6	64.7
Middle West	21.7	37.5	40.8	7.4	41.3	51.3	7.4	28.2	64.4
Far West	8.7	43.7	47.6	4.5	33.3	62.2	2.6	31.6	65.8

[a] Based on 2,054 teachers in 1924, 2,228 in 1930, and 2,529 in 1936.

[b] Nine per cent of all village teachers, ranging from 5.1 per cent in the South to 13.2 per cent in the Far West, had postgraduate degrees.

ment per school. The range was from one to 80. Most schools had from 6 to 15. The scheme received quite general approval in the communities where it operated; and, in the main, it did not appear to be difficult to find worth-while tasks for the recipients of grants to do. Several schools put these students on simple but desirable research. A number had them repair books. Girls frequently assisted in preparing the hot lunches for needy youngsters in the grades. Boys worked on repairs and on beautifying school premises. Both sexes were used for supervising recreation of the grade-school pupils. Commercial department students assisted in the clerical work of the school. One community undertook the prepa-

TABLE 58

AVERAGE ENROLLMENT IN VILLAGE AND COUNTRY SCHOOLS

By Region and by Size of Village, 140 Villages

Region and Size	*Per Village Elementary School*			*Per Village High School*			*Per Country School*		
	1924	*1930*	*1936*	*1924*	*1930*	*1936*	*1924*	*1930*	*1936*
All regions	277	304	306	129	151	205	28	27	28
Middle Atlantic	213	218	225	99	138	176	25	25	27
South	300	379	414	110	150	202	52	50	61
Middle West	310	302	236	164	177	192	23	22	20
Far West	378	456	454	173	220	283	27	32	34
Small villages	183	195	183	85	105	128	...	...	...
Medium villages	271	276	264	131	161	184	...	...	...
Large villages	412	498	379	186	224	293	...	...	...
Towns	...[a]	...[a]	676	...[a]	...[a]	369	...	...	...

[a] Included with large villages.

ration of a classified directory of homes in the area catering to tourists.

Length of term.—One of the effects of the depression was a general shortening of the school term. In the villages, by the school year 1935–36, the situation had recovered to approximately the 1924 and 1930 levels. Then only one system had a year of less than 160 days. In the year 1935–36, 3 were operating on that basis, 2 of them had less than 140 days, 105 held school for 180 days or more.

For the open country, reliable data cannot be presented. Reports to fieldworkers often indicated the legal school year, which often had slight relation to the actual number of days the school functioned. In a number of cases, the report was "we will keep the schools open as long as the money holds out" or "if the money comes in."

Typical of the situation existing in a number of the states where there was little or no state aid to schools is that in Kansas. Even early in the school year, "51 rural schools were without funds, 107 others were without enough funds to complete the present school year, in addition to 26 town school districts in a similar situation."

Serious as such conditions are, they represent real improvement over 1933–34. They raise the question, however, of what has happened to the quality of school work and the program of studies during such times of stress. To this subject the discussion now turns.

Curriculum changes.—These surveys, for obvious reasons, have never attempted technical curriculum studies. In each of them, however, an endeavor has been made to summarize changes in the curricula. Between 1924 and 1930, 200 changes were made. The answers to a questionnaire sent out in April, 1932, reported 137 additional changes. This latter 2-year period showed as many courses or departments dropped as the 6 years from 1924–30. The situation can be summarized as follows:

Period	*Courses or Depts. Added*	*Courses or Depts. Dropped*	*Total Changes*
1924–30	164	36	200
1930–32	*101*	*36*	*137*
1932–36	*230*	*46*	*276*
1930–36	331	82	413

It is quite evident that the period from 1930 to 1936 was one of far greater activity in curriculum reorganization than the first inter-survey period. In fact, the number of changes was twice as great. This coincides, of course, with a period of growing interest in curriculum reorganization in the whole field of public-school education. It must be remembered, nonetheless, that changing names of courses does not reveal how fundamentally actual content has been altered.

It will be noted that the ratio of departments or courses dropped to all changes has increased in the second period, as compared with the first, but that this ratio was not as high from 1932 to 1936 as from 1930 to 1932. In the total 12-year period, expansions of the curriculum outnumbered eliminations 495 to 118. In the main, the changes occurred in the junior and senior high schools. The increased activity of the period 1930–36, despite the increased number of eliminations and despite the depression with the necessity for economy, resulted in expanded offerings; though, as a previous section of the chapter shows, at lower costs.

Even the changes listed above do not tell the whole story, for 16 schools undertook complete revision of their curricula. Three of these enlisted the co-operation of the schools of education at state universities. Three others adopted a state program, recently launched in Virginia after much study. Four other schools changed their elementary-school work from a formal to an activity basis. It should also be stated that in listing changes some school superintendents or principals did not put down courses dropped in 1933 or 1934 but restored in 1935–36. No changes that thus cancelled each other were therefore listed. There were a number of such, especially in the field of the cultural arts.

Certain trends appear reasonably clear from the total figures. The social sciences have become far more important than formerly. In the period from 1930 to 1936, 75 village school systems, or more than one-half, added courses or departments in this field, not counting history. Almost half these additions were made between September, 1930, and April, 1932. The subjects here combined under this heading are, sociology, economics, social problems, social civics, social studies, government, and (2 cases) international relations. Counting the old-fashioned civics, all schools had, in 1936, some work in this field. In addition, 8 systems dropped the old division of history into ancient, medieval, and modern, and substituted world history. The net result was a decrease in the total time given to history but, it is claimed, a better, more interesting, and socialized presentation. Social or economic geography was also added in 4 schools.

The next major change related to vocational education. In the last report, attention was drawn to the rapid increase in commercial education, but also to the fact that there seemed to be hesitation as to the wisdom of this move, since net gains for this field were only half the gross. This hesitation seems to have disappeared since 1932. Between that year and 1936, 32 schools created departments, or expanded offerings, in commercial subjects; and only 2 contracted courses. There are now 107 of these villages with work in commercial education, as against 94 in 1930, and 100 in 1932. They are turning out graduates far in excess of the power of their communities to absorb them; and if the slackening of urban opportunity for rural youth should continue, if technological developments outstrip changes in training, the development in this field may come under fire. Questions were being raised in a few communities at the time of the 1936 study.

Agriculture still shows a fluctuation; but, as in previous studies, made a net gain. Twelve schools added it, 5 dropped it between 1932 and September, 1936; a total of 102 now have departments in this subject, as compared to 87 in 1930. In about half a dozen places, this work was credited with markedly improving agricultural practices in the community. Home economics made a sharp gain, being added or expanded in 15 schools, and dropped in only 2. There was also some increase, to a total of 10 courses, in shopwork, mechanical drawing, and manual training or arts.

The next trend of importance in these schools seems to be the beginning of an effort toward facilitating mental adjustments, and toward guidance. The curriculum additions in this field since 1932 include 4 courses in home relations, 4 in psychology, 2 in child care and psychology, and one in personal grooming. Many schools introduced work in guidance; mostly, of course, vocational. In 1930, only 5 were attempting guidance, 12 added it between 1930 and 1932, and by 1936, 50 additional schools had also instituted vocational guidance. Four-fifths of the Middle Atlantic villages offered guidance work, two-thirds of those in the Far West; the other 2 regions fell below one-third. A number of other schools were making some informal efforts along this line, so that this development may expand. The quality of much of this work, judged by the best standards, may be open to question; but a gain from zero to 67 in 12 years is at least significant of the interest in the field.

It is quite evident that Latin and modern languages are under pressure. Latin was dropped in 6 schools between 1930 and 1932, and in 8 more in the next 4 years. Modern languages were also attacked. French or Spanish was dropped in 8 schools, but added in as many. German made a gain of 2.

The contraction of various history courses into one general course was paralleled in science in a few cases, as well as in mathematics. Five schools dropped physics or chemistry and substituted general science; and 5 eliminated specialized mathematics courses and replaced them with general mathematics. In other schools, the plan of putting the sciences and some mathematics on an every-other-year basis, which began between 1930 and 1932, was followed.

Despite the agitation against "fads and frills," the cultural arts, sometimes so classified, survived the depression quite well in these communities. Music was introduced, or expanded, in 15 schools, but eliminated in 2; art or art appreciation in 6, but dropped in 2; drama in 4; folk-dancing in one. In a considerable minority of the systems, the extracurricular activities in music, drama, and debating were given some academic credit. Courses variously called "public speaking," "forensics," or "speech" were added in 12 schools, physical education in 9, and health and home-nursing in 7. Other changes included one or 2 courses in consumer education, photography, journalism, photoplay appreciation, Diesel engineering, and highway safety.

In view of the difficulties through which these schools have passed, some evidence of which has been given, the curriculum expansion is quite remarkable. It is to be explained, in part, by the opening of the high-school doors to unemployed youth for a year of postgraduate study. This was forced in about one-tenth of these villages, in part by the decline, noted later, in the proportion of graduates going on to college. It is to be explained more by skillful and efficient reorganization of the time of students and teachers, and in some places by a fusion or correlation of the offerings. But, most of all, the explanation lies in the willingness of the teachers, who as noted are better trained as a rule than in previous years, to add to their responsibilities to meet needs that they saw. Never before in the 12-year study of these communities have children and taxpayers been getting more and better education at less cost. But it must be remembered that this improvement still lacks much of reaching the standards of many urban schools, and that the open-country grade schools have lost rather than gained during the depression.

Clearly the school men of these village-centered rural communities are not satisfied with things as they find them; and clearly, too, they have a growing desire to have their students understand society better, to be better equipped vocationally, better adjusted and enriched by the cultural arts. The wisdom of some of these curriculum developments may be questioned by experts, but the trends are clear, though of unequal force.[4] So far as measured comparably in the three surveys, these trends are summarized in Tables 59 and 60. The latter shows the frequency of various combinations of these subjects.

The regional distribution of offerings in these subjects is shown

[4] For a discussion of the social and sociological implications of the school curriculum, see J. H. Kolb and Edmund deS. Brunner, *A Study of Rural Society* (Boston, Houghton Mifflin Company, 1935), Chapter XVII.

in Table 61. It will be noted that there is a slight difference among the regions in the proportion of schools offering agriculture or domestic science.[5] Nearly all in the Western regions have, however, introduced commercial education. Curiously enough, the Middle Atlantic region has the lowest record in this respect. In music and art, the South clearly lags in comparison with the other regions. Drama has made much more headway in the Western regions than in the other 2.

Perhaps more interesting is the number of these newer subjects in each school. Seventeen have all 6, 41 have all but one, the omitted subject in two-thirds of these being either drama or art.

TABLE 59

SCHOOL CURRICULA

Number of Villages with Specified Subjects in the Schools

Subject	*1924*	*1930*	*1936*
Music	117	130	120
Art	...[a]	...[a]	55
Drama	...[a]	...[a]	66
Agriculture	86	87	102
Domestic science	90	106	115
Commercial education	55	94	107
Vocational guidance	0	5	30
Manual training or industrial arts	68	73	80

[a] No data.

Thirty-two schools have 4 of the 6. In other words, two-thirds of the schools have two-thirds or more of the subjects under discussion. Twenty-eight, or an additional one-fifth, have 3; only 2 have none; and 6 have only one each. The remainder offer 2; all but one of the combinations having one or both parts vocational. But there can be no doubt that over the years the more purely cultural of these subjects have gained far more rapidly than the purely vocational.

Two other developments should be noted. North Carolina passed a law requiring the high schools of the state to teach sociology

[5] All told, about 5,000 rural high schools have classes in vocational agriculture. About three-fourths of these have chapters of the Future Farmers of America, the national organization of boys studying vocational agriculture.

TABLE 60

THE COMBINATIONS OF SPECIAL SERVICES IN THE CURRICULA OF VILLAGE SCHOOLS

140 Selected American Agricultural Villages, 1936

Combinations of Services [a]	*Number of Curriculum Services Given*						
	0	*1*	*2*	*3*	*4*	*5*	*6*
0	2						
1		1					
2		2					
4		3					
1, 2,			7				
1, 3,			2				
2, 4			2				
3, 4			2				
4, 5			1				
1, 2, 3				5			
1, 2, 4				6			
2, 3, 4				8			
2, 4, 6				2			
3, 4, 5				4			
3, 4, 6				2			
4, 5, 6				1			
1, 2, 3, 4					15		
1, 2, 4, 6					3		
1, 3, 4, 5					2		
1, 4, 5, 6					1		
2, 3, 4, 5					6		
2, 3, 4, 6					2		
3, 4, 5, 6					3		
1, 2, 3, 4, 5						17	
1, 2, 3, 4, 6						10	
1, 2, 3, 5, 6						1	
1, 3, 4, 5, 6						1	
2, 3, 4, 5, 6						10	
1, 2, 4, 5, 6						2	
1, 2, 3, 4, 5, 6							17
Total	2	6	14	28	32	41	17

[a] 1. Agriculture. 2. Domestic science. 3. Commercial subjects. 4. Music. 5. Drama. 6. Art.

and economics. Similarly, Wisconsin's legislature decreed that beginning with September, 1935, all schools must teach the principles of co-operative marketing and of consumer co-operation.

Three schools introduced a so-called Participation Diploma, awarded to those who had spent 4 years in high school, had satisfied certain minimum requirements, but had not successfully completed credits sufficient to win a diploma recognized by state boards of education for admission to state universities. This enabled these schools to hold some youth in school, usefully, and keep them from the ranks of job-seekers.

Extracurricular activities.—The extracurricular program has shown little change in the inter-survey period, though it has broadened somewhat. Athletics, of course, play a prominent part; and the increased interest in sports noted in 1930 seems to have been sustained. Basketball was played by 9 schools out of 10, usually by both boys and girls. Football and baseball were each found in 80 schools. Track has become more popular, being represented in 60 schools. Tennis, volleyball and soccer were each present in from 14 to 17 schools. Ten other competitive sports were listed from one to 4 times, including handball, hockey, golf, checkers and bridge.

TABLE 61

THE NUMBER OF VILLAGE SCHOOLS GIVING SPECIFIED SERVICES

140 Selected American Agricultural Villages, 1936: by Region

		Specified Services					
Region	NUMBER OF VILLAGES	AGRICULTURE [a]	DOMESTIC SCIENCE	COMMERCIAL SUBJECTS	MUSIC	DRAMA	ART
All regions	140	90	115	107	120	66	55
Middle Atlantic	28	20	22	13	25	6	16
South [b]	30	21	24	15	17	9	7
Middle West	60	38	49	57	58	37	20
Far West	22	11	20	22	20	14	12

[a] Twelve villages added agriculture in the school year 1936–37.

[b] Two villages in the South give none of the services specified.

Non-competitive activities were also numerous, playing quite a part in the life of these communities. There were 106 glee clubs, a gain of 6; the proportion of schools having bands rose from one-sixth to two-fifths; but orchestras dropped from two-thirds to two-fifths. Just half the schools had dramatic groups, a gain of 14. Apparently this activity was supplanting debating and the old-time literary society, which declined to 47 from 70. Plays, cantatas, operettas, pageants, concerts, and recitals by these student organizations filled many evenings in the communities whose schools had one or more of the groups mentioned. In a few schools, all these activities were included in the community part of the extracurricular program; in others, only some. The scope of the program was, of course, somewhat related to the size of the school, though it was amazing how many activities could be creditably carried on by high schools of less than 150 enrollment.

A considerable number of schools, about one-half, had one or more hobby or special interest clubs. Chief among these were the Future Farmers of America, sponsored by the Smith-Hughes teachers of vocational agriculture; but there were a large number of others, such as science, English, and history clubs, groups interested in photography and birds, and so on through a list of a score or more interests. In a number of villages, a regular period was set aside for meetings of these clubs, and bus schedules were changed on that day to accommodate those who attended the meetings. The depression took a heavy toll of school papers, only 16 being left; but examination of the village newspapers showed that a number of these were giving from a half page to a page, from once a week to once a month, to school news prepared by a student organization.

School and community.—There was a growing interest in the school's relation and contribution to the community and its life. Increasingly, school facilities were being made available to the community; in some places, not only the gymnasium, but also tennis courts, library, and the like. As one fieldworker wrote of such a situation, there seems to be no distinction whatever between school property and village property in meeting community needs. In some places, school property for community use and community parks and playgrounds were supervised by N.Y.A. students.

In one village, the school had sponsored concerts by the music department, home-talent plays, child-study classes, a father and son banquet, ice-cream suppers, a men's quartet and chorus, a lecture course, and dances, and had opened its clinics to adults. In 1935, when a new school building was asked for in this village, the bond issue carried 13 to one.

Similar programs were not unusual elsewhere. Visiting nights were instituted by a number of schools. Art exhibits were noted. Fieldworkers described several school buildings as being "hot-beds of community activities." One school operated the only "movies" in the community, and had quite a tree-planting program. All these activities, of course, are contributions to the social life of the community, are an addition to the social life available through non-school agencies, and are described in Chapter X.

Parent-Teacher Associations.—In many communities the community work was conducted chiefly through the P.T.A. Here the program was more conventional, following the usual well-known lines described in the previous reports in this series. The summary given above of the schools' contribution to community life leaves out of account, of course, offerings in adult education, which are described in Chapter IX.

Not all schools fell in with this trend. As one school principal put it, "the school is clearly an institution separate and apart from the community and has no sense of community responsibility."

Youth problems.—One reason for the interest of the school in providing some social and cultural life for the community has been the plight of many of its recent graduates caught in the depression. Indeed, quite generally one of the problems that has captured public imagination in the depression years has been that of youth denied a chance to secure college education, or opportunity for employment either at home or in the city. The sharp increase in the high-school enrollment in these communities is one indication of this. It is only in small part a function of increased population. In about one-seventh of the schools, postgraduate work had been started and had attracted a small number of former students.

Despite the sharply increased high-school enrollment, the number of high-school graduates going on to other institutions of learning, which had gained nearly 40 per cent between 1924 and 1930, remained almost stationary, as Table 62 shows, between 1930 and 1935. The proportion continuing their education was 35.7 per cent, a decline of more than 5 points. The 2 Western regions but slightly exceeded 25 per cent. The Middle Atlantic schools sent 30.7 on for further training; the South, 45.3 per cent. As in the previous studies, it is clear that those able to finish high school at all in the South have a better chance than elsewhere to go on to college.[6] The Middle West states slightly bettered the Far Western record. However, a higher proportion of graduates continuing their education went to college than ever before. This is due in large part to the decline in the number of normal schools. If the per cent continuing their education in college and normal school be taken together, there is only a slight difference in the total. Nor are there significant differences according to the size of the center.

The number of graduates going to college turned, in part, on the nearness to the community of small colleges: liberal arts, teachers, or junior. Near such institutions, where home living or tuition adjustments were possible, the proportion of high-school graduates going to college was larger than elsewhere, especially in the Middle West.

If barely one-third of the 1935 high-school graduates went to other institutions of learning, the question arises as to the rest.

[6] These figures obviously do not include Negroes. They had less than one-twentieth as many high-school graduates as the whites in these villages in 1935, but three-tenths of these Negro high-school graduates went on to additional training.

About one-fourth had found employment by the time of the field survey in the spring of 1936. This means, of course, that of the total number of 1935 high-school graduates in these communities, two-fifths, or over 2,000, were unemployed in the spring of 1936, as Table 62 shows. Moreover, many of those classed as employed

TABLE 62

TOTAL NUMBER GRADUATING FROM HIGH SCHOOL IN 1935 AND OCCUPATION IN 1936

140 Selected American Agricultural Villages

Region	*Number of Graduates*	*Number Employed*	*Per Cent Employed*	*Per Cent Continuing Education*	*Per Cent Unemployed*
All regions	5,095	1,262	24.7	35.1	40.2
Middle Atlantic	776	209	27.0	30.7	42.3
South	965(71 [a])	190(7 [a])	19.7	45.3	35.0
Middle West	2,242	537	23.9	25.5	50.6
Far West	1,112	326	29.3	27.8	42.9

[a] For those Negro village schools reporting.

were admittedly working on the home farm or in the family store. This is one reason for the high relief ratio of agricultural laborers shown in Chapter XIII. As nearly as can be estimated, this means that 50 to 75 per cent more of these graduates were livng at home than would have been the case under the conditions of the 1920's. Girls were more involved in this than boys, especially in the open-country population.

Obviously much of this employment is unsatisfactory in terms of the youth. Taking the place of the farm hired man, often at less than his wages, gives even youth so employed small hope of getting ahead. Many are qualified for better things and regard their present occupations as temporary, though they see no opening. More wish for further training that they cannot now afford. The desire for broad programs of adult education was phrased frequently and in a variety of communities, especially in the Middle West and in villages. The description of the adult education program in the schools in Chapter IX, and the critique of this program, take on more significance in the light of this fact.

If the local leaders' estimates are correct, the unemployed of the high-school class of 1935 constituted only about one-half the unemployed youth in these 140 communities. The average number per community in this category was 29, with the Middle Atlantic and Middle West regions close to the average, the Far West 10 below it, and the South having 42. The Negro average per community in the South, where secured, was 60. In general, too, the larger the community, the larger the number of unemployed youth. Towns had 46; medium and large villages were practically average; and small villages had only 22.

Despite this record, in only 68 communities did school men and other leaders admit that there was a youth problem. All regions were close to an even division on this point, except that the Middle Atlantic villages appeared especially fortunate, only 10 admitting the problem, while in the Middle West more than one-half did. The youth question was also more difficult in the towns and large villages than in medium and small village-centered communities.

This summary of the replies by adult interviewees as to whether or not there was a "youth problem" in the community is not necessarily the whole truth. Sometimes, though by no means always, negative replies meant either a failure to recognize the problem or a refusal to admit its presence. This was frequently evident to the fieldworker on the basis of observation and interviews with the youth themselves. A somewhat worse than average incident illustrates the point. In one Middle West medium-sized village, the leaders testified that there was no peculiar problem with youth. The school superintendent reported to his board that there were so few unemployed that he was opposed to an adult education program. The school janitor pointed out, however, that whereas a decade ago the only loafers in town were those who had quit high school before finishing, now the loafers were high-school graduates unable to secure steady work. From mid-afternoon to midnight every day, a score or so congregated around the creamery. It was by just such groups that the interest in adult education was expressed.

Attitudes of youth.—In the main, though with individual exceptions in almost every community and some exceptions in terms of whole localities, youth seemed to be making the best of the situation, especially if there was some work available. The spirit and attitude, as judged by and reported to fieldworkers, was good.

But it was equally true that individuals everywhere, and whole groups in some places, were becoming discouraged, fatalistic, bitter, cynical. This in turn has undermined morale. Jobs with low remuneration were often refused. Loafing, drinking, petty gambling, have followed and have undermined the fiber of boys and girls alike. Morals suffered as well in such places.

The diagnosis of the leaders who admitted the presence of youth problems in their communities agreed with the above. Loafing, drunkenness, delinquency, and immorality were reported. It must be recognized, of course, that such charges are not limited to the depression period. Informants felt, however, that they were present either to an unusual degree, or that they were manifested chiefly by the unemployed or poorly employed youth.

In a majority of cases, this array of problems was coupled with a full understanding of the underlying causes, such as lack of jobs, delayed marriage, and, less often and less basic, a lack of adequate organized leisure-time activities likely to appeal to youth.

There is not a little irony in the whole youth situation. Many of them crave better opportunities, are sensitive to their handicaps, and believe some of the difficulties could be overcome if the communities would only act. Again for years the wisdom of the rural-urban migration of youth has been questioned by some, and proposals have been made whereby home and school could reduce it. Yet now when economic forces have reduced it, there is some tension and much concern.

Remedial measures.—Among the nearly 70 communities in which a very real youth problem existed, no solutions had been attempted in 22, or practically one-third. Like the youth, the community appeared to be waiting "for something to turn up." In 11 villages the school program was enlarged either in terms of postgraduate courses or adult education or, occasionally, both. In 9 other centers, school or community organizations, with or without co-operation from the W.P.A., expanded recreational offerings and facilities. In 2 cases, both these steps were taken; and in addition the service clubs exerted themselves, in one informally, in the other through a council, to secure employment. In one town, the superintendent of schools, with the aid of the service clubs, did an excellent job. In 2 years, he has secured N.Y.A. help for 100 high-school students and for 16 graduates who then went to a near-by college. Others he guided into C.C.C. camps. A Resettlement Administration project was initiated in the neighborhood, and this school man was instrumental in the employment of 50 of his out-of-work youth. Thirty-eight villages found some help for their problems from other Federal agencies than the N.Y.A., such as those mentioned. All but one of these also had the N.Y.A.

Not all efforts were as wise. In one village, open-country youth must be out of town by 4 P.M. The merchants sponsored this ordinance. In another, the youth were urged to enlist in the army or navy. In a third, the chief concern seemed to be to secure "benefit of clergy" for "shotgun marriages."

Before a final balance can be struck on this issue, several things must be remembered. There was no abnormal problem in a number of these communities. As already noted, about one-tenth felt the depression very little. These account for about one-fifth of the "no problem" answers. Again, the social life and organization in some of these places had improved measurably, as will be described in Chapter X, and this had had an influence.

Certainly in a number of communities the plight of youth had attracted some attention. Despite losses, in part recovered by the spring of 1936, the village schools in these communities were functioning at a better level of achievement than when previously studied; and, in the main, were more alert and keen to try to improve. One evidence of this has been the expansion of adult education, not only in the schools, but in the work of another tax-supported agency, the Agricultural Extension Service. The next two chapters consider developments in these fields.

VIII

Adult Education: Agricultural Extension

THE YEARS 1930–36 have seen great changes in rural adult education. With the coming on of the depression, adult education work, as a relatively new development, quickly suffered. Schools which in the late 1920's were showing real interest decided in many cases to dispense with such activities. The slow advance in the number of county libraries was checked, and in some years losses were recorded. Even the Agricultural Extension Service suffered. In closing their review of rural adult education in early 1933, Landis and Willard viewed the situation pessimistically. They saw the enterprise buffeted about by the economic gale, and had doubts as to its survival. They set forth seven requisites on which progress seemed to depend; but expressed scant hope that their suggested program could be achieved.[1] Their program follows:

1. A greater degree of experimentation particularly by existing organizations than is going on at present.
2. More contacts between rural adult educators which will enable them to educate each other.
3. The selection and direction of the research that is needed.
4. The development of greater financial resources by governmental and voluntary means.
5. Better planning and strategy on a state and county basis.
6. Better provision for the training of professional workers.
7. National guidance and consideration of the above and of the discussion of problems, methods, and goals.

Less than 4 years have passed since this appraisal was made; but the changes that have occurred are perhaps of greater significance than would have been expected even in these days of rapid

[1] B. Y. Landis and J. D. Willard, *Rural Adult Education* (New York, The Macmillan Company, 1933), Chapters XIV and XV.

change. In the main, the situation has improved. The newer changes indicate at least the major course of development in the years that lie just ahead, although progress has been neither uniform nor wholly encouraging along the lines of such thoroughgoing and statesmanlike procedures as Landis felt to be not only necessary but fundamental.

The developments of the last 6 years will be summarized, first in terms of the major agencies at work, and then in terms of the general situation. This chapter deals with the co-operative Agricultural Extension Service of the Federal and state governments; the following chapter with the library and school, and also with the contribution to rural adult education of privately supported agencies, such as churches, women's clubs, and the like.

This order has significance. Though the present set-up of agricultural extension is only 25 years old, extension activities by the state colleges began more than half a century ago. The present organization is, therefore, the oldest nation-wide effort in adult education drawing upon tax funds. The recent developments of this service, viewed against this history, are therefore important in appraising the educational and social desires of the rural, and especially the farm, population. Libraries have long existed in rural areas, but have never succeeded in fully occupying the field. Newer methods, through which real progress has been made, came into being at approximately the same time the Agricultural Extension Service took its present shape. The program of the school is far more recent and sporadic; but it is now expanding, and seems in part to be following lines roughly comparable to those clearly traceable in the evolution of the Extension Service.

THE AGRICULTURAL EXTENSION SERVICE [2]

Incomparably the largest and best-financed agency in the field of rural adult education is the Extension Service in agriculture

[2] This section is based on the results of a questionnaire generously responded to by the directors of extension and the state extension rural sociologists in 40 of the 48 states and on a study of the annual reports of the Extension Service so far as published, as well as on the field work in the 140 village-centered agricultural communities.

and home economics operating out of the various state colleges of agriculture, and supported jointly under the Smith-Lever Law of 1914 by Federal, state, and county funds.

But before beginning this discussion, it is also important at least to list some of the social forces that have brought adult education into a position of greater importance than it formerly occupied, and that seem to the writer to emphasize the still greater value this enterprise holds in the future for American society. Obviously one of these forces is the steady increase in the average age of our population. This trend is now observable in both city and country, and nowhere is it more pronounced than in agricultural villages. Adult education is one means of safeguarding a rapidly changing society against the effects of an aging population. The possibilities of increased leisure are too well known to require elaboration. Technology has invaded the farm and the farm home. The opening chapters described the recent gain in the use of tractors, combines, and other machinery. The cotton-picker appears to be on the horizon. The implications of these inventions go beyond the possibilities of increased leisure. They involve as well new skills for their operation, drastic changes in farm management, vast possibilities for the reorganization of agriculture to supply on a sounder economic basis the optimum dietary needs of the American people. Moreover, in the trend toward regional planning, perhaps best exemplified in the Tennessee Valley Authority but apparent also in other developments initiated or planned, lies a vast opportunity for rural adult education. Here whole populations may traverse in relatively short periods the distance from the traditional agricultural economy of the later nineteenth or early twentieth century to an economy of increased industrialization, with an agriculture integrated with the needs of a population changed in its characteristics and its occupational distribution. Further, the results of such regional planning cannot but affect, in ways as yet unpredictable, the economy and social organization of many rural areas in the United States.

It is against this background that the events and developing trends in rural adult education must be viewed and criticized.

A new epoch in extension.—The historian of tomorrow will look back on the years 1932–36 as the most significant epoch in the development of the Agricultural Extension Service since those first 5 years when, before its formative period was over, it faced the emergency demands of the World War.

For its first 15 years or so, the major emphasis of the Extension Service was upon increasing production and later, along with that, upon marketing. It was in short largely vocational in nature in both its agricultural and home economics work. Then came the changed world conditions that lost us world markets for our food and fiber, and finally the A.A.A., with its program of adjusting production more nearly to domestic consumption. This sent the Extension Service off in a new and uncharted field in which it was necessary for its personnel to acquire new kinds of information, more knowledge of economics and sociology. Many who did not possess this knowledge had to secure it on a catch-as-catch-can basis while operating the new program. Moreover, even in the 1920's, social projects began to creep into the program; and in the latter half of that decade, they absorbed about 6 per cent of the effort and money of the Extension Service.

The field covered.—In 1930, a larger proportion of the counties of the nation were being served by agricultural and home demonstration agents than at any time since the World War. The Service suffered somewhat in some states in the early years of the depression, though less than did any other rural educational agency. These losses were more in a financial way than in the aggregate of personnel employed. With the coming of the Agricultural Adjustment Act, expansion was rapid; for the Department of Agriculture naturally turned to this well-organized and trusted agency to instruct the farmers in the purpose, meaning, and operation of the new law. By 1934, the employed personnel reached an all-time high of over 7,500. By April 30, 1936, the total number of professional employees, exclusive of Washington headquarters, was 8,527. This represented a gain of 709 over the previous year. Of these, 370, or 4.4 per cent, were engaged full time in boys' and girls' club work. The rest, 95.6 per cent, were giving most or all of their time to adults.

The steady increase in the number of countries served, following the immediate post-war deflation, is shown in Table 63.

TABLE 63

PER CENT OF COUNTIES HAVING AGRICULTURAL AND HOME DEMONSTRATION AGENTS

By Years

Year	*Per Cent Counties with*	
	AGRICULTURAL AGENTS	HOME DEM. AGENTS
1915	37.0	11.4
1918	79.3	55.8
1920	66.2	25.5
1925	69.1	30.2
1930	77.2	43.3
1934	91.1	41.8
1936	93.7	52.8

Use of volunteer leaders.—One of the most interesting aspects of this program of adult education in rural America is the large development in the use of volunteer local leaders who are given some training, assistance, and supervision; and who then carry the details of the local program. Without the success of this device, agricultural extension could never have become as influential or as educative as it has. These local leaders serve without pay, and bear their own expenses to training conferences. They contribute an average of 17 days a year to the work; and the number has shown a definite upward trend as the tabulation below indicates.

1925	208,582	1932	416,858
1930	318,387	1933	432,463
1931	377,027	1934	380,099
1935	424,951		

The part these volunteer leaders play in the total movement will be illustrated at several points in the chapter. It is a device that has now stood the test of time with reasonable success. It is doubtful whether the township and county crop committees of the Agricultural Adjustment Administration could have functioned as smoothly as they seem to have without the experience derived from nearly two decades of finding, training, using, and supervising volunteer leaders by the Extension Service. The willingness of rural people so to volunteer is perhaps but a twentieth-century equivalent of the neighborly co-operation at barn-raisings, corn-huskings, and the like in the nineteenth century. The success with which these volunteers have functioned should at least be considered and more emulated than it has been by other adult education agencies.

As has been indicated, the emergency created by the depression, and the efforts to meet it, laid new burdens upon the Extension Service. The usual activities suffered, at least from the point of view of the time-investment of the agricultural agents; which accounts, in part, for the drop in the number of volunteer leaders in 1934. There were those who viewed this with alarm; while others believed that the emphasis of the Service must change permanently. These attitudes still persist.

The issue is not yet settled. It is, however, important to record this real modification in the Extension Service program; and to note that it is continuing as the new Soil Conservation program, substitute for the old A.A.A., gets under way. The modification is evident, too, in other aspects of the program, as will be indicated. Moreover, if the functions of extension are to continue the present trend, the implications for the training of the professional staff are considerable. Training in the skills of agriculture and home economics alone will not suffice. Economics will have to be called upon, as will the sociology of group formation and rural organization. Methods of securing group consensus will have to be used, as well as indoctrination of specific skills or methods.

It is, however, with social trends that this study is more concerned; and attention must therefore be centered upon the increasing and highly significant cultural contributions of the Extension Service to rural America.

Local planning conferences.—Certainly one of these most closely allied to both normal and emergency programs was the effort to bring the farmers of a county together to look at their agricultural enterprise in the light of the changed local, state, national, and world conditions, and to plan for the future. Such efforts had been made by a few counties in 1932, and the published results aroused wide interest; but in the winter of 1935–36, planning conferences were held in over 2,000 counties. This effort to challenge existing procedures, to develop the agricultural enterprise on the basis of facts and constantly changing conditions, may have wide significance in the future. Interestingly enough, the criterion for such planning is the use of land in such a way as to win a better standard of living, including both material and non-material elements.[3] Local papers in the 140 villages uniformly gave much space to recording the results of these conferences. The 1936–37 series seems quite likely to give some attention to the social issues, as well as to the economic and purely vocational. As will be seen, this appears to be an inevitable evolution in the procedures.

Public affairs discussions.—But changing conditions not only affect farm management, but raise issues of national importance which in a democracy must be understood by the citizens. Opinions on such issues are often formed from insufficient evidence or are swayed by propaganda. The Extension Service, therefore, in some states organized discussion groups which considered public affairs, using materials that stated all viewpoints on a given issue. The plan began experimentally in the winter of 1933–34 in 10 states, and was greatly expanded the following year. The total number of groups varied greatly with the states. One had 1,700, another 800. Ten others averaged 121 each. Still others organized more intensively on a county basis and reported from 4 to 35

[3] Kolb and Brunner, *A Study of Rural Society*, p. 443.

counties operating. Procedures in organization also varied. In some states these discussion groups were specially organized, with all who were interested invited. In some, there were special groups for men, women, and youth. In others, existing agencies such as the Grange, Farm Bureau, and Farmer's Union were used, and the discussions were fitted into their regular programs. In New Jersey, picked leaders from each county were brought to the Agricultural College each week through the winter for a day's discussion under national leaders, and many of these held local meetings.[4]

The material used also varied widely. A few states issued pamphlets, one on each major topic discussed. Others contented themselves with mimeographed suggestions. Apparently the best discussions were secured on an informal basis and with simple topical outlines and bibliography. One farmer interviewed by a fieldworker about this program expressed the opinion of many when he said, "We sure learned a heap about what makes markets and prices."

An example from Virginia.—In Virginia the two projects of local planning and the discussion of current issues were combined, and the set-up and preparation afford an interesting illustration of Extension Service procedures, as well as possibilities in adult education.

The project was first considered at one of the meetings of the entire extension staff, at which several discussion techniques were utilized and thereby demonstrated. Next, regional meetings held in the various parts of the state were attended by the county agents and an average of three leaders from each county. County training meetings followed, to which were invited leading farmers, especially A.A.A. committeemen, farm organization representatives, professional and business men, officers of civic organizations, school officials and teachers. The attendance averaged 38

[4] The New Jersey plan, financed in part by a nongovernmental agency, the American Association for Adult Education, antedated the department's plan, as did somewhat similar developments in a few other states, notably Wisconsin and Iowa.

per county. On the basis of these meetings, the local community discussion groups were set up. Of the total number of leaders, 86 per cent were farm owner-operators, and 6 per cent more were farm owners. Six series of problems were discussed by an average of 400 local groups, though some series were used by over 500. At the end of the program, almost three-fourths of the groups expressed the desire to continue to meet throughout the year.

In Wisconsin, the number of counties with discussion programs increased from 2 in 1931–32 to 11 in 1934–35, with an average of 10 groups per county, each of which borrowed from the university an average of 3 loan-package libraries on the subject selected for discussion.

No national summary of the 1935–36 program had been compiled by the Department of Agriculture up to the time of going to press. Summaries for 19 Middle Western and Far Western states, however, give some indication of the scope of the program. It operated in 735 of the 889 counties in the 10 Middle Western states, or 82 per cent, and in 231 of 316 counties in the 9 Far Western states, or 73 per cent. Thirty-three individuals gave full time to the program, and 123 part time. There is no way of determining how many meetings were held within each county. The reactions of the farmers were reported as generally good or favorable from all the states. Criticisms related almost entirely to inadequacies in census data, or to the mechanics of organization and the scope of source materials.

Socialization of activities.—The depression stimulated two other lines of development, both of which had been begun before 1930. One of these relates to the whole field of family welfare, including especially child development and parent education. The other embraces the entire range of leisure-time activities.

Because of the depression and a developing philosophy of adult education, much of the work in clothing, nutrition, health, home furnishings, and similar phases of home demonstration became less merely technical and more and more socialized. In several states the emphasis was placed on appreciation of beauty in the home and a utilization of materials at hand. It is impossible to do more than illustrate this trend. Thousands of families in the aggregate renovated furniture, reseated chairs, rehung pictures, and re-finished floors and walls. Home Bureau clubs made tours to museums and to attractively furnished homes. Art exhibits were arranged and circulated among the groups. In one state, 2,000 persons were enrolled in a project that eventuated in home flower gardens and so-called outdoor living rooms.

Nutrition work grappled with the problem of adequate diet in the face of declining income, and this activity quickly expanded beyond the home and into the school. In Massachusetts, for instance, the Extension Service co-operated in a study of the school-lunch situation along with the State Departments of Education and Public Health, the P.T.A.'s, and the Federated Women's Clubs. As a result, a co-operative effort was made with the W.P.A. to serve a hot dish in the schools to supplement lunches brought from home.

In Missouri, 249 Home Bureau clubs supplied hot dishes or whole lunches daily to more than 6,500 children in 344 rural schools. In addition, 412 Home Economics Extension clubs assisted in improving the plane of nutrition in their communities from which W.P.A. nurses had reported some thousands of cases of malnutrition among children. These instances are simply illustrations of a wide variety of activities stimulated by Home Economics Extension and carried through by the local groups under their own leadership. One interesting development growing out of all this has been greatly increased attention to the knotty problem of consumption and consumer education.

The socialization of the program is well represented by a typical set of objectives for Home Economics Extension in Massachusetts:

To make it possible for groups of homemakers to come together with a leader to discuss their problems and, through an interchange of knowledge and experiences, to get a store of information and a sense of values upon which to base choices, decisions, and accepted standards of living.

To encourage and inspire homemakers to think, not only upon the immediate problems of family life, but upon those social and economic problems which affect the family and the community.

To interest prospective homemakers in the study of problems which pertain to successful individual, family, and community living.

To assist community leaders in analyzing present resources and utilization of these resources by all the people of the community.

In this state, nearly 24,000 families were represented in study groups concerned with actualizing these objectives; and 3,700 local volunteer leaders co-operated with the professional staff in the entire program in this field.

Child development and parent education.—It is a short step from such projects to the whole field of child development and parent education, and extension has taken that step. There is now a specialist in this field on the national staff, and 21 states have also employed state specialists. The programs are varied, and reflect somewhat the interests of the state specialist in charge, the needs of the local co-operating groups, and the age of the activity. Two quotations from annual reports, the first from an Eastern, the second from a Middle Western state, illustrate the types of activity.

The trend of parent education for the year has been definitely toward family relationships which are essential to maximum development of the individual and the welfare and happiness of the family group. The time has been divided between laying the foundation for successful living in the early years of the child's life and a more intensive study of the problems of adolescence.

In the former project, the discussion centers around such relationships as are essential to developing the spirit of co-operation, self-reliance, and a sense of security. In the latter project, problems of adolescence—physical, mental, social, and emotional growth and development—are the basis for study and discussion by the parents.

Because of the limited contacts with groups, this type of information seems more helpful as it serves as a background for working out techniques of guidance and a philosophy of family life. In order to work more intimately with groups and the individual members, the specialist has conducted more community groups and has visited those led by leaders.

In addition to reaching every county in the state in some manner, and working intensively in five counties through lay leadership, the specialist, in the capacity of chairman, has devoted much time to the organization and development of a state council of parent education. This organization seems essential to the development and co-ordination of parent education through the various agencies in the State.

This represents perhaps the leading type of activity in most states. Another popular phase is represented in the next quotation.

Leading other phases of child development work was the interest in immunization against diphtheria, with the result that 5,978 children were so immunized. In other phases of disease prevention or defect correction, 3,634 children were examined in eye clinics, 3,354 in dental clinics, 3,575 inoculated against typhoid, and 962 vaccinated against smallpox. Correction of defects found in clinics was stressed in club work, with the result that 174 children got glasses recommended, and 857 had the dental work done that was needed. There were 198 crippled children examined in clinics, and of these 59 were treated.

This development is an important illustration of a point made earlier in the chapter concerning extension's contribution to adult education. Child guidance and parent education have been growing interests in educational circles for 25 years; but the development has been largely urban and professional. It made little progress in rural America. Parent-Teacher Associations in rural schools had possibilities in this direction, but turned out far more often than not to be little more than auxiliaries for the school. Moreover, they had a high mortality rate. Their life depended upon, their program reflected, the interest of the school superintendent. Then home economics extension entered this field. It possessed the machinery to reach local groups, the technique for developing volunteer leadership. It knew that professional leadership in parent education, even on a county basis, was an ideal impossible of achievement in any predictable future. It followed the tested procedures in developing this interest. Within the realm of its resources its accomplishments are very great.[5]

Leisure-time activities.—But perhaps the greatest development has taken place in the field of leisure-time activities, especially those of drama, music, art, reading, and recreation. This type of work also antedated the 1930's, but developed surprisingly, especially in the present decade.

Of the 40 states responding to a questionnaire, 32 had well-defined programs in general recreation, and the other 8 were all doing "a little." Drama was part of the program in 26, music in 20, arts and crafts in 12, reading in 8, training in speech in 2, and folk-dancing in one. In 3 other states nothing is being done along these lines, because such activities are cared for either by the state universities or by the state board of education.

A list of the total number of recreational activities would tax the space available for this chapter. Games of many kinds are included, both group and athletic, for home and community, as is dancing, especially folk-dancing. Home-talent chautauquas are frequent. In North Dakota, because of the cold winters, it is perhaps not surprising to find considerable attention paid to indoor games suitable for both the family and the community.

Twenty-four states hold state-wide or district institutes or schools for the local volunteer recreation leaders. Many of these are, or have been, in co-operation with the National Recreation Association. A few put on such schools or courses at the annual Farmers' Week, which is a feature of the program of every state college of agriculture. In Illinois, for instance, 300 attended a course, and in addition 339 communities were represented at district recreational conferences held by the extension rural sociologist at strategic centers in each region of the state.

In Montana, despite its huge distances and low population density, district recreational training schools have enlisted in one year as many as 1,100 local leaders, both men and women, from

[5] It is only fair to state that in some urban areas and among some groups of parent educators large use has been made of volunteer leaders, but this procedure is still a controversial issue.

444 local organizations and 32 counties. In some states, county recreational councils have been organized to co-ordinate activities. A frequent goal is to have some recreation at every Farm or Home Bureau or club meeting, and, judging by the reports, considerable progress is being made toward this end. This is especially true in the Homemakers' Camps which are becoming more and more popular on both a state and county basis in a large number of the states. Of course, the emphasis on recreation is most pronounced in the youth activities under the 4-H Clubs, which are dealt with in Chapter X.

An extension rural sociologist in an Eastern state writes:

> In the field of recreation, stimulation does not seem to be necessary. Our entire efforts are going into the field of local leadership training and making program materials available to local leaders. The demand for social recreation arose very rapidly during the depression, and so far is holding its own very well. Many people have found the joy of creating their own recreation. There is a great deal of interest in the old traditional games, especially singing, folk-games and square dances.

This quotation sums up the testimony of a goodly majority of the directors of extension. Two-thirds report increasing requests for assistance along recreational and cultural lines. A number say this increase is "tremendous," or "beyond the power of our present staff to handle." But meanwhile these staffs continue to hold the training institutes, and to speed out a steady stream of monthly program suggestions, materials, and helps to local groups, as well as some bulletins.

Drama.—Most interesting, perhaps, of recent developments has been the great interest in drama. The training of local leaders has proceeded in the same way as with recreation. Literally thousands of rural groups have participated. Many of the colleges of agriculture maintain loan libraries of plays to assist groups in their selections. In one Middle Western state alone, 4,040 plays were loaned to such groups in 1935. But many of the plays are original (often the work of farmers' wives) and utilize local materials. Some of these are of very good quality. Some states are stimulating the development of the drama by holding play-writing contests; and these report that the quality of the manuscripts submitted improves with each year.

In the best organized states, the local groups put on county drama festivals, and the best companies, or those with the most significant plays, are selected from the entire state to appear at the state college during Farmers' Week.

The annual reports of the extension directors or extension rural sociologists present a vivid picture of the strength of the movement. In one small New England state, there are drama groups in 100 communities. Oregon, where the work is newer, already has 90. In Tennessee, rural men and women came from all over the state to 5 regional drama leadership training schools (each of which lasted 4 days) and returned home to assist local community leaders in their counties. In New York, 10 demonstration drama festivals and 20 county festivals were held, culminating in a state festival. In Iowa and Wisconsin, where the work is older than in some states, there are hundreds of groups; and the number has been growing each year. Despite the high density of population in Massachusetts, and its numerous large towns and cities with all their available facilities for commercial recreation, drama work in rural parts of the state has been very popular. Training meetings are held which cover, as do most such efforts elsewhere, play selection, organization for production, directing, acting, staging and lighting, costuming and make-up. Plays are discussed, and a demonstration cast acts as a laboratory group. This indeed is the usual set-up in the drama training work, though some states add assistance in speech and other related topics.

The growth of the drama work in one of the states where it began some time ago, Wisconsin, is shown in the number of counties organized for this program by years:

1926	2	1930–31	31	1934–35	41
1927–28	6	1931–32	33	1935–36	39
1928–29	17	1932–33	30		
1929–30	19	1933–34	30		

In some states, the drama work has been tied in with the public schools, either directly or by using 4-H Club groups.[6] These and other procedures have resulted in a considerable development of dramatic, and also of musical and artistic, activity in high schools, a discussion of which will be found in Chapter X. There are also, as Chapter X shows, numerous drama groups and music groups in the villages.

The illustrations presented were selected from the reports as representative. The activities under this head in the 26 states having them can perhaps be illustrated by quoting from a representative report from Ohio as to activities in the last few years:

a. County leadership drama training meetings in 68 counties; 3 counties, 1935.
b. Home talent lyceum course, rural community theatre, or play exchange in practically all of 88 counties; 42 counties have organized Home Talent courses.
c. At least one stage remodeled or built new, scenery and lights, in each of 68 counties where leadership training meetings were held; 6 new ones in 1935.
d. Courses in dramatics at summer youth conferences in camp.
e. Play loan service—several hundred copies on file for loaning for inspection; 4,040 copies loaned in 1935.
f. Planned rural talent programs at Farmers' Week; at least one night on each program since 1935.
g. Bulletins (mimeographed) on directing, acting, stage and scenery construction; new ones under process of preparation at present. See "Directing and Acting" and "Rural Community Theatres in Ohio."
h. Miniature stage used as model for stage and scenery construction.
i. Rural Dramatics Festival, Alexandria, Licking County, August 31, September 1-2, 1935. More than 700 different persons took part.
j. Which Way Agriculture? Washington County pageant, July 27, 1935.

Music and art.—In the other cultural activities of the Extension Service, the set-up is much the same as in that for the drama. This is true in reference to organization, leadership training, and county or regional festivals or demonstrations, as well as to the

[6] M. E. Kramer, *Dramatic Tournaments in the Secondary Schools* (New York, Teachers College, Columbia University, Bureau of Publications, 1936).

appearance of local orchestras, bands, choruses, glee clubs, opera groups, and the like at state college Farm Weeks, or at state fairs, or on radio programs. These enterprises are being carried on in 20 states; and are therefore second only to drama in their popularity. The Extension Service assists, not only in training, but also in organizing, such groups when requested.

The program is not limited to participation alone. Some states have a definite program in music appreciation, and use phonograph records which are loaned, explanatory notes, lectures, and demonstrations on the air. In South Dakota, there was a study course in music appreciation in which 16,000 farm and village women enrolled. Every home demonstration club in the state was represented. An example of the type of work carried on is furnished by an Iowa pamphlet entitled, *Marching through History*. This tells how music began to be related to marching, and then gives the history and setting of some of the famous march music of the world, together with a little about the composers. Suggestions to chairmen of local music groups conclude this neatly illustrated, popularly written document.[7]

Twelve states are engaged in a wide variety of art projects; and this work, in most states, is closely co-ordinated with the other phases of the extension program. Beauty in color, line, and design is demonstrated and developed in home and community life: in clothing, in the beautification of houses, grounds, and parks, and in planning for new projects in these fields of activity. Art appreciation has been encouraged through demonstrations, by loaning copies of prints of old or new works, by holding exhibits of original productions, by arranging for groups to visit museums or galleries where available, and by issuing simple suggestions for the hanging of pictures in the home.

Unfortunately, art activities and those of the drama have been combined only now and then. Where they have been, the art program has been worked out in connection with stage settings and

[7] The author is Fannie R. Buchanan.

costumes for rural drama groups, and in pageants depicting local history or life in the lands from which the original settlers of given communities came.

It may be said here that in the states possessing an art program, there has been, to some extent at least, a development of crafts. Hooked rugs, block printing, wood carving, quilting, metal work, and similar activities attract their different groups. Some of these projects have been developed to the place where they have commercial value. In one state, the craft work specializes on using local products.

As the first part of this section indicated, the Extension Service has still other activities of a cultural nature, especially in literature appreciation and reading; these will be dealt with in the next chapter. Mention should also be made of the fact that the older youth, of post-4-H-Club age, have been recruited in large numbers in many of these activities. The plight of the 18 to 24 year-old group in the depression years has been real and in a number of states special attention has been given by the Extension Service to developing activity programs fitted to the peculiar problems of this group. Most of this work is too new to appraise.

Agricultural Extension for Negroes.—What has been written, and the appraisal that follows, apply for the most part to Agricultural Extension Service activities for the white race. The Negroes are not utterly neglected by any means, but they do not receive service in proportion to their numbers. Only about 5 per cent of the entire extension staff is working exclusively for and with the Negro farmers, though 12.5 per cent of our farmers are of this race. The discrepancy on the side of technical agriculture is not as serious as it appears, for the share-croppers at least must take their orders from the white plantation owner or manager who has full access to the Extension Service specialists. On the social side, the handicap is greater. No state has a Negro extension sociologist. Yet here the needs are very great, and concern, not only the desire for expression through the cultural arts, but more elemental needs relating to health and the organization of resources for social and economic objectives. Here the Extension Service has a potentially great contribution to make, along with the vocational teachers and supervisors of the schools.[8]

Cultural values of extension work.—The cultural values of the Extension Service can best be summarized, perhaps, in a quotation from the introduction of a forthcoming study of this subject by Marjorie Patten:[9]

> It is a story of the rise of a host of homespun leisure-time activities among farm people during the troubled years since the World War. These activities are deeply rooted in the soil and already form an important part of the agricultural program sponsored by federal and state authorities to improve conditions in rural communities. Over wide areas farmers are interested now in corn and hogs and opera, in cheese and cream and drama, in wheat and cattle and folk-dancing.
>
> An *Extension Service Bulletin* issued by the Ohio State Agricultural College carries this quotation from Edman, "Leisure is an affair of mood and atmosphere rather than simply of the clock. It is not chronological occurrence, but a spiritual state. It is unhurried, pleasurable living among one's native enthusiasms."
>
> Among the cultural activities in which farm folk were found to be engaged in the communities studied by the author of this volume were plays, festivals, operas, choruses, bands, orchestras, folk-dancing and folk-music, choric speech, puppets, marionettes, hobby shows, art exhibits, playwriting, crafts, radio hours of music, drama, and art appreciation. They bear witness to the fact that farm people have taken as their own something of the Edman philosophy in their endeavor to see that culture remains in agriculture. They have demanded it in spite of, and in many cases because of, depression conditions. . . .
>
> We are accustomed to hearing the voices of the Little Theatre in cities and larger towns; vacationing America has long been entertained in an excellent fashion by the professional and semi-professional groups of actors, dancers, and musicians who move from cities to summer resorts

[8] In this connection, see a particularly valuable contribution by Maurice E. Thomasson, *A Study of Special Kinds of Education for Rural Negroes* (Charlotte, N. C., Johnson Smith University, 1936), Chapters II and IV, and also pp. 28-40 and 97-100.

[9] A project of the Department of Adult Education of Teachers College, Columbia University, under the direction of Edmund deS. Brunner.

annually. We are not so accustomed to the new voices now making themselves heard from the plains, the prairies, and the mining communities, and from little places back in the mountains. They are coming up from the tall corn, from the wheat fields, the sugar-beet fields—yes, and out of the dust bowl.

They have nothing in them of the commercial. They are the voices of men and women who have struggled through drought, thaw, drifts, impassable roads, dust, and hail storms; who have fought grasshoppers, cinch bugs, and rust.

When one has listened to a seven-hundred-voice chorus of farm folk in Iowa singing Cadman's "Marching through the Clouds with God"; when one has found literally hundreds of one-act plays being produced in isolated little communities in Wisconsin in spite of twenty-two-foot drifts and temperatures down to forty below zero; when one has danced the Cserebogar in a cold little Grange hall far from any centre, but to which over two hundred farmers had travelled miles to a Farm Bureau meeting which included music and folk-dancing as a matter of course; one becomes vitally aware that there is something new under the American sun, a program full of romance, adventure and challenge, something new but of the same spirit as that which marked the old pioneer days.

Whenever one has had the opportunity to witness this far-flung program, one finds that it is events like these that are propping up, strengthening and enriching the economic side of life in the region.

Whole counties, districts, states, and regions have been revitalized because of the new developing enthusiasm for home-grown entertainment. It is their own vivid way of interpreting the idea as old as Aristotle: "The whole end and objective of education is training for the right use of leisure time."

The local community picture.—The real appraisal of the Extension Service is made by the people in the local community. Its contributions in local terms are to both the adult education and social or community life. Of this the field study of the 140 villages produced numerous illustrations. The latter topic will be considered in Chapter X, on social life and organization. The following cases deal with the observed impact of the Extension Service on the adult education of local communities.

In one Far West community which covered over 600 square miles, the county agent organized the farmers into classes in the various neighborhoods for a careful consideration of the various emergency government programs. Out of these grew a keen interest in the broader aspects of economics and especially of sociology. Classes of college grade were started in these subjects with the aid of lecturers, not only from the agricultural college, but from several of the other state institutions of higher education.

In an Eastern state, the Granges of a county became very much interested in the drama program. A teacher of the drama was employed to divide her time among the locals in the county. The group from one of the 140 village communities was selected to go to the Farm Week Drama Contest, and won first place. The community was thrilled; and the achievement, which had brought many together to work in the common interest, had incidental value in a number of ways.

In a Southern county, the home demonstration agent was discontinued after 17 years, as an economy measure. The work meant so much to the people that in one of the communities studied, the people kept the program going with their volunteer leadership with the aid of suggestions from the state college. This happened in 2 other centers in as many regions.

In one large Middle West community, there were 24 units of Farm and Home Bureaus with a membership of 412 men and 208 women. There were 80 volunteer leaders. In connection with the A.A.A. and Soil Conservation programs, 324 meetings were held in 1935, and these were attended by 15,567, or an average of 48 for each meeting. In addition, 6 other programs dealing with technical agriculture and homemaking were carried through.

For 8 years, Miami County, Ohio, has sponsored home-talent lyceum courses, with 3,300 people on the subscription list. Plans are arranged by leaders from 11 communities, with headquarters in the County Extension agent's office. At the close, a roundup of all the cast participants is held for an evening of fun, group-singing, one-act plays, quadrilles, social dancing, and refreshments. There are 2 complete circuits of 6 communities each. This plan for providing a county with wholesome entertainment is resulting in the discovery of new talent; is demonstrating new ways to develop leisure-time activities of interest to young and old; is giving encouragement to community co-operation, to the development and maintenance of an appreciation for clean entertainment at low cost, and to the promotion of good music; and is inspiring all who take part with a new sense of satisfaction in accomplishment.

Agricultural extension was reaching almost all of the 140 village communities; home economics extension about half. It is not without significance that school authorities in over 60 per cent of the villages spoke in high terms of its contribution to the farmers. Few did so in 1930.

THE RADIO

It is axiomatic that the radio has become a powerful agency of adult education. In 1930, 20.8 per cent of all farm homes had radios, 33.7 per cent of all rural homes. There was considerable variation in the percentage of homes having radios in 1930. Even in 1930, except for the South, 40 to 50 per cent of village homes were equipped with some sort of radio reception device. Of course towns and cities had higher ratios. By 1936, moreover, the estimates of commercial agencies credit three-fourths of the nation with radios. These estimates credit one-third of the rural farms and over one-half of all the rural homes with radios. This means that the number of families with radios among both the farm and rural non-farm people has doubled since 1930. Almost 7 million rural families are estimated to have radios in 1936, as against the census figure of 3,332,506 in 1930. The increase in farm families so equipped was from 1,371,073 to 2,300,000.

Programs of special interest to rural people are available from 3 classes of stations: the large regional stations of the 2 national networks; the smaller, local commercial stations; and the publicly owned stations operated by state universities and colleges of agriculture. The best-known agricultural radio program is the National Farm and Home Hour, made possible by the co-operation of the United States Department of Agriculture, and broadcast over more than 40 stations. It is a combination of national news of interest to farmers, such as developments in the Agricultural Adjustment Administration, crop reports and prices; of educational talks on technical agricultural procedures; and of musical features. Addresses at meetings of national farm organizations are also broadcast when they occur. This feature comes daily, except on Saturdays and Sundays. Inevitably, since this program aims at interesting the farmers of the entire nation, the content must cover subjects in a general way. The materials cannot apply to one region or to one crop. To remedy this difficulty, there is a Western Farm and Home Hour; and the United States Department of Agriculture operates several other radio services, including daily Farm Flashes and Housekeeper Chats, and less frequent talks on the weather, the agricultural situation and services available from Uncle Sam—all of which give more attention to local conditions.

These services are sent in mimeographed form to local stations, commercial and public, and are frequently given local application by the state agricultural colleges. This indicates the place of the smaller commercial stations. They give attention to local problems and events. Some have developed highly useful programs, including talks, forums, question-and-answer periods, and dialogues covering successful farming and community organization practices.

In proportion to the total amount of time on the air, the stations of the colleges of agriculture naturally give the greatest amount of service to farmers and villagers of their areas. The total programs of such stations cover many features. One of the most appreciated items is the frequent broadcasting of market reports.

Comparable service is given homemakers. The weekly half-hour for this group in one state produced in a year more than

170,000 requests for copies of the talks given. Homemakers are also usually mothers interested in children; and talks on clothes, diet, child psychology, children's books and plays have brought much favorable response. In the presentation of such programs, practically all the college and university stations use faculty members as speakers. Some of these stations are conducting ambitious adult educational enterprises, often under the name of College, or School, of the Air. In these radio projects, other state agencies often co-operate. Thus in Wisconsin, 10 courses were offered in 1934–35, with no charge for tuition or study helps. There were nearly 14,000 enrollments. Only one course, "Farm Life and Living," applied directly to rural people; but they enrolled freely in the others, which included such subjects as "Everyday Economics," "Social Problems of Today," "Rediscovering Wisconsin," "The World of Music," "Science at Work," and courses in both American and foreign literature. Ohio has been a pioneer in this sort of service, which has been conducted with growing success and covers a wider field of subjects.

One other interesting radio service should be mentioned: that of the New York College of Agriculture at Cornell. It co-operates with 24 stations in its state in many ways, and issues quarterly an attractive advance program of the broadcasts from these stations of special interest to rural people. These are indexed under 50 separate headings that cover very well the technical, social, and economic interests of rural New York.

A most obvious and possibly most important contribution of the radio is the opportunity it affords the homemaker to gain some enjoyment or profit during the time spent in such routine household chores as dishwashing, mending, or dusting. In an extensive inquiry, one of the rural women's magazines found that over half the women reporting utilized the radio in this way.

Organizations in town and country are making increased use of the radio in their programs, as is evident from the growing correspondence of the Radio Institute of the Audible Arts, to which reports of such use have been voluntarily sent. A Home Demonstration Agent in New England writes of the frequent use of the radio, and especially of radio plays, in the Home Bureau groups of her county. Another in Iowa tells of the 4-H Club girls studying the operas broadcast. A State Grange lecturer in the South and another in the East tell of Granges that enjoy broadcasts at their regular meetings and some that use radio music for dancing, much to the delight of the young people. In fact, this last point has been stressed again and again by rural people. The radio seems to have made the hard years of depression a bit easier for some rural young people who can no longer afford to visit the near-by city as often as they would like.

RESETTLEMENT ADMINISTRATION

A new factor has been introduced into the tax-supported adult education field through the Resettlement Administration. It has been found increasingly necessary to educate the clients of this agency, whether the effort was for rehabilitation on the home farm or resettlement in colonies. To bring from several score to several hundred families together under new conditions in a settlement that had its beginning with their arrival is at best a difficult piece of social engineering. But these families were for a variety of causes disadvantaged both economically and socially. In the Crandon Land Purchase area, for instance, the relief families, prospective clients of the Resettlement Administration, with a family income only 9 per cent less than that of non-relief families, were found to have spent less than one-third as much for "advancement" items in their budgets; only one-seventh as much on insurance; and little more than one-half as much for personal items.[10] Moreover, in their leisure time the relief clients were found in the past to have devoted far less time to group activities than the non-relief families. Interestingly enough, the smaller the proportion

[10] E. C. Kilpatrick, "Needed Standards of Living for Rural Resettlement" (Madison, Wis., 1936, mimeographed).

of relief in the total family income, the larger the number of hours spent in group activities. To make functioning communities out of these resettlements, then, required adult education. In some places the hope had been to utilize local agencies for this, especially the Agricultural Extension Service; but in a number of places, including 2 resettlement communities within the service areas of villages studied, a special worker or two had to be employed. In one place, this influenced the older population in favor of adult education. In the other, it resulted in requests from the community for service from the Resettlement Administration.

A special educational effort of the Resettlement Administration relates to the rehabilitation clients, that is, those who were being assisted, because of temporary distress, to regain self-support on the farms they occupied when their difficulties arose. Special advice and help on planning and managing farm and family resources were given these families, which in the aggregate have amounted to several hundred thousand. This has been essentially an educational job to poorer farm people. This program has been intimately associated with the Extension Services in many states.

Summary.—The expansion in the total program of Agricultural Extension indicates a definite trend away from the conception of the past and the old idea of demonstrations as its chief teaching tool. But the old subject-matter fields have continued. The new services and trends have simply been grafted onto the old. There may be a danger in too great a subdivision of the field, the danger that as the state specialists naturally and properly seek to develop their fields, the two primary units of rural life, the family and the community, will be overlooked. Agricultural Extension, and indeed all adult education, needs to see these units whole as well as in their component parts. Specific programs need to be integrated in the total life of the community. The growing demands upon the Extension Service, and its growing opportunities, make planning for all the needs of the field the *sine qua non* of maximum efficiency and success.

Such planning would lessen a certain opportunism in the development of Agricultural Extension programs. The development of groups for the discussion of public affairs meets one of the needs stressed in the opening pages of this chapter, that of keeping an aging population alert to changing social conditions. But this work does not yet extend into the villages. Similarly, the cultural activities described are in a measure an answer to the opportunity of increased leisure. The larger social changes resulting from changes in farm management and regional planning have not yet influenced the program to any degree. With the intense activity forced on Agricultural Extension by the Agricultural Adjustment Act and succeeding soil conservation legislation, it is too much to expect that cognizance of these items should have been taken. But it is not too much to hope that these social changes will influence increasingly the program of this huge and well-financed agency of rural adult education.

IX

Adult Education: All Other Agencies

IN THIS chapter, all agencies for rural adult education other than the Extension Service of the colleges of agriculture will be considered, with special reference to the trends of the years 1930–36. Most of the discussion is based on data secured by field work in the 140 village-centered rural communities, but, as elsewhere in this report, other sources of information have been drawn upon. The chapter begins with libraries; and turns next to the adult education program of the public schools, including both the activities locally financed and operated and those of the Federal emergency adult education program. Finally, some attention is given to those phases of the work of the multitude of voluntary social organizations which have educational implications.

THE RURAL LIBRARY SITUATION

Libraries are highly important agencies of adult education, but in respect to them, rural people, as compared with urban people, have long been handicapped. This study shows, however, that rural people place great value upon having at least some semblance of such a social utility as a library. The various devices they have resorted to in their endeavor to supply the need will be noted in this section. The most important attempt to meet the problem of rural library service has been to organize tax-supported county or district libraries with branches in local communities and depositories in neighborhoods and crossroads homes, in stores, churches, and other such places. The deposited books are changed periodically. This movement began in the early 1900's. By 1920 there were 99 county libraries; by the end of 1930, there were 225. One-fourth of these were in California and

New Jersey, the only states with more than half of their counties so organized.

In 1936, there were 228 counties with annual appropriations of $1,000 or more each for library systems. There were also 2 joint-county libraries serving 4 counties in California; and 10 district libraries in New England. This computation excludes 4 counties in Hawaii. In addition, there were 88 counties that appropriated from $100 to $1,000 to libraries, usually in county seats, to secure service to all county residents who wished to avail themselves of it. In most of the county libraries the appropriations are, of course, considerably in excess of the minimum $1,000 figure. The states with 10 or more counties giving county-wide service are:

State	Counties	State	Counties
California	46	Ohio	10
Indiana	15	Texas	14
Montana	11	Wisconsin	10
New Jersey	11	Wyoming	19
North Carolina	11		

County or district service is probably the best device yet used to meet rural reading needs. Under normal conditions, the movement will doubtless spread, especially if the developing drive for state aid achieves measureable success.

Village libraries.—County and district library organizations increased but little during the depression, and the 140 communities also either held their own or in some respects bettered the situation existing in either 1924 or 1930.[1] Eighty-two, or practically 3 in 5, had public libraries. In 24 more the school library was open to the public,[2] and 21 received traveling libraries from the state library commission or a comparable agency at periodic intervals.

[1] As in the 1930 survey, many of the facts in this section were secured through the co-operation of the American Library Association, which sent out a questionnaire. Fieldworkers supplemented this information.

[2] In one village, the library, when it had to be discontinued because of financial difficulties, was turned over to the school. In 4 villages, school library service to the community was discontinued because with reductions in the size of the teaching staff it proved impossible to assign a teacher to this service.

In 9 additional places the school library was also the depository for state traveling libraries. Only one in 10, therefore, was without any library facilities. In this respect, the 2 Western regions made the best record, all but one of the Far Western villages and two-thirds of the Middle West having public libraries. Though this was true in only one-sixth of the Southern communities, all but 3 of the 30 in this region had some facilities.

The larger the village, the more likely it is to have a public library. In 82 per cent of towns, 70 per cent of the large villages, 57 per cent of the villages of medium size, and 45 per cent of the small villages there were public libraries. Fortunately, only one-sixth of even the small villages are without library facilities of any type. Six per cent of towns, 10 per cent of large villages and 7 per cent of medium-sized villages also lack them.

This discussion is concerned only with the regular, organized independent libraries in the 140 communities. In passing, it may be noted, however, that some of the makeshift arrangements just referred to unquestionably met a real need with some success. For instance, in a Far West community of 2,300 population, there was no library except the 2,800 volumes in the school, which were available to the public at certain non-school hours. Yet the circulation in the year 1935–36 was 40,000. Out of such situations may eventually grow a demand for better service, especially if the demand is stimulated by state leadership.

These village libraries varied, of course, in many respects in the quality and quantity of service they could give. More than two-fifths were open less than 16 hours a week, while only one-fourth were open more than 32 hours; and the remaining third ranged between 16 and 32 hours. As a rule, the larger the village, the more likelihood there is of longer hours.

Support.—Almost three-fifths of the 82 libraries were supported entirely by taxes, except of course for fines and incidental revenue, either from the local village or the village in co-operation with township or county. There were 7 cases in which townships co-operated in library support to insure service for their open-country population. In 11 more communities, private contributions were supplemented by tax funds. In one of these cases, the open-country share was raised by taxation, that of the village entirely by private support. Only 14 libraries, about one-sixth, depended entirely on free-will contributions; but this was 3 more than in 1930. While appropriations were cut in some places, the net loss of only 3 communities in 82 in the number receiving tax funds is encouraging.

The income, however, was small, averaging $1,204.[3] The Middle Atlantic and Middle Western libraries fell slightly below this figure; those in the Far West exceeded it by 25 per cent.[4] The average income of Southern libraries was only $286. Income varied by size also, from $2,219 in the towns and $1,961 in large villages to $411 in small ones. The village of medium size raised $920 for library purposes. Nearly four-fifths of the libraries reporting received more than 60 per cent of their income from taxation. Seven more averaged about one-half. Only 10 of those sharing in tax funds received less than 40 per cent of their funds in this way. These variations in support, both as to income and source, reflect variations primarily *in wealth*,[5] but also in community attitudes and leadership.

The American Library Association has suggested that a desirable minimum expense for libraries is $1 per inhabitant, although it adds that the small town must often spend more for the minimum essentials or reduce unit costs by increasing the service area. If these library incomes are calculated on this basis, using the village population only, the result would seem to show a not too discouraging approximation of the dollar-per-capita standard.

[3] No comparison can be made here, as budget data were very incompletely reported in the 1930 questionnaire of the American Library Association.

[4] In Missouri the average per rural library was barely $600 a year, but those that were tax-supported averaged almost $1,100 or close to the average noted above. See E. L. Morgan and M. W. Sneed, *The Libraries of Missouri* (Columbia, Mo., University of Missouri, College of Agriculture, Research Bulletin 236, April, 1936), pp. 48-53.

[5] Brunner and Kolb, *Rural Social Trends*, p. 379.

Moreover, some of these 82 libraries are open only to villagers or serve the open-country population only on the basis of membership fees of $1 or more. On the other hand, the whole tendency is, and should be, for the library, like the school and social organizations, to accept responsibility for the community area. On this basis, the income per inhabitant is but 31 cents, as against 75 cents when figured only on village population. An unpublished study by Anita Brenner, under the Department of Adult Education, Teachers College, Columbia University, in 1933, showed that a vast improvement over present rural service could be achieved at this figure if the organization were on a county or district basis. Unfortunately, relatively few of the libraries are so organized. Moreover, the South is way below this average, as Table 64 shows.

TABLE 64

AVERAGE INCOME PER INHABITANT, 82 VILLAGE LIBRARIES

By Region

Region	*Income per Inhabitant, in Cents*	
	VILLAGE	TOTAL COMMUNITY
All regions	75	31
Middle Atlantic	79	35
South	9	5
Middle West	73	29
Far West	90	37

Table 65 distributes the same data on the basis of income per borrower and per single circulation.

Librarians.—The chief items of expense for libraries are books and salaries; but one-fifth of the libraries in the 140 villages had volunteer librarians. Often these were furnished in rotation by members of some women's club. Judged by American Library Association standards, such institutions are, of course, in the same class as the one-room school and church, or worse. From another point of view, as has already been pointed out, this contribution of time, year in and year out, is an evidence of the value rural people place on having at least some library service. It is com-

TABLE 65

AVERAGE INCOME PER BORROWER AND PER SINGLE CIRCULATION OF 82 VILLAGE LIBRARIES

By Region and Size

Region and Size	Income per Borrower in Cents [a]					Income per Single Circulation in Cents [b]				
	0–49	*50–99*	*100–149*	*150–199*	*200 up*	*2–5*	*6–9*	*10–13*	*14–17*	*19 up*
All regions	11	18	15	10	8	23	24	10	3	4
Middle Atlantic	1	2	4	1	5	6	3	2	1	2
South	3	0	0	0	0	1	1	0	0	1
Middle West	5	12	8	5	0	10	15	4	1	1
Far West	2	4	3	4	3	6	5	4	1	0
Towns	2	2	3	3	3	3	4	3	2	0
Large	2	4	2	1	2	4	5	0	1	1
Medium	5	8	7	4	2	12	10	5	0	1
Small	2	4	3	2	1	4	5	2	0	2

[a] Twenty libraries did not report.
[b] Eighteen libraries did not report.

parable to the considerable contribution of time made to the Agricultural Extension Service by rural people, which is noted in the chapter on that activity. All but 2 of the unsalaried librarians were in the small and medium-sized villages.

There was no difference in the number of years of general education received by the salaried and the non-salaried librarians. The average was one year beyond high school for librarians in villages of all sizes in all regions, and 2 years for librarians in the towns. This is a poorer record than that of the Missouri librarians in the Morgan-Sneed study alluded to. Of the 68 salaried librarians interviewed in that study, 23 had been professionally trained, 28 had not, and 17 did not answer the question. Presumably they had not had such training. A majority of those professionally prepared for their work were associated with county library systems.

Use of libraries.—The primary purpose of a library is to render book service to its constituency. Do these village community libraries fulfill this function, especially in view of the small collections and the limited hours? To answer this question it is necessary first to examine the size of the collections.

This averaged 4,835 volumes, a gain of nearly 18 per cent over the 1930 total of 4,110. This rate of increase was only a bit more than one-half that of the 1924–30 period. The Middle Atlantic and Far West village libraries approximated the national average, the Middle West exceeded it; the South had only three-fifths as many, but, with the Middle Atlantic villages, showed the greatest proportionate increase in the size of its collections, as will be seen from Table 66.

Small villages, regardless of region, recorded little increase. The real gains were made in the large villages and towns. Apparently book gains in small villages barely balanced discarded volumes. This situation is improving somewhat, however, as the average library added 300 volumes in 1935; the range being from 218 in the South to 325 in the Far West, and from 164 in the small village to 400 in the towns, with the large and medium-sized village slightly exceeding the average. This 1935 gain was nearly 3 times the average annual increase for the period, and probably indicates that the libraries have shared somewhat in the economic recovery.

These libraries, therefore, especially those in the smaller centers, are small. Moreover, the quality of the collections was not studied. Some obviously contained books of little value, relics perhaps of early donations that helped start the library. The villager and farmer probably have interest in reading as varied

TABLE 66

AVERAGE NUMBER OF BOOKS OWNED PER LIBRARY 1930 AND 1936 [a]

By Region and Size of Village

Region and Size	*1930*	*1936*
All regions	4,110	4,835
Middle Atlantic	3,641	4,889
South	2,150	3,023
Middle West	5,153	4,315
Far West	4,654	4,330
Towns	... [b]	7,213
Large	5,434	7,075
Medium	3,858	4,480
Small	2,100	2,114

[a] Source: Questionnaire circulated by American Library Association.
[b] No data for 1930. Included with large villages.

as has the urbanite, but it is often beyond the power of a small library to supply their needs. In a number of states this problem is met, in part, by drawing on the resources of the state library. Where there are county libraries, these furnish an additional resource between the local collection and that of the state. Use of such assets, however, demands that either the reader or the local librarian know just what book to request. In Missouri, in the 8 years from 1927 to 1934 inclusive, according to the Morgan-Sneed study, the public libraries of the state averaged only 351 requests a year to the State Library Commission, as compared with nearly 600 by schools. An average of more than 4,000 individuals a year wrote directly, as did about 1,000 study clubs and 325 community organizations. These figures include rural and urban; but even if all rural, the service rendered by the state would not bulk large against a rural population approaching 2 millions. Indeed the total circulation from this source averaged less than four-hundredths of a volume per rural inhabitant. At best then, this auxiliary service, while highly valuable to users, does not make much impression on the need of rural people for improved library service.

Circulation.—An important index of the service rendered by these local libraries to their constituencies is, of course, the circulation. This was 4.3 volumes per inhabitant in 1935, or about half the American Library Association's standard for places of less than 10,000 inhabitants. Circulation increased markedly in the Middle Atlantic states, and somewhat in the Southern; but remained about stationary in the Western regions, as Table 67

TABLE 67

CIRCULATION PER INHABITANT AND PER BORROWER

82 Village Libraries by Region: 1935

Region	*Circulation per Inhabitant*			*Circulation per Borrower*
	1924	*1930*	*1935*	*1935*
All regions	... [a]	... [a]	4.3	16.3
Middle Atlantic	2.9	2.7	3.7	20.3
South	1.1	0.5	0.9	7.8
Middle West	3.0	4.8	4.9	17.4
Far West	3.6	4.5	4.3	13.9

[a] Not computed. Circulation per borrower, all regions, was 9.6 in 1924 and 14.6 in 1930.

shows. One explanation of the failure of circulation to grow may rest in the quality of the collections and the small number of additions from 1930 to 1934.

It is possible that in 1932 or 1933 the circulation was higher than in 1935. One librarian in California reported that in 1932 circulation rose 25 per cent over 1930, and then dropped 35.2 per cent by 1935, or 20 per cent below 1930. Another town librarian gave circulation by years and by thousands as follows:

1930	32.4	1933	30.1
1931	40.2	1934	25.3
1932	35.4	1935	27.5

Fiction and non-fiction.—The distribution of these collections between fiction and non-fiction is also of importance, and probably a function of circulation. In 2 out of 3 of the 44 libraries reporting on this point, the percentage of fiction in the book collections was 60 or above; in one out of 9 it was above 80 per cent. On the other hand, one-fifth of the libraries had less than one-half fiction; and of these a majority had less than two-fifths.

Sixty-two libraries reported on the use of non-fiction books; and of these, almost three-fourths stated that the demand for this type of book had increased. On the other hand, one-fifth noted a decrease, especially in the last 2 years. In the others there was no change.

One illustration of the interest of rural people in library service, gathered in the field work, is well worth recording. It is unique in its details among the 140 villages, but more or less representative in its spirit. In one Southern village of about 1,100 population, a library was established as a C.W.A. project. Seven hundred and six books and magazines were collected, catalogued, and made available on December 1, 1935. By May 1, 1936, the number had increased to 1,234. The circulation during the first month was 557. In March, 1936, it was 3,196, evenly divided between villagers and farmers. The W.P.A. furnishes the librarian. The upkeep and purchase of books and magazines are now financed by an appropriation of $15 a month from the county, by box suppers, penny and nickel lotteries, and the sale of coffee. In addition to its primary function, the library puts on a story hour for children whenever the schools are not in session.

In the main, rural library service has been strengthened during the years 1930–36, though not as much strengthened as the trends of 1924 to 1930, if continued, would have accomplished. But rural people are standing loyally by such libraries as they have, the county movement has again shown a gain, and the new plan for district or regional service, the latter already approved by the legislatures of 6 states, should under normal conditions result in a further forward step in the huge task of bringing library service to rural America closer to the plane it occupies in the city. The movement for state aid to libraries also holds hope in achieving this objective. New Jersey and Pennsylvania are already making grants to aid in establishing county libraries; the Illinois legislature appropriated $600,000 at its last session to assist existing libraries; and campaigns for similar action in a number of other states are under way and will be acted upon by state legislatures in 1937. Library leaders are obviously following those in the field of the public school in urging state aid, and for the same reasons.

Contribution of the Agricultural Extension Service.—One agency that furnishes reading material to rural people is the Agricultural Extension Service; its activities in this field are often overlooked. It follows several plans. Its greatest contribution is, of course, in the actual publication of bulletins and the so-called simpler circulars. The circulation of these titles is very large: in only a few states is it below 100,000 a year, and in several it exceeds a million. In a majority of states it exceeds half a million annually. Total circulation is in part related to population, but not wholly so. Thus Maine and Mississippi have an annual distribution almost equal; which means that for every bulletin shipped by the latter state, 7 are sent out by the former. The discrepancy here is partly the result of the Negro population in Mississippi.

The average Texas farm and village home requests a pamphlet every 3 weeks. In New York, a request comes from every rural home about 6 times a month.[6] It should be recalled that in more than two-thirds of the states, publications are sent out, with a few small exceptions noted later, only on request, so that the recipient has spent at least one cent for a postal card and the time involved in writing.

The fluctuations in distribution are interesting. In most states, the circulation turned downwards in either 1931 or 1932; and began to increase, often sharply, with 1933 or 1934. Distribution in Kansas, in 1935, for instance, was more than 3 times the 1933 total. In New York and Missouri, 1935 circulation showed a 25 per cent gain over 1934, and in Texas more than 50 per cent. These fluctuations reflect both reduced publishing in the first years of the depression for economy and heightened interest in many subjects later on.

Distribution is in part related to the number of titles issued. These range from 6 to more than 100, with an average of 27 per state. It should be remembered that the range of subjects is equally diverse. They cover every phase of work of the Extension Service, as described in an earlier section of this chapter. Publications on interior decoration, child development, and remedies for hog cholera may go to the same family in the same week.

The question may arise as to whether this demand is stimulated by high-pressure methods of various sorts. All the states announce their publications in the press; and, if facilities are owned or available, over the air. Beyond that, little is done. A few carry a general advertisement on the back cover of the bulletins. Six have display racks of current issues in county agents' offices. Two mail announcements to selected lists, and 2 others enclose announcements in letters.

[6] These comparisons include all circulation of state bulletins with no deduction for out-of-state and urban circulation, which is propably relatively small. The circulation of Federal bulletins is not included.

All states send bulletins without request to one or more agencies or groups, as follows:

To	Smith-Hughes vocational education teachers	28
	Local libraries	25
	Mailing lists of selected farmers	12
	State colleges and normal schools	6
	Local papers	4
	Grange lecturers	3
	Banks, creameries, and chambers of commerce	1 each

The huge distribution is probably sufficient evidence of the value rural people place on this literature. No state has any machinery for testing the reader reactions, or any criterion of readability. Few give any hints to authors; and these few, nothing beyond the suggestion to write for adults of seventh-grade or eighth-grade schooling. Quite a number give careful editorial attention to manuscripts. But nearly all pointed to the continuing and increasing volume of requests as proof that the needs of readers were being met.

The Extension Service is trying, in 8 states, to meet reading needs and deficiencies in library service in other ways. In 2 or 3, the home demonstration agents have organized reading groups which pursue a definite course. In one small New England state, an average of 50 women in each county pursued the work. The State Library Commission co-operated here and elsewhere in lending the books. In Missouri, 1,176 rural clubs had magazine or book exchanges; and to stimulate reading, 309 of these reviewed 742 books at their meetings. The State Library Commission co-operated splendidly in furnishing 65 loan libraries and over 2,500 additional books to these clubs. In Kentucky, the reading course was on "knowing your state through books." Texas put on a series of radio talks on readings, stimulated local community studies of reading resources, and offered suggestions for improving them. It also conducted radio periods on poetry and literature appreciation, as did a few other states.

There are numerous, though scattered, instances of local Home

Bureaus assisting local libraries, or campaigning for county or district library organizations. In one community the Home Bureau raised the fund for library quarters, purchased books and equipment, and paid the librarian for 2 years, until the library was taken over by the township. At least one state has a very popular book hour on the air, during which books are reviewed or read. As an outgrowth of this, there is a library of over 1,000 titles of standard fiction and non-fiction which may be borrowed by paying return postage. Its circulation is approaching 30,000 yearly.

As a result of this work, and of the publication program, Extension Service offices have been receiving in these last years a growing volume of requests for advice about what to read. These, in most cases, are referred to the state specialists concerned; but in one-eighth of the states the burden of this work has grown so heavy that at least part of the time of one person is set aside for what librarians call readers' advisory service.

It is quite evident that neither this device nor the publication program of the colleges of agriculture meet all the needs of the situation indicated earlier; but they do help materially in supplying certain types of reading material; and the contribution made should be taken into account in evaluating the total situation in rural America as to the need for and supply of desired reading material.

But it also seems clear that rural library progress between 1930 and 1936 has not been marked. Libraries have not had the advantage of additional funds, such as have come to the Agricultural Extension Service; nor has there been, in the library field, anything equivalent to the emergency adult education program of the Works Progress Administration, which is discussed later. The libraries are handicapped by the restricting boundary lines of governmental units. Their support, except in the relatively few cases of county or district organizations, has had to rest on small, somewhat weak units of local government. There are few library districts comparable to consolidated school districts. Moreover, the weakness of the library situation has resulted, in part, in other agencies, such as the school and the Agricultural Extension Service, offering some facilities. These are needed, worth while. But it may be questioned if they offer a final solution. Such co-operation as exists is good, but there is often little knowledge on the part of any of these agencies of what the others are doing, or can do. Some opportunities for the expansion of rural library service lie in such co-operation on a planned basis. The meeting of the larger, developing needs of rural people by the libraries must await not only such co-operation, but the overcoming, by legislative or other means, of some of the other handicaps noted. This in itself is an adult education problem of large proportions.

Museums.—Recent years have seen the beginning of a movement by museums to extend adult education into rural areas. No instances of this were found in the communities studied; but it may be worth while, in considering rural adult education, to list a few of the experiments now going on. The Worcester Art Museum circulates exhibits and records, especially through the schools. The Brown University Community Art Caravan circulates art exhibits throughout Rhode Island. Grange halls, schools, vacant stores, and libraries were used to house the exhibit, which stayed an average of 3 days in each of 21 centers. Total attendance averaged about 200 for each center. Exhibits of all sorts travel over New Jersey from the Newark Museum. This is a movement that has hopeful possibilities and can be well related in time to the developing interest in pageants in rural America, especially in pageants dealing with local history. Several communities studied were making plans for centennial celebrations in which pageants seemed likely to play a considerable part.

THE SCHOOLS AND ADULT EDUCATION

One of the marked educational changes noted in the 1930 survey was the more than twofold increase in the number of village schools undertaking work in adult education: 22 as against 9 in 1924. There can be no question that such a step is logical. The school is an omnipresent organization. Its building is unused when adults are free; and it is supported by and belongs pre-eminently to the taxpayers. But adult education is relatively new within the program of rural education, and in the early years of the depression it was one of the first activities to be curtailed or dispensed with. With the development of the various relief activities, however, a far-flung program of adult education, Federally financed through the Emergency Relief Administration, was initiated. It was shared in by some schools that never before had had offerings for adults. In a few, it displaced or succeeded the regular program. In others, the two programs were operated side by side. In more, the Relief Administration made possible the first venture of the educational authorities into adult education. Therefore this section on the schools and adult education has two parts. The data relating to adult education supervised and financed by the local school or county will be considered first. Then will follow a description of the emergency program, its scope, influence, and results.

Between 1930 and 1931, two school systems discontinued adult education because of the financial situation. One of these had had one of the best programs. Several others reduced their offerings. From then on, despite the depression and despite the resources of the emergency adult education program, there was a steady increase in the number of village school systems offering courses to adults. The 1935–36 figure was 34, or one less than a fourth of the 140 communities. This represented almost a fourfold gain over 1924, and a very significant increase over 1930. In 1936–37, 44 schools conducted adult classes.

Adult education in these villages was strongest in the Far West, where 2 out of 5 schools had offerings. Largely, this was because of the excellent record of California, a state which has had a considerable and successful experience with adult education, partly as a result of an active state council of adult education. The other regions all fell slightly below the national average, but none dropped below one-fifth.

Size was also a factor in whether or not a community had adult education. It was found in just over one-third of the towns and large villages; in just under one-fourth of the medium-sized centers; and in only one-sixth of the small villages. Moreover, the number of small villages with adult education remained constant between 1930 and 1936; but there were increases in the other size-groups. Among the regions, the gain in the Middle West lagged behind the others. These data are summarized in Table 68.

TABLE 68

ADULT EDUCATION: NUMBER OF VILLAGE SCHOOL SYSTEMS GIVING COURSES FOR ADULTS AND NUMBER OF COURSES OR SUBJECTS OFFERED, 1931 AND 1935

By Region and Size

Region and Size	*Number Villages*	*Number Villages Giving Courses*		*Courses or Subjects Offered*	
		1931	*1935*	*1931*	*1935*
All villages	140	20	34	55	83
Middle Atlantic	28	2	6	2	6
South	30	3	6	15	16
Middle West	60	10	13	18	23
Far West	22	5	9	20	38
Towns	17	3	6	6	26
Large	20	2	7	7	15
Medium	61	8	14	14	30
Small	42	7	7	7	12

Number and type of courses offered.—An attempt was made to list the number of courses offered to adults by these schools. The data presented above understate the situation. Frequently the school authorities reported not by courses but by major subjects.[7] With this qualification, the data can be examined. In 1931, there was an average of 2.75 subjects, or courses, for each school offering work in adult education. In 1936, the figure was 2.5. Those schools that continued their adult education throughout the intersurvey period had increased the average number of offerings to

[7] For instance, in one community which reported vocational agriculture it was discovered by accident that there were 4 courses in this field.

above 3; the schools newly embarking on this activity averaged about 2.[8] This confirms the theory of educators of adults that a program of this sort starts in a small way and gradually expands.

In the Middle Atlantic villages, there was but one course or subject for each school, usually vocational agriculture. At the other extreme were the Far West villages with an average of over 4. The California influence was again important here. Schools in small villages had fewer offerings than others, but above the 1,000 population mark there was little variation except for the towns. These data are also shown in Table 68.

The poorer record of the small village schools is understandable, but it creates a problem. They have small faculties, and the teachers often have heavier loads. But more than two-thirds of America's villages fall in the category of under 1,000 population. If the public school is to contribute measurably to rural adult education, some means must be found to enable the educational systems of small villages to enter the field. It is now quite clear that the centers of over 1,000 population can, if they wish, enter the adult field, but that 10 per cent of the rural population in and tributary to the place smaller than this will have at best inadequate adult education service from its public school.

More important than the mere number of courses are the subjects offered. Twelve topics were listed by these schools in 1930, 16 in 1935–36. There will be 20 in 1936–37. Vocational offerings comprised three-fifths of the total number in 1931, but were slightly less important in 1935–36. Cultural offerings doubled in number, but comprised less than one-sixth of the offerings. The total list for the 140 villages is given in Table 69 for the 2 years 1931 and 1935.

It is possible that this table indicates a parallelism between the Extension Service and the public schools in the development of adult education. Both clearly began with strictly vocational sub-

[8] The South did not follow this pattern. In one of its schools, the depression sharply reduced the number of offerings. In the other cases, there is reason to believe that understatement, as noted in Footnote 7, entered into the result.

jects. In 1924, practically all the work in the 9 village schools offering courses to adults was of this character. As time went on, need and the demand of the constituency broadened the offerings, just as the previous chapter showed that the extension program had been broadened. But of this more later.

Attendance.—The acid test of adult education, and the one most easily applied, is attendance; for those enrolling are under no compulsion to come to class sessions, and no truant officer asks

TABLE 69

COURSES OR SUBJECTS OFFERED IN ADULT EDUCATION

140 Villages, 1931 and 1935

Course or Subject	*Frequency of Course Given by School System*	
	1931	*1935*
Total	55	83
Agriculture	19	19
Americanization [a]	4	4
Art	2	3
Commercial subjects [b]	5	7
Foreign languages	0	1
Forum	1	5
Home economics [c]	5	10
Literature	1	1
Manual training	4	7
Music	3	7
Parent education	0	1
Physical education	4	9
Public health	1	3
Recreation	3	3
Social science [d]	0	1
Miscellaneous	2	0

[a] Includes citizenship and English to foreigners, illiterates, and semi-illiterates.
[b] Includes typing, stenography, and bookkeeping.
[c] Includes interior decoration, sewing, knitting, cooking, and home beautification.
[d] Includes government, history, psychology, economics, sociology, and law.

embarrassing questions if they drop out. Sixteen of the school systems offering adult education in 1931 were able to report on the enrollment, based on those completing the work. These 16 had 1,323 students, an average of 82.7. The average in the Far West was 120; in the South, 167; but in the Middle West, 40; and in the Middle Atlantic region, only 20. Interestingly enough, the 4 villages that dropped adult education between 1931 and 1935 averaged only 20 persons enrolled. It appears that the schools that gave up their programs during the depression were, therefore, the least successful; and that economic motives were perhaps not the only ones influencing the action. Their programs had not yet won their communities.

In 1935, with 34 schools offering one or more classes to adults, the average enrollment for each school was 81.4, practically the same as that in 1931. The average enrolled in each course was 21. The averages per school for each region maintained the same relative position as in the earlier year, save that the Far West, with 148, outdistanced the South with 104. The Middle West average increased to 64.5; but that for the Middle Atlantic region dropped slightly to 17.3.

It will be noted in the following discussion of the emergency adult education program financed by Federal work-relief funds, that the emergency classes attracted larger enrollments than those in the regular school program.

In large measure, this appears to be due to the type of program offered by the schools, which was predominantly vocational in nature, as has been noted elsewhere. Moreover, a large part of the vocational offerings appealed to farmers rather than to villagers. The emergency program, however, catered to both groups; and the villagers responded. This fact lends point to the subsequent comments on the adult education program offered by the village schools.

A critique of the program.—The preponderance of vocational work in the adult education programs of these schools is due in large part to the number of Smith-Hughes vocational teachers in the village schools, and to their policy, in their professional associations and through the vocational section of the Office of Education at Washington, to promote adult activities. Teachers in other branches have neither the tradition nor the pressure that sends them into adult education; nor do their professional duties bring them as constantly into touch with adults as is the case with the teachers of agriculture whose supervision of their students' farm plots takes them constantly to the students' homes.

This explanation is not necessarily a justification. In few schools was a balanced program of adult education found. In the total group of offerings for the 34 schools having adult education, and the 10 more planning to initiate it in the fall of 1936, vocational subjects far outweigh any others. Moreover, their bulk is out of all proportion either to the normal distribution of adult education offerings in other types of communities or to the distribution of adult interests where recorded and measured by adult education agencies. Indeed, some indication of these interests is found in the course offerings under the emergency program of adult education discussed in the next section of this chapter. Vocational education in these programs was equaled or surpassed by cultural courses and those for adult elementary students.

This unbalance in the adult education offerings of the schools in these village-centered rural communities constitutes a major problem in the proper development of such activities. It limits the appeal to certain selected groups. Because of the major emphasis on agriculture, it favors farmers as against villagers. This deprives it of active village support when budgets are under fire. The home economics work, of course, appeals to persons in both groups; but the interests of adult women extend beyond the scientific conduct of the home. In the day school, the pupils have a reasonably well-balanced educational ration. In the night school in a number of these villages, they must take vocational subjects or nothing. In the communities studied, moreover, the vocational offerings are not yet as much socialized as in the Agricultural Extension program described in the previous chapter. Here and there, as in the professional literature of the field, there are indications that the same trend is beginning. But it has not progressed as far; and there is some doubt whether under the provisions of the Smith-Hughes law it can.

This is not to say that the vocational offerings in these schools should necessarily be reduced. The records show that they have a constituency. The argument does raise the question, however, as to the necessity for a better-balanced program in adult education in these communities. And it should be added that not everywhere in these communities had an understanding been reached as to the relative responsibility of the Smith-Hughes vocational teachers in the schools and the county agents of the Extension Service of the state colleges. In some places, the two were splendidly co-operative and complementary; in some they operated independently of each other; in a few, there was indefensible overlapping and conflict.

Some sample programs.—These data summarizing the total situation can be illumined by certain specific illustrations of adult education programs under the public schools.

In a California town, the development of the offerings is clear from a comparison of courses and enrollments, 1931–32 and 1935–36:

1931–32		*1935–36*	
Course	*Enrollment*	*Course*	*Enrollment*
Music	45	.....	135
Commercial educ.	15	.....	25
Wood working	15	.....	15
Art	35	.....	20
Dramatics	30	.....	35
Total	140	Spanish	18
		World problems	29
		First aid	40
		Physical educ.	125
		Total	442

In this community, the people are enthusiastic, and members of all occupations and social groups are included in the enrollment.

A large village in the Middle West listed the following classes with enrollments of from 8 to 45, and a total of 246: cooking, sewing, home-nursing, commercial education, art, practical electricity, auto mechanics, social dancing, dramatics, and Americanization. More classes were requested in this community; but the teaching staff could not undertake more.

Another list from a Middle Western village included Spanish, typewriting, drama, story-writing, interior decoration, tap dancing, orchestral music, and current events. In another case, the program began in 1934–35 with a course in shopwork and another in homemaking. These were continued, and offerings in agriculture, music, dramatics, and flower gardening were added. The program met with an unexpectedly enthusiastic response, and could be enlarged if the staff were able to carry an additional burden.

A rather typical expansion in vocational courses for adults follows: In 1931–32, there was a class of 42 in agriculture and of 18 in food nutrition. In 1935–36, these two classes attracted 38 and 33 respectively; and a course in farm management with 38, and one in clothing with 19, had been added. Agricultural Extension agents and others frequently credited improved agricultural practices to the agricultural work of the school, both for high-school youth and adults. In 4 or 5 places, the vocational agriculture teacher not only conducted adult classes in the village school but also, to save the farmers' gas, went out to from one to 4 neighborhoods. In all such cases the work was welcomed and well attended.

Some schools, especially in smaller villages, had been quite ingenious in utilizing other agencies to assist in their adult education activities. One enlisted a near-by municipal university to staff courses in world problems and public speaking; called upon the Red Cross for offerings in home-nursing and first aid; and used its own staff for the vocational subjects.

In another village of just over 1,000 population, through the help of the joint extension department of the state college, well-attended courses were started in sociology, psychology, education, and economics. These carried college credit if students desired to have it. The enrollments ranged from 12 to 15.

Granting that the present improvement in the finances of these school districts continues or stabilizes, the future will see, in all likelihood, a considerable expansion in their adult education offerings. Forty-four schools, 10 more than in 1935–36, had arranged for courses in the school year 1936–37. In a few additional cases, plans were under way for 1937–38. In all, these schools had decided on a minimum of 93 courses or subjects, though some hoped to be able to finance more. Again it should be emphasized that, for reasons already explained, this is a decided understatement of the actual number of courses. As in the present offerings, vocational subjects loomed large in the list. As Table 70 shows, the greatest expansion will take place in the Far West, especially on the Pacific coast. It is influenced here, of course, by the experience of California, which has probably one of the best state programs

TABLE 70

PLANS FOR ADULT EDUCATION: PER CENT [a] OF SCHOOLS PLANNING TO INITIATE OFFERINGS IN ADULT EDUCATION 1936–37

By Region and Size

Region	*No. Villages*	*Planning*		*Size*	*No. Villages*	*Planning*	
		NO.	%			NO.	%
All regions	140	44	31.4	All villages	140	44	31.4
Middle Atlantic	28	10	35.7	Towns	17	7	41.2
South	30	8	26.6	Large	20	6	30.0
Middle West	60	16	26.6	Medium	61	20	32.8
Far West	22	10	45.4	Small	42	11	26.2

[a] All percentages, except totals, based on less than 100.

in the United States and one that has been operating for about a decade with increasing success. In this state, aid is given school districts with an adult education program on a per pupil basis just as with the day schools.[9]

School authorities in several other villages expressed the hope that finances would permit adult education to begin soon. None were counted in the above table, however, unless courses had been definitely approved and announced to begin in September, 1936.

The problem of instruction.—The development recorded raises

[9] For a typical program in a California village, see Landis and Willard, *Rural Adult Education,* Chapter IV, or Kolb and Brunner, *A Study of Rural Society,* pp. 446-47.

some interesting questions in regard to the future training of village high-school teachers, since the most serious criticism of the existing work was the failure of the instructors to adjust adequately to the requirements of teaching adults as contrasted with youth. This is serious, because the rural high school cannot afford to employ full-time adult teachers. The work will be successful, then, only as persons with a flair for adult education, or with training for it, are employed. It will suffer when such persons leave a community, if they are not succeeded by those of similar capacities. This consideration applies also to many city school systems that offer courses to adults. It would appear that if the public schools are going seriously to enter the adult education field, which many feel is their obligation and their opportunity, teacher-training institutions will have to begin offering at least a single introductory course in this subject. Failing this, a program of in-service training must be devised, such as operates, for instance, in Delaware under the State Board of Education.

The experience of the schools in these village-centered rural communities that do offer adult education leads to one other observation. A serious effort in this field, operating on a reasonably permanent basis, would seem to call for at least one additional person on the teaching staff, so that those able to teach adults could be relieved of one day-school class in order to assume night-school work.

The criticisms implied in portions of the two previous paragraphs apply with particular force to the emergency adult education program to which the discussion now proceeds.

THE EMERGENCY ADULT EDUCATION PROGRAM

In view of these trends in the adult education program of the school systems in these 140 communities, special interest attaches to the adult education activities and influence of the Works Progress Administration in this field under the so-called emergency program. In summary, it may be said that a surprisingly large number of the communities studied availed themselves of this service. There was a high turnover of both communities and teachers, a very uneven success; but where successful, there was a gratifying response from the community for a program invariably broader in scope than that usually offered by the public schools.

All told, 76 communities, or 54.3 per cent, participated in this work; not all of them in each year it was conducted. The South and the Far West made the most use of the facilities offered by this agency, about three-fourths of the communities in these regions participating. In the Middle West, less than one-half used it; in the Middle Atlantic states, about 2 in 5. The size of the community was also influential. Only one-third of the small villages, three-fifths of the medium, two-thirds of the large villages, and three-fourths of the towns had emergency adult education programs.

These are the total figures for the years 1934–35 and 1935–36. But while 76 villages shared in the program, only 24 operated in both of these years. In the former year, 57 villages and, in the latter, 43 villages used the opportunity offered through Federally aided adult education. In other words, after a year's trial, 33 communities, or well over one-half, dropped the work, while only 19 attempted it for the first time in 1935–36. The reasons for this are doubtless to be found in the criticisms of the Federal program given later in this section. There may be some relation between this decline in the emergency program and the gain in the regular program already noted. The number of courses offered did not decline as rapidly as the number of schools. There were 170 in 1934–35, and 152 in 1935–36. In other words, where the program was reasonably successful, as in the 24 places continuing it, offerings were expanded if personnel was available. Thus, despite the smaller number of schools in 1935–36, the average number of courses per school increased from 3 to 3.5. This was the trend in all regions except the Middle West, which region with the Far West registered the largest losses, while the Middle Atlantic region gained. These data are summarized in Table 71.

Courses offered by emergency program.—The courses offered under the Federal emergency program cover very much the same general subjects as those appearing in the adult curricula of the schools that had their own programs, but the emphasis was different. Proportionally only about one-half as many were vocational, doubtless in part because this phase of the work is better cared for in the regular program. Adult elementary courses for illiterates, or near illiterates, bulked about as important as the vocational offerings. Cultural subjects such as art, music, and drama equaled the vocational in 1934–35, but declined by one

TABLE 71

ADULT EDUCATION UNDER EMERGENCY SPONSORSHIP

Number Village School Systems Giving Courses for Adults through Emergency Adult Education Program and Number Such Courses, 1934–35 and 1935–36, by Region and Size

Region and Size	*No. of Villages*	*No. Villages Giving Courses 1934–35*	*No. of Courses*	*Av. No. Courses per Village*	*No. Villages Giving Courses 1935–36*	*No. of Courses*	*Av. No. Courses per Village*
All regions	140	57	170	3.0	43	152	3.5
Middle Atlantic	28	4	9	2.3	7	33	4.7
South	30	17	67	3.9	18	77	4.3
Middle West	60	21	53	2.5	11	20	1.8
Far West	22	15	41	2.7	7	22	3.1
Towns	17	12	39	3.2	9	28	3.1
Large villages	20	8	19	2.4	8	26	3.5
Medium	61	25	78	3.1	19	76	4.0
Small	42	12	34	2.8	7	22	3.1

third in the following year to about the proportion given in the regular program. Forums, though all 5 of those operated by school systems had been successful and were scheduled for continuance, dropped from 9 to none in the emergency set-up, though 2 of these were taken over by other agencies in the community. On the other hand, social science proved increasingly popular, the number of offerings more than doubling in the second year, at which time this field had more than 11 per cent of all offerings. Its popularity may carry a suggestion for those in charge of the regular school programs of adult education in the villages. The details here summarized are set forth in Table 72.

Numerical measures.—The enrollment and attendance figures of the emergency program contain much of interest. The villages that gave offerings in 1934–35 but not in the following year operated an average of 3.5 courses each with an enrollment of 41.3 persons per village, or 11.8 for each course. Regional variations were slight. In contrast, those villages that had emergency

TABLE 72

FREQUENCY OF COURSES UNDER EMERGENCY ADULT EDUCATION PROGRAM, 1934–35 AND 1935–36

Type of Course	*Frequency*	
	1934–35	*1935–36*
Total	170	152
Agriculture	6	7
Americanization	14	14
Art	11	6
Commercial education	14	11
Dramatics	10	4
Elementary subjects	32	23
Foreign languages	1	4
Forums	9	0
Home economics	18	20
Literature	5	8
Manual training	2	5
Mathematics	0	5
Music	14	9
Parent education	3	3
Physical education	4	1
Public health	6	5
Recreation	5	3
Science	2	0
Social science	7	17
Workers' education	2	4
Miscellaneous	5	3

adult education classes in 1934–35 and continued them in 1935–36, averaged 94.6 persons each in the first of these years and 138.3 in the second. The places that initiated this program for the first time in the latter year enrolled an average total of 101.5 each. Obviously, the villages that continued their program through both years or began it in 1935–36 were more successful in appealing to their constituencies than those that availed themselves of the facilities of the emergency program only in 1934–35.

The regional variations in the enrollment figures are significant; they show again the large place filled in the South by the emergency program, as well as its relatively unsuccessful appeal in the Middle West. The South was, however, lower in average attendance. These facts are set forth in Table 73. This table also shows that while villages that discontinued the program had not been able to attract large enrollments, they had succeeded in holding the interest of those who came.

Where the emergency program succeeded.—To the authors, these figures indicate that the potential future of adult education in village-centered rural communities is large. When the handicaps mentioned elsewhere in this section are considered, the enrollment and attendance figures indicate a real interest. It remains for the schools to capitalize this, which it would seem they can do if they offer a broad program rather than one overweighted on the vocational side and if the program they offer will appeal to both villagers and farmers rather than to either group alone.

The evaluation of the emergency program is important, but very difficult. In some places it was highly successful, especially in the South. In one community, for instance, 4 courses in "general culture," including literature, public affairs, art and music appreciation, had an enrollment of 143 and an average attendance of 100 for the entire academic year of 1935–36. In another large Southern village, the record for the year was:

Course	*Enrollment*	*Av. Att.*	*Per Cent Att. of Enrollment*
Agriculture	188	150	80.0
Home economics	89	75	84.2
Public affairs	37	32	86.4
Literature	118	96	81.4

The average attendance figures rivaled those of the high school in this community.

TABLE 73

AVERAGE ENROLLMENT AND AVERAGE ATTENDANCE PER SCHOOL FOR THOSE VILLAGES WITH EMERGENCY ADULT EDUCATION PROGRAMS

Region	*Offering Program in 1934–35, not in 1935–36*		*Offering Program in 1934–35 and 1935–36*				*Offering Program 1935–36 only*	
			AV. ENROL.		AV. ATT. %			
	AV. ENROL.	AV. ATT. %	*1934–35*	*1935–36*	*1934–35*	*1935–36*	AV. ENROL.	AV. ATT. %
All regions	41.3	.76	94.6	138.3	.68	.62	101.5	.77
Middle Atlantic	48	.70	48	58	.70	.87	58	.87
South	24	.63	141	210	.62	.60	186	.79
Middle West	41	.79	104	81	.77	.58	47	.51
Far West	41	.79	48	59	.68	.63	...	...

In one of the Far Western states, the adult education work was done by correspondence because of the low density of population. In the 2 villages studied in this state, courses were being taken in arithmetic, auto mechanics, business law, consumer education, Diesel engines, English, forestry, journalism, photography, psychology, typewriting, and blueprint reading. Papers were sent to the state department of education to be graded, criticized, and returned. Participants seemed to be getting a good deal out of the experience.

The Negro program was much more generally successful, where it existed, than was that for whites, especially where it taught the three R's, which came under the program for illiterates. Average attendance was higher in these classes than among the whites. The Negro work was generally approved by the whites except in one village where there were workers' education classes for Negroes working in a small textile mill.

The best illustration of the success of the emergency adult education program in these centers comes from a Middle Western village where, until spring planting interfered, 1,500 persons were enrolled in 24 classes, including government, grammar, elementary and advanced typewriting, bookkeeping, play-production, art, business training, parliamentary law, orchestral music, Spanish, German, chemistry, mechanical drawing, commercial arithmetic, manual training, shorthand, home economics, agriculture, choral singing, and Bible.

The discussion of the emergency program thus far has been in relation to offerings in the school buildings in the village center. These offerings were, of course, open to farmers as well as villagers; and in many communities, especially in the Far West, some of the open-country population attended. But open-country schools also shared in these activities to some extent. No complete statement can be made, however, as the expense of visiting every open-country school was prohibitive. Most of the data on these institutions were secured from county superintendents who did not always know the details. It is conservatively estimated, however, that about 10 per cent of the open-country schools shared in the emergency adult education program. The preponderance of this work was in the South, where it majored on courses designed for illiterates and near illiterates, both white and Negro. In the main, it was reported to be successful, as it was in a few isolated Middle West communities where Smith-Hughes vocational teachers of agriculture had been doing extension work and took it upon themselves to organize classes, especially in modern social problems, speech, music, English literature, and sociology. These were all centered in neighborhoods, and held an average attendance of from 22 to 80 over a 2-year period. Teachers for the most part were unemployed college-trained persons. Apparently such open-country work as existed was more successful as a rule than in the villages. The small volume of it was accounted for by the inability to find teachers.

Reasons for large proportion of failures.—Unfortunately there is another side to the question. In 33 of the communities that shared in this enterprise in 1934–35, it was discontinued in 1935–36, because, as nine of the school superintendents in these places phrased it, they and the school boards were "completely disgusted." Others who were less emotional and more analytical gave, with surprising unanimity from all sections of the country, quite a list of criticisms, among them these:

The quality of the teaching was poor. This was charged in 18 cases. Even in 22 places where the teachers were adjudged fair, and in the 31 where they were well prepared in their subjects, it was frequently stated that they were too young or too inexperienced to instruct adults and that they were inferior to the regular public-school staff. In only 26 of the 76 communities was the quality of instruction adjudged "good" by the educational authorities. Especially where there was, or had been, good adult education in the schools or other agencies, as frequently in California, the emergency work suffered by comparison. Indeed the most frequent comment where the teaching was classified as "good" was, "work commendable considering lack of preparation and background."

The turnover of teachers was high. As times improved, the better qualified teachers went back to regular jobs. Despite some efforts at training teachers in adult education techniques, the quality of teaching was thus progressively lowered.

The program was handicapped by red tape, constant changing of regulations, and lack of proper supervision. The worst illustration of this comes from the community used for the last illustration above. The school superintendent alleges that the work here was discontinued because, despite repeated promises, not a cent was paid either for materials or for the instructors. Interest among the people was keen, instruction was good, the program was adjudged one of the very best in the state. The program was killed, according to the local people, by administrative bungling.

The relief, rather than the educational, features were emphasized. This hurt morale and made it difficult and in some cases impossible to secure good teachers who were unemployed but could not yet qualify for relief. Indeed a number of communities that desired classes were unable to have them for this reason.

The choice of subjects offered was not always determined on the basis of the needs and interests of the constituency, but on the basis of the interests and skills of relief teachers.

Less frequently, other causes for the failure or mediocre success of the work were mentioned. In some places, the people looked on the program as "made work," organized "to give a few people jobs." Also they objected to the time required and the heavy assignments. Occasionally, too, there were problems everywhere common to adult education which teachers were not competent to handle, such as the attempt to merge in one group social classes between which a strong sense of social distance existed, or the tendency of a few vocal people to monopolize the discussion.

W.P.A. officials concerned with these programs agreed with many of these criticisms, but added in 8 cases that the "lethargic" or "non-co-operative" attitudes of the school officials or boards explained the lack of success. This was admitted by some of the school superintendents, who averred that the program competed with the regular school offerings, especially among upper-class students and potential postgraduates. They argued for the inclusion on a Federal-aid basis of one more teacher on each high-school staff to free enough teaching time to enable the school itself to put on a continuing adult education program. This suggestion ignored of course the necessities for relief.

Even where the program was fairly well done, its values were sometimes not turned to account locally. The county directors appeared to have little freedom of action. The program was something handed down from above. There was no effort to let the local people share in the planning. It was something to be passively accepted and used until withdrawn.

Probably the basic determinant of success or failure was the quality of the leadership and teaching; for it did succeed in some places. Moreover, there were by-products that may in the long run add more or less to the credit side of some final evaluation.

But the importance of the quality of leadership underscores again the necessity for any permanent program to look well to the training and quality of its leadership. The broad social forces implementing this new interest in adult education in rural America call for leaders and teachers who can relate the content of their courses to the on-going tides of these forces. The too-long continuance of opportunism in training public-school educators of adults, and in building programs of adult education, spells only loss to the movement and to the community, whether rural or urban.

The subject of the emergency program must not be left without a word as to the Federal Theatre and the Federal Art projects. In some of the Southern states especially, drama groups and art exhibits have gone on the road and have aroused considerable interest and support. Rural people have visited them in numbers, and have enrolled in classes in painting, weaving, and modeling as well. Here is a new factor in rural adult education, accepted willingly while it lasts, but showing the eagerness of rural people to share in cultural goods too long the property of only the larger urban centers. The experience here has been of the same sort as that given the cultural program of the Agricultural Extension Service. It raises questions of importance for the planners of the rural adult education of the future to consider, because it reveals so much of the unexpected desires and interest which rural people have.

One other Works Progress Administration contribution to rural adult education should be noted. Rural schools have long been deficient in the teaching of music. Works Progress Administration teachers went into thousands of such schools; and in many cases their service was expanded to include organization of "social music activities" on a community basis.

Community judgments.—Surveyors attempted to discover in their various interviews what community attitudes were toward adult education itself. In a majority of the communities, there was probably no change; and in the great bulk of these the current attitude was one of indifference, due largely either to lack of information or lack of a sense of need. This was especially true in the village centers and as related to possible contributions of the public school. Farmers were quite generally in favor of the adult education activities of the agricultural college Extension Service, though they seldom had considered them as affording adult education. That term they applied almost exclusively to school programs.

On the other hand, in 25 communities there was a good bit of evidence from the spoken reactions of the people that attitudes toward adult education had become more favorable in the intersurvey period, especially since the emergency programs had got under way. In only 11 places was the attitude less favorable or adverse. There was a clear-cut relationship between the amount of preparation and the quality of the work of the teachers in their subject-matter fields, and the reactions of the community, as Table 74 shows.

Nor was this confined to expressions of opinion, significant as these were when voiced along with the criticisms detailed above. As more than one person put it, "This emergency adult education was poorly done, but it was enough to show me what could be done and how valuable it would be."

TABLE 74

INFLUENCE OF PREPARATION OF TEACHERS AND QUALITY OF THEIR INSTRUCTION UPON THE SENSE OF RESPONSIBILITY FOR ADULT EDUCATION IN THE SCHOOL SYSTEMS OF 76 VILLAGES REPORTING

140 Selected American Agricultural Villages, 1935

Preparation of Teachers in Relation to Quality of Instruction	*Has the Emergency Adult Education Program Dulled or Quickened a Sense of Responsibility for AE in the School System*			
	QUICKENED	DULLED	NO CHANGE	NO ANSWER
Well prepared—good	6	1	9	2
Well prepared—average or fair	2	...	5	1
Well prepared—poor	...	...	...	1
Well prepared—no answer	...	...	3	...
Average—good	4	...	4	...
Average—average	6	1	1	1
Average—poor	1	2	2	...
Average—no answer	...	...	...	...
Poor—good	...	...	...	...
Poor—fair	2	2	4	...
Poor—poor	2	5	1	...
Poor—no answer	2	...	...	...
No answer—good	...	...	...	...
No answer—average	...	...	1	...
No answer—poor	...	...	1	...
No answer—no answer	...	1	...	2

In some places the school system has already taken over the work on a local-support basis. One town in the Middle West had 10 emergency classes in 1934–35 with an enrollment of 1,035, and an average attendance of 796. These were changed into 5 emergency classes and 4 conducted by the local school in 1935–36. In 1936–37, all the offerings will be under the auspices of the local school district and all Federal aid will be discontinued.

In 10 other widely scattered centers, plans had been made to initiate adult education on a permanent basis when the emergency program ended. Their distribution is shown in Table 75. This is in addition to the 10 villages that were added to the 34 already having adult education as part of the regular school program when the school year 1936–37 opened. If these plans all carry through, 55 of the 140 school systems will have adult education. In almost all of the communities planning to take over the emergency program in whole or in part, the school authorities said their plans had been undertaken because of requests for the service received from the community after the emergency program had got under way. Moreover, it was the broader than average program that was demanded in such places.

TABLE 75

IN THOSE COMMUNITIES HAVING AN EMERGENCY ADULT EDUCATION PROGRAM WILL THE SCHOOL SYSTEM MAKE AN EFFORT TO CONTINUE ADULT EDUCATION WHEN, AS, AND IF FEDERAL AID IS STOPPED

140 Selected American Agricultural Villages, 1935: by Region and Size of Village

Region and Size	*Yes*	*No*	*No Answer*
Middle Atlantic	1	9	1
South	3	13	7
Middle West	4	16	7
Far West	3	8	4
Town	5	5	3
Large	4	7	2
Medium	2	27	7
Small	0	7	7

NON-SCHOOL ADULT EDUCATION AGENCIES

The discussion has thus far dealt with adult education agencies wholly or partly tax supported. There are, however, in any community of more than several hundred population, many organizations with programs that are educational to some degree. These village-centered rural communities were no exception. As Chapter X shows, practically all of them had agencies interested in the socio-economic phases of life to the number, including Granges, of about 200. A regular feature of the program of each of these agencies, most of which met weekly, was a lecture. There were also numerous special-interest groups organized around some specific activity, such as art, music, or drama. Some of these were wholly educational, like the Parent-Teacher Associations, some of which were responsible for lecture courses, others for winter lyceums, and many for study clubs. Practically all the churches of 100 members or more, and a number of those that were smaller than this, had some adult education, though usually this was confined to religious instruction. Many of these agencies were constituent members of state or national bodies with salaried staffs from whose offices issued a steady stream of program suggestions, and from which speakers could often be obtained. The total amount of educational activity in these communities from the sources just listed was and is large. Excluding the Extension Service activities and those of schools and churches, it is probable that there were about 3 gatherings a week per community which had some educational features for adults.

An evaluation of the quality and influence of these activities is another problem, and within the limits of this study it is insolvable, at least in precise terms. It is the purpose of this section merely to set down some illustrations quite representative of the better programs found, and all definitely superior to the usual run of activities described in the paragraph above.

In a large Middle West village, after an attempt by a local "patriotic" organization to prevent a meeting of which it did not approve, a strong group of business and professional people organized a University Extension Forum dedicated to the "full and free discussion of political and economic subjects." The extension division of the state university co-operated with suggestions and in sending speakers when requested. The school auditorium was used. Because of the quality of the program and the standing of its sponsors, this enterprise has been quite successful since its inception in the winter of 1933–34.

The forum idea has spread, slowly however, in these communities. In 2, forums initiated in one case by the emergency adult education program and in another by a strong church have been taken over by community organizations, one of them a committee representing the leading social groups of the village. In another instance, the school had to drop its adult education work because of financial difficulties. A community church took the work over, and utilized its fine parish house for the dramatic and musical activities as well as for a popular forum. This church also housed the library.

All told, there were 10 community-wide forums in these villages sponsored by private agencies, twice as many as by the schools. Two of these were by community organizations, 2 by Roman Catholic churches, 6 by Protestant churches, 15 all told. Perhaps the most successful was conducted by the churches of a Far West medium-sized village where an average of 400 persons attended a series of monthly meetings devoted in 1935–36 to international affairs, economic problems, and race relations. Speakers and discussion leaders were secured from the universities of the state. This total of 15 forums for these 140 communities includes only those that were community-wide in their appeal. No account is taken of the use of the forum procedure by specific organizations such as farm groups or women's clubs.

Of one village of less than 1,500 population, the fieldworker wrote, "The Chamber of Commerce and Lion's Clubs have really excellent programs on local, state, national, and international topics." They co-operate closely with the school, which contributes to the expense of the high-grade speakers who address the high-school student-body as well as the businessmen. Often the business groups open these meetings to the community at large, or have a joint affair with the Women's Club, which in this place has a $5,000 clubhouse and a full complement of "departmental" work.

Co-operation between women's clubs and men's luncheon clubs was found in several other places, and in such cases the high quality of the program was always a matter of comment. One such combination drew one-third of its lecturers from a university about 50 miles away.

In another village of less than 1,000 population in the Middle West, the adult education program was started by a group of unmarried youth, all graduates of the local high school. The professor of sociology from a neighboring university was brought in for an 8 weeks' lecture course on "The Family." This was followed by a course in home-nursing.

One interesting enterprise is reported from the South, which has also cemented village and country relations. The state has an extensive drama movement under the extension sociologist of the state agricultural college. There are a number of rural drama groups in the county, and these perform in turn at the local moving-picture theater. The manager of the theater has promoted the idea. Several groups of various kinds have been formed in the village, and community affairs of educational or good-grade recreational content now are booked once a week at the theater. All told there were 10 theater guilds in these villages, not counting the drama groups under Agricultural Extension.

The effort of a school principal to broaden the interest of his staff resulted in another interesting effort, a book club in which each member bought some quite recent book of his or her own choice for review. The club soon aroused interest in the community and its meetings had to be transferred to the school building.

Some churches went beyond the traditional program already alluded to. A few have lecture courses, some are doing quite a lot with music, and one Negro church had an extensive and successful program devoted to the study of Negro history and culture. In the main, the adult education of the churches, while of better quality, was sharply less in quantity than in 1930. The depression, or other causes, had evidently ended some of the efforts described in the previous report.

One interesting new development was the educational work being undertaken by some of the co-operatives, especially consumer organizations. Still embryonic, it is nonetheless the first indication in this series of studies that the co-operatives in these villages were learning what comparable agencies learned long ago in Europe: that education is the only safe cornerstone of continuing and successful economic co-operation. This may be one phase in which rural adult education will see a considerable expansion in the next decade.

Summary.—The outstanding impression of this review is that the adult education movement in rural America grew and flourished during the inter-survey years and despite the depression. The Agricultural Extension Service has been enlarged, and its program expanded. The library movement has made less progress, but has somewhat better than held its own. Adult education is winning its way in the public schools, and an expansion seems to be indicated. The emergency program set back adult education in some communities, but appears to have helped it in more. Programs of non-school agencies aroused more favorable comment from fieldworkers than ever before. There was constant reference in their reports, and in comments of professional men and women in these communities, to the wider interests and broadened attitudes brought by these last years.

In terms of the local community, the picture is somewhat blurred. Here it is that the agencies mentioned function. Clearly, so far as the chief tax-supported agencies are concerned, the Agricultural Extension Service and the schools, the emphasis is overwhelmingly vocational; and just as clearly this is not the sum and essence of adult education. The former of these agencies is socializing its work to an encouraging degree. The latter, as yet, if this sample of communities is an index, is moving only sporadically and hesitatingly in this direction. Moreover, there are other state or county tax-supported agencies, such as boards of health or county health units, whose objectives involve adult education to some degree and an approach to the local community as well. The non-tax-supported agencies, more often than not, represent some one leader's interests rather than the needs of the community; or they are dependent to a greater or less degree upon the suggestion of national or state federated agencies for their programs. In some of the communities, even where adult education activities are going on, there is no real concept of adult education. In some of them, progress is made on a hit-or-miss basis, motivation is by hope rather than by knowledge and ideas.

Obviously, the weakest spot in rural adult education is the village. The Agricultural Extension Service is making a considerable and growing contribution to at least the larger half of the farm homes of the nation. But it is doing little if anything in the village and town centers so closely related to its original constituency. Even the work of the village schools has thus far, because of its emphasis on vocational agriculture, been somewhat farm-centered. This is unfortunate. Moreover, excellent as the work of these two agencies is, and broadening as their programs seem to be, they are still one-sided as judged by the total scope of adult education in cities.

In the field of adult education, rural America possesses, at least in terms of budget and personnel, a closer approximation to the aggregate of urban resources than in almost any other of our accustomed social utilities. But the over-emphasis on a few aspects of the total field, and conversely the under-emphasis on many other essential features largely chargeable to the laws under which the work is carried on, bid fair to introduce into this field also an otherwise avoidable inequality of opportunity. If adult education is the social necessity it has frequently been proclaimed in these recent years, if it is a promising tool for conserving democracy in a tumultuous and rapidly changing world, it is doubly unfortunate to permit this inequality to persist. Clearly the broader and more socialized programs of the Extension Service must be rapidly expanded. Clearly, too, this service with its trained personnel should be placed at the disposal of villages, at least to the extent that the villages are not already meeting their needs through the schools.

The direction a more adequate school program might well take has been indicated. It is probably worth while to indicate also that well-rounded adult education programs by the school will fit directly and usefully into the present interest of education in school and community relationships.

Implicit in the foregoing interpretation of the data presented is the fact that no agency concerned with adult education is looking at either the total field or the total community; yet indisputably the adequate use of the total resources available would go far toward the construction of a reasonably adequate and acceptable program.

This raises two questions. Is there adequate co-operation among the agencies engaged in rural adult education? Would a consultative and planning body organized as a state council of adult education help strengthen the whole movement?

In terms of the local community, the first question is soon answered. In only a very few of these communities was there anything approaching a thoroughgoing co-operative approach to the adult education field, though it should be recalled that, far more than in 1930 or 1924, there were co-operative arrangements between pairs of agencies. Some of these have been described.

Even among the tax-supported agencies, co-operation was none too frequent, despite the mutual interest of all such agencies, especially those on a state basis, in the same constituency. The question was therefore put to the directors of Agricultural Extension, in the questionnaire mentioned in the first section of this chapter, as to the extent of their co-operation with other state agencies. Of the 40 directors replying, nearly one-half (18), did not answer this question; of the other 22, 20 reported some co-operation with one or more agency. Six of these stated that there was co-operation on one or more specific projects with all state-tax-supported agencies. One reported only incidental co-operation.

The other 15 said there was co-operation, usually only as needs arose, with:

Boards of health in	10 cases
State library commissions	7 "
Board of education	6 "
Smith-Hughes vocational supervisors	2 "

In one state, all executives or directors of state agencies held monthly meetings for the consideration of mutual problems, to exchange information, and to plan the best possible approach to the state for each agency. In one other state, where there was reasonably continuous and effective co-operation, the Extension Service and the vocational department of the board of education co-operated very closely, even freely exchanging or lending personnel and delimiting functions and spheres of influence in local communities, to achieve the greatest possible results with a maximum of efficiency and a minimum of expense. With these two exceptions, co-operation was less thoroughgoing; and usually it was on a project-by-project basis.

On the question as to whether or not a state council of adult education would help the situation, 26 of the 40 directors of Agricultural Extension replied, 4 with an unqualified negative. Three other negative responses were qualified; one saying the field was too large for overlapping and therefore no council was needed, another that the field was too well defined. A third remarked that he was personally in favor, but such a move would not be permitted by the Federal Department of Agriculture, a statement that may be questioned. The other 19 were in favor of a state council of adult education, 2 qualifying by limiting the enterprise to a consultative basis only. Generalizing from the letters, it is fair to say that with one exception the greatest need for some such agency was felt by the more rural states.

In view of the data presented, primarily from the questionnaire but also from the field surveys, it seems to the authors that the progress of rural adult education, especially among the non-farm village population, will be haphazard, marked by numerous avoidable failures and its tempo slower than need be, unless by some device in both states and communities the problem can be somewhere viewed as a whole and programs and procedures worked out on that basis. Otherwise rural adult education will depend upon the breadth of vision of agencies traditionally vocational, upon age-groups and sex-groups with objectives in part at least institutional, and upon the often ephemeral development of special-interest groups. But it has depended upon just these assets throughout its history; and the record set down in these two chapters shows that despite the depression, substantial progress has been made since 1930.

This progress, however, has been in terms of the accepted measures of progress, and in terms of the obviously improved character of the programs of the volunteer or private agencies. In terms of the larger problems alluded to at the opening of the preceding chapter, there has been little progress; nor does there seem to be as firm a foundation for such progress as is apparent in the Agricultural Extension Service. The impending expansion of vocational education by means of the George-Deen Act may help build that foundation, especially if that work is broadly conceived. Advantageous, too, would be a broadening of the basis of the Agricultural Extension Service so that in co-operation with the schools and other agencies the facilities of its cultural and socio-economic programs could be put at the disposal of the village population.

X

Social Organizations[1]

SCHOOLS and churches are the dominant social institutions of the rural community. They do not, however, satisfy all the needs and desires of rural people for social life and association. Many and various other organizations have therefore grown up. These will be considered in this chapter.

Social organizations, and indeed recreational and social life, have experienced changes in these communities since 1930. Some of the changes confirmed trends discovered at the end of the first inter-survey period. They were due to the ordinary processes of community life. Other changes were induced by the depression, and some were caused by the emergence of new habits, or perhaps fads, in the use of leisure time. Organizations of different kinds fared differently during the period under survey. Some became stronger, some declined. Some that are of new types came into existence. Their inclusion in the tables of this chapter made it necessary to reclassify all social organizations existent in 1930 in order to present comparable data. Therefore the 1930 figures of this chapter are in slight disagreement with those given in *Rural Social Trends,* in which the results of the previous study of the 140 villages appear. This classification follows:

Athletic: Baseball, basketball, tennis, golf, fishing, clubs, and the like.

Bridge.

Civic: Organizations designed for the good of the community, as W.C.T.U., charitable and welfare agencies, or fire departments, when social organizations.

Educational: Parent-Teacher Associations, literary and study groups.

Fraternal: All lodges or secret orders of the fraternal type.

Musical: Bands, orchestras, glee clubs, choral societies.

[1] Edmund deS. Brunner, Jr., is co-author of this chapter.

Patriotic: American Legion and its auxiliary, G.A.R., Sons of Veterans, D.A.R., W.R.C.

Political.

Social: Community social clubs, card clubs other than bridge, and all other organizations chiefly sociable in purpose, regardless of other but more minor functions.

Socio-economic: All businessmen's organizations and service or luncheon clubs.

Socio-religious: Ministerial associations, social organizations under religious but not local parish auspices, the Young Men's Christian Association, Knights of Columbus and its women's organizations.

Youth-serving: Hi-Y and Pioneers, Boy and Girl Scouts, Camp Fire Girls, and any others for children and young people except junior lodges and 4-H Clubs.

4-H.

Farm Bureau (including Home Bureau).

Grange.

Townsend and Social Justice Clubs.

It will be seen from this that, as previously, the subsidiary organizations of schools and churches are not here considered. They are noted in the chapters on these institutions.

Moreover, the analysis of the social organizations has been carried further than in previous studies. As formerly, the data on all organizations are presented. But, in addition, there are analyses of the trends shown in those agencies which have functioned throughout the entire period of 1924 to 1936 and which in each type are therefore the most stable.

High turnover among organizations and its causes.—The outstanding characteristic of rural social organizations between 1930 and 1936, as between 1924 and 1930, was their heavy turnover. Nearly one-third of all the organizations existing in 1930 had become inactive or had died away completely by 1936. Barely two-fifths of those found in 1924 were still functioning. During the 1930–36 period the number of new or reorganized groups amounted to only about one-fourth of those functioning in 1930. In the 1924–30 period, the births of new organizations slightly exceeded the deaths of old ones. In the 1930–36 period, the reverse was true. No doubt a portion of this relatively high mortality resulted in part from the leaner purses of rural folk during the depression. Social organizations became unwarranted luxuries when dollars were sorely needed for food, shelter, and clothing. Along with economic compulsion for less support of organized groups came a trend, already noticeable before 1930, toward unorganized and informal recreation requiring little direction or management. This trend appears in the emphasis on parks, playgrounds and community centers, with their facilities for games; in the rise of soft-ball teams and leagues; and in bridge clubs. Thus in one community of 3,311 persons, half of whom lived in the village, 150 men participated in 10 soft-ball teams playing 3 or 4 nights a week, while perhaps twice as many looked on. Fieldworkers also reported more than once, "life in this community revolves around the school" or the community house. There were reports of more fishing, hunting, and camping than formerly. Furthermore, people not too seriously affected by the depression turned to the automobile, the dance hall, and the roadhouse for amusement, apparently preferring to spend their money in this way than on community facilities for recreation or on social organizations.

There are villages, moreover, where social organizations simply are not needed as once they were, where the social life of the village centers about an institution or community center. The chief social interests of the people in one Pennsylvania community, for instance, are the churches, which hold a number of annual festivals, anniversaries, and special services. Family reunions and picnics seemingly fill the other gregarious needs of the conservative villagers. In contrast to this village, the social life of one in the South revolves giddily about a pool hall, where cockfighting, billiards, and gambling are carried on nightly to the embarrassment of the ministers and their allies. In other circles of the village's society, no opprobrium is attached to one's presence in the pool hall, as most of the people go there. A Middle Western village is happy in putting on a colossal annual fair which grows each year. Everybody in the community works and co-operates to make this big affair a success. The fair lasts three days; discussion and preparation occupy 362. And likewise, the villagers of a Middle Atlantic community are perfectly content, with or without social organizations, while they amuse themselves and guests from all over the countryside in their beautiful and completely equipped parks and playgrounds.

CONTRIBUTIONS OF FEDERAL AGENCIES TO LOCAL SOCIAL LIFE

Two Federal agencies, one well and long established, the other emergency in character, also touch the social life of these communities and contribute to it. They are the Agricultural Extension Service and the W.P.A. They will be considered in that order.

Agricultural Extension.—The chapter on adult education has shown conclusively that under the aegis of the Agricultural Extension Service, rural and especially farm people have organized effectively for cultural activities that have social values as well. But this service through the state colleges of agriculture helps in the organization of social life as such. Community development through planning to meet community needs and working toward the actualizing of those plans is one of its major interests in many of the states. Many of the Farm and Home Bureau groups whose existence is reported in this chapter felt the influence of this work and shared in it in one or more ways. By way of summarizing these varied activities, the report of the director of Agricultural Extension in a representative state of the Middle West is condensed.

Clubs to the number of 834 reported some of the following activities: improved schools; provided Sunday School or church services; provided playground equipment at the school or community playground; encouraged the organization of sports; beautified highways or community buildings; improved cemeteries; built new or repaired community buildings; organized choruses, bands, or orchestras; arranged for lectures, classes, or study groups for adults or older boys and girls not in school; organized educational or social opportunities for young people. Sanitation measures, usually in relation to the disposal of human wastes, or the drainage of swampy places to get rid of mosquito breeding places, were reported taken by 189 clubs.

Local leaders in 858 clubs put on 2,676 meetings for the entire community, men, women, and children, at which the chief activities were games and songs. In addition, these clubs arranged over 1,000 good times of various sorts just for young people; 549, nearly two-thirds, had one or more plays, and 224, more than one-fourth, joined with others in community or county choruses.

Most of the states with extension rural sociologists reported also numerous requests to help in the organization of community associations and in planning their programs. Moreover, rural people wish to house their activities in buildings. One-third of the states recorded an unprecedented demand for assistance in planning adequate community buildings; and another one-sixth reported some requests along this line. This movement was stimulated by the availability of W.P.A. labor. One of the more rural New England states alone reported having assisted in planning for 100 such buildings which had been erected by the time of this study, while 55 more, approved by W.P.A. administrators, were in process of being planned.

It is entirely possible that in those states where this phenomenon was evident there may be, as a result, an increase in the number of active neighborhoods, or at least that a cohesive and stabilizing force will have been introduced into neighborhood life.

The youth work of the Agricultural Extension carried on under the name of 4-H Clubs, and already alluded to, is an extremely important adjunct of rural social life which reaches over 900,000 youths. The programs cover a wide variety of activities, covering projects in livestock, crops, home economics, forestry, and handcrafts, as well as a number of projects in community service and recreation. One hundred thousand boys and girls attended over 1,700 camps. Nearly twice as many went on almost 5,000 tours. Music plays a prominent part in the programs, and there are many 4-H bands, orchestras, choruses, and quartets. The state colleges have issued a large amount of material on the music phases of the program. The local leadership for these groups is carried by nearly 100,000 men and women, three-tenths of whom were themselves once 4-H Club members.

These activities, like others of the Agricultural Extension Service, as is pointed out in Chapter VIII, are much more available to the open-country than to the village population. They are likely to continue and develop. Except in a few states, where the Extension Service gave its facilities freely to villagers as well, the only government assistance to the social life of villages was through the recreational program of the C.W.A., and later the W.P.A. Obviously this was an emergency measure open to the same handicaps as the emergency adult education program, already discussed. It was, however, of importance because of both its successes and its failures; and it is to a consideration of the influence and contribution of this activity to the social life of these villages that the discussion now turns.

The W.P.A.—The effect of the emergency recreational program, over and above its civic improvements elsewhere discussed in its governmental aspects, has already been mentioned several times in this chapter; but it has had such a marked influence in some communities that it must be described in more detail.

A Far Western village, for example, now possesses a fine recreation park, conveniently located, built at a cost of $32,000 by E.R.A. and W.P.A. labor. This park is well equipped with a heated swimming pool, showers, dressing rooms, life guards, playground apparatus, baseball diamonds, tennis courts, and flood lights. The people of this village are turning increasingly to this park for the use of their leisure time. The county fair has been discontinued; and it is very likely that existent social organizations will suffer from loss of interest in them.

In a Southern community, a low swampy area has been changed to a spot of beauty and usefulness, a lake covering 25 acres having been built. In addition to this, 9 Federal fish hatcheries have been constructed and 1,000 pecan trees have been set out on the grounds. Additional plants and shrubbery have been set out to add beauty to the lake, swimming pool, and fish hatcheries.

Such projects were sometimes conducted quite independently of any assistance from the emergency programs. A small Middle West village secured an 11-acre tract half a mile from its boundary, which it converted into a park. An old gravel pit on other property has been converted into a swimming pool. The wooded area is used for a picnic ground. The money to purchase the tract was acquired by gifts from citizens and organizations, but the upkeep is a charge on the tax budget.

In spite of recognized benefits, however, many rural people have expressed dissatisfaction with the W.P.A. program. A major objection is against the large sums of Federal money spent on the projects. The grants seemed large in proportion to normal local expenses. The working personnel, particularly the administrative part of it, is the recipient of much adverse criticism. W.P.A. officials have in some cases earned the undesirable reputation of being inefficient and ill-fitted for their jobs, and laborers employed by the agency are occasionally thought to be not properly industrious, and to be unwilling to accept private employment. W.P.A. activities, especially in the fields of adult education and organized recreation, have been handicapped by regulations governing the organization, as already noted in the chapter on adult education.[2]

[2] A sample regulation is appended. "Supplies and materials for instruction requisitions will soon be received by Federal heads designated as buyer. Prior to the purchase of any material you will submit to this office a list of the proposed purchases and will not make them until this list has been returned to you bearing my signature or that of W.D.Z. In this connection remember that your purchases will be divided into expendable and non-expendable material. The expendable material is

One rule, requiring that teachers and leaders be qualified for relief, has been detrimental to the success of this type of work, since under this rule good personnel has not often been available. Nevertheless, in spite of faults real and imagined, it is evident that in rural villages the W.P.A. has been a new force which has contributed measurably to their social and civic welfare.

WHY SOCIAL ORGANIZATIONS DIED

The drift away from social organizations already alluded to reflects a lack of interest in them caused by their inability to perform some valuable function for their members and for the community. An active group supplies to its members goals to work for, and thus an opportunity to work with other persons and to express themselves in community life. Once the desired ends have been attained, however, leaving the organization with no definite course to steer, its members are bound to lose interest and turn to other things. Membership, attendance, and financial support drop off, and death follows shortly after. The need for an active program, on the other hand, sometimes causes two or more organizations to compete for the opportunity to perform some function or service for the community. Bitter conflict often results, in which a stalemate is reached. Each group is unable to make any progress, and is consequently likely to die away.

Another problem of some types of organizations is the spread of county-wide organizations. Some of these, like the Grange from its very start, and the newer Rotary and Kiwanis, have made it

---

accounted for by a statement of the uses to which it was put. All expendable material lost, broken or in any other way passing out of your possession must be accounted for and you are not only personally but also financially responsible for its proper distribution. For example a baseball purchased with government funds is lost; make an exact record of the time, place and have a statement signed by two witnesses. A baseball bat is broken, it may not be thrown away until it has been inspected and a clearance certificate issued by a proper government official. The slightest deviation from the government provisions relative to procurement and accountability for government property will inevitably result in a deduction from your pay check."

their policy to build local groups into county-wide federations. But some of the other newer agencies, largely of a special-interest type, have used the county as their smallest unit of operation, especially in areas of good roads, and this has reduced the time that those interested could spend in local organizations. This same trend was noticed in connection with economic co-operative agencies.

Rural schools, in attempting to co-ordinate their activities, hold meetings which are attended by representatives from all sections of the county. The Federal emergency agencies have also been responsible for constantly bringing village and country people to the county seat, as have farmers' co-operatives, farmers' economic associations, and 4-H Club programs. Apparently some social organizations are seeking the strength and quality of leadership available in county-wide set-ups, and this has in some measure sapped local groups indigenous to separate villages. Such reasons for the decline of local social organizations have constructive elements, some of them many. On the other hand, the conflicts already alluded to are always unfortunate, and for that reason a few representative cases will be illustrated.

Community conflicts.—Wherever people are concerned, as in social organizations, the interaction of their personalities and characteristics is a strong force affecting the fate of the groups to which they belong. In those instances in which strong leaders are present, persons who express but also suggest and guide the will of the group, organizations have better chances for life and success. Such persons, however, are not always present or may move away. A group bereft of good leadership, like one without objectives, is liable to pass out of the picture. Leadership is not the only problem confronting social organizations. Conflict within them and within the community caused by the opposing beliefs of members on matters of local importance, religion, civic improvements, politics, and the like, is liable to split groups asunder with fatal results. In one Middle Atlantic village, for example, strife between wealthy Quakers who formerly dominated community life and the new "lower" element of Democratic party affiliations has brought the activities of most social organizations to a standstill. It has also prevented the conversion of an old academy building into a much-needed community house and gymnasium. The younger Quakers, who have children, are in a dilemma. They would like to obtain the proposed facilities for their children, yet feel that they should support the viewpoint of the older Quakers.

The social life of a Middle Western village is being seriously interfered with by religious differences between Polish Catholics who live in one section of the village and German Lutherans who live in another. These differences have prevented social organizations and community enterprises from progressing. Young people in the village have no organized activities to which to apply their energies, and they are dissatisfied.

Another village is now suffering from violent conflict over a proposed sewage system. According to the fieldworker, "a few enlightened citizens are for it, but most of the property is owned by a few men who are violently opposed to it."

In one or two cases, conflicts were caused by the battle between two leading families to gain both economic and social control. Everyone perforce must take sides, the community inevitably suffers, and the social organizations within it as well.

Difference of opinion as to politics still at times seriously divides a village into two factions. Naturally a richer and more abundant social life has difficulty in flourishing in warlike environments such as these described here. However, situations of serious conflict are present only in the small minority of the communities, and social groups in the main have not been much handicapped by them. Generally a state either of co-operation of one group with another and with the people of the community exists, or there is a live-and-let-live attitude. In a Far Western village, for instance, a committee of representatives of all the village clubs is working out a recreational program for the benefit of all the citizens. In several villages the American Legion is aided by other groups in putting on its annual Memorial Day program. Parent-Teacher Associations often receive valuable co-operation from businessmen's clubs in their work on behalf of school children; and the latter organizations are in turn given a helping hand by other groups in carrying on annual fairs, Farmers' Days, and the like. In the main, the depression seems to have brought more, rather than less, co-operation among social organizations.

The vital statistics of social organizations.—The effects of the various factors causing changes in the number of social organizations of the different types are summarized in three tables which are introduced here. Table 76 shows the changes in the number of social organizations by type between 1930 and 1936.

TABLE 76

CHANGES IN NUMBER OF SOCIAL ORGANIZATIONS, BY TYPE

140 Selected American Agricultural Villages, 1936

	Organizations in 1930		*Organizations 1930 to 1936*		*Organizations in 1936*		
Type of Organization	TOTAL NUMBER	AV. PER VILLAGE	INACTIVE OR OR DEAD	NEW OR REOR-GANIZED	TOTAL NUMBER	AV. PER VILLAGE	*Net Change*
All types	2,925	20.9	946	774	2,753	19.7	*−172*
Athletic	94	.7	49	24	69	.5	*− 25*
Civic	293	2.1	88	50	255	1.8	*− 38*
Educational	187	1.3	58	68	197	1.4	+ 10
Fraternal	906	6.4	230	74	750	5.4	*−156*
Musical	80	.6	32	16	64	.5	*− 16*
Patriotic	256	1.8	33	41	264	1.9	+ 8
Social	223	1.6	94	85	214	1.5	*− 9*
Bridge	195	1.4	75	160	280	2.0	+ 85
Socio-religious	25	.2	8	7	24	.2	*− 1*
Socio-economic	142	1.0	47	51	146	1.0	+ 4
Farm Bureau	111	.8	48	35	98	.7	*− 13*
Grange	55	.4	13	13	55	.4	0
Political	...	...	...	4	4	.0 [a]	+ 4
Townsend and Social Justice	...	...	...	59	59	.4	+ 59
Youth-serving	192	1.4	77	48	163	1.2	*− 29*
4-H	166	1.2	94	39	111	.8	*− 55*

[a] Less than .1.

The total number decreased from 2,925 to 2,753 in that period, or about 6 per cent; and the average per village fell from 20.9 to

19.7. This was despite a gain in population. This 1936 total is 85 organizations less than in 1924, when there were 20.3 per village. Groups devoted to athletic activities dropped off sharply, as did 4-H Clubs and youth-serving organizations. Civic, musical, and fraternal organizations also experienced a thinning of their ranks. The decline in civic organizations is due to the elimination of 37 Red Cross chapters and 16 cemetery associations that had apparently ceased all social-welfare activities formerly engaged in, and which operated purely on the basis of an annual business meeting.

The greatest decline in the actual number of groups occurred in those of a fraternal nature, despite the inclusion of a considerable number whose charters had been suspended. This was done on the assumption, true in some cases, but probably not in all, that the suspension was caused by administrative difficulties with the national overhead organization. Reports of fieldworkers from all over the country indicate that interest in the various lodges is rapidly dying out. In one village alone, 8 died between 1930 and 1936. The average loss was 2.5 per village. Lodge membership has also dropped, and attendance is poor. Young people are uninterested and decline to join. In many cases the organizations are held together only by the desire of their members to preserve the insurance equities which they hold. The number of fraternal organizations is still, however, approximately triple that of any other type of social organization, the next most numerous being bridge clubs, which have increased phenomenally in the past 5 years.

Table 77 will serve to show how the different types of organizations have fared. It gives the birth rates and death rates of social organizations by type for the 1930–36 period.

For all organizations, the death rate exceeded the birth rate; and this is true for each type of organization except educational, bridge, patriotic, and socio-economic, whose numbers increased. Four-H Clubs, athletic clubs, musical and fraternal organizations suffered particularly from an excess of deaths over births. It is evident from the data of this table that the turnover among social organizations is high. The most stable types of organizations were the ones that gained in number. Bridge clubs are an exception. Although their death rate was high, their birth rate more than doubled it. Granges remained the same in number, while social and socio-religious groups declined very little.

It may be worth while to examine these data further. The decline in athletic and musical organizations is clearly attributable to the depression. These are costly agencies. Their per capita expenses were 2 to 3 times higher than any other type. A number of villages discontinued tax support for their bands, which resulted

TABLE 77

BIRTH RATES AND DEATH RATES OF SOCIAL ORGANIZATIONS

By Type

Type of Organization	*Rates per Hundred*		*Points of Net Gain or Loss, 1930–36*
	BIRTH	DEATH	
All types	26.7	32.3	*– 5.6*
Athletic	25.5	52.1	*–26.6*
Civic	17.1	30.0	*–12.9*
Educational	36.3	31.0	+ 5.3
Fraternal	8.2	25.3	*–17.1*
Musical	20.0	40.0	*–20.0*
Patriotic	16.0	12.9	+ 3.1
Social	38.1	42.1	*– 4.0*
Bridge	82.1	38.4	+43.6
Socio-religious	28.0	32.0	*– 4.0*
Socio-economic	35.9	33.1	+ 2.8
Farm Bureau	31.5	43.2	*–11.7*
Grange	23.6	23.6	0
Youth-serving	25.1	40.1	*–15.0*
4-H	23.5	56.6	*–33.1*

in the disbanding of these organizations. The increase in patriotic groups, whose birth rates and death rates alike were low, was caused in part by the reorganization of American Legion posts brought on by the bonus agitation. The decline in Farm and Home Bureau groups is more apparent than real. In a number of communities the local organizations lapsed, and the work was put on a district or county basis. Actually it is a safe estimate that the Farm Bureau had a larger membership in these communities in

1936 than in 1930, and certainly larger than in 1932 or 1933. Similarly the number of 4-H Clubs may be an under-enumeration. In a few communities, internal evidence suggests that fieldworkers treated all clubs as one unit. Nationally the 4-H organization has a membership of over 900,000 rural youth and has probably never been more influential. It is unquestionably the largest rural youth organization in the nation.[3]

One of the new types of organizations appearing for the first time in the reports of this series of studies is the Townsend Club.

Townsend Clubs.—With the depression came many fantastic schemes for its cure, notable among which was the Townsend Plan. The promoters of this plan have been organizing Townsend Clubs throughout the country in the interest of realizing, through political means, the operation of the $200 a month pension for the aged. Townsend organizers have penetrated to about 100 of the 140 villages and have succeeded in establishing Townsend Clubs in 55 of them, 20 in the Far West. There were also 9 Social Justice Clubs. They were aided in their task by the fact that the depression had left in its wake many unemployed, dissatisfied elderly persons, in addition to those normally unemployed and dissatisfied, who saw in the Townsend Plan a solution of their difficulties. While Townsend Clubs are fairly numerous, have large memberships, and fair attendance, they are not highly regarded by most of the outstanding citizens of the communities. Most of them were losing influence rapidly at the time of the survey. The notes of a fieldworker who surveyed a Middle Atlantic village are of interest in this connection:

> The president of the organization is a man who went into debt to everybody and then went into bankruptcy. Mr. M———, assistant editor of the S——— Record and a very intelligent and public spirited individual, says, "not a member of the (Townsend) club as it stands at present ever earned $100 a month, to say nothing of $200. And what's more, they were more than contented on that sum. Every member of that club is in the organization not because he or she feels that it is a good administrative policy, but rather because of the possibilities of personal gain."

[3] Its present membership is only about one per cent below the 1930 peak.

Prevalent also among the attitudes of village citizens who do not belong to the Townsend Clubs is the opinion that their leaders are often former members of the Ku Klux Klan. Furthermore, Townsendites have the reputation of being heavily indebted individuals, some of whom suffered foreclosures in recent years.

Although the Townsend Clubs are not well thought of, they are sometimes feared for their political potentialities. Their leaders (who are generally between 50 and 70 years of age) claim great strength; but up to the time of the survey there had been little opportunity to test this question. And in the meantime Townsend Clubs are clearly declining in strength. In fact, many had dropped below the minimum number of members required for a local branch of the movement and gave this as the reason for refusing data on membership to the surveyor. The data on these clubs in Table 81 are a decided overstatement of the actual situation; but only the largest clubs gave information. It should also be noted that the number of communities in which attempts to organize Townsend Clubs failed almost equaled the number in which they succeeded. Outside organizers started the clubs, drummed up enthusiasm for a time, and then left, with the result that members are losing interest. It is quite likely that Townsend Clubs will die away in rural villages, especially with the return of prosperity.

Regional differences in social organizations.—Table 78 shows the change in the number of social organizations by regions. Villages of the Far West have, as in 1930, the greatest number of organizations per village. It was also the only region in which the number of social groups increased. The South has, as previously, the least number of organizations per village. Undoubtedly this is partly a function of the economic situation in the South. In all regions there was a heavy turnover in social organizations, births and deaths being frequent; but the Middle Atlantic showed the greatest stability. Though the total number of groups is less than in 1924, the Middle Atlantic and Southern regions still have more now than then. The losses in the 2 Western areas have been quite sharp.

Distribution of organizations.—Changing the basis of comparison from the number of organizations to the number of villages having each type of organization affords another method of measuring the changes which have taken place in the 1930–36 period. In general, fewer villages had athletic, civic, educational, fraternal, musical, bridge, Grange, youth-serving, and 4-H organizations in 1936 than in 1930; the number of villages having athletic, musical, youth-serving, and 4-H Clubs dropped off considerably. While fraternal organizations were represented in only one less village, and indeed were found in all but 2 communities, it will be recalled that their actual number decreased sharply. Bridge clubs, on the other hand, appeared in fewer villages; but their actual number rose substantially. In spite of smaller representation in other regions, in the South athletic and educational organizations were present in more villages than in 1930. Other types of organizations did not show much change in representation, except for youth-serving and 4-H Clubs, whose numbers decreased, leaving more villages without them. It will be noted that Townsend and Social Justice Clubs are well represented except in the South. The data for the foregoing are given in Table 79, which shows the number of villages having each type of social organization by regions.

When the representation of social organizations by size of village is examined, it is apparent that fewer villages of each size had various types of organizations in 1936 than in 1930. This is particularly true of small and medium-sized villages, and to a lesser extent of large and town-sized villages. No generalizations can be made about the changes in representation of each type of organization according to size of village. Figures on these changes are given in Table 80, in which the frequencies of occurrence of each type are tabulated by size of village.

It will be seen that athletic organizations appeared in fewer villages of all sizes in 1936, with the exception of large villages. This type is best represented in the towns. Civic and educational groups are well represented but occurred less frequently in all

TABLE 78

CHANGES IN NUMBER OF SOCIAL ORGANIZATIONS, BY REGION

140 Selected American Agricultural Villages, 1936

Region	*Number of Villages*	*Organizations in 1930*		*Inactive or Dead*	*New or Reorganized*	*Organizations in 1936*		*Net Changes in Av. No. of Organizations*
		TOTAL NUMBER	AV. PER VILLAGE [a]			TOTAL NUMBER	AV. PER VILLAGE	
All regions	140	2,925	20.9	946	774	2,753	19.7	*−1.2*
Middle Atlantic	28	565	20.2	133	94	526	18.8	*−1.4*
South	30	408	13.6	167	145	386	12.9	*−0.7*
Middle West	60	1,362	22.7	424	293	1,231	20.5	*−2.2*
Far West	22	590	26.8	222	242	610	27.7	+0.9

[a] In 1924 the average number of social organizations was 20.3 for all villages. Regional averages were: Middle Atlantic, 16.9; South, 10.6; Middle West, 23.2; Far West, 29.6.

but the town-sized villages; and more medium-sized villages had educational groups in 1936. Musical organizations appeared in more towns, but in fewer of all other villages. Patriotic, socio-economic, and youth-serving groups generally occur more frequently as the size of the village increases. The reverse is true of 4-H Clubs. The most stable types of organizations with respect to frequency of occurrence are fraternal, socio-religious, the Grange, and the Farm Bureau. Organizations belonging to these types have been long established, and more often than not have national affiliations.

CHANGES WITHIN ORGANIZATIONS

Membership has decreased.—Between 1924 and 1930, membership in social organizations decreased somewhat; and this trend continued up to 1936. Between 1930 and 1936, the average membership for all organizations dropped from 60.0 to 55.6. It will be remembered that the Townsend and Social Justice organizations, with their very large reported memberships, partly obscure the amount of decline in average membership of social organizations. If Townsend and Social Justice Clubs had been eliminated, the number of social organizations would have declined even more significantly; and obviously the average membership would have been even less. This decrease occurred despite increasing population in the 140 villages, and apparently reflects declining interest in the various types of groups and clubs. Table 81 indicates in detail the changes in the average membership of social organizations between 1930 and 1936, by type of organization, and by region.

While the average membership for all organizations dropped off, a majority of the separate types evidently succeeded in adding members to their rolls. Athletic clubs made a substantial gain; 4-H Clubs, youth-serving, musical, social, socio-religious, socio-economic, and Farm Bureau organizations also increased their average membership, while all other types experienced losses.

TABLE 79

VILLAGES HAVING EACH TYPE OF SOCIAL ORGANIZATION, BY REGION

140 Selected American Agricultural Villages, 1936

Type of Organization	*No. and Per Cent of All 140 Villages Having Specified Social Organizations, 1930 and 1936*				*Number of Villages in Each Region Having Specified Social Organizations, 1930 and 1936*							
	ALL VILLAGES				MIDDLE ATLANTIC		SOUTH		MIDDLE WEST		FAR WEST	
	1930		*1936*		*1930*	*1936*	*1930*	*1936*	*1930*	*1936*	*1930*	*1936*
	No.	*Per Cent*	*No.*	*Per Cent*								
Athletic	57	40.7	44	31.4	12	11	2	3	34	23	9	7
Civic	117	83.6	109	77.8	26	26	24	19	50	48	17	16
Educational	95	67.9	94	67.1	18	17	25	29	39	38	13	10
Fraternal	139	99.3	138	98.6	28	28	29	30	60	59	22	21
Musical	66	47.1	53	37.9	18	16	12	8	33	27	3	2
Patriotic	115	82.1	115	82.1	20	22	18	17	56	55	21	21
Social	68	48.6	72	51.4	13	13	7	9	40	42	8	8
Bridge	64	45.7	58	41.4	11	10	13	16	28	23	12	9
Socio-religious	20	14.3	20	14.3	4	4	...	1	15	15	1	...
Socio-economic	91	65.0	91	65.0	16	15	15	16	40	42	20	18
Farm Bureau	46	32.9	47	33.6	12	10	8	10	21	21	5	6
Grange	35	25.0	34	24.3	20	19	1	2	4	4	10	9
Political	...	...	3	2.1	...	...	...	2	...	1	...	...
Townsend and Social Justice	...	...	54	38.6	...	14	...	1	...	19	...	20
Youth-serving	104	74.3	89	63.6	21	23	19	13	43	35	21	18
4-H	54	38.6	44	31.4	10	10	8	6	24	19	12	9

Losses in membership were particularly noticeable in fraternal organizations, which, it will be recalled, also declined in number. It is evident, however, that no relationship generally exists between changes in number of organizations of each type and changes in their average membership. Townsend and Social Justice Clubs, gathering to their ranks the impoverished aged and dissatisfied, enjoy by far the highest average membership of any type of organization, though here the figures are skewed by the refusal of

TABLE 80

VILLAGES HAVING EACH TYPE OF SOCIAL ORGANIZATION BY SIZE OF VILLAGE[a]

140 Selected American Agricultural Villages, 1936

Type of Organization	*No. of Small Villages*		*No. of Medium Villages*		*No. of Large Villages*		*No. of Towns*	
	1930	*1936*	*1930*	*1936*	*1930*	*1936*	*1930*	*1936*
Athletic	14	12	28	18	5	5	10	9
Civic	29	27	54	49	19	18	15	15
Educational	26	25	42	43	15	14	12	12
Fraternal	42	42	60	59	20	20	17	17
Musical	16	15	33	21	11	9	6	8
Patriotic	28	30	53	50	18	18	16	17
Social	16	17	30	34	11	12	11	9
Bridge	11	12	30	26	10	12	13	8
Socio-religious	6	5	6	7	7	7	1	1
Socio-economic	18	16	41	44	16	16	16	15
Farm Bureau	14	13	16	18	10	9	6	7
Grange	13	11	14	15	5	5	3	3
Political	...	...	...	1	...	1	...	1
Townsend and Social Justice	...	13	...	24	...	5	...	12
Youth-serving	30	25	41	34	17	15	16	15
4-H	18	15	26	19	5	6	5	4

[a] The total number of villages is divided as follows: small, 42; medium, 61; large, 20; town, 17.

small groups to divulge their membership. The Grange comes second in average membership. Table 81 shows that the average membership in social organizations declined in each geographic region, especially in the Middle Atlantic. This region, however, still shows the highest average membership, and the South, which had the least decline, the lowest.

While the average membership of all social organizations has decreased in the last 5 years, it is interesting to note that in this respect farmers' economic organizations have made gains. Although the number of these organizations has declined somewhat in number, average membership has risen, as a result of increases in the Middle West and the Far West; in the South and Middle Atlantic the reverse was true. It is possible that these changes in average membership have some relation to the A.A.A. program.

TABLE 81

MEMBERSHIP IN SOCIAL ORGANIZATIONS, BY TYPE AND REGION

140 Villages

Type of Organization	*Number of Organizations*		*Number Reporting*		*Average Membership for Those Reporting*	
	1930	*1936*	*1930*	*1936*	*1930*	*1936*
All types	2,925	2,753	2,495	2,381	60.0	55.6
Athletic	94	69	82	51	41.0	57.3
Civic	293	255	264	240	51.8	50.6
Educational	187	197	159	168	65.9	57.0
Fraternal	906	750	834	700	91.1	79.2
Musical	80	64	79	57	26.6	30.6
Patriotic	256	264	244	258	52.5	44.7
Social	223	214	185	198	33.2	34.7
Bridge	195	280	114	152	14.3	13.5
Socio-religious	25	24	25	23	68.8	75.1
Socio-economic	142	146	133	139	40.5	47.9
Farm Bureau	111	98	83	78	45.6	50.9
Grange	55	55	51	50	121.4	120.3
Political	...	4	...	4	...	32.0
Townsend and Social Justice	...	59	...	15	...	293.7
Youth-serving	192	163	172	152	29.6	30.8
4-H	166	111	70	96	19.4	23.9
All regions	2,925	2,753	2,495	2,381	60.0	55.6
Middle Atlantic	565	526	481	454	75.9	68.0
South	408	386	367	370	50.1	48.9
Middle West	1,362	1,231	1,197	1,066	56.3	52.5
Far West	590	610	450	491	61.0	55.7

In the Middle Atlantic region, where the A.A.A. was inoperative for the most part, average membership declined slightly. In the South, the decline was much greater, perhaps because the cotton program caused a reduction in the number of farmers. But in the Middle West and the Far West, where the A.A.A. program received heavy participation and stimulated farmers to co-operate and to organize themselves, farmers' economic organizations enjoyed substantial gains in average membership. The data are given in Table 82, which shows membership in farmers' economic organizations, by region, for 1930 and 1936.

Organizations with continuous history.—One measure of these changes is the number of organizations that had a continuous history over the two survey periods or simply the second one, as well as those which had lapsed after 1924 and been reorganized, compared with the number of agencies that had died. In this comparison, as in subsequent ones on the same basis, only those four-fifths of the organizations for which complete data were secured are considered.

TABLE 82

MEMBERSHIP IN FARMERS' ECONOMIC ORGANIZATIONS [a]

By Region: 140 Villages

Region	*Number of Organizations*		*Number Reporting*		*Average Membership for Those Reporting*	
	1930	*1936*	*1930*	*1936*	*1930*	*1936*
All regions	166	153	134	128	74.4	78.0
Middle Atlantic	51	50	50	48	118.7	113.5
South	11	16	9	15	66.8	47.9
Middle West	64	43	43	29	45.3	64.9
Far West	40	44	32	36	46.4	53.8

[a] Farmers' Union, Gleaners, Farm Club, Farm and Home Bureaus, and home economics organizations.

Membership contrasts among older and younger organizations.—When the average membership of organizations that have existed throughout both survey periods is considered, some interesting facts are disclosed. In the first place, the 1924 memberships of the more stable and enduring organizations were almost double those of social organizations that died between 1924 and 1930; and their 1930 memberships were more than double those of groups formed after 1924 but prior to 1930 which failed to survive until 1936. They were also sharply larger than clubs that had been reorganized between 1924 and 1936, or those born after the depression began.

Apparently size is related to survival, and apparently also groups organized during the depression found it much harder than formerly to recruit new members, since the trends noted above hold for practically every type of social organization except bridge clubs, and for all 4 regions.

Contrasting with these data, however, is the fact that the average membership of these older groups among the social organizations of the 140 communities lost in membership between 1924 and 1936 by 15.5 per cent. Most of this decline, as with the entire group of agencies, took place after 1930. On the other hand, the younger organizations, enumerated for the first time in 1930 and continuing through 1936, had maintained their smaller total membership practically unchanged through the depression. Possibly those persons who did join new groups were so much interested that maintaining the loyalty and interest was easier. Possibly the factor of novelty entered into the record of these newer groups.

Despite the heavy mortality among athletic and musical organizations, those that did survive ran counter to the trend of declining memberships. In both cases, they showed increases that carried their totals to sharply higher levels than in 1924. Average membership in the continuing Farm Bureaus and social economic groups also showed gains over 1930. Educational groups lost, but were still substantially above 1924.

Ratio of open-country members increases slowly.—The proportion of open-country members in the membership had no influence on the stability or survival of these organizations. There was almost no difference between the continuing, new, or lapsed organizations in this particular, though the general trend for all groups is toward a slowly increasing proportion of open-country members in the various agencies of the community. For all types of organizations, this proportion increased slightly from 34.2 to 35.3 between 1930 and 1936. It decreased in the Middle West and increased in the other regions, especially in the Far West, which now has the highest percentage of any region of open-country members. Certain figures in Table 84 which shows the proportion of country members by region and by type of organization, are outstanding. Athletic groups, for example, have a relatively high percentage of country members, although it has fallen considerably in the last 6 years. The percentage for civic organizations in the South and the Far West has risen a good deal; the same is true of educational organizations in the South. Open-country people in the Far West contribute largely to the membership of musical organizations in that region, and to a much greater degree in 1936 than in 1930. From social clubs in the South, and from bridge clubs in all regions, however, country people have been excluded or else have not cared or been able to join. Socio-religious organizations, on the other hand, are more likely to include a relatively large proportion of country members. This is also true of Townsend and of 4-H Clubs; and, of course, of the Farm Bureau and Grange. In the South and in the Far West, the Farm Bureau had a smaller portion of its members from the country in 1936, indicating greater interest among villagers in these groups; but for the nation as a whole the situation was the reverse.

Larger proportion of women in social organizations.—In all social organizations in the 140 villages there was a higher proportion of female members in 1936 than in 1930, the increase being from 40.5 per cent to 43.7 per cent; correspondingly, the proportion of male members fell off. Women are particularly prominent numerically in educational, social, bridge, and civic organizations. Men are predominant in all other types. In patriotic, Farm Bureau, and youth-serving organizations there exists approximately equal division between the numbers of male and female members. The percentages of female members increased between 1930 and 1936 in many types of organizations, educational, fraternal, musical, patriotic, bridge, Farm Bureau, and youth-serving. In every geographic region, also, the proportion of female members has risen since 1930, and is highest in the Middle West. Table 85 gives the

TABLE 83

AVERAGE MEMBERSHIP IN IDENTICAL ORGANIZATIONS

Type of Organization	*Identical Organizations Existing at Each Period*				*Identical Organizations Starting between 1924 and 1930*			*Identical Organizations Existing in 1924 and 1930 but Dying between 1930 and 1936*		
	NO. REPORTING	*1924*	*1930*	*1936*	NO. REPORTING	*1930*	*1936*	NO. REPORTING	*1924*	*1930*
All types	1,178	80.5	79.8	67.5	410	43.9	43.8	376	53.2	54.7
Middle Atlantic	236	98.3	100.8	88.1	122	49.4	50.5	42	58.6	55.5
South	135	75.7	72.7	58.4	69	46.9	43.7	73	50.8	46.1
Middle West	609	78.1	74.1	62.5	159	33.9	37.8	172	56.1	59.4
Far West	198	69.7	77.4	64.6	60	55.9	45.9	89	47.4	52.5
Athletic	12	81.2	73.9	102.9	22	44.6	44.6	18	17.8	18.9
Civic	137	59.2	55.3	50.5	48	64.4	56.3	40	46.3	35.9
Educational	75	57.6	77.3	69.8	30	71.0	72.5	16	50.6	72.0
Fraternal	518	110.6	109.1	84.2	49	69.9	49.6	144	70.8	64.6
Musical	24	25.5	29.2	32.3	19	30.3	29.4	14	22.9	23.3
Patriotic	173	51.2	56.1	48.1	32	36.2	39.4	28	33.6	27.7
Political	0	...	...	...	0	...	...	0	...	...
Social	75	38.3	28.3	27.4	37	28.5	37.9	29	37.1	43.4
Bridge	18	15.1	14.2	13.7	23	16.0	14.8	10	13.5	11.3
Socio-economic	39	61.6	52.9	59.3	37	35.9	45.6	24	69.3	130.2
Farm Bureau	22	54.9	51.4	60.5	22	42.1	41.3	21	49.3	57.1
Grange	30	172.9	161.2	158.4	9	44.7	63.4	10	87.5	90.7
Socio-religious	11	132.2	101.9	95.8	6	47.3	50.7	7	51.9	39.0
Townsend	0	...	...	...	0	...	...	0	...	...
Youth-serving	43	28.6	31.0	35.9	52	30.4	30.6	13	30.0	23.7
4-H	1	20.0	31.0	58.0	24	29.1	42.8	2	15.0	30.5

proportion of males and females in the membership of social organizations by type, and by region.

When the social organizations are classified by age on this point, some interesting facts appear. In the main, the tendency is for the newer organizations to have a larger proportion of females than the older ones. For instance, no women were members of athletic groups that had been organized prior to 1924 and were still functioning; but they made up more than one-fifth of the membership of such clubs formed since 1930. This same tendency was noted in the musical, socio-economic, and patriotic groups. Interestingly, white females make up barely two-fifths of the membership of the older patriotic groups; they comprise seven-tenths of the members enrolled in the more recent of these agencies.

On the other hand, there was a significantly larger proportion of men in the membership of the newer groups devoted to educational and civic purposes than in the older ones, though even in these the percentage of men in the total membership had gained.

Average attendance improved.—While membership in social organizations dropped during the depression, the remaining members attended meetings better. Educational, fraternal, musical, patriotic, and bridge clubs enjoyed better attendance in 1936 than in 1930. Bridge players have an almost perfect record in this respect. Meetings of musical groups are also well attended. Several types of organizations, however, experienced a falling off in attendance, athletic organizations being most seriously affected. A probable explanation in the latter case is that the new recreational parks of many villages have attracted to them for informal recreation people who would otherwise have attended meetings of athletic organizations. Data on changes in attendance between 1930 and 1936 are presented in Table 86. It will be noticed that attendance has improved in every region, particularly in the South and the Far West.

The younger an organization, the higher is the proportion of its members who attend meetings, at least in the aggregate in all

TABLE 84

PROPORTION OF MEMBERS FROM THE COUNTRY IN SOCIAL ORGANIZATIONS, 1930 AND 1936

By Type of Organization and by Region: 140 Villages

Type of Organization	All Regions		Middle Atlantic		South		Middle West		Far West	
	PER CENT		PER CENT		PER CENT		PER CENT		PER CENT	
	1930	*1936*	*1930*	*1936*	*1930*	*1936*	*1930*	*1936*	*1930*	*1936*
All types	34.2	35.3	35.8	39.4	30.3	34.6	33.2	30.8	36.2	40.7
Athletic	30.2	23.5	63.3	45.7	0.0	10.1	17.1	14.1	42.0	38.3
Civic	14.4	19.9	11.8	9.9	8.8	29.2	14.4	14.0	19.3	38.3
Educational	25.6	27.8	29.8	20.0	16.3	36.7	25.2	26.0	26.7	25.0
Fraternal	32.8	32.7	27.8	33.6	35.7	37.1	32.9	29.4	34.9	36.1
Musical	24.4	24.1	11.5	23.9	12.2	14.3	28.9	23.6	57.2	86.0
Patriotic	31.9	33.6	30.6	29.2	26.0	31.7	29.9	33.0	42.2	39.0
Social	27.6	36.0	14.8	37.9	5.5	13.4	37.4	33.8	32.2	44.2
Bridge	6.6	6.9	1.5	0.0	.9	7.5	6.2	6.3	12.2	8.4
Socio-religious	53.8	44.8	38.7	40.3	...	...	61.0	46.2	29.4	...
Socio-economic	23.8	13.5	8.6	13.0	6.6	3.0	45.8	16.3	21.1	13.9
Farm Bureau	69.4	81.3	57.7	68.7	95.6	69.8	70.5	92.3	62.4	61.6
Grange	88.6	84.8	85.9	81.4	89.4	91.1	92.7	81.9	96.3	91.0
Political	...	18.7	...	...	...	22.2	...	21.0	...	...
Townsend and Social Justice	...	75.5	...	22.1	...	...	...	40.0	...	63.5
Youth-serving	24.7	27.6	20.7	22.5	11.0	21.2	25.5	29.1	34.2	33.8
4-H	73.5	89.2	72.9	79.6	71.3	82.2	64.1	87.3	76.9	157.2

regions and among a majority of the types of organizations. In no case does the attendance ratio of the older groups exceed that of the younger by any considerable figure. This is only to be expected. Interest is usually highest in the early years. The surprising thing about the attendance data, however, is that the percentage of members present at the meetings of the organizations that died was higher than for the continuing organizations. This was also true of all regions and most types of organizations. Apparently it was

TABLE 85

PROPORTION OF MALES AND FEMALES IN THE MEMBERSHIP OF SOCIAL ORGANIZATIONS

By Type and Region: 140 Villages

Type of Organization	*Number Reporting Sex of Members*		*Per Cent Males*		*Per Cent Females*	
	1930	*1936*	*1930*	*1936*	*1930*	*1936*
All types	2,437	2,190	59.48	56.28	40.52	43.72
Athletic	79	41	87.24	92.29	12.76	7.71
Civic	259	222	30.85	35.66	69.15	64.34
Educational	152	151	24.47	23.12	75.53	76.88
Fraternal	826	642	68.61	64.71	31.39	35.29
Musical	78	50	76.32	60.11	23.68	39.89
Patriotic	243	258	54.58	51.46	45.42	48.54
Social	183	173	32.61	36.54	67.39	63.46
Bridge	100	142	17.13	11.78	82.87	88.22
Socio-religious	25	22	71.05	73.06	28.95	26.94
Socio-economic	130	136	90.64	90.14	9.36	9.86
Farm Bureau	76	75	56.61	48.76	43.39	51.24
Grange	50	42	53.58	56.49	46.42	43.51
Political	. . .	4	. . .	78.12	. . .	21.88
Townsend and Social Justice	. . .	9	. . .	59.10	. . .	40.90
Youth-serving	172	150	61.53	53.43	38.47	46.57
4-H	64	73	58.35	58.90	41.65	41.10
All regions	2,437	2,190	59.48	56.28	40.52	43.72
Middle Atlantic	476	420	60.47	59.04	39.53	40.96
South	360	338	65.32	61.20	34.68	38.80
Middle West	1,165	1,013	57.55	53.49	42.45	46.51
Far West	436	419	58.88	55.81	41.12	44.19

not initial lack of support that led to their early demise. Other explanations must be sought for their failure to survive. One of these has been given, namely, their smaller size. General factors outlined earlier in this section also account for some deaths, but only further research can clear up the problem. It might, for instance, be that the members of many lapsed organizations came from the less stable elements in the community, the more volatile, those more ready to migrate. It would be interesting to compare the membership rolls of present and lapsed churches of the more emotional sects with the rolls of lapsed social organizations to discover if any relationships existed.

Finances follow the business cycle.—While for all organizations, membership has decreased and attendance has improved,

TABLE 86

ATTENDANCE IN SOCIAL ORGANIZATIONS

By Type and Region: 140 Selected American Agricultural Villages

Type of Organization	*Number of Organizations Reporting*		*Per Cent of Attendance*	
	1930	*1936*	*1930*	*1936*
All types	2,189	2,211	39.8	43.3
Athletic	25	35	93.2	45.8
Civic	245	226	51.3	51.8
Educational	160	173	58.8	61.1
Fraternal	790	678	25.2	28.5
Musical	65	54	79.6	85.2
Patriotic	227	248	34.0	40.7
Social	169	170	60.4	57.7
Bridge	90	148	94.5	99.8
Socio-religious	20	20	34.0	36.7
Socio-economic	116	129	69.2	61.1
Farm Bureau	36	55	41.8	57.0
Grange	49	47	29.9	29.5
Political	...	4	...	51.6
Townsend and Social Justice	...	10	...	48.3
Youth-serving	152	144	75.8	71.4
4-H	45	70	87.8	91.4
All regions	2,189	2,211	39.8	43.3
Middle Atlantic	432	432	35.2	38.6
South	325	359	41.5	50.2
Middle West	1,044	987	40.2	41.4
Far West	388	433	43.5	48.0

per capita expenditures declined during the 1930 to 1936 period by almost 30 per cent. This is a slightly smaller decline than was experienced by the churches. Athletic groups cut their per capita expenditures more than one-half; but they still remain relatively high. The per capita expenditures of all types of organizations except socio-religious and the Grange fell in the depression years. Musical groups now have the highest expenses per member, and Townsend Clubs the lowest. Per capita expenditures fell in every region, and with especial violence in the Far West. Villages have more organizations per village in this region than in any other; and consequently financial support has been spread among more units of organization than in other parts of the country. Table 88 shows the per capita expenditures of social organizations by type and the per capita expenditures by region for 1930 and 1936.

The contrast between the continuing and the lapsed social organizations in the matter of per capita costs suggests another cause of the death of the latter. In the Middle Atlantic and Middle West regions, which had two-thirds of the lapsed organizations that lived for only one enumeration, and on which records were available, the per capita contributions were on the average more than 25 per cent above those of the continuing organizations. For those organizations found in both 1924 and 1930 which died before 1935, this tendency was accentuated and observable in all regions. For the whole group, the per capita costs averaged 35.2 per cent above those of the organizations that survived. By 1930 they had dropped 47.1 per cent, against a drop of only 3 per cent for those that survived the entire period. Apparently whatever other causes entered in, these clubs started too ambitiously and were unable to hold their members on the sharply restricted program that became necessary.

Illustrations of activity and change.—Underlying all the various statistics on social organizations are the stories that figures only partly reflect. The figures tell nothing, for instance, of the Kiwanis Club in a village of the Middle West which is proving a good Samaritan to the underprivileged school children by helping them where no parental or civic budget has provided for their welfare. Last year the club did a number of things: bought a pair of glasses, paid for a tonsillectomy, raised $280 for their work through a home-talent play, sponsored the junior band, and paid an orchestra

TABLE 87

RATIO OF ATTENDANCE TO ALL MEMBERS IN IDENTICAL ORGANIZATIONS

Type of Organizations	*Identical Organizations Existing at Each Period*				*Identical Organizations Starting between 1924 and 1930*			*Identical Organizations Existing in 1924 and 1930 but Dying between 1930 and 1936*		
	NO. REPORTING	*1924*	*1930*	*1936*	NO. REPORTING	*1930*	*1936*	NO. REPORTING	*1924*	*1930*
All types	1,042	32.5	31.1	34.4	339	53.6	55.5	264	37.2	39.4
Middle Atlantic	211	31.8	28.3	31.1	109	46.9	51.4	51	35.5	33.6
South	117	30.3	31.2	35.0	64	50.5	51.1	62	37.8	44.5
Middle West	540	31.9	31.0	35.7	118	61.5	57.0	104	36.7	40.7
Far West	174	37.2	35.7	35.7	48	59.1	67.0	47	39.1	38.3
Athletic	1	10.9	100.0	50.0	4	31.5	41.4	0	...	...
Civic	118	47.7	46.7	51.4	44	51.5	57.6	36	46.3	49.2
Educational	71	60.1	55.3	51.5	28	53.8	51.6	10	60.3	52.7
Fraternal	482	23.0	22.4	25.3	43	25.8	31.0	106	27.1	29.8
Musical	19	84.6	86.7	89.5	16	76.3	83.1	8	74.7	80.0
Patriotic	160	39.5	34.1	38.1	30	43.3	43.7	19	46.0	40.5
Political	0	...	...	...	0	...	...	0	...	...
Social	67	75.0	71.2	76.1	33	81.6	70.5	25	57.0	50.7
Bridge	18	92.3	86.7	89.5	19	98.7	98.2	8	94.3	100.0
Socio-economic	32	56.7	64.9	54.6	31	72.9	55.1	15	55.0	64.0
Farm Bureau	7	63.5	43.8	62.7	16	70.2	62.0	8	60.6	65.6
Grange	27	39.0	28.9	26.3	8	42.2	38.4	10	26.2	24.1
Socio-religious	8	17.9	26.5	28.6	4	52.4	55.5	5	40.1	49.1
Townsend	0	...	...	...	0	...	...	0	...	...
Youth-serving	32	76.9	84.3	80.5	45	71.3	68.6	13	69.5	81.5
4-H	0	...	...	...	18	84.4	85.3	1	75.0	83.8

leader to direct the band. This club has also interested itself in meetings. It conducts an "Old Settlers Day" which is attended by large crowds of from 10 to 20 thousand people. On this day, 4-H Clubs exhibit their work; and the best of this is sent to the State Fair. The Kiwanis Club enables the village 4-H Clubs to compete by contributing $100 for the prize fund of the State Fair. This club, like many businessmen's organizations, is in reality as much

TABLE 88

PER CAPITA EXPENDITURES OF SOCIAL ORGANIZATIONS

By Type and Region: 140 Villages, 1930–36

Type of Organization	*Number of Organizations Reporting*		*Per Capita Expenditures*	
	1930	*1936*	*1930*	*1936*
All types	1,774	1,732	$ 5.67	$ 4.03
Athletic	58	34	18.55	8.66
Civic	212	181	6.17	5.97
Educational	108	137	1.69	1.41
Fraternal	656	549	4.33	3.89
Musical	55	45	14.83	10.45
Patriotic	192	211	6.20	3.79
Social	130	119	6.46	1.62
Bridge	54	98	1.98	1.22
Socio-religious	22	16	3.87	4.90
Socio-economic	98	106	18.79	8.42
Farm Bureau	28	42	5.74	4.63
Grange	36	33	1.91	2.55
Political	...	3	...	2.39
Townsend	...	4	...	.35
Youth-serving	105	107	3.27	2.19
4-H	20	47	1.63	1.01
All regions	1,774	1,732	5.67	4.03
Middle Atlantic	379	365	5.25	4.56
South	157	278	5.49	4.24
Middle West	944	839	4.76	3.49
Far West	294	250	8.71	4.55

a civic as it is a socio-economic organization. This factor is one reason for the decline of purely civic organizations.

The desire to obtain a community clubhouse has unified and filled with life several clubs of a Southern village. Four Home Demonstration clubs and a women's club have formed a single organization, and for 2 years have been actively pushing their project with all the zeal common to women with a purpose. The results will undoubtedly be of value to the whole community, as the experience of one Eastern village may indicate. Here the Grange has succeeded in establishing a community center which has proved very popular. A field report gives detailed information on the achievement of the organization. "The outstanding interest of this group is the Grange encampment which holds its sixty-second meeting this year. The camp grounds, which lie west of the village, are enclosed and have several buildings for exhibit and meeting purposes. This encampment was started as a village Grange picnic, and has been growing steadily. Some years ago the camp grounds were improved and now have both electricity and water supply.

"The organization now owns tents which are rented for $8 a week to those who wish to use them. Some families bring their own tents which are wired for them for a small fee. Last year 400 tents were set up on the grounds and more than 10 thousand people were present during the 2 most eventful days of the week. The program is very similar to that of a county fair and replaces it in this region. It is run in close co-operation with the state and county Extension Service." Community centers of the kind described here are becoming more popular in rural villages. Sometimes they are owned by some organization, the Grange in this case. Lately, parks, playgrounds, and halls have been requested of the Federal work relief agencies and have been built, as was mentioned earlier in the chapter.

In spite of the depression, and partly because of it in some cases, many social organizations have lived and flourished in the last 5 years. They provided escape and relief from the economic dismalness of daily life. Groups turned to activities which tended to ameliorate the depression's bad effects on the community. The various projects undertaken by different clubs and organizations are as numerous as those of the W.P.A. Businessmen's clubs were generous in their aid of school children; they also were instrumental in supporting community enterprises, athletic teams, parks, and libraries, for which they often sought Federal aid. Public forums were conducted under their aegis, often in co-operation with other groups. Finally, organizations of this type attempted to improve the business of their members by enlarging the trade areas of their villages and by attracting country people to them. Parent-Teacher Associations naturally concentrated their energies on helping school children, for whom they provided food, medical attention, clothing, and amusement. Patriotic organizations also aided schools and pupils, and furthermore contributed to civic improvement, sponsored public forums, and community musical and athletic groups. Women's clubs are apparently beehives of activity, as they entered fields normally worked in by all other types of organizations. A partial list of accomplishments of a Southern women's club is given as example.

> Perhaps in the educational field the club can find its greatest accomplishments. More than a thousand dollars has been spent by the club members for the benefit and improvement of the school. The following school improvements can be listed as the most important work along this line:
>
> building of septic tank
> contribution to basketball equipment
> building of bookcases in library
> contribution to building of primary room
> erection of drinking fountains
> installation of shower baths for boys
> purchase of stage scenery for school auditorium
> payment of expenses of a girl for attendance at domestic science classes at Athens
> donation of some equipment to domestic science dept.
>
> In addition to the work for the school, the women's club has sponsored educational programs for its members, waged campaigns against adult illiteracy, and has made possible a library for the people of the town.

With the return of prosperity, more records of achievement such as this are being made by many rural social organizations. People are now in a better mental and financial condition to support their local groups.

The village American Legion posts are another type of organization whose activities often transcend the category of patriotic as usually understood. A typical post in a medium-sized village organized an annual community-wide picnic, financed band concerts, supported Boy and Girl Scouts, placed traffic signs on the streets, sent flowers to invalids, planted trees and worked for village beautification, and gathered and distributed clothes to the poor. In addition to most of these activities, many other posts engaged in such activities as supporting their own and the high-school basketball or baseball teams, and sometimes both. Several wired the new parks so that there could be tennis and even football and baseball after dark.

Co-operative undertakings.—Quite apart from these cases of organizational activity, and from the informal social and recreational life, there were numerous enterprises that involved the cooperation of more than one agency. One community in 6 had Fourth of July celebrations; one in 4, Memorial Day exercises. One in 10 celebrated Armistice Day, and an equal number had community celebrations of Christmas. One in 9 conducted elaborate programs related to agriculture, such as harvest or blossom festivals. Old Home Weeks or Old Settlers Days were sponsored by one-tenth of these places. Eight had marked their centennials in the inter-survey period with elaborate festivals, including pageants, fairs, addresses, and historical papers. Half a dozen conducted fairs of the type described elsewhere in the chapter. In the main, however, there seemed to be less interest in community festivals centering in the traditional holidays, and more interest in the dignifying of functional interests.

Summary.—This chapter has reviewed the many varied manifestations of social life and organization in the communities under survey. It is a record of both loss and gain. Pre-eminently it is a story of change, of changes that vary in kind and in tempo with the regions, changes that are a response to the play of cosmic social and economic forces upon local communities, changes that reflect the adaptation of communities and their leaders to these forces.

Thus the fraternal orders, products of the era of isolation in rural America when mutual needs and hardships placed a premium upon neighborly fraternity, are seen yielding ground to activities and agencies that socialize neighborliness in terms of effort for community betterment and that meet the age-old need for charity through organization and the resources of the state and nation.

Thus, too, the interests and thoughts of men and women have broadened with the process of the years. In a period when bread itself became a prime necessity for millions, the conviction deepened that man lives not by bread alone. Increasingly, rural people have sought to understand, perchance to utilize, the forces that baffled them. They have recognized the end of their isolation, the inevitableness of interaction among all groups. Increasingly, too, they have sought outlets for expression in drama, in community service, in recreation. Often in this they have followed blindly urban pathways even to the bridge table. But frequently and encouragingly they have given a cultural turn to activities in terms authentically expressive of rural America.

True, there are backward communities as there are retarded individuals. True, too, there are conservative, unimaginative, even defeatist localities and persons; and there are those whose every nerve, to the point of exhaustion, must still be strained to meet the problems of survival and subsistence. But viewing the record of social life and the previous story of the progress of adult education against the background of economic stress and suffering described in the opening chapters of this report leads to the conclusion that rural America is on the move toward a better, more wholesome and more functional social life, and warrants the high hope that the impetus already developed may be powerful enough to achieve and hold that good.

XI

Notes on Government and Health

THIS chapter will discuss a considerable variety of manifestations that are related to the general theme of social life. Many of the topics were covered much more completely in the previous studies but had to be omitted to a considerable extent from this one because of budgetary limitations. The data here included, however, especially those dealing with local government and health, are believed to give real indications of changes in these fields in the 140 communities.

LOCAL GOVERNMENT

Few changes noted.—Local government in rural areas was reported in the 1930 study as having experienced less change than any other type of organization. It has remained almost unchanged throughout the 1930–36 inter-survey period. In only one community were changes made in the structural set-up of the government organization. These changes, which consolidated offices and introduced a more efficient and economical administration and gave the taxpayers more and better service at less cost, were introduced after a careful survey by the Bureau of Agricultural Economics of the United States Department of Agriculture. This is the only instance in these communities in which desired economy was wisely and scientifically secured.

One village increased its boundary slightly to take in persons just over the line who were receiving town water and light and fire protection at lower cost than the villagers.

Two badly governed villages revolted. In one, the reform party, after 4 years in power, lost by a narrow margin. In the other, it remained in power; and as a result, the village bonds which had dropped to half their par value had been restored to par. The indebtedness had been reduced by $100,000.

Governmental expenditures reduced.—The depression naturally reduced the average tax revenues of village government. Exclusive of revenues from school districts and municipal utilities, the average village receipts dropped from $13,579 to $10,665, or 21.3 per cent. This was practically the same rate of decline as for the school districts. The rate of decline from 1930 to 1935 was quite constant among all regions except the Middle Atlantic, where the decrease was 7.2 per cent. The other regions ranged from 22.0 to 26.4 per cent. The large villages and towns suffered more severe losses than the smaller-sized centers. These data are detailed in Table 89, which also shows that in all regions except the Middle Atlantic the decline in village tax revenues set in before 1930.

TABLE 89

AVERAGE TAX REVENUES PER VILLAGE FOR SUPPORT OF VILLAGE GOVERNMENT EXCLUSIVE OF SCHOOLS AND UTILITIES [a]

Region and Size	*1924*	*1930*	*1935*
All regions	$14,301	$13,579	$10,665
Middle Atlantic	9,456	11,874	11,014
South	11,504	10,077	7,873
Middle West	15,419	14,435	10,649
Far West	22,364	17,740	13,731
Small	... [b]	6,320	5,013
Medium	... [b]	12,835	10,361
Large	... [b]	20,076	15,437
Town	... [b]	28,473	21,551

[a] Table based on 136 villages for 1924 and 129 identical villages for 1930 and 1935.
[b] Not computed for 1924.

It should be noted that this decrease in budget occurs despite an increase in relief expenditures in some of these communities. Such an item was negligible in 1924 and not very large in 1930. This means that the normal activities have been cut by more than the percentage of reduction shown in the total expenses in order to make place for the new item of expense. Comparing the decline in tax revenues from 1924 to 1935, the results show a drop of 25.3 per cent for the total group of villages. This figure, however, is made up of an increase of 16.5 per cent in the Middle Atlantic, and decreases of 46.1, 43.9, and 38.6 per cent for the Southern, Middle Western, and Far Western regions, respectively.

Decreases such as these are considerable when viewed in the aggregate; but the relief for the individual taxpayer is not very large, although, because of increases in the population of the villages, the percentage decline in the per capita tax burden is somewhat larger than the decline in the total tax funds raised. The per capita taxes paid are shown in Table 90.

Many civic improvements.—Two other influences on local government were frequently mentioned. The vast majority of these municipalities have enjoyed honest, though not always efficient, government. The present inter-survey period saw gains in efficiency

TABLE 90

PER CAPITA TAXES BY REGION

140 Villages

Region	*1924*	*1930*	*1935*
All regions	$10.81	$10.05	$7.41
Middle Atlantic	8.39	10.54	8.81
South	8.49	7.27	5.37
Middle West	11.77	10.95	7.69
Far West	14.29	11.34	7.67

and a broadened social outlook. The cause of this change is locally reported to be the increasing amount of co-operation between local and Federal officials in connection with work relief and other recovery projects. The number of these projects is considerable and they cover a wide range of types. Streets were built or resurfaced in 32 villages. Thirteen places constructed sewers. Twenty constructed parks. Eighteen built swimming pools; and 5, municipal tennis courts, not counting, of course, pools and courts built as part of the park equipment. Ten community houses were erected, together with from 3 to 6 firehouses, town halls, and libraries. Seventeen municipal water systems were installed or existing systems much extended, and 4 new reservoirs were constructed. Six municipal electric light plants were built. Plans for improvements of all these various kinds were under discussion in other communities at the time of the survey. In addition, there were several cases of planning for each of the following betterments: municipal parking spaces, rest rooms and comfort stations for farmers, gymnasiums, hospitals, post offices, and airports. There were also numerous projects in civic beautification including the setting out of hundreds of trees in the average community.

All told, it is a very impressive list of civic improvements that have been made in the last 3 years; and the facilities in question were being regularly used by the people. This is one of the distinct gains from the depression for these 140 communities and they have helped bring the farm population into the informal recreational life of the community. Such enterprises were in line with the traditions of local government in the villages. The 1924 study showed that local people thought of their municipal government chiefly in terms of improvements of various sorts.

Some of these developments were described in detail in the previous chapter. It may be of interest here simply to list the projects in 2 villages, one in the South, the other in the Far West, both with less than 1,500 population. The list covers the period from the organization of relief in 1933 to the time of the survey in the spring of 1936.

1. The stone steps at the courthouse which were originally placed there to prevent cattle from roaming into the courthouse grounds, were removed.
2. The cemetery was cleaned up, shrubbery planted.
3. The roadsides were cleaned up and in some instances made more attractive.
4. The Methodist Church was renovated and the grounds surrounding it were cleared and leveled. At the Baptist Church, the leveling of grounds, planting of shrubs, as well as the beautification of the parsonage grounds was somewhat more extensive.
5. A syrup-blending plant and a cold-storage plant are under construction.

6. Some property formerly owned by the Boy Scouts was developed and the grounds were cleared; stoves, tables, benches and bath houses were built for what will really be a community park, about 4 miles out from the village center.
7. A similar piece of work is in progress at a pool owned by the Girl Scouts about 2 miles out of town.
8. Extensive sidewalk repairs were undertaken, and later 8,000 feet of sidewalk were constructed.
9. A county library was established.

The second list is shorter, partly because the village was smaller, partly because the need for work-relief was considerably less acute.

1. Two and one-half miles of streets paved.
2. Library building erected.
3. New city hall built.
4. Gymnasium for school and community.
5. Public park greatly improved.
6. New water system in schools.

The other result often reported of this co-operation with the Federal government was a lessening of the bitterness between political parties and factions in the villages. Community-wide co-operation was required to secure these benefits, and for the most part the citizens demanded and secured that co-operation. Some villages reported also that, as a result of the Federal program, it was easier to secure real leaders for public office.

Rural electrification.—One of the evidences of the struggle for higher standards of living in rural America, reported in the previous report of this series,[1] was the increase from 7.0 to 13.4 per cent of the total in the number of farm homes lighted by electricity. One reason for this low figure has been the fear of the high investment necessary to give service to a population of low density. According to the Federal Power Commission,[2] 60 per cent of 1,273,085 rural customers average from six-tenths of one cus-

[1] Brunner and Kolb, *Rural Social Trends*, p. 63.

[2] *Rural Electric Service*, Rate Series No. 8 (Washington, United States Government Printing Office, 1936), p. 127.

tomer to 9.5, per mile of line. Obviously, this means far higher construction costs per customer than in cities. To help in the extension of central station electric service to farmers, Congress made permanent the Rural Electrification Administration founded in May, 1935, by executive order. With 10-year appropriations of over 400 million dollars, great impetus is thus given to the extension of rural electrification.

The great interest in rural electrification, stimulated among other things by the Rural Electrification Administration, thus lends significance to the number of municipal electric light and power plants in these communities. All told, there were 22 at the time of the survey, 16 of them in the Middle West, 4 in the Far West, and 2 in the Middle Atlantic. In 7 other centers, municipal plants were under construction or had been approved at the time of the survey. In still others, the issue of municipal as against private utility was being actively debated.

Thirty-one communities were already co-operating with the Rural Electrification Administration, whether through private companies, municipalities, or co-operatives; and others expressed interest in such co-operation as soon as the opportunity offered. Farm Bureaus, Farmers' Unions, and Co-operatives were all actively at work on the extension of rural electrification. In this connection it is interesting to note that, excluding California because of the large amounts of energy used there for irrigation purposes, the average revenue per kilowatt hour for 693 private utility companies was 5.3 cents as against 3.4 cents for the 730 municipal plants. These figures cover more than one-half million farm customers, less than 10 per cent of whom were serviced by municipal plants.[3]

Back of these simple statistics lie many interesting stories. One of the communities in this study received national publicity because of a suit entered to prevent the municipality's earning profits on its electric power plant. These profits were applied to regular

[3] *Ibid.*, p. 17.

municipal expenses. The State Public Service Commission ruled that this was not a proper procedure, but the decision was overruled by the Court of Appeals. The rates in this village were already lower than those in other communities in the same area.

Typical of several situations is that of a Middle Atlantic village in which, with Rural Electrification Administration help, the municipal plant has been enlarged and by January, 1937, expects to serve 984 farm homes on 269 miles of line. Similar co-operation was being extended by the Rural Electrification Administration to farmers' co-operatives whether they were co-operating with private or municipal plants or planning to erect their own. In a Middle West village, a municipal plant with a long record of successful operation had agreed to supply open-country sub-centers for one and one-half cents per kilowatt. Private companies in all regions were forestalling competition from municipal or co-operative plants by reducing rates. In the Tennessee Valley Authority area, reductions in the villages studied averaged 50 per cent. In one Middle West community, rates had been reduced 4 times in 5 years, each time resulting in a sharp increase in energy consumption. In another where there was a successful municipal plant, the Rural Electrification Administration allotted $120,000 for expansion of plant and lines to serve the contiguous farming area. In a third community of 414 farm homes without electric service, 300 signed up to install current under a co-operative agreement aided by a Federal grant.

This accelerating activity in the expansion of rural electric service was too recent to show results that could be appraised; but it seems very probable that any future visit to these communities will show not only a huge expansion in the number of homes with electric service but also the usual by-product results from the introduction of labor-saving machinery in the farm home and barn and the improved lighting of homes, schools, Grange halls, and other meeting places of farm people.

Health.—Health, as an item in the local community budget, is of little importance. Increasingly, health work is being carried on by counties under so-called County Health Units. Rural America had 615 counties or other districts with full-time health officers in January, 1932, 3 times as many as in 1922. This number declined to 530 by December, 1933. Then the tide turned. In 1936, there were 647. This type of work seems likely to increase under the provisions of the Social Security Act. There was a quite general increase in community interest in health and health provision despite the depression. Clinics had increased in number, in part because of the use of W.P.A. nurses.

The contribution of one county health unit was clear from the report of a Southern village whose community area covered a large part of the county. Local, state, and Federal appropriations provided a budget of $7,000 for a full-time doctor and nurse. A year later a sanitary inspector was added. In the third year, 1935, an additional nurse was employed. Doctor and nurse have reached each open-country school at least once. Clinics have been held, water supplies examined. The weekly paper carries a front-page article on health by the doctor in each issue. The undertaker complains of the sharply lowered death rate, as well he may. The incidence of typhoid has, for instance, been cut 90 per cent in the last 2 years, as compared with 1931.

The 1930 report showed that doctors in rural areas were growing both older and fewer. This was based on a study of the directories of the American Medical Association.[4] No similar data were secured this year; but the Metropolitan Life Insurance Company in its August, 1936, Statistical Bulletin reports an analysis of the American Medical Directory of 1936 which contains much of interest in connection with the field of rural health. They report as follows:

In the first place, it shows that the proportion of physicians to population steadily decreased up to 1929, when there was one doctor to every 797 inhabitants. Since then there has been a steady increase in the ratio

[4] Brunner and Kolb, *Rural Social Trends*, pp. 276-82.

of licensed physicians. This statement applies, particularly, with minor variations, to the industrial states of the Northeast and to most of the Mountain and Pacific Coast states. Apparently, the diminished opportunities offered by the business world in recent years have caused a larger proportion of medical graduates to go into actual practice than was customary during the boom years following the World War, when a considerable number of graduate physicians were attracted into industrial and other fields where their medical training could be better capitalized. At least, this seems to be true, in general, of the large centers of population.

Medical practice in the rural sections, as a rule, still has little or no attraction for the newly graduated medical student. This is evidenced by the fact that in such states as Mississippi, Alabama, Georgia, North and South Carolina, and the Dakotas, where from 70 to 85 per cent of the inhabitants reside in the rural areas, the number of persons per physician ranges from 1,196 in South Dakota to 1,541 in South Carolina. On the other hand, in the states of Rhode Island, Massachusetts, New York, Illinois, and California, where the rural inhabitants constitute less than 27 per cent of the total population, the ratio of persons to physicians ranges from 519 in California to 737 in Rhode Island. In other words, the average physician in South Carolina has nearly three times as many prospective patients in his locality as has a doctor in California or New York.

The drift of doctors to the large medical centers is further revealed in a study of the ratio of persons to physicians in certain of the leading cities of the country. In the Borough of Manhattan, New York, for example, there are only 287 persons per physician; in Boston there were 290; in Washington, D.C., 297; in San Francisco, 345; and in Los Angeles, 384.

It is possible, however, that in village-centered agricultural communities the decline has been checked, whether temporarily or not remains to be seen. At least the number of physicians increased about 7 per cent, on the basis of field-work figures, over 1930. Though the totals are not yet up to 1924 for the total group of villages, in the 2 Western regions this level has been exceeded.

The number of dentists also increased about 10 per cent between 1930 and 1936. The gain was distributed unevenly over all regions, as Table 92 shows.

The distribution of doctors and dentists naturally varied according to the size of the village; but even in the small communities, the number held at least to the 1930 levels, as will be noted from Table 93.

There has also been a significant increase in the number of hospitals in these communities since 1924. Most of the increase came between that year and 1930, by which time there were 53, slightly more than twice the number in 1924. By 1936 the total was 55. The larger a community, the greater the likelihood that it would have one of these hospitals. A number of these institutions were little more than a few beds in a doctor's home, used for little more than emergency cases. Others were county-seat hospitals with some approach to modern standards, though in the main these hospitals appeared to fall woefully below the standards achieved in the rural demonstration hospitals assisted by the Commonwealth Fund.

TABLE 91

DISTRIBUTION OF DOCTORS BY REGIONS [a]

Region	*1920*	*1930* [b]	*1936* [b]
All regions	504	417	447
Middle Atlantic	100	70	83
South	132	89	95
Middle West	196	182	197
Far West	76	76	78

[a] There are slight discrepancies between these 1930 figures and those in *Rural Social Trends*, which were based on census records. This is accounted for in part by differences in classification.

[b] Based on field work.

TABLE 92

DISTRIBUTION OF DENTISTS BY REGION

140 Villages

Region	*1930*	*1936*
All regions	242	269
Middle Atlantic	37	45
South	39	46
Middle West	125	131
Far West	41	47

COMMUNICATION

City dailies gain rural circulation.—The last years have also seen a great development in the facilities for communication. The number of radios was everywhere reported to have increased, as was noted in the discussion of adult education in Chapter VIII. Radios were kept even when telephones were discontinued. Where measured in 1930 urban newspaper circulation had increased sharply, the median gain being about 50 per cent over 1924. This factor was not measured, save in one community, in 1936; but from most villages and rural route carriers the report was that "Nearly every one receives city papers." In the one community where a count was made, a county-seat town in the northern part

TABLE 93

DISTRIBUTION OF DOCTORS AND DENTISTS BY SIZE OF COMMUNITY

140 Villages

	1930			*1936*		
Size	*Number Villages in Each Group*	*Number of Doctors*	*Number of Dentists*	*Number Villages in Each Group*	*Number of Doctors*	*Number of Dentists*
Towns	12	85	45	17	95	51
Large villages	23	82	53	20	93	51
Medium villages	57	172	104	61	181	123
Small villages	48	78	40	42	78	44

of the South, 367 of the 420 white homes took a city daily, about double the 1924 proportion. A number of others received the Sunday editions of either New York or Philadelphia papers. A New York tabloid circulated widely among the Negroes on Sunday.

Local papers improve.—Interestingly enough, the local papers which had seemed very much on the downgrade in 1924 and barely holding their own in 1930, survived the depression. It was noticeable that they carried far more national news than formerly, and frequently related it to local manifestations of Federal activities. It was also noticeable on reading these papers from every major region in the United States that anti-administration editorials were frequently of almost or quite identical wording, while pro-administration editorials were in no case discovered to be similar. That is not to say that stories from Federal press bureaus were not found. They were quite frequent. In the main they were of two types: human interest, or factual question and answer.

Transportation.—Chapter IV has already noted the increase in farm-to-market roads. All agree that these roads have increased the frequency with which farm people come to the center. Existing roads have also been improved in most of the communities. Train service had been cut quite sharply by 1930, and some further reductions in service were made, but an increase in bus and truck service was quite generally reported.

RACE RELATIONS

The relations that exist between races in communities in which two sharply different racial groups exist side by side are an important factor in social life. Outside the South, and to a less extent the Far West, the localities studied are quite homogeneous. The foreign born in the Middle Atlantic and Middle West regions are of northern European stock, have been long in the United States, and for the most part are completely assimilated. One indication of this is the high mortality of foreign-language social organizations which has been going on at an accelerating rate since 1924. One Southern community has had a foreign-born colony since 1923. These foreign-born farmers were then none too welcome. They shared none of the social or religious traditions of the South, cared naught for cotton or tobacco farming, but sought by intensive agriculture on small holdings to supply a near-by urban market with vegetables and dairy products.[5] The changed attitude of the native stock is remarkable as shown in the fieldworker's report:

[5] For an extended study of this community as of 1927, see Brunner, *Immigrant Farmers and Their Children* (1929), Part II, Chapter I. This is a publication of the Institute of Social and Religious Research, distributed by Harper & Brothers, New York.

Over a period of years these farmers have gained the respect and admiration of the community, and their farms are models for the entire Southeastern section. The people are hard workers and thrifty, and their children for the most part are leaders in the village schools. The co-operation of the various elements of this community is remarkable. There are two co-operative truck associations, a community house which is active all the time, and church schools in which the mother languages are taught. The young people sponsor gatherings throughout the year, and these have proved so popular that outsiders from miles around come to enjoy the good-will and fellowship that is to be found there.

Relations with Negroes.—The main problem of race relations as touched by these studies is, of course, that of the Negroes in the South. In these communities there has been little ruffling of a peaceful *status quo*. The segregation of the Negro is complete. He has his own churches, schools, and few social organizations. The Negro has drawn relief funds as is shown in Chapter XIII. He has had some educational facilities, though highly limited, as is clear from a study of these school systems. The Negro quarter usually stands by itself, off from the village, often on the far side of the railroad tracks, a stream, or other barrier. The houses are poorly built, frequently unpainted. The windows are often only shutters and usually unscreened. Primarily these people are dependent upon seasonal labor related to the cotton cycle and on odd jobs. Without relief, the situation in at least some of these communities would have been serious indeed, and perhaps less peaceful. Now and then also the basic social attitudes flare up, as in one village when the Tennessee Valley Authority proposed to establish a community library for the benefit of all the citizens, Negro and white. There was apparently little business of any sort transacted in this village until the Tennessee Valley Authority abandoned its original proposal and constructed 2 libraries, one for each race.

Somehow the Negroes have supported their churches, at an unbelievably low level as the next chapter shows; but there seems to be but one expenditure absolutely vital to this group in many of the communities, namely, their insurance and burial policies. The weekly fees ranged from 10 cents to $1 and were estimated quite often to reach 10 per cent of the family income. In many communities, these burial associations are the only organizations other than churches to which the Negroes belong.[6] Sometimes they are helped by white landlords who find this a cheaper device than paying for Negro burials.

One of these organizations is specially interesting in illustrating how one agency can do many things. It was founded in 1906. Dues were 25 cents a month. Surplus was invested in land until at present 340 acres are owned. Rent from this, plus dues, gives the society a budget of over $800 a year. The society pays $1.50 sick benefits to members, cares for the old, and attends to the burial of members. Until 10 years ago it secured flour and fertilizer for its members by purchasing in carload lots and selling at cost. Opposition of the landlords is said to have ended this co-operative buying.

The discussion now turns to another aspect of organized social life, the religious.

[6] In the Far West, very few of the communities had any problem of race relations. There were Mexicans, of course, but they were in separate groups, almost as strictly segregated as the Negroes. The feeling against Japanese and Armenians, quite strong in 1924 and still noticeable in 1930, had disappeared. Both are now accepted as permanent residents.

XII

Rural Religion

THE CHURCHES of rural America have in some respects felt the strain of these last years more acutely than other social institutions. Their recovery from the low point has not been as marked as in the case of the schools. In part, this is a natural result of the type of organization that has characterized organized rural religion for half a century at least. The country church had numerous unsolved problems before the depression began, problems of competition, undersized congregations, inadequate ministerial service, sub-standard programs. The record in the inter-survey period of 1930–36 is therefore one of loss in many, though not in all, aspects of the religious situation.

Number of churches declines.—In the previous inter-survey period, 1924–30, the birth rate and death rate of village churches almost balanced; in the open country, there was a net loss of nearly 11 per cent. Between 1930 and 1936, 70 village churches died, one in 11; but the net loss, because of new churches formed, was only 13, bringing the total to 771. This loss was almost exclusively among the white Protestant churches and in the Middle Atlantic villages. The Negro group made a net gain of 2, raising the number to 74; the Roman Catholic group lost 2, bringing their total to 71.

The open-country churches, as in the previous inter-survey period, had greater difficulty. Of the 552 churches in these communities that were outside the village boundaries in 1930, 115 died in the 6-year period, almost 21 per cent. However, 88 new churches were formed, or reopened, and several were added as a result of enlarged community boundaries. The net loss was therefore 19, or 3.4 per cent. Again, the loss was almost exclusively white Protestant and outside the South. Thus the net loss was less than one-half that of the earlier inter-survey period. Excluding the South, the loss was 16.8 per cent. The chief explanation lies in a depression-induced phenomenon. Ministers unable to secure charges, and former clergymen who had lost their positions, opened up a number of abandoned churches, especially where living quarters were available, and served the people for anything they could secure in cash or kind. In a few instances, such reopenings were alleged to be in violation of county agreements. Some of the new churches, 26 in all, were added because of enlarged community boundaries. If these be deducted, the net loss in terms of the number of churches reported in 1930 will of course be larger. The facts on net numbers of churches in the three surveys are recorded in Table 94.

TABLE 94

VILLAGE AND COUNTRY CHURCHES BY CREED, COLOR, AND REGION, 1924–36

140 American Agricultural Villages

	Village Churches			*Country Churches*		
Region	*1924*	*1930*	*1936*	*1924*	*1930*	*1936*
			ALL CHURCHES			
All regions	780	784	763	619	552	533
Middle Atlantic	137	137	126	120	101	88
South	183	193	188	274	255	286
Middle West	299	300	296	178	157	131
Far West	101	154	153	47	39	28
			WHITE PROTESTANT CHURCHES			
All regions	648	639	618	515	468	439
Middle Atlantic	121	121	110	118	99	87
South	123	124	118	184	178	201
Middle West	263	260	257	168	153	125
Far West	141	134	133	45	38	26
			NEGRO PROTESTANT CHURCHES			
All regions	62	72	74	91	77	84
South	57	64	66	88	76	83
			ROMAN CATHOLIC CHURCHES			
All regions	70	73	71	13	7	10
Middle Atlantic	15	15	15	0	1	1
South	3	5	4	2	1	2
Middle West	34	38	34	9	4	5
Far West	18	18	18	2	1	2

Members per church continue to increase.—The average number of members per church in all regions increased in the last inter-survey period, as in the first, for all types of churches, as Table 95 shows.

It now amounts to 171 in the village and 93 in the open country, or, for the dominant white Protestant group, to 163 and 86, respectively. This represents a gain of 16.5 in the village and 18.1 per cent in the open country for this group since 1924. The greater part of this gain was made in the second period, 1930–36.

As would be expected with the increasing average membership of these churches, the proportion of very small churches is declining. In 1924, 25.5 per cent of village and 43.3 per cent of open-country churches had less than 50 members. The 1936 per cents were 20.1 and 30.8, respectively. Conversely, the proportion with 200 or more members, which were 24.3 and 6.0 per cent for village and country, respectively, in 1924 had risen to 32.2 and 8.0 per cent in 1936.

There are two explanations for this trend toward larger memberships. In the first place it is obviously the smaller and weaker churches that succumb to the pressure of social forces and die. This automatically raised the average membership of the surviving group. In the second place while many ministers reported a lessening of interest in religion during the depression, others reported that people had been turned to spiritual concerns by their troubles.

It is probable that the replies on this point bear some relation to the condition of the church. There was general agreement among the more doctrinally conservative clergy that the depression was a heaven-sent punishment for the excesses of the 1920's. There was also frequent mention of the fact that attendance dropped both because people lacked clothes fit for Sunday wear and because of the demands for money by preachers, especially in churches that had building debts on their hands.

Two tests of the net result of these trends are to be found in the proportion of the total population belonging to local churches and in the average attendance at services. The first of these shows that in the total group of communities, the sharp decline in the proportion of the population in church has been checked. However, the regions behaved differently in this respect. In the Middle Atlantic and the Middle West, the decline continued. In the South and the Far West, where there had been sharp losses between 1924 and 1930, there were sharp gains between 1930 and 1936, which carried the ratio in the latter region to above 1924 levels as Table 96 shows.

The explanation of these changes lies in part in population movements. Open-country Negroes moving into villages apparently joined churches, and Middle Western farmers fleeing to the Far West from drought areas swelled church memberships there. But there was probably also some increased interest in religion as such.

These figures should, of course, be corrected by the proportion of inactive members among the total membership, which amounted to 18.1 per cent in 1930. Data on this point, however, were not secured in 1936, both because of the expense involved in a name-by-name examination of the rolls of some 1,300 churches and because it was known that at least some churches were carrying on the rolls above-average proportions of persons who had ceased contributing because of financial stress.

Attendance declines further.—The test of attendance is, therefore, probably the fairest index of interest in the activities of the church. The record on this point shows a decided falling off on the part of resident members. On the basis of the data on attendance furnished by the churches, two measurements were made, one on the basis of resident members, the other on the basis of community population. It is recognized, of course, that there is always some non-member attendance; but obviously attendance could not be separated as between members and non-members.

Crediting all attendance to resident members, there appears to have been a falling off of more than one-fifth in rural church attendance in the last 6 years. This decline was at 3 times as rapid

TABLE 95

AVERAGE RESIDENT MEMBERSHIP OF VILLAGE AND OPEN-COUNTRY CHURCHES

By Creed, Color, and Region, 1924–36

Region	ALL CHURCHES			WHITE PROTESTANT			NEGRO PROTESTANT			ROMAN CATHOLIC		
	1924	*1930*	*1936*	*1924*	*1930*	*1936*	*1924*	*1930*	*1936*	*1924*	*1930*	*1936*
	Village Churches											
All regions	148	155	171	140	149	163	83	76	81	287	308	377
Middle Atlantic	162	166	179	151	161	165	...	...	...	274	226	319
South	136	149	158	154	164	181	89	84	85	...	...	...
Middle West	172	173	195	153	160	178	...	...	...	328	315	388
Far West	105	112	135	92	100	112	...	...	...	217	227	336
	Country Churches											
All regions	80	82	93	73	77	86	117	114	115	134	125	195
Middle Atlantic	51	57	55	51	57	55	...	...	...	...	...	...
South	94	91	94	81	83	90	121	114	116	...	...	...
Middle West	84	89	118	82	87	116	...	...	...	...	...	...
Far West	57	61	100	55	59	77	...	...	...	...	...	...

a rate as in the first inter-survey period. Every region shared in this decline. The loss was again especially severe in the Middle West. It seems hardly possible that a drop of this magnitude could be accounted for on the basis of the depression difficulties of church members who lacked gas for their cars or adequate clothes for Sunday wear. These factors clearly operated to some extent; but they were offset by a rigorous pruning of the church rolls, which in many congregations eliminated inactive members and especially non-resident members. The proportion of non-residents to total members, for instance, declined from 12.5 to 9.0 per cent between 1930 and 1936. Moreover, many ministers reported that their

TABLE 96

RATIO OF RESIDENT CHURCH MEMBERSHIP TO COMMUNITY POPULATION BY REGION

140 American Agricultural Villages

Region	*1924* *Per Cent*	*1930* *Per Cent*	*1936* *Per Cent*
All regions	35.3	32.9	32.8
Middle Atlantic	37.9	35.9	34.0
South	38.4	34.9	37.6
Middle West	36.5	35.8	32.1
Far West	24.6	21.0	25.5

attendance was better when the weather was inclement than when it was clear.

On the basis of total community population, the decline in attendance was 12.7 per cent. In the Middle West, it exceeded 30 per cent. The gain in the Far West kept the national average from sinking lower. This gain is due to the increase in the Roman Catholic membership, and to the large curiosity attendance at services of some of the emotional sects such as the Four-Square Gospel. Table 97 contains the regional data on these comparisons.

The acceleration in the rate of decline in rural church attendance in the face of the improvement in the professional training of the ministers, reported later, should prove disquieting to church leaders. The explanations, other than that indicated above, appear reasonably clear from the data presented throughout this chapter. Small, competing churches, poorly trained ministers, feeble programs will not impress the constituency of the rural church, especially in the light of the more interesting, richer, steadily improving social life described in the last chapters. If the church puts its institutional forms and emphasis upon the minutiae of doctrine about the needs of the people, it must expect to pay the price in lowered attendance, lowered contributions, and declining loyalty.

Open-country members of village churches increase.—One element of importance in the church situation is the proportion of open-country members in village and town churches. Up to 1930 this had been steadily increasing. It was long ago pointed out in

TABLE 97

ATTENDANCE INTEREST IN CHURCHES, ALL DENOMINATIONS

Region	*Average Monthly Attendance* PER PERSON IN COMMUNITY POPULATION			PER RESIDENT CHURCH-MEMBERS		
	1924	*1930*	*1936*	*1924*	*1930*	*1936*
All regions	1.2	1.1	.96	3.9	3.6	2.8
Middle Atlantic	1.1	1.1	.91	3.5	3.1	2.5
South	1.1	1.0	.95	2.5	3.1	2.4
Middle West	1.6	1.4	.97	5.4	4.0	3.0
Far West	0.8	0.8	.98	4.5	4.0	3.75

this series of studies that the churches at the center unconsciously competed for members with those in the open country; often the wealthier and better educated members of the open-country neighborhoods were the ones attracted by the better services of the village, and the competition, therefore, frequently resulted in the death of open-country churches. The less prosperous members of these churches then either were lost to organized religion or they joined emotional sects whose representatives had begun working among them. This latter phenomenon was summed up in the generalization that the killing range of the village or town church was greater than its service range.

Between 1930 and 1936, the proportion of open-country members in the total membership of village and town churches increased somewhat in every region, and in every size-group of villages. This gain was not phenomenal, being only from 35.5 per cent to 38.2 per cent of the membership, a gain of 2.7 points or of 7.7 per cent in the proportion. However, this increase follows one of comparable scope between 1924 and 1930. Among the white Protestant churches alone, the proportion is 34.9 per cent. In the 1920 study of 26 counties, the ratio of open-country members to total village church membership was only 20 per cent. There seems to be no doubt, therefore, that rural religion, like other rural social institutions, is more and more centralizing in the village and town centers of rural communities. The rate of the progress of this movement differs among the regions and the denominations. It has gone further with the Roman Catholics than with the Protestants, further in the Middle and Far West regions than in the others; but the trend is the same in all groups and areas. This is one important explanation of the decline in the number of open-country churches; and, as was pointed out in previous reports, it sets for the church at the center the problem of adequate ministry to those in the rural hinterland who have lost their own churches but have not joined those in the village center. Were this problem more efficiently handled, the attendance losses described above might be checked. Table 98 carries the detailed figures.

Church support sharply lower.—As might be expected as a result of the depression, the per capita contributions to churches declined drastically between 1930 and 1936. Interestingly, the drop in the open-country churches was proportionately less than in those of the village, being 33.8 and 36.2 per cent, respectively. Moreover, the village decline followed a 3 per cent drop between 1924 and 1930, whereas, in the open country during this period, there had been a gain of about 5 per cent. The proportionate loss in per capita contributions in open-country churches about equaled the decline in the per pupil cost of instruction in open-country schools. In the villages, the drop in church gifts was proportionately almost twice that of school costs. On the other hand, per member contributions to social organizations, as Chapter X shows, dropped only 29 per cent.

Had this survey been undertaken earlier, however, the declines would have been more drastic. Financially, churches were obviously sharing to some extent in the recovery, as there were numerous congregations that in 1935, or in the fiscal year April 1, 1935, to March 31, 1936 (the dates for the fiscal year of a number of

TABLE 98

PER CENT OF MEMBERS FROM OPEN COUNTRY IN VILLAGE CHURCH

Region and Size	*Per Cent of Members from Open Country*	
	1930 [a]	*1936*
All regions	35.5	38.2
Middle Atlantic	28.0	30.4
South	25.8	30.2
Middle West	40.8	42.7
Far West	46.0	47.5
Small villages	34.1	45.4
Medium villages	34.2	39.8
Large villages	27.3	31.0
Towns	... [b]	35.9

[a] In 1924, the proportion for all villages was 31.6 per cent.
[b] Included with large villages in 1930.

the larger denominations), were reducing indebtedness on current expenses and on ministers' salaries. Table 99 gives the details.

This drop in per member contributions has apparently not been as severe in these village and open-country churches as among all churches. The Federal Council of the Churches of Christ in America quotes the United Stewardship Council [1] as showing a drop of 43 per cent in per capita contributions between 1928 and 1935 for all churches and all purposes, and of 45 per cent for congregational purposes only. There was an increase of less than one per cent between 1934 and 1935. The total figures were $23.38

[1] *Information Service*, March 21, 1936.

given for all purposes per member in 1930, and $18.08 in 1935.

The total expenses per Protestant church also declined: in the villages, from $2,402 to $1,910, or 20.5 per cent; in the open country, from $709 to $560, or 21 per cent. The lower rate of decline in the total budgets as compared with the per capita contributions is due to the larger memberships already noted, and to the fact that for a number of the weaker churches it was not possible to secure fiscal data. In numerous cases, far more than ever before, the minister was given the collection without a record being kept of the amount, or he was paid in part in farm products. As one Southern elder put it when questioned as to salary, "we jes' do the best we can." Essential repairs and janitor service were contributed.

TABLE 99

PER MEMBER EXPENDITURES IN VILLAGE AND COUNTRY PROTESTANT CHURCHES BY REGION

	Village			Country		
Region	*1924*	*1930*	*1936*	*1924*	*1930*	*1936*
All regions	$16.89	$16.38	$10.45	$8.13	$ 8.57	$5.67
Middle Atlantic	17.09	18.61	12.70	12.40	12.34	8.30
South	16.33	15.22	8.51	5.38	5.40	3.02
Middle West	17.81	16.25	9.93	12.39	12.57	8.81
Far West	19.35	19.54	12.79	12.33	16.13	6.68

Regional differences, by size of village, on both total church expenses and per capita contributions indicate that Middle Atlantic churches and those in large villages had the largest budgets, that the Middle Western open-country churches had the largest per member expenses for this group, while per capita expenses in the South were less than one-half those in the other regions.

The Negro churches reported an average current expense of $289, or $2.56 per member per year, a decline on both items of about 50 per cent. The Roman Catholic church budgets dropped slightly more than one-fifth to $2,490 per church; but the per member offerings declined to $6.20 from $12.03, or almost half.

The reduced funds of these churches were spent in a somewhat different way than in 1930. As the depression grew more severe, the problem of survival, especially for the open-country churches, grew more acute; hence there was less money for the benevolence work of the denominations. The salary of the pastor and bills for coal and light had to be given first consideration. Of the total per member gifts in the village churches, therefore, only $1.79 went for missionary and benevolent purposes. This was a decline of practically one-half from 1930, and of more than two-thirds as compared with 1924. In the open-country churches, the amount was $1.13, a drop proportionately almost, but not quite, as large as in the village churches.

This decline set in sometime after 1924. The drop to 1930 was quite severe; and was clearly associated, in part, with declining interest in missionary activities abroad and impatience with the competitive use of benevolence funds at home in grants-in-aid. The subsequent decline was more influenced by the depression than by other considerations. The distribution of expenditures, reported in Table 100, in reality overstates the proportion given

TABLE 100

DISTRIBUTION OF EXPENDITURES IN VILLAGE AND COUNTRY PROTESTANT CHURCHES

Expenditure	*Village Churches*			*Country Churches*		
	1924	*1930*	*1936*	*1924*	*1930*	*1936*
Total	100.0	100.0	100.0	100.0	100.0	100.0
Salary	43.6	49.4	49.9	48.3	51.4	56.2
Benevolences	31.8	21.6	17.1	32.0	24.9	20.0
Other	24.6	29.0	33.0	19.7	23.7	23.8

to benevolences. It is based on the records of only four-fifths of the churches. As is elsewhere explained, a larger minority of the congregations than in previous studies, especially the very small and weak churches, no longer kept financial records. These, for the most part, gave nothing at all to benevolent causes. A few churches had dropped benevolent offerings by congregational action. For all Protestant churches in the United States, as reported by the source quoted above, 22.8 per cent of the contributions were devoted to benevolences in 1930, and 17.5 per cent in 1935–36. These rural-giving trends, therefore, follow those of all churches rather closely, though open-country churches clearly give a larger proportion of their money to benevolences, despite the poor programs and other handicaps of these congregations.

Recruiting holds its own.—One test of the interest in the church, and of its power to survive, is the degree to which it can recruit from its youth persons willing to enter its ministry or missionary service on a professional basis.

This factor has been measured in each of these studies. The level of recruiting among white Protestant churches seems to remain nearly constant in these communities. Only a minimum of the churches, about one-fourth in the villages and one-seventh in the open country, produce recruits in any half decade; and the chances are that if one is found, there will be two, as the average per church furnishing persons for professional Christian service is 1.8, as it has been since the first study.

There has been, however, a tendency everywhere except in the Far West for the number of candidates to decline slowly. This is especially true in the Middle Atlantic region. Among the open-country churches, the trend is not clear, except for the Middle Atlantic decline. In the Far West, the increase has been startling. It is perhaps related to the increased interest in religion, as shown by the gain in the proportion of the population in church reported above. It is also clearly an indication of the success of such special groups as the Four-Square Gospel and other emotional sects to gain recruits for starting new churches of such sects, which are stronger on the Pacific coast than elsewhere.

Very sharp, too, as Table 101 shows, has been the gain in the number of Negroes entering the ministry. This is unusual at a time when many observers hold that the Negro church is losing influence. On this point, it must be remembered that there are more Negro churches in these communities than previously and that memberships have held their own. Quite possibly the serious losses in Negro education in these last 6 years and the difficulties of other professional groups serving Negroes have made the ministry appear more desirable to youth than formerly.

It is interesting to note that two-fifths of the village Roman Catholic churches, though none of those in the open country, furnished men to the priesthood in the last inter-survey period to the number of about 4 per church. In proportion to membership, this is only slightly above the number for the Protestant group, whose congregations are considerably smaller than the Catholic. Over four-fifths of these recruits to the priesthood came from the Middle

TABLE 101

CHURCH MEMBERS ENTERING PROFESSIONAL CHRISTIAN SERVICE

Region	*1919–24*	*1925–30*	*1931–36*
		VILLAGE WHITE PROTESTANT	
All regions	225	250	253
Middle Atlantic	61	43	29
South	35	45	40
Middle West	116	127	104
Far West	13	35	80
		OPEN-COUNTRY WHITE PROTESTANT	
All regions	60	80	63
Middle Atlantic	21	10	9
South	9	21	20
Middle West	26	47	27
Far West	4	2	7
		TOTAL WHITE PROTESTANT	
All regions	285	330	316
		NEGRO PROTESTANT	
South	10	48	141

West, where slightly less than half the churches of this body are located. The Middle Atlantic and Far West regions furnished almost none.

Program of the church.—The programs of these churches showed an intensification along the more traditional lines and an apparent slackening in some of the more socialized aspects of the program.

Of first rank in the Protestant churches are the Sunday schools, which are possessed by all but the smallest organizations and by some of the emotional sects. More than nine-tenths of all village churches, and more than four-fifths of those in the open country, have Sunday schools. This represents practically no change since 1930 or 1924. Village enrollments declined very slightly. Those in the open country increased about 13 per cent over 1930. Average attendance in the villages likewise was practically unchanged, but increased in the open country. Perhaps this increase is due to the inability of country people to share as much as formerly in social life outside their neighborhoods, which drove them back to the Sunday school as one avenue for social contacts.

Other features of the religious education program showed marked improvement. Almost one-third of the churches now have classes to prepare for church membership, a gain in the proportion of about 50 per cent. There were comparable gains with mission-study classes and daily vacation Bible schools. More than a fourth of the churches now operate this adjunct to the religious education program.

As Table 103 shows, the gains were quite generally distributed among the regions, but were particularly striking in the South, especially with the Negro churches. The explanation for these generally distributed gains probably lies in two factors. In the first place, with the sharp rise in the proportion of ministers trained in college and seminary, more churches than formerly had pastors equipped to lead such enterprises. In the second place, the steady pressure of the denominational agencies upon the churches to add the features under discussion to their religious education work is probably taking effect in rural America.

Social program.—In 1930, three-tenths of the village churches reported lectures and concerts, and one-seventh reported holding classes. One-tenth of the open country also reported the first two items. An effort was made in this study to secure more details regarding such activities under the general category of adult education. This effort failed. Either such activities have been discontinued, or they were so sporadic as not to seem worth dignifying

TABLE 102

ENROLLMENT AND ATTENDANCE IN PROTESTANT VILLAGE AND COUNTRY SUNDAY SCHOOLS

Region	*Average Sunday School Enrollment*						*Per Cent Attendance of Enrollment*					
	VILLAGE			COUNTRY			VILLAGE			COUNTRY		
	1924	*1930*	*1936*	*1924*	*1930*	*1936*	*1924*	*1930*	*1936*	*1924*	*1930*	*1936*
All regions	111	127	125	67	66	75	69.4	64.0	63.8	62.6	65.2	69.3
Middle Atlantic	144	145	156	67	64	67	59.7	61.6	62.7	58.2	61.5	65.4
South: White	126	151	140	67	71	77	66.7	65.2	62.2	68.6	62.9	67.7
South: Negro	52	55	51	53	54	69	65.3	65.0	62.8	69.8	63.3	68.2
Middle West	108	132	131	74	70	83	75.9	63.0	63.3	71.6	69.5	72.7
Far West	98	111	111	51	57	85	70.4	67.4	69.2	41.2	71.8	80.7

as adult education by the pastor, or fieldworkers failed to record the information. Another possible explanation known to apply in some communities is that the W.P.A. recreational and educational programs superseded activities formerly conducted by churches.

The results of the study on the community and on the broader educational program of the churches reveal, of course, the clash of philosophies about the function of the church, as well as conflicting social philosophies.

In about a half-dozen cases, churches had community houses which were open to the public and in which well-rounded programs of recreation and adult education were being carried on. Four of these programs included successful forums. Another

TABLE 103

RELIGIOUS EDUCATION PROGRAM, PROTESTANT CHURCHES

	No. Churches Reporting		*Per Cent Churches Having* CLASSES IN PREP. CHURCH MEMB.		MISSION-STUDY CLASSES		DAILY VACATION BIBLE SCHOOL	
Region	*1930*	*1936*	*1930*	*1936*	*1930*	*1936*	*1930*	*1936*
All regions	1156	1185	23.4	32.0	20.1	28.7	18.1	27.9
Middle Atlantic	209	196	31.1	45.4	21.5	29.1	27.8	30.6
South: White	285	321	8.1	17.4	19.3	25.2	8.1	19.0
South: Negro	125	144	1.6	9.7	3.3	14.6	0.8	0.7
Middle West	396	355	36.6	47.3	25.0	35.5	23.7	45.9
Far West	141	169	25.5	30.8	24.8	32.5	23.4	27.2

church conducted successfully "a complete, modern, rural church program." Three other churches had quite ambitious programs of recreation, welfare, religious education, and general adult education, the latter including lectures on current events and psychology. Seven churches, 5 of them in the South, were carrying on well-organized welfare and relief programs forced by depression conditions. In each case, this work was heartily commended by Federal relief officials. In another village, a socially-minded pastor, concerned over the obvious revolt of youth against moral conventions and mores, initiated a program of activities and discussion for the young people of the community. To compete with roadhouses, weekly dances were included. The response of the youth was almost unanimous. Immediately, quite unanimous opposition arose from the other churches. Proselyting was charged. The program was, therefore, discontinued; and the youth problem rapidly assumed more serious proportions. In another village, a young people's program in a well-equipped community building was offered to the W.P.A. recreation officials; but the building was closed and the program discontinued when it was discovered that W.P.A. leadership meant that persons of any church could be admitted.

One Negro church is conducting a full program of recreation, including athletics and education on Sunday afternoons, which has proved very popular. Despite criticisms from the ministers of other churches of both races, this program is locally credited with measurably improving conditions among Negro youth.

Clashing philosophies also are apparent in the attitudes of clergy and laity. Contrasting with the forums and classes noted above is the church in which the men's organization insisted on discussing the religious implications of modern social and economic problems, but was opposed by the pastor on the ground that such activities were not "spiritual." The contrasting incident is that of a young, socially-minded pastor who lost his church after a discussion of the Soil Conservation program of the Department of Agriculture under the title "Our Stewardship of God's Land." The leading laymen of this church explained the action thus: "When we really need rain God will send it. And, brother, we won't attend a church where a minister uses notes; for the Lord has said he would fill their mouths."

There was great concern among the clergy over the return of legalized liquor, and much denunciation of youth and women for drinking; yet, in the main, with the exceptions noted in the discussion of the youth problem in Chapter VII, the testimony of the school men, physicians, and other leaders among the laity was to the effect that moral conditions were better than in the latter half of the 1920's and were improving. This was true even where the churches were clearly declining in influence. In fact, some of the worst situations apparently existed in the half-dozen and more villages where the churches had been strong enough to prevent chaperoned dances or other activities deemed too liberal in the local community, thereby forcing those interested in such activities into seeking them under commercial auspices.

It is quite clear that the issues involved in an individualistic, as against a social, interpretation of religion are by no means settled; and that in fact there is also an issue between the generations as to church policy. Rural youth is not interested in an interpretation of religion solely in terms of doctrine or ritual. This was found even in a number of Roman Catholic churches. It is not interested in denominational divisions. It is resentful in the extreme when such divisions balk "going" programs. Three times as many pastors reported that youth were losing interest in the church and its program as felt that the interest of youth was quickening. Where the latter report was made to fieldworkers, the churches concerned were catering to youth in terms of youth's needs. These issues appeared more serious than at any time since this series of studies began.

MINISTERS

As the salaried leaders of their congregations, the ministers are in a strategic position in determining the program and policy of the churches they serve. It has long been recognized that the personnel problem was crucial in the whole situation in which the rural church in America finds itself. The large number of small congregations has made it necessary to utilize untrained leaders, or else to assign groups of churches to the care of a single minister. In either case, it has been difficult for churches so served to make progress. They received either too little or too inefficient leadership; and without better service they have not won their communities. Great efforts have been made by the denominations for 20 years to solve this problem. Mission boards giving grants-in-aid have employed for the most part only men trained in college and seminary. They have conducted in-service training through institutes and summer schools.

Ministers better trained.—With respect to their professional training, the inter-survey period has shown marked improvement for the first time in this series of studies. Of all ministers, 43.9 per cent, in 1936, were trained in college and seminary, as against 33.2 per cent in 1930, and 35.0 per cent in 1924. The number of college graduates without theological degrees dropped slightly from 19.5 to 17 per cent. Even so, more than three-fifths of the clergy were college graduates or better, as against slightly over half in 1930, and slightly less than half in 1924. This still leaves, of course, nearly two-fifths who have not had college training. A few of these, 7.6 per cent of all ministers, have graduated from so-called Bible schools; but 31.5 per cent have not had any specific training. The majority of these are serving either in the South or with churches of the more emotional sects. As in the previous studies, the non-resident pastors, that is, those serving groups of churches and not residing in their parishes, made a poorer record than the resident ministers; but even this group showed sharp improvement, as Table 104 shows.

This general improvement has brought the level of training of the rural clergy nearer to that of the rural schoolteachers in these communities, though a far larger proportion of the clergy than of the teachers lack any professional preparation.

These data, encouraging as they are, are open to two corrections. The percentages given above are based on total figures and therefore include the records of some 50 Roman Catholic priests, practically all of whom were trained in college and seminary. They also include about 90 Negro clergy who, for obvious reasons, are the most poorly trained group. The total figures, as it turns out, are therefore almost identical with those of the clergy of the white Protestant churches, so far as the data were secured.

Information on training, however, was not available for about 10 per cent of the Protestant clergy, either because the ministers lived outside the communities and could not be reached, or because the information was refused. There was greater sensitivity than previously in admitting lack of professional training. This 10 per cent, judged by the type of churches they served, were highly unlikely to be trained men; and the under-enumeration on this point as compared with the previous studies results in a more favorable result than complete data would show. But even allowing for this error, the situation has unquestionably improved.

The reasons for this improvement are not hard to find. The depression has made more trained men available in the churches, as well as in the public schools. City churches have had to release assistant pastors or directors of religious education. Overhead agencies of the denominations have been forced to reduce staff. The slow but sure decline in the number of churches, especially in the open country, has reduced the number of available jobs. The efforts of the denominations to train men, as described above, are beginning to bear fruit, especially since fewer city jobs have been available to men so trained, whose better records in their parishes under normal conditions would have resulted in calling a number of them to urban parishes.

Residence of ministers.—Next to training, one of the most important influences in the development of the rural church is the amount of time it receives from its minister. Many surveys have shown that churches with full-time resident ministers make the best progress. In this respect, there has been no significant change since 1930. Each resident minister in these communities averaged 1.7 churches under his care. Deducting those that served but one church, the average was slightly over 2. The average non-resident minister had 2.9 churches, as against 3 in 1930 and 2.9 in 1924. The fact that a number of non-resident ministers could not be reached, as noted above, may account for this small change. In short, the situation on this point is practically the same as in 1930.

TABLE 104

TRAINING OF ALL PASTORS BY RESIDENCE [a]

	Per Cent of Pastors Graduated from									All Others		
	COLLEGE			BIBLE SCHOOL OR SEMINARY			COLLEGE AND SEMINARY					
	1924	*1930*	*1936*	*1924*	*1930*	*1936*	*1924*	*1930*	*1936*	*1924*	*1930*	*1936*
Grand total	14.2	19.5	17.0	13.6	10.5	7.6	35.0	33.2	43.9	37.2	36.8	31.5
Resident	15.1	19.0	17.8	13.8	11.2	8.9	40.8	40.0	48.1	30.3	29.8	25.2
Non-resident	12.2	20.5	14.5	13.0	9.0	3.4	21.8	19.5	30.7	53.0	51.0	51.4

[a] Percentages based on 811 pastors in 1924, 564 resident; 866 in 1930, 578 resident; 740 in 1936, 561 resident.

Ministers' salaries lower.—In common with the decline in all financial indices, the compensation reported by the ministers declined. For all denominations the average annual salary was $1,059, as compared with $1,433 in 1930, and $1,441 in 1924. Among the white Protestant ministers, the drop was from $1,531 in 1930 to $1,127 in 1936; which, as for all ministers in that period, was a decline of slightly over 26 per cent. This was at a somewhat higher rate than the loss in total expenses. It was also a larger loss than was suffered by schoolteachers. The rate of decline differed with the regions. It was most severe in the South and least in the Middle Atlantic. Table 105 gives the details.

It may very likely be that even these data on pastors' salaries overstate the truth. Especially in the South, ministers laughed rather ironically when salary was mentioned and gave the "official salary" rather than the amount received. In one case in which the minister reported his salary as $500, his wife stated that up to the time of the survey in June, 1936, but $30 had been received on account. A number of similar stories were reported by field-workers. A small number of ministers stated they were on relief. It is possible that more were, and that this accounts for the lack of accounts and information as to salary in some churches.

RELATIONSHIPS OF CHURCHES: COMPETITION AND CO-OPERATION

For a quarter of a century, Protestant church leaders have given considerable attention to flaying the evils of competition among rural churches and to working for co-operation. This involves, of course, the whole question of the relationships among churches. It must be recognized that the denominational differences apparent in the religious scene have historical causes and often current sociological sanctions. There is, first of all, the great division between Roman Catholics, Protestants, and Jews, though the rural work of the last named body is negligible. The Protestant group is also divided into certain broad groups. Some denominations, such as the Episcopal, Lutheran, Reformed, and Moravian, share

TABLE 105

AVERAGE SALARIES OF MINISTERS BY REGION AND RESIDENCE

Region	All Ministers								
	ALL MINISTERS RESIDENT AND NON-RESIDENT			RESIDENT			NON-RESIDENT		
	1924	*1930*	*1936*	*1924*	*1930*	*1936*	*1924*	*1930*	*1936*
All regions	$1,441	$1,433	$1,059	$1,530	$1,571	$1,158	$1,148	$1,107	$ 765
Middle Atlantic	1,506	1,621	1,390	. . . [a]	1,696	1,387	1,165	1,359	1,407
South	1,456	1,309	864	. . . [a]	1,624	1,090	1,081	969	621
Middle West	1,435	1,495	1,136	. . . [a]	1,582	1,178	1,208	1,201	889
Far West	1,396	1,279	926	. . . [a]	1,327	934	1,122	1,085	833
	White Protestant Ministers								
All regions	. . . [a]	1,531	1,127	. . . [a]	1,649	1,202	. . . [a]	1,208	858
Middle Atlantic	. . . [a]	1,664	1,411	. . . [a]	1,745	1,411	. . . [a]	1,379	1,413
South	. . . [a]	1,564	1,023	. . . [a]	1,863	1,269	. . . [a]	1,162	719
Middle West	. . . [a]	1,520	1,139	. . . [a]	1,619	1,178	. . . [a]	1,204	903
Far West	. . . [a]	1,345	933	. . . [a]	1,392	941	. . . [a]	1,128	829

[a] Not computed for 1924.

a common liturgical tradition. Others are bound together by the ritual of immersion, especially the Baptist bodies. Foreign-language groups have their own churches. The extreme emotional groups are another major division. These include a large number of bodies such as the Holiness and the Four-Square Gospel. Finally there is a large and important group, largely English in their tradition, such as the Presbyterian, Methodist, and Congregational. It has long been recognized that co-operation within such groups was easier to achieve than co-operation between them, even though the significance of the differences is lessening. For instance, it is well to remember that the United Brethren represent a reaction against the formalism of the Lutheran and Reformed churches, particularly the latter. It is significant that wherever a United Brethren church is found there will also usually be a Reformed church close by. The United Brethren appealed to the more or less emotional types in the community, and were a manifestation of the Methodist influences among the Germans a century or so ago. That there continues to be this division is merely a revelation of the fact that the forms of our institutions continue long after their reason for existing has passed. In other words, these people are not different in their mean cultural backgrounds. They are different only in their religious habits, which have been handed down from a previous generation.

Even within such groups, differences among the several churches of a given community often reflect social and economic cleavages more than they do theological ones. Thus the farm-owners may belong quite generally to one congregation, the farm-tenants to another, the professional and better-off business group to a third. In many Southern communities that are both agricultural service stations and textile-mill towns, each important denomination has separate churches in both the village proper and the "mill hill."

But granted all this, there still remains, even within groups, a degree of competition that has long been denounced as unjustifiable over-churching. The competition splits communities, prevents a better-unified social life, results in small, inefficient congregations, poorly paid ministers, barren programs. This in turn makes it difficult for the church to gain, and results in the loss of religious interest among the population. Specific illustrations of the workings of these forces in individual communities have been given in previous reports in this series. More could be produced from the current survey; but the point is so well known and has been so often illustrated that it would be but emphasizing the obvious. In passing, it should be recalled, however, that previous studies have shown that when there were fewer than two churches per 1,000 population, average membership, membership gains, total budget, per capita contributions to current expenses and benevolences were uniformly higher than when there were more churches.

Rather, attention may be directed to the results of the continued inability of Protestantism to control, in any large or effective way, this situation. In 1924, there were exactly 1,400 churches in these 140 village-centered rural communities. In 1936, there were 1,304. As was pointed out earlier, the gross losses have been considerably larger than the net. The birth rate among churches has been high, in the villages practically equaling the death rate. Moreover, enlarging community boundaries have added to the number of churches in the areas studied. Considerably less than one-tenth of the nearly 400 churches that have passed out of existence in these communities since 1924 have been closed as a result of co-operative efforts. Most of the churches that have been born also had slight sociological or economic justification.

Meanwhile, the slow but sure operation of social forces results in a slowly declining number of churches, both actually and relative to the population. This involves bitter struggle, bitter competition, and bitter death. The number of churches per community has declined from 10 in 1924 to 9.5 in 1930 to 9.12 in 1936. The number per 1,000 population has dropped more rapidly, from 3.3 in 1924 to 2.4 in 1936; and, as noted, the proportion of the population in church is lower now than at any time since this series of studies began. The losses are exclusively among the Protestant group. Roman Catholics have held their own. As Table 106 shows, the total loss reported above is shared in by every region and by practically every size-group.[2]

It seems likely that these forces will continue to operate. Field-work reports showed that in 37 churches there was active discussion at the time of the survey as to whether or not services should be maintained any longer. Moreover, the closing of a church seems to be an individual matter. No case has been found in these surveys where, when action was locally taken, arrangements were made for the religious care of the members by some surviving church.

Here then is a large and still unsolved problem for the Protestant bodies. Some progress, however, in meeting it can be recorded. There is an increasing amount of interchurch co-operation on the community level, and there is less competitive home mission aid. With reference to the former aspect, field-work reports showed 40 communities with regularly scheduled union services. In 5 of these, such services were held in community parks during the warmer portion of the year. Union daily vacation Bible schools were held in 27 communities, union teacher-training classes in 14. Three centers co-operated in the use of school busses to bring country people to services at the center. Interchurch attendance was reported to be increasing and widening the religious view-points of the people. A few cases were found of church co-operation in recreational programs for enrollees in near-by C.C.C. camps. There were a few cases of Protestant-Catholic co-operation in community affairs; and in one of these the Lutheran church on purchasing a new pipe organ donated its old one to the Roman Catholic church, which had none.

Home mission aid.—One of the factors in relationships among churches is the granting of subsidies by denominational treasuries

[2] The gain in the large villages of the South is due to the separate tabulation of towns.

TABLE 106

CHURCHES PER 1,000 POPULATION

By Region and by Size of Village

Region	*All Villages*			*Small Villages*			*Medium Villages*			*Large Villages*			*Towns* [a]
	1924	*1930*	*1936*	*1924*	*1930*	*1936*	*1924*	*1930*	*1936*	*1924*	*1930*	*1936*	*1936*
All regions	3.3	2.8	2.4	4.7	3.9	3.1	2.9	2.7	2.5	2.8	2.3	2.3	1.9
Middle Atlantic	3.6	3.1	2.7	5.0	4.5	3.6	2.8	2.3	2.6	2.7	2.3	2.0	2.5
South	3.6	3.1	3.2	4.5	4.2	3.7	3.7	3.2	3.3	3.0	2.5	3.6	2.2
Middle West	2.9	2.6	2.0	4.8	3.1	2.6	2.6	2.5	2.0	2.4	2.2	1.6	1.7
Far West	3.1	2.3	1.9	4.4	3.4	2.4	2.3	2.3	2.2	2.8	2.0	1.9	1.7

[a] Towns were included with large villages in previous studies, since the number of such places was considerably smaller in 1924 and 1930 than in 1936.

to local congregations that otherwise could not exist. As was pointed out in previous studies, this practice is one important factor in the matter of so-called over-churching. Between 1924 and 1930, the number of aided churches increased despite efforts on the part of a number of denominations to improve the situation. Since 1930, these efforts have progressed to the point of definite agreements among five or six major bodies to limit competitive grants. Such efforts were aided by the depression which reduced the funds available for this purpose. The result of these two forces is clearly evident in the data on this point. In both the villages and the open-country areas, the number of communities and of churches aided and the size of the subsidy declined.

It is significant, however, that while this was the trend, there was one sharp variation. The agreements alluded to concern national boards of home missions operating for the most part outside the South and in the newer sections of the country. The so-called self-supporting states, which do not depend on national bodies for help, extend aid in their own territory through their own agencies. Such state agencies then are responsible in the Middle Atlantic region for an increase in the number of communities and churches receiving this so-called home mission aid. The total amount of aid to village churches in this region, as a result, actually increased between 1930 and 1936, though only by one per cent. Elsewhere the total amount of aid dropped 49 per cent. Indeed, despite relatively strong councils of churches in both New York and Pennsylvania which have worked to reduce competition, more villages now receive aid than in 1924; and the total amount of aid has increased from $4,260 to $5,418, or 27.2 per cent.

It has often been pointed out that interdenominational competition was most severe in the villages; and it is significant that state home mission agencies in the Middle Atlantic region put their money into these centers. In the open country they cut more drastically than they did in the other regions.

With this exception, however, the situation with respect to home mission aid conforms more nearly than ever before to the protestations of co-operation and comity that have resounded from the platforms of interdenominational conferences for two decades. Indeed, the total amount of open-country home mission aid in these communities declined 58.6 per cent between 1930 and 1936. The average grant per church dropped from $393 to $289 in the villages, 26.4 per cent; and from $153 to $125, or 18.3 per cent, in the open country. The number of aided churches declined one-fifth in the villages and one-half in the open country. The regional details are clear from Table 107.

TABLE 107

HOME MISSION AID IN WHITE PROTESTANT VILLAGE AND COUNTRY CHURCHES BY REGION

140 Villages

Region	*Number of Communities with Aided Churches*			*Number of Aided Churches*			*Average Amount of Home Mission Aid*		
	1924	*1930*	*1935*	*1924*	*1930*	*1935*	*1924*	*1930*	*1935*
				VILLAGE CHURCHES					
All regions	71	68	55	92	89	71	$350	$393	$289
Middle Atlantic	12	11	14	15	14	18	284	384	301
South	18	12	13	19	18	16	333	450	214
Middle West	26	27	16	38	32	21	367	335	280
Far West	15	18	12	20	25	16	383	425	364
				COUNTRY CHURCHES					
All regions	35	37	23	63	87	44	198	153	125
Middle Atlantic	7	7	5	17	18	11	155	130	57
South	9	14	8	24	46	21	149	113	103
Middle West	14	10	5	13	15	6	184	185	195
Far West	5	6	5	9	8	6	430	362	254

It must be pointed out, however, that certainly some of the home mission aid that still exists is competitive. The tendency has been when one church was aided, that one or more others were also helped. To some extent this still holds. In the villages, the average number of churches aided per community receiving aid remains at 1.3. In the open country, however, it has declined from 2.3 to 2.0. It must be remembered in this connection, that some of the sociological reasons for denominational differences obtain with as much, or with even greater, force to the whole problem of home mission aid. Religious traditions which have become fixed through several generations are not easily set aside, especially since sentiment, loyalty, and conviction loom so large in religious expression. Religion roots deeply in the affections of people, especially the older people, and naturally they wish to perpetuate in their children something which they prize so highly. Then there is always the egocentrism of the religious group, the feeling that each has something which the others do not have and which sets him above them. The Baptist has the superior, Biblical form of baptism; the Presbyterian is proud of his correct doctrine; the Methodist Episcopalian insists that the church member must be "converted"; the Wesleyan Methodist is convinced that he is the true follower of the Wesleys. It is true that these attitudes are not nearly as strong as formerly; but they lie deep and still linger, and out of them grow what is often called over-churching or competition, sustained especially in the older states by home mission aid.

Despite the facts listed above, the number of united churches of all types in these communities has increased very slowly. There were 19 in 1924. One of these died, 9 others have been formed, making 27 in 1936. This group now comprises 2.1 per cent of all churches, as against 1.3 in 1924.

This review of the fortunes of the institutionalized religion in these communities finds the churches still losing ground, and at a more rapid pace than during the first inter-survey period, despite the fact that average memberships per church are larger. Possibly this very fact blinds the eyes of those most concerned to the lowered attendance, declining interest, and falling contributions, and to the general inefficiency and planlessness in the face of the operation of social forces. Individual churches grow or maintain themselves; but institutionalized religion continues to decline, as measured in the aggregate and compared with its total opportunity.

XIII

Relief in Rural Areas

PRODUCTION in the years of the recent depression was curtailed, workers were unemployed, wages were cut, there was industrial failure, farm purchasing power was reduced, and farms were foreclosed. It was a period of commercial decline: new capital issues ebbed, turnover of demand deposits shrank, interest rates were lowered, and many banks failed. The series of graphs depicting each of those items from 1928 through 1935 all descend to the depression, which resulted not only in the abridgment of physical values, but, more tragically, in the deterioration of human resources.

Of all the institutions in the alphabetic succession designed by the Federal government to spell recovery, none was more certainly directed to save human resources than was the Emergency Relief Administration, and none affected more individuals as individuals.

This chapter is concerned with the operation of relief in the villages that were resurveyed for the third time in 1936. The persons living in incorporated villages, i.e., in places having populations ranging from 250 to 2,500, are rural by census definition; and by the same token, the village is a non-farm community. The village population is rural non-farm. It is rural in the sense that the village is not highly urbanized, and non-farm in that the people do not live on farms. The village center is made up of persons who depend upon the contiguous farming community. Villagers do not live on farms; they live *off* them. If the surrounding farming community suffers a crop loss, a price decline, or inequality in purchasing, the agricultural village center must suffer inevitably. To it the consequences of farm distress are a tightening of money, the freezing of assets, a stagnation of trade, the dismissal of employees, an impoverishing of farm laborers, and the expansion of poor rolls.

The depression on the farm and in the agricultural village may stem from the same ultimate causes; but there the essential likeness ceases. The depression resultants are different; relief measures that may mitigate the severity of the burden for the farmer will not necessarily moderate it for the villagers. There are essential differences between rural farm relief and rural non-farm relief. It may be a statistical convenience to categorize rural farm and rural non-farm relief under the rubric of rural relief; but it is a convenience that avoids the reality of the human resources which are being saved for society.

Through the co-operation of the Works Progress Administration, the rural non-farm relief loads of 133 of the 140 agricultural villages were obtained as of June, 1935. Each relief family was reported with the number of persons on relief, their ages, occupational status, and work status. For the purposes of this study, the summaries of the data are compared with the statistics of the Federal census of the same villages in 1930.

The incidence of relief in June, 1935, may be expressed in ratio to the total population in 1930. In the 133 villages, the ratio of the June, 1935, relief population to the 1930 total population varied from a low of about one-third of one per cent to a high of almost 33 per cent. The incidence of relief in the village having the highest relative load was 87 times the relative load in the village with the smallest load. The 19,763 persons on relief in the 133 villages during June, 1935, constituted almost 11 per cent of the total population enumerated in the villages in 1930. By region, the median of the distribution of the relative relief-load ratios is used as index. The Middle West has the highest median ratio of 11 per cent; the Far West, 9 per cent; the South, eight and two-thirds per cent; and the Middle Atlantic villages only 8 per cent. The spread of relief varies greatly as the data reported in Table 108 indicate. The higher average relief ratio in the Middle

West villages may be attributable to the successive crop failures due to drought and soil depletion.

The relationship between relief and retail sales per capita on a community population base may indicate whether the higher relief loads are associated with greater community need. Consequently

TABLE 108

DISTRIBUTION OF THE RATIO OF THE NUMBER OF VILLAGE PERSONS ON RELIEF IN JUNE, 1935, TO THE TOTAL VILLAGE POPULATION IN 1930 CENSUS BY REGION

133 Villages

Ratio of Relief, 1935 to Population, 1930	*Middle Atlantic*	*South*	*Middle West*	*Far West*	*133 Villages*
31–32.99	...	1	...	...	1
29–30.99	...	...	...	...	...
27–28.99	...	...	2	...	2
25–26.99	...	1	...	1	2
23–24.99	...	1	1	1	3
21–22.99	1	1	1	2	5
19–20.99	...	...	5	1	6
17–18.99	1	1	3	1	6
15–16.99	...	...	5	...	5
13–14.99	3	2	6	1	12
11–12.99	3	2	6	1	12
9–10.99	4	4	9	2	19
7– 8.99	3	6	4	2	15
5– 6.99	2	3	6	5	16
3– 4.99	2	4	3	2	11
1– 2.99	7	2	4	1	14
0– 0.99	1	...	3	...	4
Number	27	28	58	20	133
Median of the ratios	8.00	8.67	11.00	9.00	9.68

the 133 villages were grouped into four categories of relief load: lowest quarter, from 0 to 5.52 per cent of relief to 1930 total population; second quarter, from 5.53 to 9.67 per cent; third quarter, from 9.68 to 14.45 per cent; and highest quarter, over 14.46 per cent. The per capita retail sales per community population in 1929 and in 1933 were:

Relief Load	*Quarter*	*Per Capita Retail Sales per Community Population*		*Ratio of 1933/1929 per Capita Sales*
		1929	*1933*	
0 – 5.52	I	286	132	46
5.53– 9.67	II	344	150	44
9.68–14.45	III	294	112	38
Over 14.46	IV	268	120	45

The decrease in per capita sales is associated with higher relief loads in the first three quarters, but not in the highest quarter. The highest quarter of relief villages, however, had the lowest per capita sales in 1929. The probabilities are that the highest quarter relief communities were in the poorest situation in 1930, and that the next three years merely intensified their economic problems. It is significant that, whereas the number of retail stores increased between 1929 and 1933 in the two low relief groups, the number of retail stores declined in the two highest quarters.

Using the same partitions for relief groups of villages, an analysis was made of the industrial gains and losses between 1930 and 1936. The facts in the table show that relief in these villages is not associated with the number of industries lost, the number of industries, or the average number of full-time employees.

Relief Quarter	*Number of Industries Present in*		*Average Number of Full-Time Employees*	
	1930	*1936*	*1930*	*1936*
I	154	123	28	29
II	143	137	16	16
III	170	124	30	20
IV	97	96	14	14

In the lowest relief group of villages, moreover, 66 industries had gone out of existence in the period 1930–36 while 35 industries had been begun in the same period, leaving a net loss of 31. The death rate and birth rate for industry in the second quarter were 58 and 50; in the third quarter, 76 and 31; and in the highest relief quarter, 39 and 38. The ratio of industrial deaths to industrial births in villages does not seem to be related to relief loads.

Neither can any significant relationship between relief load and population increase be demonstrated. The relief load results from a complex of events, economic, social, and political. The primary cause may vary from village to village. It may be that finer analyses will be needed to demonstrate on what basis relief loads were allocated in village communities.

Whatever the reasons for the degree of relief, the population on relief may be a better indication of policy than the method of association of economic or other variables.

The persons on relief in these rural non-farm villages differ significantly from the total population in 1930. In Table 109 are reported the age-distributions by number and per cent of the 1935 relief population and the 1930 total population. The median age of the total 1930 population was almost 30 years, whereas the

TABLE 109

AGE DISTRIBUTION, BY NUMBER AND PER CENT, OF THE VILLAGE POPULATION AS OF 1930 AND OF THE RELIEF POPULATION IN THE SAME VILLAGES AS OF 1935

133 Villages

	Number Distribution		*Per Cent Distribution*	
Age	1930 POPULATION	1935 RELIEF POPULATION	1930 POPULATION	1935 RELIEF POPULATION
All ages	180,074	19,763	100.00	100.00
Under 5	14,442	2,095	8.02	10.60
5– 9	16,523	2,564	9.18	12.97
10–14	16,300	2,665	9.05	13.49
15–19	16,193	2,261	8.99	11.44
20–24	14,243	1,486	7.91	7.53
25–29	12,762	1,059	7.09	5.36
30–34	11,749	971	6.52	4.92
35–39	11,961	1,034	6.64	5.23
40–44	11,270	1,018	6.26	5.15
45–49	10,726	958	5.96	4.85
50–54	9,891	882	5.49	4.46
55–59	8,567	702	4.76	3.55
60–64	7,820	644	4.34	3.26
65–69	6,624	574	3.68	2.90
70–74	5,158	400	2.86	2.02
75 and over	5,717	391	3.17	1.98
Age unknown	128	59	.07	.30

median age of the 1935 relief population is 21 years. The relief population is significantly younger than the total population in 1930. Against the well authenticated trend towards an older population which has been noted for over a century, the difference between the average age of the relief population and the total population in 1935 may indeed be greater than the 9 years. The greater youth of the relief population is better appreciated when the percentage of children in the total 1930 population is compared with the percentage in the 1935 relief population. The relief population had relatively a third as many more children under 5 years of age in June, 1935, as were present in the total 1930 population. There are relatively more children in the relief population than were in the total population in 1930. For the age-group under 5 years, the ratios were 8.02 and 10.60 for the total 1930 population and the 1935 relief population, respectively. The corresponding ratios for the age-group 5 to 10 years were 9.18 to 12.97; for the age-group 10 to 15 years, 9.05 to 13.49; and for the age-group 15 to 20 years, 8.99 to 11.44. The relief population is on the average younger, primarily because of the large number of children in relief families. More than 37 per cent of the relief population is younger than 15 years of age, as compared with the 26.25 per cent in the total 1930 population. These facts apply not only to all regions but to each region separately.

The number of persons in the average family in the total 1930 population was 3.7. In the 1935 relief population, the average number was 3.8. Of the 5,155 relief families, 695 consisted of one person each, and 1,075 of 2 persons. Another statistic descriptive of the family unit is obtained by considering the number of children under 5 years of age to the number of women of child-bearing age. In the 1930 village population, the number of children under 5 years was 14,442, and the number of women 15 to 45 years of age was 40,798. In the 1935 relief population, the corresponding figures are 2,095 children and 4,106 women. The number of children under 5 years of age to 1,000 women of child-bearing age was 354 in the 1930 total population, and 510 in the 1935 relief population.

The greater youthfulness and the larger number of children within the relief population indicates a relatively smaller potential working population. The heads and members in the relief group working or seeking work were 31 per cent of all persons on relief. In 1930, however, 37 per cent of the total population 10 years of age and over was reported as gainfully employed. Although the information regarding incapacity for work was not requested or required information, 211 family heads and 153 family members were reported as incapacitated. Work status of the relief population is reported in Table 110.

The potential workers in the relief group may be compared with

TABLE 110

COMPOSITION AND CHARACTERISTICS OF THE RELIEF POPULATION OF 133 OF THE 140 SELECTED UNITED STATES AGRICULTURAL VILLAGES IN JUNE, 1935, BY REGION

Work Status by Head and Non-Head

	Working and Not Seeking Work	*Not Working and Seeking Work*	*Not Working and Not Seeking Work*	*No Answer*[a]	*No Answer with Record of Incapacity*	*Working and Seeking Work*
All regions						
All persons	2,717	3,409	4,031	9,194	364	48
Heads	1,993	2,006	323	583	211	39
Non-heads	724	1,403	3,708	8,611	153	9
Middle Atlantic						
All persons	328	483	616	1,187	44	0
Heads	235	305	61	64	32	0
Non-heads	93	178	555	1,123	12	0
South						
All persons	648	983	815	2,214	144	40
Heads	403	546	86	139	76	32
Non-heads	245	437	729	2,075	68	8
Middle West						
All persons	1,021	1,629	1,807	4,146	156	6
Heads	740	985	140	325	89	5
Non-heads	281	644	1,667	3,821	67	1
Far West						
All persons	720	314	793	1,647	20	2
Heads	615	170	36	55	14	2
Non-heads	105	144	757	1,592	6	0

[a] Composed of those under 15 or over 64 years of age.

the gainfully employed reported in the Federal census of 1930. The usual industry of each potential worker in the relief group was coded with the broad industrial categories of the 1930 Federal census. The resulting tabulations are reported in Table 111.

As in total population in 1930, the proportion of gainfully employed males engaged in agriculture, forestry, and animal husbandry was 13 per cent. The corresponding proportion of potential workers engaged in the same broad industry group was over 30 per cent. The percentages for the broad category of manufacturing and mechanical industry were 33.7 in 1930 and 39.2 in the relief population. The percentages in mineral extraction were 1.5 and 2.7, respectively. The three broad classes of agriculture, manufacture, and mining accounted for 48.3 per cent of the gainfully employed in 1930, but for 72.2 per cent of the relief workers.

If the depression affected all industries equally, the proportions of workers on relief should have been approximately those returned in 1930. But this is not so. The depression did not affect all industries or workers equally. The males in the broad categories of professional service, trade, public service, and transportation were in relatively smaller proportion on the relief rolls than in the 1930 population. For female workers, the situation is paralleled. It is significant that although 3.7 per cent of the male workers on relief did not report a usual industry or reported that they had never worked, more than 20 per cent of the female workers on relief were thus classified. The depression forced a group of women to seek employment outside the home; so that from this younger relief population there was as large a proportion of women seeking employment as there was of the gainfully employed in 1930. Among the males, however, 46 per cent of all relief males may be classified as potential workers as compared with the 59 per cent of gainfully employed in 1930.

The occupational stratification of relief workers is given in Table 112. Of all relief males working or seeking work, 23.7 per cent are reported usually occupied as "farm laborers," and an additional 32.5 per cent as "other unskilled workers." Over 56 per cent of potential male workers are unskilled operatives.

Of the relief female workers, 7 per cent are usually occupied as "farm laborers," 5.5 per cent as "other unskilled work-

TABLE 111

USUAL INDUSTRY FOR THOSE PERSONS WORKING OR SEEKING WORK IN RELIEF FAMILIES, JUNE, 1935, COMPARED WITH THE INDUSTRY OF GAINFULLY EMPLOYED PERSONS 10 YEARS OR OVER IN 1930

By Sex: 133 Villages

Industry	MALES IN INDUSTRY *1930*	MALES WORKING OR SEEKING WORK *1935*	FEMALES IN INDUSTRY *1930*	FEMALES WORKING OR SEEKING WORK *1935*	*Total in Industry* *1930*	*Total Working or Seeking Work* *1935*
	Number Distribution					
All industries	51,627	4,499	15,529	1,675	67,156	6,174
Agriculture, forestry, and animal husbandry	6,722	1,364	332	123	7,054	1,487
Extraction of minerals	794	123	17	21	811	144
Manufacturing and mechanical industries	17,408	1,763	2,570	303	19,978	2,066
Transportation	7,397	594	810	25	8,207	619
Trade	11,838	306	2,250	86	14,088	392
Public service	1,245	23	206	7	1,451	30
Professional	3,846	65	3,673	52	7,519	117
Domestic and personal service	2,377	95	5,671	722	8,048	817
Unknown and never worked	...	166	...	336	...	502
	Per Cent Distribution					
All industries	100.00	100.00	100.00	100.00	100.00	100.00
Agriculture, forestry, and animal husbandry	13.02	30.32	2.14	7.34	10.50	24.08
Extraction of minerals	1.54	2.73	.11	1.25	1.21	2.33
Manufacturing and mechanical industries	33.72	39.19	16.55	18.09	29.75	33.46
Transportation	14.33	13.20	5.22	1.49	12.22	10.03
Trade	22.93	6.80	14.49	5.13	20.98	6.35
Public service	2.41	.51	1.33	.42	2.16	.49
Professional	7.45	1.44	23.65	3.10	11.20	1.90
Domestic and personal service	4.60	2.11	36.52	43.10	11.98	13.23
Unknown and never worked	...	3.69	...	20.06	...	8.13

ers," and more than 40 per cent as "servants and allied workers." The overwhelming characteristic of the relief workers is general lack of skill. Their lack of skill may not have been the primary cause of the need for relief, but it is the lack of skill that made these persons marginal in times of economic distress.

From data secured for another study,[1] the characteristics of the relief population may be deduced as reported from 138 counties in the following areas: East Cotton, West Cotton, Appalachian-Ozark, Lake-States-Cutover, Hay and Dairy, Corn, Spring Wheat, and Ranching. The age-distribution of the rural farm population in 1930 and the open-country relief population in June, 1935, and of the rural non-farm population in 1930 and the village relief population in June, 1935, are reported in Table 113, as well as the age-distribution of the rehabilitation population in June, 1935.

The ratio of the number of persons on relief in June, 1935, to the total population in 1930 is, for the open country 10.6, and for the rural non-farm, 10.4. The relief population in open-country residence is younger than the total population in 1930; the same is true for the relief group in the villages. The open-country relief population is, however, younger than the village relief population: 42.3 per cent of the open-country relief group was under 15 years of age, whereas 37.51 per cent of the village relief group was under that age.[2] Furthermore, an additonal 4.5 per cent of the 1930 population is on rehabilitation rolls in the open country, whereas a negligible proportion of the village population is receiving rehabilitation aid.

For the relief population, the usual occupation of the potential

[1] The authors are engaged on a study of relief as of June, 1935, and a study of the educational background of relief workers as of October, 1935, for the Works Progress Administration.

[2] In the 133 villages, the per cent of relief population under 15 years of age is 37.06, which is an indication of the representativeness of the survey sample of 140 American agricultural villages. It is probable that inferences from the sample of agricultural villages and also from the village population of the 138 counties may be applied logically to the totality of American agricultural villages.

TABLE 112

USUAL INDUSTRY (RELIEF CODE) OF THOSE PERSONS ON RELIEF WHO WERE WORKING OR SEEKING WORK, JUNE, 1935

By Region, by Head or Member, and by Sex: 133 Villages

Industry	*All regions*				*Middle Atlantic*				*South*				*Middle West*				*Far West*			
	HEAD		MEMBER		HEAD		MEMBER		HEAD		MEMBER		HEAD		MEMBER		HEAD		MEMBER	
	M.	*F.*	*M.*	*F.*	*M.*	*F.*	*M.*	*F.*	*M.*	*F.*	*M.*	*F.*	*M.*	*F.*	*M.*	*F.*	*M.*	*F.*	*M.*	*F.*
Agriculture	1,010	39	318	85	55	1	24	...	223	35	131	63	444	3	123	15	288	...	40	7
Forestry and fishing	7	...	3	...	1	...	1	...	2	...	...	...	3	...	2	...	1	...	...	...
Extraction of minerals	99	...	8	...	1	...	...	...	10	...	1	...	71	...	7	...	17	...	...	...
Building and construction	299	...	25	...	58	...	6	...	54	...	4	...	118	...	12	...	69	...	3	...
Iron, steel, machinery, and vehicles	40	...	5	...	9	...	2	...	1	...	...	...	24	...	3	...	6	...	...	...
Auto factories and repair shops	29	...	...	...	3	...	...	...	4	...	...	...	20	...	...	...	2	...	...	...
Lumber and furniture	111	2	11	1	7	1	1	...	43	1	7	1	24	...	2	...	37	...	1	...
Paper, printing, and allied	12	...	1	2	6	...	...	...	2	...	...	...	2	...	...	2	2	...	1	...
Textiles	36	10	9	21	24	5	6	14	9	5	2	4	3	...	1	3	...	...	...	...
Food and allied	56	25	20	40	4	2	5	4	10	...	1	3	29	8	9	8	13	15	5	25
Other and not specified manufacturing	76	2	8	14	38	2	3	11	7	...	1	...	20	...	2	1	11	...	2	2
Road and street building and repair	242	...	20	1	104	...	10	...	18	...	2	...	94	...	7	...	26	...	1	1
Other transportation and communication	238	5	30	11	41	1	3	2	32	2	6	1	118	2	16	6	47	...	5	2
Trade	397	67	99	81	43	8	19	15	94	15	26	12	193	30	41	43	67	14	13	11
Public service	74	19	13	31	4	3	5	5	9	5	6	10	42	4	1	12	19	7	1	4
Professional service	38	6	12	9	7	...	...	...	11	3	3	1	15	...	8	5	5	3	1	3
Domestic and personal service	58	354	9	418	13	33	4	33	13	149	3	162	22	119	...	188	10	53	2	35
No usual industry	546	84	474	312	57	1	66	28	157	50	102	117	268	22	251	143	64	11	55	24
Industry unknown	37	4	22	20	7	1	3	1	8	...	4	14	22	3	12	3	...	...	3	2
Not a worker	6	10	1	2	...	...	...	...	...	9	1	2	6	1	...	...	...	...	...	...

TABLE 113

COMPOSITION AND CHARACTERISTICS OF THE 1930 POPULATION; THE JUNE, 1935, RELIEF POPULATION; THE JUNE, 1935, REHABILITATION POPULATION OF 138 SELECTED UNITED STATES COUNTIES[a]

By Age and Residence: Number and Per Cent

Age	*1930* *Rural Farm Population*		*1935* *Open-Country Relief*		*1935* *Open-Country Rehabilitation*	
	NUMBER	PER CENT	NUMBER	PER CENT	NUMBER	PER CENT
All ages	1,558,601	100.00	164,982	100.00	71,280	100.00
Under 10	378,630	24.29	46,234	28.02	20,478	28.73
10–14	196,796	12.63	23,620	14.32	10,778	15.12
15–24	307,007	19.70	31,358	19.00	13,712	19.24
25–34	181,887	11.67	19,854	12.03	8,660	12.15
35–44	175,287	11.25	15,558	9.43	7,478	10.49
45–54	147,836	9.48	12,284	7.45	5,310	7.45
55–64	96,278	6.18	8,110	4.92	2,668	3.74
65 and over	74,536	4.78	7,836	4.75	1,578	2.21
Unknown	354	.02	128	.08	618	.87

Age	*1930* *Rural Non-Farm Population*		*1935* *Village Relief*		*1935* *Village Rehabilitation*	
	NUMBER	PER CENT	NUMBER	PER CENT	NUMBER	PER CENT
All ages	855,077	100.00	88,862	100.00	3,316	100.00
Under 10	187,097	21.88	21,488	24.18	1,002	30.22
10–14	83,936	9.82	11,848	13.33	508	15.32
15–24	149,395	17.47	16,846	18.96	598	18.03
25–34	124,258	14.53	10,572	11.90	374	11.28
35–44	106,020	12.40	8,958	10.08	314	9.47
45–54	83,620	9.78	8,002	9.00	250	7.54
55–64	59,683	6.98	5,748	6.47	150	4.52
65 and over	60,592	7.09	5,320	5.99	102	3.08
Unknown	476	.05	80	.09	18	.54

[a] In this table and in Tables 114-17, all based on the 138 selected counties used by the Works Progress Administration for its studies, the open-country relief population includes the farm population and all other persons living in centers, incorporated or otherwise, of less than 50 inhabitants, and as used here the term "village" refers to all rural non-farm persons living in places, incorporated or otherwise, of 50 or more inhabitants. The comparisons of open-country relief with rural farm population and of village relief with rural non-farm population are therefore not strictly comparable. The heading "village" in these tables is sanctioned by census procedure (Leon Truesdell, *Farm Population of the United States 1920*, p. 36, Table 5; and *Fifteenth Census of the United States*, *Population*, Vol. III, p. 6).

worker is reported for the open country, and for the village, in Table 114. The unskilled workers predominate in both relief groups. Over 45 per cent of the open-country relief workers are classified with usual occupation as "farm laborer" or "unskilled worker." About half of the village relief group are so classified. The open-country relief group had relatively more than 3 times as many agricultural workers as had the village relief group. The personnel of both relief groups are predominantly unskilled or

TABLE 114

COMPOSITION AND CHARACTERISTICS OF THE RELIEF POPULATION OF 138 SELECTED COUNTIES IN JUNE, 1935

Usual Occupation of All Potential Workers: by Residence

Classification	*Number*	*Per Cent*	*Number*	*Per Cent*
	OPEN COUNTRY		VILLAGE	
Usual occupation	50,032	100.00	28,510	100.00
Agricultural workers	31,066	62.09	5,970	20.94
Farm operators	16,322	32.62	2,058	7.22
Owners and managers	5,876	11.74	626	2.20
Croppers	2,724	5.44	422	1.48
Tenants	7,722	15.44	1,010	3.54
Farm laborers	14,744	29.47	3,912	13.72
Non-agricultural workers	12,212	24.41	16,952	59.46
Professional	198	.39	322	1.13
Proprietors, managers, and officials	196	.39	474	1.66
Clerical and allied	430	.86	1,188	4.17
Skilled workers and foremen	1,330	2.66	2,144	7.52
Semi-skilled workers	1,860	3.72	2,460	8.63
Unskilled	8,198	16.39	10,364	36.35
Servants and allied	1,326	2.65	2,452	8.60
Other unskilled	6,872	13.74	7,912	27.75
No usual occupation	5,032	10.06	3,894	13.66
Head not a worker	1,640	3.28	1,640	5.75
Unknown	82	.16	54	.19

semi-skilled, but differ in industrial activity. These differences substantiate the argument that relief in the village and in the open country cannot be subsumed under the same category.

From the point of intellectual endowment, the only material available is a record of the amount of formal education as a function of age. In October, 1935, the relief schedule required, for each family head and each member, a report of the last school grade completed. If normal progress had been made through the grades, a child of 6 years would have completed 0 year-grades of formal schooling; a child of 7 years, one year-grade; and so on to a child of 14, who would have completed 8 year-grades of formal schooling. For the children aged 10, 11, 12, 13, and 14, the normal expectation of grades completed would be 4.0, 5.0, 6.0, 7.0, and 8.0, respectively. The actual median grade of completed education for children of open-country relief families is 3.5, 4.4, 5.1, 6.0, and 7.0 for those respective ages. In the village relief group, the children attained median completed grades of 4.1, 4.8, 5.7, 6.6, and 7.5 for the same ages respectively. Open-country relief children are more retarded than village children. Certainly it cannot be assumed that the compulsory school requirement was abated for children on relief; nevertheless both groups of relief children are retarded from the point of view of normal progress from age 11 on. For the open country, the median retardation in year-grades is .48, .56, .90, .99, and .94 for ages 10 through 14 respectively. The village relief group is accelerated .06, .30, .44, and .10 year-grades for ages 11 through 14, respectively. Since school placement is symptomatic of intellectual endowments, it is very probable that the children in the relief population are in general less well endowed than the average of the total population. This conclusion is more clearly substantiated from the tables of age-grade status prepared for relief children from open-country residences and from village residences reported in Tables 115 and 116.

Assuming that normal placement for children of 10 and 11 years is the category grade 4.5, for 12-year-olds is grade 6, for 13-year-olds is grade 7, and for 14-year-olds is grade 8, it will be readily apparent that the percentage of children normally placed is 46.5, 59.3, 29.5, 27.7, and 29.1 for village relief children, and 37.8, 51.2, 22.0, 19.5, and 19.9 for open-country relief children at ages 10, 11, 12, 13, and 14 respectively. Moreover, if the above definition of normal school progress applies, 58 per cent of open-country relief 10-year-olds are retarded one or more terms (a half year-grade) and only 1.58 per cent are accelerated one or more terms. The corresponding percentages for village relief 10-year-olds are 48.6 per cent retarded, and 3.2 per cent accelerated.

For 11-year-olds, the percentages are 38.9 for retardation and

TABLE 115

AGE AND GRADE STATUS OF CHILDREN 10 TO 15 YEARS OF AGE AS OF OCTOBER, 1935

138 Selected Counties: by Number

Grade and High School	*10*	*11*	*12*	*13*	*14*	*15*
Children of Village Relief Residence						
0	14	16	6	6	...	14
1, 2, 3	904	470	246	158	88	68
4, 5	878	1,108	726	492	304	200
6	54	196	512	462	260	242
7	4	16	176	506	434	218
8	...	...	28	158	506	440
9	...	...	...	18	90	386
10	2	...	...	2	16	106
11	...	...	...	...	2	30
12	...	...	...	...	...	...
Grade and high school total	1,856	1,806	1,694	1,802	1,700	1,704
Unknown	32	62	42	26	38	28
All grades or years	1,888	1,736	1,828	1,828	1,738	1,732
Children of Open-Country Relief Residence						
0	112	90	54	64	34	72
1, 2, 3	2,132	1,328	892	530	348	322
4, 5	1,434	1,866	1,438	1,142	724	640
6	54	236	764	792	466	362
7	6	62	248	680	842	558
8	...	6	34	212	646	780
9	...	4	...	28	126	368
10	...	...	4	...	16	96
11	...	...	...	...	...	6
12	...	...	...	...	...	...
Grade and high school totals	3,738	3,592	3,434	3,448	3,202	3,204
Unknown	52	54	32	38	44	42
All grades or years	3,790	3,646	3,466	3,486	3,246	3,246

8.5 for acceleration for open-country relief children, and 26.0 and 11.4 for village children. For 12-year-olds, the two sets of percentages are 68.8 and 8.3 for the open country, and 56.3 and 11.8 for the village; for 13-year-olds, 72.5 and 6.9 for the open country, and 61.2 and 9.7 for the village; and, for 14-year-olds, 74.4 and 4.4 for the open country and 62.5 and 6.2 for the village. The average retardation ratio for those of the open country is 62.5 compared with the village relief ratio of 51; and the average acceleration ratio is 6 for open-country and 8.5 for village relief children.

TABLE 116

AGE AND GRADE STATUS OF CHILDREN 10 TO 15 YEARS OF AGE AS OF OCTOBER, 1935

138 Selected Counties: by Percentages

Grade and High School	*10*	*11*	*12*	*13*	*14*	*15*
Children of Village Relief Residence						
0	.7	.9	.4	.3	...	.8
1, 2, 3	47.9	25.1	14.2	8.7	5.1	3.9
4, 5	46.5	59.3	41.8	26.9	17.5	11.6
6	2.9	10.5	29.5	25.3	14.9	14.0
7	.2	.9	10.1	27.7	25.0	12.6
8	...	...	1.6	8.6	29.1	25.4
9	...	...	...	1.0	5.2	22.3
10	.1	...	...	.1	.9	6.1
11	...	...	...	...	.1	1.7
12	...	...	...	...	...	...
Grade and high school totals	98.3	96.7	97.6	98.6	97.8	98.4
Unknown	1.7	3.3	2.4	1.4	2.2	1.6
All grades or years	100.0	100.0	100.0	100.0	100.0	100.0
Children of Open-Country Relief Residence						
0	3.0	2.5	1.6	1.8	1.0	2.2
1, 2, 3	56.2	36.4	25.7	15.2	10.7	9.9
4, 5	37.8	51.2	41.5	32.8	22.3	19.7
6	1.4	6.4	22.0	22.7	14.4	11.2
7	.2	1.7	7.2	19.5	25.9	17.2
8	...	.2	1.0	6.1	19.9	24.0
9	...	.1	...	.8	3.9	11.3
10	...	...	.1	...	.5	3.0
11	...	...	...	...	...	.2
12	...	...	...	...	...	...
Grade and high school totals	98.6	98.5	99.1	98.9	98.6	98.7
Unknown	1.4	1.5	.9	1.1	1.4	1.3
All grades or years	100.0	100.0	100.0	100.0	100.0	100.0

The above figures on age-grade status apply only to relief children. For all relief members, the median grade of completed formal schooling was computed for each age-group; the data are reported by residence in Table 117. It is apparent that those persons on relief from the open-country residences had less formal schooling, in the aggregate and at each age-interval, than did the village relief group. It is significant that from age 21 on, each successive age-group had progressively less formal schooling than the preceding younger age-group.

These persons aged 16 to 25 from the open-country relief group had approximately the equivalent of elementary school graduation; and those of corresponding age from the village, about a year more of high-school work. It is noteworthy that in June,

TABLE 117

COMPOSITION AND CHARACTERISTICS OF THE RELIEF POPULATION OF 138 SELECTED COUNTIES IN OCTOBER, 1935, MEDIAN GRADES OF COMPLETED SCHOOLING

By Age and Residence

Ages	*Open Country*	*Village*
10	3.52	4.06
11	4.44	4.81
12	5.10	5.70
13	6.01	6.56
14	7.06	7.50
15	7.41	8.28
16–17	8.01	8.79
18–19	8.07	8.78
20	8.05	8.60
21	8.28	8.59
22–24	7.67	8.44
25–29	7.36	8.16
30–34	6.88	8.04
35–39	6.41	7.58
40–44	6.20	6.90
45–49	5.74	6.80
50–54	5.32	6.37
54–59	5.10	6.13
60–64	5.02	5.98
All ages	6.27	7.17

1935, in the 133 villages earlier referred to, a total of 3,747 persons aged 15 to 25 were on relief, an average of about 28 per village, and that the fieldworkers' reports from 126 of these villages gave 3,665 unemployed youths, an average of about 29 per village reporting. In less than half the villages, however, did the unemployed youth constitute a problem.

But relief did constitute a problem in many villages. The villagers' expression of opinion varied somewhat; but the general burden of their attitudes is revealed by some of the field reports. The statistical background concerning the characteristics of the relief population in the 133 villages of the survey, and in the 138 counties under study, shows that some of the attitudes have some basis in fact.

From a Middle Atlantic village with a high relief load came the report that there was a depression, and that people needed help for a time, but there never was a time that the village "could not have cared for its own needy and been glad to do it. Relief completely demoralized the people so far as resourcefulness is concerned, and the relief people make no effort whatsoever to find their own employment so long as there is the simple process of getting on W.P.A."

From a Southern village with a low relief load comes the report "that many people on relief rolls have no business there. They are as well off as many not on the rolls, and about as well off as before the depression. However it is profitable to get W.P.A. work and get seasonal work. The combination is much more profitable than either source singly."

From another Southern village comes the complaint that the high salaries paid on relief might do much to explain why some people prefer to stay on relief to working. From still another village comes the report that relief is undesirable in an agricultural area because of the effect on the morale of the population. In another Southern community, it was felt that the inception of E.R.A. coincided with the refusal of Negro labor to work in private industry, and the consequent shortage of farm laborers.

In the West, the complaints are of the same kind: "From one village the report is that the employer cannot get adequate help at a price in keeping with income; in another, P.W.A. wages are too high and spoil workers, who become unwilling to work in private industry; from another, delinquency increased because of the demoralization of the youth relief group with its attitude of the 'Government owes me a living.' "

The general tenor is that relief demoralized the recipients and that the workers would refuse private work sometimes because of the higher wage on P.W.A. and sometimes because of the fact that it was easier to get a P.W.A. salary than to work for it. Villagers were particularly bitter about the quality and the amount of work done on relief. One field report from the Middle West carried the following story which may be accepted as an attitude or as a contribution to American folklore.

A farmer came into the farm implement dealer's place shouting, "Cy, do ye want to buy some seed corn?" Cy retorted, "Weigh it up." When the corn had been weighed the farmer said, "Say, I don't want all of the price in cash. I want some W.P.A. poison."

CY: "What do you want W.P.A. poison for?"

FARMER: "Well, you know my farm is overrun with squirrels."

CY: "W.P.A. poison won't kill 'em."

FARMER: "Don't I know it, but it'll make 'em so danged lazy, I can just stamp 'em to death."

Another source of difficulty was that there were not enough skilled men to do the jobs approved under W.P.A. and P.W.A. From one village comes the criticism that the village had to go beyond the county to get men to complete projects.

Occasionally there were charges of political patronage in assigning persons to relief rolls. Such complaints came largely from Pennsylvania.

More frequently there was dissension among local merchants as to the mode of distribution of relief orders. Another cause for attack on relief is represented in the write-up of a Western village in which it is stated that "First the administration penalized people for going out and getting jobs in that they refused to put them back on relief after they had a few days of work. Some were afraid to accept work during the summer for fear they cannot get back on relief if necessary this fall."

A very frequent source of trouble lay in the fact that administration came from outside the village. The village felt that it knew the people better, understood their needs and their standards of living. The villagers felt that since it was their community and, in part, their problem, they should be allowed voice in the program of the relief agency. If more local jurisdiction had been allowed, it might have made for smaller relief loads because of local pride, and because of local antagonism to the kind of individuals admitted to relief benefits. The people on relief, claimed some of these villagers, have always been our problem; we took care of them when they were sick, fed them when they were hungry, clothed them when it was necessary. But such curtailment of relief through local intervention in some communities would have been artificial. There was need and it had to be met.

All in all, the relief program which affected most directly the greatest number of individuals also brought forth the greatest amount of individual criticism. Sometimes the criticism was so marked that persons who accepted relief were denied fellowship in the church. Two widely separated villages, one in the West and one in the Middle Atlantic region, reported such action. In one Western community, the Mennonites took responsibility for its members so that by April, 1936, only one family was still on the village rolls.

Of course, many of the communities, although sharply critical of relief as such, indicated that relief carried the village. Many villages unloaded their perennial poor cases upon the relief administration, lightening the tax load. Fairly typical is the California village report that P.W.A. money was welcomed because it did put men at work during the crisis and made city improvements possible at this time. Despite criticism, there was a general recognition that relief and other government money was the basis of much of the trade and business activity in 1935–36. In some villages the elaborate procedure in developing projects and plans has had a great influence in causing the villagers to think of their futures in terms of long-time programs, and the long list of local improvements bears witness that, though costly, the relief program produced many physically tangible assets at the same time that it attempted to save human resources for society.

Drainage ditches, extension of municipal waterworks, paving of streets, state highways, power plant, cannery, school building, sewers, repair of civic buildings, draining land, creating parks, widening streets, athletic field, new city hall, tree planting, ditching, county court house, landscaping school, sewing projects, changing river channels, are among the long list of projects completed under W.P.A. and P.W.A. auspices. Truly an imposing list of long-time gains from an emergency administration.

Relief was a mixed blessing, involving some tangible physical results with the premonition of lasting harm to some, if not all, of those who were on relief. The villagers were rather prone to think that it was relief that made the relief recipients lazy, shiftless, bad workmen, and more fecund. Such an opinion, moreover, is not only common to villagers, but to most persons not on relief. The soundness of such an attitude is, however, questionable. What the villagers considered a consequence of relief is more probably the cause. Larger family units, disproportionate number of younger children, preponderance of unskilled workers, great retardation of children in school, curtailed education of the adult population are of too long duration to be directly attributable as a consequence of the relief program, or its method of administration.

Economic stress with the additional load of poor and short crops and the tendency toward mechanization did affect the village and the open country sufficiently to make some relief program mandatory. The persons first affected and affected most were those whose contribution to society was marginal and whose assets were minimal.

Relief and cognate governmental agencies must be credited with crystallization of some of the problem areas. Social trends in

1930 indicated that mechanization of farms was increasing, that the pull of urban centers was becoming greater, but they did not indicate with sufficient clarity that persons normally utilized on the farm or in the village would become marginal. That tendency towards the marginal utility of some of the village and open-country workers is now as clearly revealed as was the tendency for some of the farming land to become marginal during the agricultural depression of the early twenties.

With the great disparity in physical assets of the rural areas as compared with urban centers, a program of equalization of comforts might offer a great opportunity for the rural community, an opportunity which cannot, however, be grasped readily, since too large a proportion of the population in the rural areas is not equipped to put it into effect. Rural electrification, for instance, requires men to locate lines, to put them up, and to service the system. A completed system would require electricians and repairmen. Are there enough persons trained in rural areas for the rural electrification needs of rural areas? Mechanization of farms has often been criticized for displacing farm workers. From a village in the Southwest came the report that outstanding in instituting changes has been the action of one big landowner who bought 5 tractors and auxiliary equipment to operate 2,000 acres which had formerly been divided into 60-acre tracts per tenant family. Under the tractor economy, selected laborers were retained to operate the machinery, while some 30 families averaging 5 members per unit were forced off the land to seek relief. It would be interesting to know what kind of laborers were retained to run the machinery on the 2,000-acre farm.

Electrification will bring about displacement just as surely as mechanization does. But the displacement will be differential—unskilled laborers must be supplanted by skilled personnel to operate the devices and to service the devices and the systems. The training of this new personnel is an important problem. The training requires the education or re-education of the adult, and the instruction of youth to take on the tasks created by newer development. Moreover, the education program is not primarily vocational. Changes in attitude, in social adaptations, in the use of leisure, in the amount and kind of information, and in co-operation are also required.

The farmer of the future will not so much require the services of farm laborers as he will need the skills of the tractor operator, the electrician, the mechanic, and the animal husbandman. Specialization of skills for the increased specialization of farm management requires a new stress on education, an education planned to adapt the adult population to the changing needs of the rural economy and to prepare youth to find its place in service to the agricultural community. Such redirection of the stress in education is needed.

It is not to be assumed that education is a panacea for the agricultural and village distress of the last 5 years. It may very well be that the persons who were marginal in the last 5 years are less well endowed than those who never needed to apply for relief. If this be true, there are definite limits to their educability. Nevertheless, if the standard of living of the population can be raised, then the marginal worker will acquire greater utility insofar as he is prepared to do new tasks.

Any program for the melioration of agricultural villages and their surrounding communities must consider the education of youth, and the rehabilitation of adults for the services that such melioration requires. That means that teachers, conscious of the social and economic problems, who know not only how to do, but also how to teach, are needed as never before in rural areas. Such teachers, after a decade of service in the communities, may do much to mitigate the effects of change in the rural areas.

Relief, in villages and in their surrounding agricultural communities, has been given to those persons displaced by agricultural failure, by economic distress, and by rural mechanization.

Such persons tend on the whole to be those who are less able to adjust to change. A suggested program of increasing physical comforts for the village and farm requires a corollary program of education and rehabilitation. The incidence of relief may be a blessing in disguise if it results in a program of social and economic planning.

XIV

Some Implications

THE PRECEDING chapter brought to an end the report of rural social trends during the depression which were revealed by a third study of 140 identical village-centered rural communities.

That report presented the factual story of the depression years, and comparisons with conditions existing when the two previous studies were made. There was some attempt at interpretation. Thus far and no farther can social science go, according to its present conventions.

But to the authors it seems that social scientists have a further obligation. The researches of the physical scientist are not produced solely for library shelves and files. Discoveries in his fields are translated into action, whether in factory or pharmacy. So, too, in the rural field the discoveries of the plant pathologist, the soil chemist, the agronomist, and scores of other experts are translated into changes in farm management on millions of fields and in thousands of orchards throughout the nation.

Thus, as one of the authors has said in another connection: [1]

> The physical scientist in his laboratory manipulates the elements with which he deals in an effort, at last with frequent success, to achieve preconceived ends. The social scientist has usually striven to emulate the precision of the laboratory without concern for his ends. He has believed that his truths would, when given to the world, produce beneficial results. This was the approach of President Hoover's Committee on Recent Social Trends, but Hoover's successor challenged social scientists themselves to act on their findings, to build and execute policy. In so doing, President Roosevelt broadened the function of the expert in modern society, who must not only discover truth, but also guide, plan and programize. This is a task of very great importance and of supreme difficulty

[1] Kolb and Brunner, *A Study of Rural Society*, pp. 601-3, quoted by special permission of the publishers, Houghton Mifflin Company, Boston.

since the human atom, unlike the atom of the physicist's laboratory, reacts to infinitely more impulses, infinitely more complex in their nature.

This is not to say that society has proceeded unplanned up to this time. That would be ridiculous. Rural America has had many plans written into law.

A great national land policy was planned in the post Civil War days and executed with considerable success under the Homestead Law. Amid all the confusion and alarms of civil strife, we planned to bring the benefits of science to agriculture on a national scale, and therefore founded our land grant colleges of agriculture. Under the necessities of a greater conflict, the World War, and under the spell of a century and a half in which each day saw more mouths to feed and backs to clothe than the day before, we redoubled our efforts to produce ever more by planning. We established and expanded our agricultural extension service, and assisted all rural high schools that desired it to have a teacher of agriculture. The extension service plan has been copied by other nations. Confronted by the problem of providing adequate credit for agriculture, we planned and created the Federal Land Bank system which measurably improved the credit conditions of agriculture. What is true in agriculture is true in other branches of our national economy. But we have had scattered and sporadic plans and have not seen that often such plans when combined produced a dilemma. We have not understood and perhaps still do not understand the difference between plans and a planning program, constantly taking all the changing factors into account.

To the authors of this report, it seems inevitable that social science must accept the challenge to interpret its discovered facts in terms of action. They recognize that this cannot be done with the same finality with which the formulae of the physical scientist can be applied, and that no final blueprints can be prepared either now or ever, to regiment the intricate group-relations of human beings. But it is believed that the way to avoid the dictatorship of force is to achieve consent for experimentation and policy making that lead to social control through reason and intelligence.

Therefore, the authors, instead of closing this report with a factual summary of findings, will attempt here to indicate some things that their findings suggest to them, either of the need for experimentation or of policies that are desirable to achieve a larger measure of socio-economic well-being in rural America.

The word planning used several times in the foregoing has begun to arouse resistances in some quarters, to connote idealistic blueprinting. The interest of the authors is simply in the use of such facts as are pertinent in the construction and implementing of policies that will strengthen the national well being. Applied social science is only common horse sense.

Along with much other research recorded in hundreds of reports, this third study of conditions in rural America as illustrated by these communities makes clear that there is sufficient knowledge for constituted authorities to begin doing some things on purpose. The implications here stated may not measure up to the obligation the authors have stated. They may be erroneous. But they will have value if their very mistakes arouse criticism in terms of policy and action in terms of experimentation.

Migration.—Paramount in public thinking at the moment are the issues of population migration and relief. They are not unrelated. The ebb and flow of migration between country and city has been noted and, in Chapter III, described in terms of the communities studied. It is well recognized that the recent increase in farm and to some extent in village population has been a result of the depression. Any sustained period of industrial expansion will doubtless restore the flow of people from the land to the city and much of the return movement will come from problem areas where social utilities are below average. This will create problems for cities, as pointed out later in this chapter.

Population movements cannot be controlled. They can be influenced. Uneconomic land areas can be closed to settlement or state aid, social institutions in areas of "rural slums" can be administered to discourage settlement. In areas of extreme need, resettlement can be attempted. In localities of continued settlement, though of probable declining population and hence of declining support for social institutions and of migrating leadership, the social servants, such as extension workers, educators, clergymen, public health officials, and the like, must be schooled in leadership and in ways and means of sustaining the necessary minimum functioning of community life.

Relief problems.—It is clear the rural problem areas have produced the most severe problems of rural relief.[2] The very bulk of the rural relief load has been a dramatic indication of changed conditions in rural America and the nation. The like of it has never been known in our previous history. In part, though in part only, it indicates that our social utilities and arrangements in rural areas have been inadequate and deficient. Too many of our population have been untrained or wrongly trained. It has become common of late to consider rural America as the reservoir of population for the nation as a whole. Care must be taken that this reservoir be not filled with the dregs of our population.

These two problems but serve as an introduction to the complex of problems of rural America. From one point of view they raise the fundamental relation of people to land.

The land and the people.—The interaction of land and people makes rural life. Seldom if ever in our history has the land factor been of more concern. We now know that this is not a permanent country, that soil fertility can be exhausted, that topsoil can be washed and blown away. We know the devices by which these processes can be checked and cured. But the wastage of our soil is the responsibility of our people. It is tied up with the early pioneers' belief that our land resources were inexhaustible. It is imbedded in the conviction that the slaughter of the trees was necessary to gain the acreage to raise our food and fiber. It is a function of our increasing tenancy, and of the type of social arrangements that make of the tenant a migrant farmer who exploits the surface wealth of the soil and then moves on every other year. Clearly there are com-

[2] P. G. Beck and M. C. Forster, *Six Rural Problem Areas* (Washington, D.C., Federal Emergency Relief Administration, 1935).

pulsions that force anti-social behavior upon hundreds of thousands; compulsions that arise in part from lags in understanding, in part from prejudices, in part from ignorance.

Experts in erosion control, in land utilization, and in farm management have their several and particular solutions; but any fundamental attack, from whatever angle begun, opens the door into the whole range of rural life problems. Take, for instance, the problem of tenancy. There is now a Presidential Commission for the study of tenancy. The proportion of tenant-operated farms in America has mounted alarmingly in recent decades, and the proportion of land operated by tenants even more rapidly. It is quite possible to devise and to recommend a better form of lease, to regularize landlord-tenant relations, especially in the South, to provide machinery whereby tenants can, with Federal assistance, become owners. Such steps would be desirable.

But the problem of tenancy will not thereby be solved. The human factors would still be unknown and unpredictable elements in the equation. Important as are the problems of land and its use, the human factor is paramount. Scores of treatises show the disadvantages of tenancy. But the previous study in this series [3] and other researches have shown that of late tenants have preferred *not* to become owners. By design, they remain below the top rung of the agricultural ladder. Simply making the conditions of ownership easier may not stimulate many of them to take the last step upward, unless not merely problems of credit are solved, to insure greater security but also problems of taxation, and those affecting soil conservation, market outlets, profitable prices, and a fair share of the national income for agriculture as a whole.

The past quarter of a century has produced a treasure store of information applicable to these problems. What is needed above all else is a synthesis of these data, an interpretation, a policy for American Agriculture, and a rural life that will not only solve the problem of erosion, and the problems of credit or

[3] Brunner and Kolb, *Rural Social Trends.*

tenancy, but that will build a well-rounded plan for agriculture and rural life behind which could be thrown the whole power of the nation.

The National Resources Board and the population specialists have forecast the probable future trend of our population within limits. They have, with the aid of other experts, forecast the food and fiber requirements of that population on varying levels of income. The possibilities of agricultural production in the nation are known. The answer to the question as to how many farmers and how many acres we need to meet these requirements in any immediately predictable future is obtainable. On such bases, we can plan and then work to train the required number of future farmers to conserve and build up our soil and our forests, thus meeting our needs and creating the reserves that will be usable and necessary when, as, and if foreign markets improve, national income rises to levels that are pronounced achievable by the Brookings Institution studies, or the chemurgic scientists develop fully the possibilities of new industrial uses for farm products.

This will raise in the minds of some the restrictions on production of the Agricultural Adjustment Administration program and the current trend toward finding some measure for controlling production. Such restriction is merely akin to reducing the production of many industrial products during a period of slow consumer demand. For the moment it appears necessary. We are still operating in a commercial economy of scarcity. But the authors reject the idea that in a better or more ideal society prosperity can be secured by inducing scarcity in any goods, agricultural or non-agricultural. As a nation, our diet is deficient in many items, not merely because of ignorance of their value but also because millions of our citizens have not the wherewithal to buy them. Here, then, planning for agricultural and rural life leads, as at many other points, into planning for national well-being.

Perhaps in the South economic progress waits upon not only

greater diversification but also upon a great educational campaign by the home economists in the schools and the Extension Service that would change and enrich the diet of the South.

Related to data such as these will be those of the farm management experts. Farms in America are growing larger at one end of the scale, smaller at the other. In the light of probable developments, what is the optimum-size farm for the various types of agricultural enterprise? [4] Present trends in size of farm are obviously a response to conditions. No one would start a 40-acre fruit and truck ranch in the dry-farming area. But the tidal wave of farm foreclosures since 1920 suggests that farm-size may have been one factor in the tragedy, and certainly farm equipment in relation to size another.

Soil experts must also play their part. At one place proper procedures can restore fertility economically. At another land may have become so seriously wounded by misuse that the healing touch of nature through the years alone can solve the problem. Hence, rural zoning must be extended.

But there are other data that must contribute to this synthesis. The human element has not been introduced. Some farmers fail, some tenants remain tenants, and some laborers stay laborers because of what they are. Agriculture with profit as the objective is not an occupation for a moron. Moreover, intelligence is no guarantee of efficient farming. Questions of capacity enter in. Human beings cannot be precisely catalogued and regimented into occupations; but just as the agricultural outlook influences crop plantings in America, a comparable occupational outlook, coupled with a socially conceived and motivated vocational education and guidance program, would lay the foundation for occupational planning and distribution that would make a more economically justifiable

[4] In one county in the East there was, some years ago, the largest farm east of the Mississippi River—it covered well in excess of 10,000 acres—while the modal family-size farm in this county was barely 3 acres. The type of agriculture was the same. The large farm failed to pay, and so did some of the modal-size farms. Were both size-groups uneconomic?

use of the most important surplus crop of rural America—the human.

Moreover, this human crop, whether in city or village or farm, lives, moves, and has its being in relation to social groupings. The best plan devisable for efficient and profitable agriculture is self-doomed if it leaves this basic factor out of account. Rural people have shown unmistakably that they are interested, not merely in living, but in living well. The struggle to raise family and community standards, to achieve the best obtainable through social utilities, clearly discernible by those who know rural America, clearly evident in this series of studies, will perhaps some day be accounted as great an epic as the conquest of the American wilderness by the pioneer. To the considerations raised in these last two paragraphs, the rest of this chapter is devoted. But first it should be noted that rural America is more ready for such a general approach to building workable policies than ever before. Rural America has raised questions, and it has studied in these last dozen years or more as never before. In the referenda on the A.A.A. crop plans, in the presidential elections of 1932 and 1936, in the revival of interest in its indigenous culture, it is showing signs the social scientist recognizes as possible indications of readiness to move in new directions. At the least, it is uneasily asking: "Whither now?"

The answer to that question involves building a program for the conservation and utilization of our resources, both natural and human. If the latter is not achieved, the former cannot be. Implied here and in the previous discussion is the need to take the individual differences of human beings into account.

If the handling of a herd, the cultivation of a field, or any other task is inefficiently done, the wastage is great. The effort of the person who could do something else more efficiently than he is performing his present task is wasted. So is the effort of him who could perform the task well, but who is busied elsewhere. And from all inefficiency, society loses. There are, of course self-selective factors. Gregarious souls do not apply for forest rangers' jobs. Some tenants would shun the responsibilities of ownership, no matter how easy the highway to that status. But the wastage of human resources is nonetheless tremendous, and it is one factor in the wastage of natural resources.

Education is of course called for, but education planned and given in terms of the known capacities of the student to acquire developable skills, information and attitudes. Socially and economically useful citizens can be produced in no other way. The addition of an extra course in character education, auto-mechanics, or typewriting, or even the raising of the legal attendance age will not accomplish the ends here envisaged, though in specific situations such things may be called for.

This means, obviously, that organized education can no longer be limited by the boundaries of nineteenth-century school districts. Education is the concern of the nation and the state; not, of course, in the way it is in a totalitarian state, but because it is anti-social and uneconomic for a democracy not to develop the capacity of its human resources to the highest achievable levels.

This means consolidation of schools, and consolidation does not necessarily weaken communities. With proper community planning by school authorities, in which Agricultural Extension could and should help, neighborhoods can be better integrated in their communities than formerly. It certainly means educational facilities in rural America equivalent in terms of equipment and personnel to the levels of the city. It may mean the co-operation of groups of districts to secure the services of psychologists, guidance experts, and others, who in addition to their professional competence know their rural America. This but applies to public education an equivalent of what the Agricultural Extension Service is to rural adult education.

The financing of this program is not as appalling as it may appear. There has been much progress in state aid for education. Vocational education is already liberally subsidized by the Federal government. A bill is before Congress that would grant Federal funds to general education. This approach does not penalize unjustly the urban centers of wealth. Between 1920 and 1930, the cities bore less than half the cost of educating and rearing the young men and women who went to work in their commercial enterprises and industries. The balance of the bill was paid by rural America which trained and reared the tens of thousands of youth who went cityward. Taking much of the burden of education off the little local rural school district is a matter of simple justice, therefore, as well as of social and economic wisdom.[5] Better rural education would be profitable to urban America.

Part of the cost can be borne by the consolidation of school districts. There are well over 100,000 such in the United States. Kansas has about 10,000, New York about 8,000. Each of these is an administrative unit with the power to tax. In these days of rapid communication and enlarging boundaries, there is no justification on any ground for this system. It is wasteful of money and of human beings. It is responsible for countless inefficiencies in teaching, in buildings, in social organization. It is completely indefensible. But at the present rate of progress it will take half a century to eliminate it, largely because the demonstration of these costly inefficiencies has been made by educators to educators rather than to the citizens as a whole.

It is not without significance here that such high proportions of the relief loads in rural America were made up of persons deficient in education as compared with the rest of the population. The conclusion is obvious from the record that the weaknesses in education have been costly in this respect.

But quite apart from such considerations, improvement in education can be financed in part within the educational process

[5] Indeed, the whole century-old system of taxation and local government needs drastic reorganization. In these fields the experts agree; little happens, however, again because of the human elements, here compounded in part of ignorance, in part of inertia, and in part of the human selfishness naturally displayed by those with vested interests in the system as it exists.

itself. In this field, as in all others, accomplishment lags behind possibilities. Curriculum reorganization indicates one way toward a more efficient organization of the necessary content, and new teaching aids and devices hold possibilities the exploration of which is just beginning.

Such a program leads into the subject of teacher selection and education. Sentiment and local loyalty must cease to dictate appointments. This is not only a matter of sanely rigorous certification standards. These have helped, though like other social arrangements they should be, as they are not, kept under continuous review and criticism in the light of changing conditions. The teachers needed must obviously be trained in content. But they must also be alert and socially conscious. The mechanics of education no more define its social ends than do the mechanics of housekeeping or the factory set the objectives of these processes. The loyalty of the teacher must be to the potential citizen who will be a member of many social groups and who, like his teacher, will be played upon by many social forces that must be understood if the individual and society are not to proceed from catastrophe to catastrophe, if they are not to be subject to irrational and emotional shifts in attitude typified in recent years by Ku Klux Klan Americanism and Townsendism.

Co-operative attitudes necessary and possible.—The plans being fabricated for the structure of the future will be executed by the child of today, and these plans will be inoperative without the support of co-operative attitudes. If the rugged individualism of certain philosophers of laissez faire is to give way, as seems likely under the impact of modern conditions, the only alternative to the control of dictators or dictator groups is democratic co-operation. Any group relationship involves co-operation; and in the economic realm in this country economic co-operation as a manifestation of democracy in economic trends has progressed further among rural than among urban people. But it has far to go. The development of co-operative attitudes and the building of understandings about the processes of co-operation which are essentially sociological are work for the schools. The results cannot be attained merely by courses, as now being attempted in Wisconsin. The whole educative process must function.

Action impossible without adult education.—But it is not wise to wait for a generation to grow up before more socially useful policies are made and put in operation. Adult education is most essential. The progress of education itself is retarded somewhat because adults are not aware of the valid sanctions for such improvement as has been made. An adult education job for the schools is the creation of attitudes in adults favorable to a finer, more functional education for children. This must be accomplished, moreover, in terms of the social justifications involved, not in terms of the institutional arguments in favor of the expansions of activities as such.

This, however, is a lesser phase of adult education. The experiences of the last years give some indication that an increasing number of adults admit the need for continuing education, and also that such education is measurably effective in teaching skills, changing practices, and altering attitudes. But the numbers reached are small compared with the reasonable possibilities. The instrumentalities are ready to hand. They need some expansion in the territory covered, such as would bring the social, economic, home, and family aspects of the Extension Service into the villages. They need also some development of the newer aspects of the work, some criticism of the older aspects in the light of changed social and economic conditions. The adult program in the schools as such is feeble but growing, and has shown its possibilities.

In this aspect of education, distinction must be made between formalized education and the more informal approaches and techniques. Adults are often reluctant to submit to the former. Hence the value of discussion groups, of the experiences in social organizations and recreation, of the radio and the printed page. Nonetheless, some skills and informations must rely chiefly on the more formalized techniques.

Education only one tool.—Important as education is, however, and absolutely essential as adult education is if democracy is to plan and chart its course, education is not a panacea, certainly not that which is institutionalized. It is one of many media. Moreover, learning goes on in many ways. It needs no school to make the farmer shift from mule to tractor, or learn to drive a car rather than a horse. But in school or out, there are limits to educability, and far more must be learned about both education and people before greater reliance can be placed upon education.

This section on education has been developed as far as it has simply as an illustration, and because specialists in many fields too often fumble badly in handling the educative procedures that might speed their programs toward their goals.

Other social organizations can play their part in the necessary policy making, organizations that can be utilized for all types of social, recreational, and cultural outlets. They function chiefly on the local level of community or county. In a democracy, commonsense policy making must include these local units; but in that policy building the local people must participate. In this the county projects described are a beginning; but as on the national stage, so on the local, planning must include social as well as economic phases. There is a need for greater integration of organizations on this level; and self-study and program planning based on it in a locality would help achieve this. The experience during the war and the year or two immediately following have produced considerable pessimism as to the possibilities of community organization. But the approach at that time was too much from the top down. Much has been learned since, and there are evidences within and without this study that economy of time and a richer social and cultural life can be attained on a community level through integration and co-operation, especially if it is based on self-study. This is a field in which Agricultural Extension through its rural sociologists can give much help. It can at least furnish the means by which the citizens of a community can look at their community and its needs in the large and construct a functional program that would meet such needs, rather than devote themselves to promoting the several organizations of which they are a part.

An enterprise of this sort requires leadership; and both the professional and lay leaders in rural communities need, among other recognized qualities, sensitivity to individual and group differences, especially such as lie in the realm of emotions. Poor and inadequate leadership can wreck a community. This has happened in some of the places studied. Not co-operation but schism has been the result of ill-advised efforts, perchance well-motivated but none the less ignorant of facts and factors in community life that made conflict inevitable.

The Agricultural Extension Service, beyond all other agencies, has developed the use of volunteer leaders, and if trends in social life and organization move as would seem to be indicated by this series of studies, it has a great contribution to make in the development of effective leadership for this social and cultural co-operation, especially if this service comes to serve, as the authors believe it should, all rural people and not simply the farm population.

The role of commerce.—Moreover, the economic agencies of the village or town, chambers of commerce, service clubs, and the like, can also profit by planning their economic services. Not all centers can possess all types of services. Marginal businesses, just like marginal banks and farms, are a liability to the community. On the other hand, a few communities have cushioned the shock of the depression, even measurably overcome it, by ingenious planning for, and development of, economic services not previously offered.

At this point also there is need for training leadership and for guidance to local agencies and their officers. State laws require doctors, dentists, lawyers, teachers, and certain other professional groups to meet certain standards before they begin to serve their fellow men. In the light of the tragedies of 1921 to 1933, is there any reason why such procedures should not be followed with banking? One or two state colleges of agriculture have studied and helped improve the rural newspapers of their states. The Department of Commerce gives much help to industry and urban business, but such helps are of small use to the village storekeeper with an annual turnover of from $10,000 to $40,000. A broadly conceived service in rural terms to such rural merchants by the Department of Commerce or the schools of business of state universities would do much to improve the economic service available to rural people, especially if it be not confined merely to penny-catching trade devices. The inevitable dependence of commerce upon the fortunes and good will of the community and the forces that affect community well-being must also be understood.

Communities village or town centered.—This is the more necessary because the daily social and economic aspects and contacts of rural life are clearly revolving more and more around the village and town center. The policies of social organizations, schools, churches, and businesses must more and more be based on that fact. Involved here, of course, is also the determination of the economic and population base needed to sustain a given service. A school does not require as large a base as a hospital. But too little is known as to the required base for any given service. Thus, large areas of rural America are deprived of certain services because in the absence of knowledge on this point none are venturesome enough to launch a given service on the trial-and-error method. Yet techniques for a more precise answer to such questions are available.

The country and its city.—The problem of village-country relations is working out its solution, though the process can be accelerated. But the relationships of rural life are increasingly broader than those of the town-centered community. What happens on the plains of Siberia or the pampas of Argentine, what is decided at a world wheat conference or a meeting of the Pan American Union, in these times is of more influence in determining the fortunes of a farm family than what happened in the next county was a century ago. At the least there is involved here an expansion of policy making in terms of metropolitan areas broadly defined, and of regions, as the past years and the work of the National Resources Board hopefully illustrate. Much of the planning within cities is from the point of view of their own benefit. Too often they look on their hinterlands as areas to exploit. The demonstrated interdependence of city and country must be hammered home, an interdependence that may vary in degree but which will not disappear even if the farm population drops to one-tenth of the national total and the total rural to one-fourth or one-fifth. Indeed, should such a decline in rural farm and non-farm population occur, the problems of interrelationship between city and country will become of extreme importance, especially to the city. It will become vitally interested in the quality and caliber of the hundreds of thousands of rural people flooding its houses and institutions. If these are not as well prepared to meet life and to live as are the city dwellers, urban standards and culture will be lowered. From this point of view, too, it is again evident that the city has a large stake in rural well-being.

This means, of course, the wholesome development of all the resources of an area and a region on the basis of a maximum of goods and services for all. Moreover, in a number of aspects such activities exist. A few city-county health departments have made records conspicuous in the whole public-health field. There are comparable developments in the library field. The stage is set in many situations for procedures looking toward an expansion of such techniques all along the line.

Socialized religion.—Nor would the authors exclude organized religion from the scope of social planning. Like education, organized religion is a social force; and it serves directly a considerable portion of the population. It is in many respects woefully weak, weaker than need be. The decline has been slow but long and steady. The procedures for improving it are known, but they cannot be applied by all the many churches that are now trying to function. The economic, and the population, base simply do not exist. A little progress has been made in attacking this competitive over-plus of churches interdenominationally, but almost none in solving intradenominational competition between village and open-country churches. The attack, moreover, is hortatory, not administrative or even honestly educative. The rural American deserves as good leadership in the church as in the school, as good as in the city. What he gets is often several grades below this. If the national religious agencies wish, they can help solve these problems. It has been done in enough places and areas to show that it can be done, both in terms of eliminating anti-social competition which introduces divisive elements into the community and actually prevents the co-operations of a desirable nature such as churches are supposed to stand for, and in terms of effective programs of service by local churches unhampered by competition. These national agencies can then, if they will, place individual and social ethics above the minutiae of creed. They can exalt, as did the prophets from Isaiah to Jesus, the social worth of human beings. They can motivate and exemplify the co-operation called for in the effectuating of needed national and local policies. They can make religion an indispensable force in the social milieu of the countryside.

Social parity.—What is being urged throughout these latter pages is that there is achievable for rural America by the application of common sense to known facts in the community, county, and state, social parity as well as economic. This parity takes national action in some particulars; but at no point can it be achieved without local effort and co-operation. It is not economically safe for sharp disparity in agricultural and industrial income to exist. It is not socially safe in a democracy for the rural half of the nation in a period of free population mobility to be served by institutions that fall below at least the average standards of urban performance, or to be deprived of services. One such deprivation relates to social security. The farmer and the agricultural laborer are among the important groups not included in the provisions of the act as at present operating. Eventually legislation must give to the farmer the same survival value, the same security as is now the possession of the industrial worker.

Certain provisions of the existing Social Security Act will, however, help to improve the health situation in rural America, an area of acute need, which like others has not been touched upon in this chapter.

Here, then, are some illustrations of areas of both social and economic interest where data exist that are capable of being forged into policies more scientifically valid than the policies which society is now using, and of areas in which recent and desirable policies would probably be fructified by bringing to bear a synthesis of data from more fields than have been used.

It is hardly likely that the suggestions here set forth will meet with the complete approval of any reader. The authors have simply ventured to interpret some results of this study in terms of possible policies because far too few social scientists have in the past essayed such attempts based on their researches. Too often, the first pronouncements on policy come only after a social scientist has assumed public office. His views then may be subjected to technical criticism; but they also perforce enter the political arena, and their defense must be in political as well as in scientific terms.

If a degree of integrated program building is to be introduced into the developing social pattern of our age, if social controls are to become more subject to reason and intelligence, the implications of researches for social policy should be criticized, debated, and measurably determined before they play their parts on the political stage. Therefore the more the attempt here made meets drastic but constructive criticism, the better the purposes of this venture will be served.

But the critics should remember that the authors have been

limited by their own research and experience. It is their deep conviction that policy building is not the prerogative of any single discipline among the social sciences, nor yet of each one separately. There is no single interpretation of social or group action, even of individual action. Mankind too often grasps at the immediate benefit and loses the lasting gain, too often allows short-term economic advantage to overcome lasting social good, too frequently responds to sentiment rather than to the common sense of the economist. The construction of socially adequate policies must be on the basis of the synthesis of the social disciplines. The representative of any field who walls his specialty off by itself, who does not humbly seek truth wherever it may be found, can no longer fit the emerging definition of the social scientist of tomorrow.

Appendix A: Acknowledgments

In addition to the acknowledgments made in the Introduction, the authors desire to express their appreciation of the co-operation of the following institutions and individuals:

Teachers College, Columbia University, for office space and facilities used during the study.

Dr. A. G. Black, chief of the Bureau of Agricultural Economics, United States Department of Agriculture; Dr. O. E. Baker and Dr. C. P. Loomis of the same organization; and especially Dr. Conrad Taeuber, for participation in field work and for constructive suggestions on the manuscript.

The Bureau of the Census, especially Mr. F. A. Gosnell of the Census of American Business, through whom the retail sales data on the 1933 and 1935 census were secured for each of the 140 villages.

The American Library Association, through whose co-operation the data on the libraries was gathered.

The following individuals who either arranged for studies in their states by staff members or students, or conducted the field work:

Alford, Harold D.
Anderson, W. A.
Benson, Ezra T.
Berg, A. C.
Bornman, Charles J.
Bradley, Ruth Campbell
Breithaupt, L. R.
Burnham, Ernest
Conrey, Amalia
Durbin, Arthur J. V.
Gillette, J. M.
Hall, Homer
Hall, O. F.
Hamilton, C. Horace
Hill, Randall C.
Hodgdon, Evelyn R.
Hoffman, C. S.
Holley, W. C.
Hollingshead, A. B.
Kolb, J. H.
Landis, Paul H.
Larson, Olaf F.
Losey, Edwin
Mallison, Dallas
Manny, Theodore B.
Matthews, M. Taylor
McCrae, J. A.
Metzlar, W. H.
Morgan, E. L.
Morgan, John W.
Mumford, Eben
Murchie, R. W.
Oyler, Betty
Patten, Marjorie
Rapp, Robert E.
Russell, Daniel
Russell, Judith
Shales, J. M.
Smudde, F. M.
Tape, H. A.
Trumper, May
Tylor, W. Russell
Wakeley, Ray E.
Wasson, C. R.
Wieland, Edwin M.
Williams, B. O.
Wilson, W. T.
Wofford, Kate V.

The following statisticians: Leonore Epstein; Jerome Salit.

Mrs. Carol Sheldon acted as Secretary-Assistant throughout the study.

Appendix B: Methodology

THE STUDY described in this volume is, as noted in the Introduction, the third that has been made of the same village-centered rural communities.

The original investigation was initiated in 1923 as a project of the Institute of Social and Religious Research. The communities were chosen after careful consultation with colleges of agriculture, state boards of education, and one or more other state agencies. These agencies were asked to select communities reasonably representative of "service station" villages in the major regions or crop areas of their states.

The regional distribution of these villages was roughly comparable to the rural population of the regions except that the Middle Atlantic was overweighted to compensate for not including New England. This region was not used because of the fact that few of its villages were incorporated. This made it impossible to secure many types of data on a basis comparable with the communities in the other regions. The chief limitation here was the lack of census data for the village centers. In New England, census data is gathered on a township basis.

The 1920 census data for these villages and 37 others not surveyed were secured in this first study and related to the field survey information.

This first study was completed in the summer of 1925 and was published in a series of volumes issued during 1926 to 1927.[1] The field schedules used and some of the field-work instructions were also published in Brunner's *Surveying Your Community*.[2]

The second survey of these communities was made as part of a study of Rural Social Trends, initiated by the Institute for Social and Religious Research in the fall of 1929, which early in the next year became the rural section of President Hoover's Research Committee on Social Trends. In this study also census data were used but on a broader base. Not only was the 1930 census of population data for the villages again specially tabulated, but census of distribution data was also secured. In addition

[1] C. Luther Fry, *American Villages* (1926); Edmund deS. Brunner, Gwendolyn S. Hughes, and Marjorie Patten, *American Agricultural Villages* (1927); and Edmund deS. Brunner, *Village Communities* (1927). These are publications of the Institute of Social and Religious Research, distributed by Harper & Brothers, New York.

[2] A publication (1925) of the Institute of Social and Religious Research, distributed by Harper & Brothers, New York.

large use was made of the agricultural census data. Much of this data was tabulated not only in terms of the villages, and for regional and national totals, but it was also tabulated for concentric tiers of counties surrounding 18 major cities in order to measure urban-rural interrelationships and the effect of distances upon these. This investigation was reported in Brunner and Kolb's *Rural Social Trends*.[3]

The third investigation was a joint project of the Council for Research in the Social Sciences of Columbia University and the Bureau of Agricultural Economics of the United States Department of Agriculture. Cooperation in field work was also extended by the Rural Research Unit of the W.P.A.

This third survey was an effort to discover before the data and the recollections had been lost what changes had been wrought by the depression. Budgetary limitations restricted the scope of the field survey in this third study as compared with the two previous investigations. The chief cut was made in connection with the churches. It is believed, however, that nothing essential to an understanding of the actual changes and trends of the depression period has been omitted.

The average community required a week of field-work time. As many data as possible were gathered in advance. These included municipal and school accounts, bank statements, and other matters of public record. Fieldworkers conducted about 100 interviews in each community, the number varying with the population. Each fieldworker also submitted a narrative interpretation of the facts secured. Considerable use was also made of the local weekly newspapers. This non-schedule material was read and all important items were recorded on cards that were indexed. The community write-ups yielded over 600 such items, about three-fifths of which were used in this report. The church write-ups produced about 400. In addition, what might be called a summary page was employed on the community schedule which called for listing all work undertaken or dropped, or shifts in auspices since 1930 in connection with civic improvements, industrial or agricultural developments, social, recreational, educational or cultural enterprises, the celebration of national or local holidays or festivals, and the like. This served as a valuable check on the field-work report and produced some otherwise unrecorded data. This material also was recorded on cards, nearly 1,000 in all. The main resource, however, was the fieldworkers' write-ups noted above.

The two previous reports in this series of studies have contained appendices describing in more detail the scope and methods of those studies.

[3] New York, McGraw-Hill Book Company, 1933.

The basic material there set forth holds, of course, for this present survey. In addition, at occasional pertinent points in the text of this report, there are brief explanations of methods used. Two methodological devices were used in the present study, however, which deserve a brief description.

In studying social organizations in 1924 and in 1930, a count was made of all social organizations in the community at each survey period. For each social organization, additional auxiliary data about membership, attendance, open-country participation, and expenditures were obtained. Trends were inferred from the differences between averages for each variable at each survey period. It was believed possible, however, that the averages had an error in that new organizations might bias the results. In order to check this hypothesis in regard to the social organization data, a new analysis was used in 1936 which traces through the statistics for identical organizations. In other words, as noted in Chapter X, in the 1924–1930–1936 group would be all organizations that were in existence in 1924 or before. If differences do exist between the averages of, let us say, membership, the inferences are clearer, since it is known precisely that these are identical social organizations. Deaths among social organizations can be located and understood without any special assumptions about the nature of the facts. It is hoped that the method of identical establishments will be elaborated and extended to include co-operatives, industries, and schools.

Another methodological development is in the use of a hitherto untapped, but potentially rich, source of sociological information. The annual or biennial reports of state superintendents of education usually give information about pupils, children of school age, teachers, pupil-teacher ratios, attendance, and school finance, which are valuable adjuncts of knowledge in a survey. An attempt was made to bring a semblance of consistency out of the reports of the various states, and to apply the tier technique analysis to the data. Trends of sociological value were revealed. Some of these are set forth in Chapter VII. Attention is called to this source of data and its uses in the hope that other social scientists may use it. If a sufficient number do, it may perhaps be possible to secure better preparation of the reports, more standardization, and possibly some useful data not now published, on the basis of which better analyses of such information can be attempted.

Index